John Millar

Elements of the Law relating to Insurances

John Millar

Elements of the Law relating to Insurances

ISBN/EAN: 9783743330702

Manufactured in Europe, USA, Canada, Australia, Japa

Cover: Foto ©ninafisch / pixelio.de

Manufactured and distributed by brebook publishing software (www.brebook.com)

John Millar

Elements of the Law relating to Insurances

OF THE

LAW

RELATING TO

INSURANCES.

BY

JOHN MILLAR, *jun.* ESQ. ADVOCATE.

EDINBURGH:
PRINTED FOR J. BELL, PARLIAMENT-CLOSE: AND
G. G. J. & J. ROBINSON, LONDON.

M.DCC.LXXXVII.

TO

WILLIAM ADAM, Esq. M. P.

COUNSELLOR AT LAW,

IN TESTIMONY OF

GRATITUDE AND ESTEEM,

THIS COMPILATION

IS RESPECTFULLY INSCRIBED,

BY HIS OBLIGED

HUMBLE SERVANT,

J. MILLAR, *junior*.

PREFACE.

THERE is no branch of law in which a compilation, uniting theory with practice, appears to be so much wanted as in that which relates to Insurance.

This, in a mercantile country, is a subject of great practical importance. It is no less a matter of speculative curiosity, as it depends on the principles of general equity and expediency, unconfined by the shackles of municipal regulation. No branch of law has, however, in proportion to its importance, been so imperfectly treated.

In a work of this nature, the primary object, no doubt, is to illustrate the practice by a collection of real cases. Nothing complete in this view could be expected from our early writers, because it is principally from the abilities of an eminent Judge still living, and from the multiplicity of insurance-questions, arising from the extensive commerce of a recent period, that

that we have acquired any great number of syftematic decifions. Even in the more full and recent compilation of *Mr Wefkett*, a great many important decifions are wanting.

In arrangement, and general reafoning, the performances of this, and of all the preceding writers, are ftill more imperfect. Among the earlier compilers on infurance-law, both Englifh and foreign, there fcarcely appears an attempt towards a natural method; and an alphabetical order feems equally contrary to practical utility, and fcientific principle.

This defect is even lefs remarkable in the arrangement of the general plan of our writers, than in the detail of particular parts. The facts which they have collected are not placed in fuch a light as to illuftrate any general principle. The decifions of judges, and the regulations of mercantile ftates, are loofely thrown together, and the bufinefs of claffing them is left to the reader.

THE

PREFACE.

THE following publication is an attempt to remove some of these imperfections. In the prosecution of this work, the first object is to make a complete collection of practical cases in insurance. And here undoubtedly the decisions of Lord MANSFIELD ought to hold the chief place. It would have exceeded the Author's plan to have collected these at full length as they stand in the Reports of Sir William Burrow, Mr Couper, Mr Douglas, or in later compilations of the same kind. It is attempted, therefore, to abridge them, as far as appears consistent with perspicuity.

A CONSIDERABLE number of English cases, likewise, which had not, when this work went to the press, appeared in any printed collection, are here inserted. These have been furnished by a gentleman conversant in the law of England, on whose accuracy the Author can depend.

THE older English decisions must likewise enter into the present collection. In the original compilations, these are sometimes given with so much conciseness, as
to

to permit of their being inserted at full length, and sometimes their obscurity will scarcely admit of an abridgment. In general, however, it has been studied to proportion the length of each decision to its importance in point of illustration. An abridgment of this kind, although it will not altogether supersede the necessity of consulting the original authorities, may, it is hoped, be of considerable utility.

The decisions of the Supreme Court in Scotland, upon matters of insurance, have never been fully collected or digested in any work of this kind. As these, however, are of importance to one part of the nation in point of precedent, and to the whole as a matter of curiosity, it has been thought proper that they should appear as completely as possible in the present publication. Many of them relate to points never expressly decided in England, and all of them afford further illustration of general principles. With the same view of illustration, a selection has been made of such foreign cases as contain any thing important or singular.

Besides

PREFACE.

BESIDES collecting these decisions, it has been the view of the Author to arrange and digest them as they naturally arise from one another, and as they contribute to illustrate the general reasoning and principles upon which they are founded. For this purpose the following order has occurred:

CONTENTS.

Introductory Observations on the Contract of Insurance.—Its Nature.—Utility of it.—History.—Subjects of Insurance,   1

PART I. OF THE CIRCUMSTANCES REQUISITE TO PRODUCE A VALID INSURANCE,   29
    CHAP. 1. *Form of the Contract,*   30
    CHAP. 2. *Effect of Fraud and Error in a Policy of Insurance,*   39
        SECT. 1. *Direct Fraud,*   48
        —— 2. *Erroneous information, or mistake occasioned by the fault of the other party,*   52
        —— 3. *Mutual Error,*   97
    CHAP. 3. *How far Parties have a right to recede from their Engagements,*   110

PART II. OF THE NATURE OF AN INSURANCE CONTRACT, AND THE OBLIGATIONS ARISING FROM IT, 115

    CHAP. 1. *Of the Duration of the Insurer's Risk,* 116

        SECT. 1. *Commencement of Risk,* 117

        ——— 2. *Termination of Risk,* 119

    CHAP. 2. *Of the Nature of the Risk; or of the Event against which provision is made by Insurance* 129

    CHAP. 3. *Of the Extent of the Insurer's Obligation when a Loss is incurred in terms of the Policy,* 206

        SECT. 1. *How the Extent of Obligation is affected by the Assured's* interest *in the Subject,* 207

        ——— 2. *In what manner the Obligation of the Underwriter is affected by the Nature and Extent of the* Loss, 279

        Art. 1. *Total Loss.—Abandonment,* ib

        Art. 2. *Partial Loss.—Digression concerning Average,* 329—331

PART

PART III. OF THOSE CIRCUMSTANCES PECULIAR TO INSURANCE, WHICH EXTINGUISH THE OBLIGATIONS OF PARTIES, AND VACATE THE POLICY, 375

    SECT. 1. *Effect of the Assured exceeding his Powers; or of* Variation *from the Policy,* 383

    ―― 2. *Effect of Failure of express Warranties, or of* Nonperformance, 468

    ―― 3. *Of Premium,—and of the Return of Premium when the Policy is vacated,* 528

ELEMENTS

OF

INSURANCE.

Introductory Observations on the Contract of Insurance.—Its Nature.—Utility of it.—History.—Subjects of Insurance.

1. INSURANCE is a contract, by which one man, for a consideration received, becomes liable for the loss arising to another, from any specified contingency.

The one party, who is called the *Insurer* or *Underwriter*, receives, or is supposed to receive, a sum of money, in hand, at the time of the agreement. This is called the *Premium*. The other party, the *Assured*, whose property is exposed to some danger, obtains an obligation of indemnification, in case the damage apprehended shall take place.

The contract of insurance differs from most other contracts, in this respect, That the consideration is given, not for a certain determinate payment or performance, but for what is merely contingent. The assured pays a sum of money in advance: But the reciprocal obligation of the underwriter depends upon an event, which is uncertain at the date of the contract. What he takes upon himself, is a mere *risk;* and it remains to be ascertained by future accidents, what is the payment or performance to which he shall be subjected, or whether he shall be subjected to any.

2. The utility of a contract of this nature, in commercial nations, is great and apparent. The underwriter, who promises to be responsible for the danger attending the conduct of any branch of trade, receives a consideration proportioned to the risk he undertakes, and therefore derives a reasonable profit from that employment of stock. On the other hand, the merchant, by abandoning a share of his expected gain, is freed from the apprehension of a loss that might be ruinous to him. The underwriter is thus enabled to participate in the profits of every different concern: He becomes a sort of temporary partner of the most extensive trading companies.

Insurance is no less advantageous to the public than to individuals, by moderating and diffusing the profits of trade, and by preventing accidental misfortunes from operating to the ruin of individuals, or companies of merchants, which might obstruct the uniform progress of commerce, and endanger public credit.

3. Confidering the manifeft utility of fuch a contract, and that it feems to be fo obvioufly fuggefted, from the circumftances of perfons engaged in any hazardous mercantile adventure, it may be thought wonderful, that the practice of infurance was in a great meafure unknown to the nations of antiquity. This muft, undoubtedly, be attributed to the limited nature of their commerce.

The Greek ftates feem to have been totally unacquainted with it. We hear of the mercantile regulations of Rhodes; part of which has been tranfcribed into the compilations of JUSTINIAN; but no paffage has been handed down to us, that alludes to fuch a bargain as infurance.

The Romans, although they were poffeffed of great wealth, had, comparatively, little experience in commerce. Their opulence was chiefly the effect of rapine and peculation in the conquered provinces. Among that people, trade and manufactures were carried on principally by the flaves and freed men of the more wealthy citizens, and were confidered as below the dignity of thofe who were born free. As a proof of the limited ftate of their trade, it has been obferved, that mercantile profits, in confequence of the little competition among merchants, were immoderately high; by which the rate of interest became proportionably great. From the fituation

ation of the Romans, there was little occasion therefore to diminish the hazard of the merchant, by insurances. It is impossible to suppose, that a bargain of this kind was totally unknown among them, but it appears to have been very uncommon.

In JUSTINIAN's Pandects, the lawyer ULPIAN seriously makes the observation, That a contract of insurance is not illegal. " Illa stipulatio, " *decem millia salva fore promittis?* valet*." Had the bargain been common, such an opinion with regard to its validity, would have been thought superfluous.

A contrivance something similar to insurance is mentioned by SUETONIUS †, as having been employed on a singular occasion by the Emperor CLAUDIUS. In order to encourage the importation of grain, he took the risk of the sea upon himself: " Negotiatoribus certa lucra proposuit, " suscepto in se damno, si quid per tempestates " accidisset; et naves, mercaturæ causa, fabri- " cantibus, magna commoda constituit." In another case, it is mentioned by LIVY, " impetra- " tum fuit, ut, quæ navibus imponerentur ad ex- " ercitum Hispaniensem deferenda, ab hostium " tempestatisque vi, publico periculo essent ‡."

In these cases, however, no mention is made of a premium paid, by the merchant, for the hazard

---

* Dig. l. 67. de verb. obligationibus.
† SUET. in Vita Claudii, c. 18.
‡ LIVY, lib. 23. c. 49.

hazard undertaken; and they are rather to be considered as examples of a bounty offered by the public, than of a mutual contract.

From the infrequency of insurance at Rome, this agreement had no name; it could only be expressed by a circumlocution; and writers, during the early period of modern ages, adopted the barbarous word *Assecuratio*.

The contract of bottomry, however, which is somewhat a-kin to insurance, or at least answers the same purpose in a more limited degree, is frequently mentioned by the Roman lawyers, and is the subject of a particular title in the compilations of JUSTINIAN [*].

Upon the downfal of the Roman empire, some part of the ancient commerce was carried on by several towns of Italy, which by their situation on the coast of the Mediterranean, were enabled to trade with many neighbouring nations, and by the Red Sea, to maintain a correspondence with India. The Moors who settled in the south of Spain, and the other inhabitants of that country, particularly about the Bay of Biscay, enjoying advantages of situation in some respects similar, were also encouraged to carry on an extensive navigation, and became early a mercantile people.

The inhabitants around the Baltic were in like manner enabled, at an early period, to procure a subsistence by fishing; to convey the rude materials

[*] Dig. De Nautico fænore.

rials of the country along the coasts of that narrow sea; and thence to trade with nations at a distance.

The southern commerce of Italy and Spain, and the northern trade of the Baltic, were followed by the manufactures and trade of the Netherlands: the ruin of which, from the bad policy of PHILIP II. laid the foundation of the commercial prosperity of Holland and England.

This progress of commercial improvement was accompanied with a corresponding extension of mercantile law. A variety of rules were laid down by different states; at first, for the regulation of navigation merely, and, at a period somewhat later, for the regulation of insurances, and other maritime contracts.

The first public enactments of this kind seem to have taken place in the Levant. What these were, is not now precisely known; but we are told, that the commercial laws established by some of the petty states in the Mediterranean, had obtained a high reputation and currency among merchants. It is unnecessary to specify the precise dates of those ordinances. The regulations of Rome, and of Amalphi, then a famous mercantile state, were made about the end of the 11th century. Those of Majorca, at that time possessed by the Pisans, and of Pisa itself; those of Marseilles; of Almeria, a town belonging to the Counts of Barcelona; of Genoa; and of the Morea, were introduced in the course of the 11th;

and

and thofe of Venice, of Conftantinople, and of Arragon, in the courfe of the 13th century*.

The enactment of fimilar regulations at the ifle of *Oleron*, in the Bay of Bifcay, when that ifland and the adjacent territory of France were in the poffeffion of RICHARD I. of England, was probably fuggefted from imitation of the ftatutes of the Levant. It is at the fame time deferving of notice, that the ifland of *Oleron*, from its centrical fituation between the maritime ftates of Italy and the Baltic; between Spain, the country which produced fine wool, and the infant manufactures of Flanders, joined to its connection with the dominions of England, and its pofition at the mouth of the Garonne, rendered it a very convenient *entrepot* for the exchange of commodities between thefe different countries. The regulations of Oleron, are faid to have been firft collected and publifhed about the year 1266.

There is reafon to believe, that infurances were not practifed at the time when the earlier regulations of the Levant, and thofe of Oleron, were arranged into a fyftem. The former have not been handed down to us; but the latter, which were probably a mere copy of them, contain no allufion to fuch a contract.

At a period fomewhat later, flourifhed the magnificent city of *Wifby*, the capital of Gothland, and

* See GIAN. Hift. Naples.———*Cafa-regi* on the *Confolato del Mare*. This laft famous compilation, which was received by the whole ftates of the Levant, was originally the production of the Kings of Arragon.

and the great mart of the Baltic; whose maritime ordinances were held in high estimation, and are, in general, still in observance among the northern states. In these regulations, there is one passage referring to a policy of insurance *.

Several French writers have ascribed to their own country, the honour of inventing insurances, together with bills of exchange. They maintain that both of these owed their origin to the expulsion of the Jews from France, who, in 1182, made use of those expedients for concealing and securing the transportation of their effects †.

This account, however, both with regard to insurances and bills of exchange, seems to be extremely improbable. It is difficult to conceive, that mercantile contracts, of such an obvious nature, were the exclusive invention of any set of people, or that they could long remain unknown in any nation possessing a considerable degree of trade. The 12th century, the period in which this invention is supposed to have arisen, was that of the first great advancement of the

---

* " Si le maistre est contraint de *bailler caution* au bour-
" geois pour le navire, le bourgeois sera pareillement tenu
" *bailler caution* pour la vie du maistre ; c'est a dire, que
" contre les hazards de la mer et de la mort, il ne peut eche-
" oir de requisition raisonnable à *bailler caution* ; reguliere-
" ment le bourgeois doit risquer son bien, et le maistre sa li-
" berté et sa vie; bien y peut estre fait *polisse d'assurance*."
Ord. de Wisby, as collected by *Cleirac, Us et coutumes de la mer.* Art. 66.

† See BORNIER,—SAVARY.

the arts, and of knowledge, in Europe. And as the Italians had then made greater proficiency in trade, and in every species of improvement, they were likely to make the first and greatest advances in relation to insurance and to exchange, as well as in every other branch of commercial transaction.

The name, accordingly, which has been adopted by the whole of Europe, for this contract, is evidently derived from the Italian word *polizza*, a promise. And the first regulations, of any consequence, that relate expressly to the subject of insurance, are those enacted by the states upon the coast of the Mediterranean. Mention is made, by CLEIRAC, of the insurance laws of Barcelona, enacted in the year 1484*. The regulations of Florence, upon the same subject, promulgated about the year 1523, refer to certain more ancient laws or customs prevalent in that city. The practice of insurance, both in England and the Netherlands, was indisputably introduced by the merchants of Lombardy.

From Barcelona, the rules and practice of insurance

---

* These *Ordonnances des Prudhommes de Barcelonne*, had been usually inserted in the editions of the *Consolato del Mare* of Arragon; but they are rejected by CASA-REGIS, as of a later date than that famous compilation. Those passages quoted by CLEIRAC, prove the practice of insurance to have been of some standing at Barcelona. See *Us et Coutumes de la Mer*, p. 224 and 235. Also see the preface to the *Consolato del Mare*, of CASA-REGIS.

furance were communicated to the different provinces of Spain: By means of a commercial intercourse with Italy, joined to a territorial connection with the Spanish dominions, they were extended to the Netherlands; and, under PHILIP II. gave rise to a considerable compilation at Antwerp.

The invention of the mariners compass, which was soon followed by the discovery of America, and of a passage to the East Indies by the Cape of Good Hope, opened a field of commercial adventure much more extensive and fertile. These discoveries were, at the same time, productive of greater variety in the nature and degree of hazard attending mercantile undertakings. They tended, therefore, of necessity, to display the advantages, and to increase the practice of insurance; and by introducing a multiplicity of provisions and stipulations formerly unknown, to render the contract more complex, and applicable to a greater variety of cases. By degrees these discoveries altered entirely the commercial state of Europe; a knowledge of navigation was more universally diffused, and the custom of insurances became more or less extensive among different nations, according as they obtained, by situation, or other circumstances, a greater share in those distant branches of trade.

From this period, a great variety of maritime regulations were enacted in most of the states of Europe; and these have been renewed and altered

tered from time to time, according to the suggestions of more advanced experience. The ordinances of the different great cities in Holland, of Amsterdam, Rotterdam, and Middleburg, which have received correction since the commencement of the present century, are particularly worthy of notice. To these may be added, the statutes of Hamburgh, of Stockholm, and Copenhagen; of Bilboa; and above all, the very complete code of mercantile regulations adopted in France by Lewis XIV. These, with others that might be mentioned, form a system of what the sentiments of professional men in different countries have determined to be just, and of what their experience has found to be useful.

In all these collections of maritime law, the regulation of insurances appears an object of principal concern. In several foreign states, its importance has rendered it the subject of jurisdiction to a separate court of justice. This is the case in France, in Amsterdam, and Middleburg, in Stockholm, and in Copenhagen.

Britain is, however, the country in which the practice of insurance has been most extensive, and in which the law of insurance has been most improved. This contract is said to have been introduced into England by a set of Italian merchants, who resided in Lombard-street, and who are still alluded to in the printed forms of British policies, by a clause, providing, that " the " contract shall be as effectual as those formerly " made in Lombard-street."

In-

In the time of Queen ELIZABETH, insurance had become so frequent, particularly at the office of the great mercantile company in the Royal Exchange in London, as to draw the attention of the Legislature. And a court of justice, called the *Chamber of Assurances*, was established, to take cognizance of all questions with regard to it.

By the statute, 43d ELIZ. c. 12. a special commission, to consist of the Judge of the Admiralty, the Recorder of London, certain doctors of civil law, and a number of *discreet* merchants, was appointed to be named by the Chancellor, for the purpose of deciding upon insurances. This Court, however, had no exclusive jurisdiction, but one merely concurrent with the courts of common law. An appeal lay from it to Chancery. From the limited nature of its powers, this commission appears never to have been of considerable utility; and it has long been laid aside.

It is pretty remarkable, that although the practice of insurance has been carried to a much greater extent in Britain than in any other country in Europe, yet we have few statutory regulations on that subject.

This circumstance may perhaps be, in part, accounted for, from the late period, comparatively speaking, at which the commerce and the insurance of Britain became extensive. The rise of Britain, as a great mercantile nation, was posterior

rior even to that of the Netherlands, and of the Dutch commonwealth. All the European nations who made advances in commerce, had enacted feparate fyftems of mercantile regulation, which however agreed in moft points. The great doctrines with regard to infurance, came therefore to be previoufly fettled by the ufage and confent of merchants; and Britain, of confequence, had lefs occafion for pofitive ftatutes upon the fubject.

Befides, in a great and extenfive empire, like Britain, the attention of the Legiflature is lefs apt, than in fmall ftates, to be directed to the improvement of private jurifprudence.

In one remarkable inftance, indeed, the practice of infurance has, perhaps injudicioufly, been limited by public regulation. The facility of combination among merchants, their activity in promoting their own intereft, together with the credit and influence which they naturally poffefs with the Legiflature, have produced an attempt to erect a monopoly in this, as well as in other branches of commerce and manufacture.

In the year 1720, two great companies, known by the names of the *Royal Exchange Affurance Company,* and the *London Affurance Company,* made application to Parliament, to obtain the exclufive privilege of carrying on, as a company, all the infurances of the kingdom. And in confideration of L. 600,000, advanced towards payment of the debt contracted upon the civil lift,

their

their requeſt was granted. By an act, therefore, 6th Geo. I. c. 18. it was provided, "That it ſhall be lawful for his Majeſty, by two charters, to erect theſe two Companies into ſeparate incorporate bodies, for the aſſurance of ſhips and merchandiſe at ſea, or for lending money on bottomry. That all other *companies* ſhall be prohibited from engaging in theſe branches of trade, except the Eaſt India and South Sea Companies, which may ſtill lend upon the bottoms of their own ſhips." Private adventurers, however, are allowed to underwrite as formerly.

When this act was made, it is probable that the ſtock of an aſſociation of merchants was neceſſary for producing ſufficient credit to carry on an extenſive trade of inſurance; and that the excluſive privilege given to the two companies above mentioned, in contradiſtinction to all other companies, was therefore ſuppoſed to be of ſome conſequence. But ſince that time, the great accumulation of wealth in the hands of individuals, has produced a proportionable confidence in their perſonal ſecurity, and enabled them to cope even with the mercantile companies in this branch of buſineſs. The ſtatute, at the ſame time, is in ſome meaſure, evaded, by making the inſurance in the name of an individual, who, by a private agreement, becomes bound to communicate with others his profit and loſs.

The ſcheme of monopolizing the buſineſs of inſurance,

infurance, has not been confined to Britain; a regulation fimilar to the Britifh ftatute above mentioned, was introduced in Paris, in the year 1686, when the exclufive right of underwriting, *as a company*, was vefted in a fociety, confifting only of thirty perfons. Limitations of this kind, it is believed, ftill continue, although with a lefs degree of ftrictnefs; and to this fpirit of reftraint, one of their own writers afcribes the little progrefs which the French have made in infurances.

The authors who have written exprefsly upon infurance in Britain, are not numerous. There have been feveral books on maritime affairs in general, which contain a few occafional obfervations, and fome practical cafes relating to infurance; but which are comparatively of fmall importance. The chief of.thefe are, MOLLOY *de Jure Maritimo et Navali;* GERARD MALYNES' *Lex Mercatoria*; POSTLETHWAITE's *Dictionary of Commerce*; BEAWES' *Lex Mercatoria rediviva*.

The firft author of note who writes exprefsly upon infurance is NICHOLAS MAGENS, merchant. His book, in two volumes, which was publifhed in 1755, confifts of a fhort effay on infurance; a collection of cafes relating to adjuftments and averages; a compilation of foreign mercantile ordinances; and a number of treaties with foreign powers. It is, undoubtedly a work of great utility and merit. His compilation of the moft important fyftems of foreign ordinances,

ordinances, must continue to be much in request. His *essay*, which is principally founded upon these, is concise, acute, and practical; and had he lived at a period subsequent to the decisions of Lord Mansfield, might perhaps have superseded many future treatises on the subject. The other parts of his book are less judicious. His collection of cases of *adjustment* and average, is excessively voluminous and prolix; and each case is stated with a minuteness of calculation, that few people have application enough to follow. It is to be regretted, that while he inserted these, and a variety of *treaties of peace*, that are extremely foreign to the subject, he should have totally overlooked that great source of equitable regulation, the decisions of courts of justice, in England, and in other countries.

The small volume on " Bills of Exchange " and insurances," ascribed to Mr Cunningham, is principally a compilation of adjudged cases, taken from Strange's Reports, and from Molloy, Malynes, and the older writers, with very little general observation, and still less method. The work by Mr Parker on the " Laws " of Shipping and Insurance," is a similar collection of the acts of Parliament, relating to these subjects, and of cases extending to a period somewhat more recent; but without any attempt at arrangement.

The late publication by Mr Wesket, in the form of a dictionary, contains by far the greatest

est collection of materials on the subject of insurances hitherto published in this country. It is unnecessary to give any account of a book so generally known; and the numerous documents it contains will sufficiently justify the use made of it by the author of the present Treatise, especially in matters of practice.

But the great improvement of English law, with regard to insurance, has proceeded from the number of decisions which our courts of justice have recently pronounced upon that subject. The trade of Britain, has, of late, been so extensive and various, as to increase to a very great degree the demand for insurance, and to bring under discussion a multiplicity of curious and interesting points. There is perhaps no subject of private jurisprudence, upon which the liberal views of the present age, and the refined notions of equity, as well as the great knowledge and abilities of the English judges, have been of late more eminently displayed. It would be presumption in the author to speak more particularly of the distinguished character to whom the kingdom is principally indebted for these decisions.

In Scotland, the improvements of this branch of law have been still later than in England, as might be expected from the slower progress of its commerce. Although the decisions of the principal court of justice have been pretty regularly collected, for more than a century, yet, the first decisions which, strictly speaking, relate to *insurance*, are all, except one, within the course of the last ten years. During this period, however, the trade of insuring has risen to a very great height ; and the decisions of the Court of Session, upon that subject, have become proportionably comprehensive and systematic.

4. The subjects of insurance may be as various as the different species of property, and the different sorts of danger to which these may be exposed. This variety has, in some cases, been limited by common law, as well as by express regulation.

It is unnecessary to enter into a minute detail of the different cases in which insurance is prohibited. The great example of restriction in this respect, those prohibitions which are calculated for the prevention of gaming, will fall to be more particularly considered hereafter.

All insurance on illicit trade is prohibited, as well as the commerce it tends to encourage. This seems to follow from the principles of common law, without positive enactment. Every person who insures contraband goods, is assisting and abetting in an evasion of the law. Nay, as the insurer takes the risk of capture and seizure upon himself, it is he, properly speaking, who is to be considered as the smuggler. Every insurance upon a trade which the parties know to be illicit, must therefore be illegal ; it is a contract *ob turpem*

turpem caufam; and the perfon who claims upon fuch a policy, muft found upon his own crime.

The principles of common law, however, upon this fubject, have very univerfally been enforced and confirmed by exprefs regulation. This is the cafe among all the foreign mercantile ftates, without exception.

In England, the Legiflature has, befides declaring the law, added the fanction of a fevere penalty on all infurance on contraband trade. By ftat. 4. and 5. W. and M. c. 15. it is provided, that " all perfons who fhall undertake, *by way of " infurance*, or otherwife, to deliver any goods, " *&c. without paying the duties or cuftoms, or " any prohibited goods whatever*," fhall forfeit the fum of L. 500; and that the like fum fhall be forfeited by the affured.

This general ftatute, with regard to illegal infurance, has been repeated and applied to particular inftances of prohibited trade *. It is only deferving of notice, that, by the Union, this, like every other ftatute regulating the foreign commerce of England, is underftood to be extended to Scotland.

The general prohibition of infurance on illicit trade, is illuftrated by the following cafe:

JOHNSTON *againft* SUTTON.

Sutton infured *Johnfton* " on goods on board " the fhip *Venus, at and from London to New*
" *York*."

---

* See the ftat. 8. and 9. W. and M.—12. GEO. II. c. 21.

"*York.*" The ship had been cleared for *Halifax* and *New York*; she had provisions on board, which she had a licence to carry to *New York*, under a proviso of the prohibitory act 16. GEO. III. c. 5.; but one half of the cargo, including the goods which were the subjects of this policy, was not licensed, and was not calculated for the *Halifax* market, but for *New York*. There had been a proclamation by Sir William Howe, allowing the entry of unlicensed goods at *New York*; but this proclamation the Commander had no authority, under the act of Parliament, to issue. The *Venus* was taken in her passage to New York, by an American privateer.

A verdict having been found for the plaintiffs, a rule for a new trial was granted; the court were clear, that this being an insurance on an illicit trade, was therefore null; and judgment was given for the defendant, by the *rule being made absolute*. Dougl. Rep. Nov. 15. 1779.

It has been the subject of doubt, how far this rule of common law, annulling insurances on illicit trade, is applicable to the case, where a branch of traffic is permitted in one country, but prohibited in another; how far ought an insurance, contrary to the law of either of those nations, between whose subjects a trade is carried on, to be supported by a foreign court of justice.

On the one hand, it has been laid down, by a
very

very eminent Scots law authority[*], that no bargain, contrary to the law of the *locus contractus*, and consequently to the duty of the contracting parties, can be effectual in any country.

"Obedience," says he, "is due to the laws of our country, and to transgress any of them is a moral wrong. This moral wrong ought to weigh with judges in every country; because it is an act of injustice to support any moral wrong, by making it the foundation either of an action, or of an exception. I give for an example, the statute prohibiting any member of a court of law to buy land about which there is a plea depending. Such a purchase being made notwithstanding, the purchaser follows the vender into a foreign country, in order to compel him, by a process, to make the bargain effectual. A bargain unlawful, where made, becomes not lawful by change of place; and therefore the foreign judge ought not to support such unlawful bargain, by sustaining action upon it."

The general line of decision in the supreme court of Scotland seems agreeable to Lord Kames's position, that the judges of one country are, so far, *ex comitate*, bound to pay attention to the laws, though merely municipal, of another. There does not occur any distinction between *revenue* ordinances, and any other species of municipal regulation.

This

[*] Princip. of Equity, b. 3. c. 8. § 7.

This doctrine is undoubtedly the liberal one; but it is attended with some difficulties. The interpretation of a foreign municipal law, it may be argued, whether consuetudinary or statutory, must, in many cases, be a matter of great difficulty; and in which our courts of justice are by no means competent to judge. To support a foreign regulation, is a very different matter from enforcing a foreign decree; because, in the latter case, the court is relieved from all question with regard to the application of the law. But there may be more danger from their misunderstanding a foreign municipal ordinance, than from their neglecting it altogether. In the one case, by disregarding the regulation, the judge only fails to support a right; in the other, by mistaking and misapplying the law, he enforces a positive wrong. These reasonings, however, do not appear conclusive.

From the opinion above stated, it follows, that wherever an insurance is illegal at first, being inconsistent with the duty of the contracting parties, such an agreement ought not to be sustained in any country whatever. Suppose, therefore, that two English subjects residing at Paris, should execute an insurance in each others favour, upon wool to be exported from England. Such a bargain, being criminal in British subjects, ought not to found action in France. Or suppose that two Englishmen, residing at Paris, insure each other on goods to be smuggled into France;

France; such a policy ought not to be sustained at London; for it was illegal at first, being contrary to the *lex loci contractus*, and therefore inconsistent with that temporary obedience which every man owes to the laws of that country in which he resides.

But a third case may be put, in which a different conclusion must be drawn. Suppose that two persons, residing in their own country, agree to insure upon goods to be smuggled into any foreign state; the bargain would probably be reprobated by the state which was to suffer the detriment; but it ought to be supported every where else; for it is an innocent bargain. The rules of natural equity, it may be observed, are obligatory every where; but those regulations which are merely municipal, like the *revenue* ordinances of a country, have no obligation beyond the jurisdiction of the enacting power. The revenue laws of any nation, are, in the view of foreigners, mere measures of expediency, adopted to supply the necessities of government. They are matters of fact, which foreigners are not supposed to know; and restrictions upon natural right, in which, although known, they are not bound to acquiesce. This is established by the following decision:

In the month of July 1778, *Planché* and *Jacquery, merchants in London*, procured insurance, from *Fletcher*, " upon goods on
" board

" board the *Maria Magdalena*, a Swedish ship,
" *at and from London and Ramsgate to Nantz,*
" *with liberty to call at Ostend,* being a gene-
" ral ship in the port of London for Nantz."
It was understood, that she was to go directly to *Nantz,* without touching at *Ostend*; but the ship's clearances from the customhouse in London were all made out as for *Ostend* only. At the same time, the captain, while at London, with a view of evading certain French duties, signed bills of loading, in the French language, bearing to be made at *Ostend,* and representing the goods as shipped at *Ostend* for *Nantz.* The proclamation for reprizals on French ships having appeared previous to the ship's sailing, she was taken by a King's cutter, and the goods were condemned.

Lord MANSFIELD said, " the reason for clear-
" ing for Ostend, and signing bills of lading as
" from thence, did not fully appear. But it was
" guessed at. The *Fermiers Generaux* have the
" management of the taxes in France. As we
" have laid a large duty on French goods, the
" French may have done the same on ours, and
" it may be the interest of the farmers to connive
" at the importation of English commodities, and
" to take Ostend duties, rather than stop the trade
" altogether, by exacting a tax which amounts
" to a prohibition. But, at any rate, this was no
" fraud in this country. *One nation does not*
" *take*

" *take notice of the revenue laws of another**." Dougl. Rep. Nov. 15. 1779.

Another prohibition has been very generally adopted among the maritime states of Europe; that of insurance, by seamen, upon their own wages. This has been introduced, from the view of securing the diligence and activity of that class of men in the preservation of ship and cargo. As this prohibition, however, has no foundation whatever in common law, it can only be considered as taking place in those countries where it has been enforced by positive enactment. Views of expediency, however great, are not of themselves sufficient to establish what is law. In Britain, accordingly, where the Legislature have made no provision upon the subject, an insurance, by seamen, upon their own wages, must undoubtedly be held as valid. It does not appear that the point has been expressly decided; but, in Scotland at least, such insurances are by no means without

---

* It is material to observe, that, in this case, there was a declaration in the policy, that the insurance was made on account of *Vallée & Dupleffis, Monsieur Luffeau le jeune, Guillaume Albert, et Poitier de la Gueule*. From these names, and from the condemnation, it was assumed by the defendants counsel, that the interest was French. But Lord MANSFIELD said, " It does not appear that the goods are " French property. An Englishman might be sending his " goods to France in a neutral ship."

without example, and have never been the subject of challenge *.

Many of the foreign mercantile states prohibit insurance on *lives:* A prohibition arising from the jealousy naturally entertained in an ill regulated government, of whatever may serve as a motive to the commission of great crimes. The same jealousy is yet more apparent in some of the Italian states, where insurance is not only prohibited on the lives of great men, but on any political occurrence, and even on *marriages* and the *birth of children.*

In this country, insurances may relate chiefly to three different subjects. 1*st*, A man may insure his house and effects from the accidents of fire. 2*dly*, A person who has a revenue or pecuniary advantage depending on his own life, or on the life of any other person, may insure the continuance of that revenue for a time specified. And, *lastly,* A man may insure his property from the risk attending its transportation from place to place, either by sea or land.

Of all these, by far the most important, and that which opens the most extensive and curious field of enquiry, is the insurance upon property exposed to the hazards of the sea. In speaking of

---

* The case of *Kay against Young* (quoted under *Concealment, p.* 1. *ch.* 2.), was an insurance by the captain on his own wages. Although it was keenly litigated, this point was not started.

of infurance, therefore, it will be underftood, that, in general, this laft, or what may be called *maritime infurance*, is meant. At the fame time, notice fhall be taken of any peculiarities that occur with regard to the infurance on *lives*, and from *fire*.

Infurance on a maritime adventure may be either on the *fhip*, the *cargo*, or on the *freight*, that is, on the wages which the fhip ought to earn by the carriage of goods from port to port.

We are told alfo, that mercantile adventurers, particularly in the Mediterranean, were formerly accuftomed to infure their perfonal liberty. The effect of this agreement was to fubject the infurer in the ranfom, if the affured was made a captive. It is imagined an agreement of this kind is now very uncommon; but where it takes place, it is not materially different from an infurance againft the lofs of a fhip or cargo; and therefore does not feem to deferve a feparate confideration.

5. In treating of this fubject, I fhall confider, *firft*, How the contract is entered into, or the circumftances requifite to produce a valid infurance. *Secondly*, What are the obligations arifing from it. And, *laftly*, What are the circumftances by which the obligations of parties may be extinguifhed, particularly thofe peculiar to this agreement.

ELE-

ELEMENTS
OF
INSURANCE.

PART I.

Of the circumstances requisite to produce a valid Insurance.

THE great circumstance essential to the constitution of insurance, as well as of every other contract, is the *consent of parties*.

Upon this subject, we may consider, *first*, the *form of words*, or writing, in which this consent must be expressed.

2*dly*, The consent of parties, in order to produce a valid obligation, must be free from *force*, from *fraud*, and, in certain cases, from *error or mistake*. It will open an extensive and curious field of enquiry, to examine the operation of the general principles of law, with respect to several of these particulars, when applied to a contract of so peculiar a nature as that of insurance.

Lastly,

Lastly, We may examine whether consent alone, although free from the intervention of fraud and error, and expressed in a formal deed, will be sufficient to produce a complete contract of insurance; or, how far, after such legal consent, parties have a *right to recede from their agreement.*

CHAP. I.

Of the form of an Insurance-contract.

THE importance of the contract of insurance, and the singularity of those obligations which it is intended to create, have, in all commercial states, rendered a deed in writing essential to its validity. In most countries where insurance is practised, printed forms of policies are used, varying according to the object of the agreement, with blanks for the circumstances in which one adventure may differ from another. In the expression of these, there is considerable variety in different countries. The following is offered, as a neat and concise example of a maritime policy * :

" *Lion*,—SHAW, *from New York to Clyde, at two guineas* per cent.

" IN the Name of GOD, AMEN. Know all men, by these presents, that we subscribers, merchants in Glasgow, have assured, likeas, we, each

---

* For the London form, see the appendix; as well as for the form of a policy on lives, and from fire.

each of us for ourselves, do, by these presents, assure to, and in favour of, *Messrs A. B. and Co. merchants in Glasgow, for themselves, or for whom it may concern*, the several sums of money annexed to our respective subscriptions underwritten, upon *the hull, boats, materials, and other furniture, of and in the Lion; likewise, upon the freight of said Lion, and upon all and whatsoever kinds of goods and merchandise, laden or to be laden, on said account, aboard of said Lion*, burden—————tons, or thereabout, whereof *John Shaw*— is master, for this present voyage, or whosoever else shall go master in the said ship, or by whatever other name the said ship or master is, or shall be called; beginning the adventure upon the said *hull and aforesaids, at and from New York, and upon the said freight, and goods and merchandise, at and from the lading thereof aboard the said Lion, and to continue and endure, until she shall arrive at Greenock or Port-Glasgow, and be safely moored twenty-four hours, and said freight, and said goods and merchandise be there safely landed.* The said *hull and aforesaids*, are and shall be valued at one thousand pounds Sterling, and said freight at five hundred pounds Sterling, and said goods and merchandise, as value may hereafter appear by invoices; according to which particular sum, all losses that may happen upon the said *hull and aforesaids*, are to be repaired by us, proportionably to the several sums annexed

to

to our subscriptions, in manner underwritten. Touching the adventures and perils, which we, the said assurers, are contented to bear, and do take upon us in this voyage; they are of the sea, men of war, fire, enemies, pirates, rovers, thieves, jettezons, letters of mart, and countermart, surprisals, takings at sea, arrests, restraints, and detainments, of all Kings, Princes, or people, of what nation, condition, or quality soever, baratry of the master and mariners, and all other perils, losses, or misfortunes, that have, or shall come, to the hurt, detriment, or damage of the said *hull and aforesaids*, or any part thereof, during this adventure. And in case of any misfortune or loss, it shall be lawful for the assured, their factors, servants, or assigns, to sue, labour, and travel for, in and about the defence, safeguard, and recovery of the said *hull and aforesaids*, or any part thereof, without prejudice to this assurance, to the charges whereof we the assurers will contribute each of us for ourselves, according to the respective sums assured by us in manner underwritten. And it is agreed by us, the assurers, that this writing and assurance shall be of as much force and effect, as the surest policy, or writing of assurance made at London. And so we the assurers, do hereby bind and oblige us, each of us for ourselves, conform to the sums of money annexed to our respective subscriptions underwritten, our heirs and successors, to the saids *Messrs A. B.*
and

and Co. their heirs, executors, and affigns, for the true performance of the premifes, and to repair any lofs they fhall fuftain upon the faid *hull and aforefaids,* or any part thereof, to the extent of the fums at which the fame are particularly valued, in manner above written, during the continuance of this adventure; confefling ourfelves paid the confideration due to us for this affurance, by the affured, after the rate of *two guineas per centum.* And it is further agreed, that in cafe of average lofs, not exceeding *five* pounds *per* hundred, upon the faid whole fhip, tackle, apparel, boat, and other furniture, and upon the whole goods and merchandifes, laden or to be laden aboard the faid fhip, we are not to pay, or allow any thing towards repairing fuch lofs."

"And it is further agreed, that in cafe any difpute or difference fhall arife, relating to a lofs on this policy, it fhall be referred to two indifferent perfons, one to be chofen by the faid affured, and the other by us, who fhall have full power to adjuft the fame; and in cafe they cannot agree, then fuch two perfons fhall chufe a third perfon to be overfman and umpire betwixt them; and any two of them agreeing, their fentence and award fhall be obligatory to both parties: With and under the burden of which three laft named provifions thefe prefents are granted, and no other ways. In witnefs whereof we have fubfcribed scribed these presents*, (printed on stamped paper, conform to act of Parliament,) at Glasgow, the *first* day of *January,* One thousand seven hundred and eighty *six* years, before these witnesses, *C. D. merchant in Glasgow, and D. F. merchant there,* by whom the blanks, witnesses names and designations are filled up."

" *N. B.* Insurers are not liable for any average-loss upon grain, fish, fruit, wine, provisions, or other goods which in their own nature are liable to perish or decay, by continuing long on board, or being faulty or decayed before shipping: But the owners of such goods shall recover, on a general average, when any part of them are thrown overboard, for the preservation of the whole; and on a particular average, when the damage happens by stranding or bulging."

All contracts of insurance agree in certain general clauses, which may be considered as essential. Every policy must settle the following particulars:

1*st,* The person in whose favour the insurance is made.

2*dly,* The subject insured, whether house, life, ship, goods, or freight.

3*dly,* The sort of danger from which the subject is warranted.

4*thly,*

---

* This clause is peculiar to policies used at *Glasgow*. It has the effect of making the policy a complete deed, according to the Scots form of writings.

4*thly*, The confideration or premium given by the affured. And,

5*thly*, The fubfcription of the underwriters, with the place and date of each fubfcription.

To thefe five articles, it fhould feem, all the claufes that in Britain ufually enter into an infurance-policy may be reduced.

With regard to the perfon in whofe favour the infurance is made, this head of the policy comprehends all thofe claufes which may be prompted by an anxiety to prevent miftakes in this matter; fuch as, that the infurance fhall be valid " in favour of whoever fhall be proprietor of the " fubject;" or with regard to the point, how far the policy may admit of *affignment*.

The *fecond* head comprehends all thofe circumftances of defignation and defcription that may appear neceffary to identify the fubject; and thofe claufes which ferve to afcertain what proportion of the fubject is fecured from hazard. This, in infurances on lives and from fire, is generally executed by a particular ftipulation, expreffing to what extent the infurer fhall be refponfible. In maritime infurances, which are frequently underwritten by a number of individuals, it is done by a fum of money being adjected to each fubfcription. Claufes *valuing* the fubject infured, have a fimilar effect, and are extremely common.

The

The *third* article of the policy, the *danger* to which the infurer is fubjected, feems to depend upon two particulars; the extent of the lofs which may be incurred, and the nature and circumftances of the adventure from which that lofs may arife. To afcertain this laft, which is of the utmoft confequence, it is neceffary, in maritime infurances, to fpecify when the rifk fhall commence and terminate; the port of loading, and that of the difcharge of the veffel, together with the different places at which, during the voyage, fhe may touch.

Under this head may likewife occur a variety of exceptions and conditions, which are explanations of the adventure undertaken, and farther limitations of the danger to which the infurer fubjects himfelf. The underwriter on fire, for example, fometimes excepts from his obligation the danger of fire from *foreign invafion*. The infurer on lives fometimes thinks it of fufficient importance to infert the exception of death by *fuicide*, or *the hand of juftice*.

With refpect to the two laft articles, the receipt of the premium muft be acknowledged by the underwriter, for reafons to be afterwards explained. And the policy is fubfcribed by him alone, becaufe it is the underwriter alone who comes under an obligation to a future performance.

In foreign, and in many Britifh policies, there is a claufe by which parties bind themfelves to fubmit submit any questions that may arise, to the decision of arbiters. But this in Britain is not understood to exclude an application to the judicial establishments of the country. Foreign policies likewise contain a clause fixing the *forum* in which the contract shall be made effectual. But this is never practised in Britain.

It does not appear, that, naturally, any form of words whatever is essential to an insurance contract, provided it contains the clauses above mentioned. All the foreign commercial states, however, who have attempted any regulation on this head, have prescribed a particular style to be employed. Among some of them *, this form is necessary to the validity of the contract. In others †, the deviation from it is attended with a penalty, but without annulling the deed.

In England, where few statutory regulations have taken place upon insurance, every man, it should seem, may adopt that form of expression which pleases his own fancy. Writing seems, however, to be indirectly rendered necessary, by a statute now to be mentioned.

In this country, the frequency and importance of the contract of insurance has pointed it out to government, as a proper source of public revenue. Accordingly, by stat. 11. Geo. I. *c.* 30. § 44. it was provided, that, " when any vessel " or merchandises shall be insured, a policy, du- " ly stamped, shall be issued or made out, within
" three

---

* Antwerp, Florence.　　† Spain.

" three days at farthest, under the penalty of
" L. 100 upon the insurer, to be recovered like
" all other penalties, in relation to the stamp-
" duties." And promissory notes, unstamped,
for assurances of ships or merchandises, are declared null.

With regard to the amount of this stamp-duty, it was provided by 8th Geo. III. *c.* 25. that property extending to L. 1000, might be insured with a 5 s. stamp, and all above it with two 5 s. stamps; but that without these, the insurance shall be void, and the premium shall remain the property of the insurer*. By stat. 16th Geo. III. *c.* 24. an additional duty has been laid on, of one shilling on every policy †.

The effect of these statutes, therefore, seems in one view to be this: A bargain of insurance may be entered into, by any writing, or even verbally;

---

* The *onus probandi* lies upon the insurer, that a policy properly stamped, had been made out. Betts, *qui tam &c.* against Carman. Betts brought an action on stat. 11. Geo. I. c. 30. § 44. against *Carman*, to recover the penalties from the defendant, for underwriting without a stamped policy.

Ashurst I. held, That the plaintiff did enough to support his case, if he proved the contract; which he did, by a letter from the defendant, acknowledging the receipt of the premium: That it was incumbent on the defendant to shew the actual execution of the policy, within the terms of the act; and that a stamped policy, made three days after, was no defence. The Court confirmed this judgment, by refusing the defendant a new trial. *Mich.* 24th Geo. III. B. R.——M. S.

† Similar duties are exigible on fire and life policies.

verbally; but after three days, it cannot afford a ground of action, unless extended on paper stamped in terms of the act. The assured, likewise, shall have no action to recover his premium, and the insurer shall forfeit L. 100, as penalties, for attempting to defraud the revenue.

The requisites above mentioned being attended to, and the policy expressed in intelligible language, the contract of insurance is complete, as to form.

CHAP. II.

Of the effect of Fraud and Error, in a Policy of Insurance.

IT is abundantly evident, that direct fraud among contracting parties, must be destructive of the validity of any engagement. The person who practises fraud in his dealings, is criminal. The sympathy and indignation of the public are interested, to redress the sufferer; to prevent the other party from acquiring an advantage by his own delinquency, and even to subject him to punishment.

This principle is particularly applicable to the bargain of insurance. In this agreement, the situation of parties supposes a mutual confidence and good faith, in a peculiar degree; and the notion of *fraud* meets with a more extensive construction from the law, than in other contracts.

In many other transactions; in the sale of any commodity, for example, it is enough if the vender does not actually impose upon the purchaser, by representing his merchandise as different from what it is in reality; it infers no fraud that he does not disclose all its defects. The merchant submits his goods to the inspection of the purchaser, who is supposed, in a certain degree, to trust to his own skill; and if, confiding in appearances, he should reject a better commodity, and chuse a worse, or if he should be mistaken in the market-price of it, the merchant will not be deprived of the advantage arising from his own duplicity and concealment in this respect.

But insurance is an agreement, not with regard to a subject already existing, but a future contingency. There is nothing presented to the senses for ocular inspection; the question is with regard to the amount of a probability; and all those circumstances on which that probability depends must be disclosed, before the subject of the intended bargain can be fairly judged of.

The full communication of every particular relating to the risk, is peculiarly incumbent upon the assured. The assured is often the owner of the ship: He is, in all cases, more connected with the owners than the underwriter is: He has far better opportunities, therefore, of being acquainted with the nature of the adventure, the strength of the ship, the condition of the

the cargo, the perils of the voyage; and, with regard to any peculiarity in these respects, the underwriter must depend on the information of his assured. It becomes absolutely necessary to guard, with the utmost circumspection, against fraudulent conduct on the part of the assured, for which he has so much temptation and opportunity.

Not only, therefore, is the smallest degree of deceit, and direct *misrepresentation* sufficient to destroy the policy; but every intentional *concealment* of circumstances, which may any way affect the consent of parties, is a breach of that peculiar trust and confidence reposed by the one party in the other; and it vacates the agreement as a species of fraud. All *intentional concealment*, of circumstances which vary the risk, *is fraud*, in insurance.

The effect of *error and mistake*, in destroying the consent of parties to an insurance policy, is no less worthy of observation.

A policy of insurance resembles other contracts, in requiring that parties should be fully agreed about the nature and qualities of the subject of their bargain. If, whether from *fraud* or from *error*, the subject is considered by one of the parties, as *materially different* from what it is in reality, the agreement is, in fact, incomplete, and the person who suffers is entitled to redress.

Put the case, that one person sells a horse, which has some important latent defect, such as, if known, would put a stop to the bargain; the purchase must be invalid; for the horse is, in fact, materially different from that which the other party intended to buy; and consent, the essential circumstance of a contract, is here really wanting.

The same thing holds in a policy of insurance. The assured, for a premium given, purchases indemnity upon a specified event; and the insurer, for the consideration received, subjects himself to a risk. If that event appears to the insurer in a light materially different from what it is in reality, the risk undertaken becomes different from what was understood; the contract entered into is, in fact, different from that which was intended, and must be null, as wanting the consent of parties.

In ordinary contracts, in a sale, for example, a distinction may be made betwixt various kinds and degrees of error. The most striking instance of error occurs, where one individual subject is mistaken for another; as when a person is commissioned to purchase a particular horse, and by mistake purchases another instead of him. Nearly connected is that degree of error which relates to the *essential qualities* of a subject; suppose, for instance, a horse is bought for the plough, and it appears, upon trial, he has never been broke to that service.

The

The purchaser of any commodity, no doubt, when it is fairly submitted to his inspection, is understood to depend, in a certain degree, upon his own skill in estimating its value. But there are certain qualities which every vender must be supposed to *warrant* to the purchaser; the merchant is understood to warrant the commodity as not materially deficient in respect of its principal uses. And if it should turn out to be, in a high degree, incapable of being applied to those purposes for which such a commodity is intended, although there should be no fraud in the vender, the losing purchaser must be freed from his bargain.

The question however recurs; What are those qualities which the vender is supposed to warrant? The defect of any commodity is a matter of degree; and how far may a latent defect extend without annulling the contract? It may be answered, the merchant is supposed to warrant those qualities which have been essential to the agreement, and without which there would have been no agreement. It is, therefore, such error only as *gives rise to the bargain*, that can render it invalid; such as, if corrected in proper time, would have totally prevented the contract from taking place.

With regard to mistakes of inferior importance, as to the nature and qualities of the subject, such as, if corrected in time, could not have prevented the bargain altogether, but only altered ed the terms of it; they never can be sustained to annul the agreement; although, where they are very apparent, they may operate as a reason for a deduction from the price. Still less attention seems to be due to errors in the *market-value* of any commodity. A mistake as to the nature and qualities of a subject may be unavoidable; but every purchaser may inform himself as to the ordinary market-price; and he is therefore more readily supposed to trust to his own skill with regard to it. By the Roman law, a remedy was allowed against such error when it rose to a very great extent; but modern mercantile nations have refused any redress whatever against errors in the market-price of commodities, as prejudicial to the interest of commerce.

The same views, it should seem, with regard to the effects of error and mistake, which apply to other covenants, extend likewise, in general, to contracts of insurance. If a vessel has been insured, and it is afterwards discovered that she was so leaky and rotten at the commencement of the adventure, as to be *insufficient* to perform the voyage, even although there may have been no fraud or concealment on the part of the assured; yet there is here such a degree of error as will invalidate the consent of the insurer.

These reasonings, however, with regard to *error*, are only applicable where a mistake has occurred, which is not imputable to any *fault* of either of the contracting parties. It is only where

where the merchant has submitted his goods fully and fairly to the inspection of his customer, that no mistake will annul the sale, except an *error in substantialibus*, a mistake which had given rise to the agreement.

But, what if one of the parties has, without fraudulent design, from culpable inattention and negligence merely, or from ignorance, misled the other by erroneous information? In such a case, it will not be necessary, in order to annul the contract, that the mistake committed should be of a nature so important. Any mistake, whether it respects the *qualities* or *value* of the subject; not only such as *led to a bargain* at first, but such as *enhanced the price* of the commodity, will invalidate the consent of parties.

Of this variation from the general effect of error, the contract of insurance affords several examples.

Suppose, on the one hand, the merchant should *communicate information* to the underwriter, that the vessel was safe in port, when, in reality, the fact was otherwise; or, suppose, on the other, he *conceals* a *letter of advice*, informing him that the ship had sailed before a particular day. If either the *misrepresentation* or *concealment* was intentional, the policy is void, as being founded on fraud. But granting the assured to have acted without design, from mere oversight, or ignorance of what was proper to be done;

done; the question will be, Whether the misrepresentation or concealment is *material?* that is, whether the insurer's hazard is affected by it; and if the smallest variation of the *risk run* from *that intended*, is thereby produced, the consent of parties must still be invalid.

The *insurer*, in the cases above stated, is seeking to be free from a bargain which he considers as unequal; he is therefore endeavouring to *avoid actual loss*, as well as the assured. He has been drawn into that bargain without any misconduct of his own; for he acted reasonably in trusting to the information of the other party; and he was entitled to expect from him a full communication with respect to the extent of the risk.

But the *assured* does not appear free from the imputation of fault in the transaction in question. Every person who engages in insurances knows, or ought to know, how much the underwriter must depend on the information of his assured; and the latter ought therefore to be upon his guard not to communicate what may *mislead*. He ought to be aware of the situation of mutual trust and confidence in which he stands with his party; and he ought to be extremely careful not to *conceal*. A moderate degree of attention might prevent both; and he appears guilty of gross negligence, who falls into either.

This

This diſtinction between the effects of *ſimple error*, and *miſrepreſentation* or *concealment*, is farther ſtrengthened by views of expediency.

In the caſe of a miſtake which has not ariſen from the information given by either of the parties, there is no harm in ſuſtaining the contract, unleſs the miſtake is of great magnitude: But it would be highly dangerous to give ſupport, in any extent, to a bargain, where an error has originated from the act and deed of one of them. This would be opening a door to diſhoneſt artifice; and the pretence of inattention and ignorance would be always at hand, as a cover to fraudulent intention.

Every inſtance of miſrepreſentation and concealment, therefore, however unintentional, *if it varies the riſk undertaken,* in the minuteſt particular, *from that underſtood,* deſtroys the conſent of parties, and annuls the contract. It implies, not only miſtake, but *miſtake founded on fault.* " *Culpa lata,*" ſay the civilians, " *æquiparatur* " *dolo.*" *Miſrepreſentation* and *concealment,* in all caſes of inſurance, carry with them a degree of groſs negligence, which is a ſort of *conſtructive fraud* in the eye of law, to the effect of deſtroying every obligation founded upon it.

Theſe principles now ſtated, with regard to fraud, error, and fault, will be found to operate in a variety of queſtions that occur in the ſubject of inſurance. We may, in this view, conſider, the effect of *direct fraud* of any kind;—of *erroneous information*;—of *mutual miſtake.*

SECT.

Sect. I. *Of direct Fraud.*

1. Whenever, in the *first* place, the consent of either the assured or underwriter has been elicited by direct fraud, or by dishonest artifice of any kind, there can be little doubt that such consent must be totally without effect. The contract is null and void from the beginning.

Of this a variety of examples may be produced; as where a person insures a rotten ship, and contrives to have her sunk; of which we have an instance in the case of *Firebrass* v. *Perkins*, quoted in MOLLOY*. Or where a person insures goods not shipped, or relands them, with a view to defraud the underwriters; of which likewise a variety of examples must suggest themselves. But the following case may afford sufficient illustration of so clear a principle.

WHITTINGHAM *v.* THORNBOROUGH.

J. S. and others came to the insurance-office, and brought a policy to insure, for a year, the life of A, upon which they had no concern or interest depending. The policy run, "Whether "interested or not interested." In order to draw in subscribers, they agreed with M, a known merchant upon the Exchange, and a leading man in such cases, to subscribe first; but in case A died within the year, M was to lose nothing

* B. 2. c. 7. § 5.

nothing, but, on the contrary, was to share what should be gained from the other subscribers. Upon the credit of M's subscription, several others having enquired of M. about A, who was his neighbour, subscribed likewise. A died in four months, and the bill was to be relieved against this policy. These facts being all confessed by the answer, the policy was decreed to be delivered up, and the premium to be repaid, the plaintiff deducting thereout his costs. The court said, " In-
" suring was first set up for the benefit of trade,
" that when a merchant happened to have a
" loss he might not be undone by it, the loss
" in this way being borne by many. But if such
" ill practices were used, it would turn to the
" ruin of trade, instead of advancing it." *Preced. in Chancery.* 20. *Hil.* 1690. 2. *Eq. Abr.* 635.

2. Direct fraud in insurance, not only vacates the obligations of the innocent party, but renders him who has been guilty of it, the proper object of punishment.

" Any person," says the Ordinance of Stockholm, " making use of artifice, fraud, and fal-
" lacy, in any matter of insurance or average,
" shall not only make good to all parties concern-
" ed, all the inconveniencies and damages they
" may have received thereby, but likewise, on
" account of his offence, shall, according to the
" circumstances of the case, and the prescription
" of the penal laws enacted in our ordinance a-
" gainst

"gainst criminals, be punished in his estate, honour, and life*."

From similar views, where fraud has intervened in a contract of insurance, the obligation of the innocent party is not only vacated, so far as it appears to have originated from the deceit employed, but it is cut down altogether, as a punishment for dishonest intention. Thus, if a merchant fraudulently insures his ship or cargo beyond its real value, the insurance is not restricted to the real amount, but the policy is reduced *in totum*.

The different species of fraud in relation to insurance, as they differ from each other in kind and in degree, are in Britain the subjects of an arbitrary punishment. There is one species of fraud, however, which has been declared felony, by express statute. I mean the fraudulent destroying or sinking of ships.

It is unnecessary to recite the earlier statutes which have been enacted upon this subject. By an act of 4th Geo. I. it is provided, "That if any owner of, or captain, master, mariner, or other officer, belonging to any ship, shall wilfully cast away, burn, or otherwise destroy the ship, of which he is owner, or unto which he belongeth; or in any manner of way direct, or procure the same to be done, to the prejudice of any person or persons, that shall underwrite

---

* See the foreign ordinances, *passim*. *Mag.* v. 2.

"underwrite any policy or policies of infurance
"thereon, or of any merchant or merchants,
"that fhall load goods thereon, he fhall fuffer
"death."

And by another act, 11th GEO. I. it is enacted, "That if any owner of, or captain, mafter,
"officer, or mariner, belonging to any fhip or
"veffel, fhall wilfully caft away, burn, or other-
"wife deftroy the fhip or veffel of which he is
"owner, or to which he belongeth, or in any
"ways direct or procure the fame to be done,
"with intent or defign to prejudice any perfon
"that hath or fhall underwrite any policy of in-
"furance thereon, or of any merchant that fhall
"load goods thereon, or of any owner of fuch
"fhip or veffel, the perfon offending therein,
"being thereof lawfully convicted, fhall be deem-
"ed and adjudged a felon, and fhall fuffer as in
"cafes of felony, without benefit of clergy."

From fome peculiarities of expreffion in thefe ftatutes, which have been fuppofed applicable only to the Englifh mode of trial, it has been doubted how far they extend to Scotland. The queftion has been tried in two cafes; that of *Samuel Lampro*, in 1751; and that of *Herdman, M'Iver,* and *M'Callum,* fo late as the 1784. In *Lampro's* cafe, the Judge-admiral refufed to fuftain action upon the ftatutes. In that of *Herdman, M'Iver,* and *M'Callum,* the Judge-admiral had found, that the ftatutes *did extend* to Scotland; but his fentence was reverfed by the
Court

Court of Justiciary. It is unnecessary to enter into the particulars of these cases, as by a recent statute of his present Majesty, in the course of the summer 1786, an express enactment has taken place, remedying the imperfection of the law of Scotland in this respect, and declaring the crime of fraudulently sinking or destroying ships, to be punishable with death in that country as well as in England [*].

Sect. II. *Effect of erroneous Information; or of Mistake occasioned by the fault of the other Party.*

Erroneous information comprehends two species, which differ in form, though not in substance; *misrepresentation* and *concealment*. In both cases, the principle is the same, whether a falsehood be suggested, or a truth suppressed.

"Insurance," says Lord MANSFIELD, "is a
"contract upon speculation: The special facts
"upon which the contingent chance is to be
"computed, lie most commonly in the know-
"ledge of the insured only; the underwriter
"trusts to *his* representation, and proceeds upon
"confidence that he does not keep back any cir-
"cumstance in his knowledge, so as to mislead
"the underwriter into a belief that the circum-
"stance does not exist, and to induce him to
"estimate the risk as if it did not exist; *the*
"*keeping*

---

[*] In the act regulating the Court of Admiralty.

" *keeping back such circumstances is a fraud;* and
" therefore the policy is void."

" Although the suppression should happen by
" *mistake*, without any fraudulent intention, yet
" still the underwriter is deceived, and the policy
" is void; because the *risk run is really diffe-*
" *rent from the risk understood and intended to be*
" *run* at the time of the agreement."—

—" The policy would equally be void against
" the underwriter, if *he* concealed; as, if he
" insured a ship, on her voyage, which he pri-
" vately knew to be arrived; and an action
" would lie to recover the premium."—

—" The question, therefore, must always be,
" Whether there was, under all the circumstan-
" ces, at the time the policy was underwritten,
" a fair representation or a concealment? Frau-
" dulent, if designed; or, though not design-
" ed, varying materially the object of the policy,
" and changing the risk understood to be run."
In *Carter* v. *Boehm*.

Under this head, several cases may be distinguished.

I. Upon the principles already stated, if there be any thing peculiar in the *construction of the ship*, or the *nature of the cargo*, which is productive of extraordinary risk, it ought to be expressed in the policy, otherwise the insurer cannot be subjected to the consequences of such peculiarity.

arity. In judging of the extent of the infurer's obligation, we muft confider what circumftances were in the view of parties at the date of the contract. The infurer is entitled to fuppofe, that every thing refpecting the fhip is in its ordinary fituation; and he will not be obliged to anfwer for misfortunes, of which he was not aware, and therefore which he did not mean to undertake. Thefe peculiarities, however, muft in general be known to the affured, and the infurer ought to be freed from the effect of a confent, which, fo far, appears founded in improper and faulty concealment.

By the regulations of many foreign countries, accordingly, there are certain commodities which cannot be included under the general denomination of *goods* or *merchandife*, but muft be fpecified by name. Thus, by Ord. *Rotterd.* 1721, and *Amfterd.* 1744, " Ammunition, arms, gold, filver, " and jewels, muft be exprefsly declared."

By the *French* Ordinance, all goods fubject to leakage, muft be expreffed in the policy; and by the *Pruffian*, all goods fubject to corruption and leakage. In infurances made on flaves or cattle, by the Ordinance of *Spain*, this circumftance muft be declared in the policy, otherwife the infurers run no rifk. Similar regulations are introduced by the Ordinances of *Hamburg*, which make an exception, among others, of " goods " prohibited by powers at war;" by thofe of
Sweden;

Sweden; by the *Spanish West-Indian Laws;* and by those of *Florence* in 1526 *.

It was formerly observed, that insurance is prohibited upon contraband goods; and therefore it follows, that the underwriter is not liable for any loss on such goods. The principle now explained presents another reason, wherever the insurer has been ignorant that the goods were contraband, *viz.* that he appears to have been led by fraud and concealment to underwrite a cargo which was attended with extraordinary risk.

Another illustration occurs, although the principle does not seem to be carried its whole length. By the Ordinance of *Amsterdam* and of *Copenhagen,* "if a ship be *fir-built,* it must be expressed, "otherwise, in case of loss, the insurer is only "liable for *half* the damage."

In all these cases, the insurer suffers a loss by the concealment: He undertakes a risk greater than he intended; the circumstances concealed might, if discovered, have prevented the insurance altogether, or altered the terms of it; and the suppression of these circumstances implies *fault* in the assured.

II. Upon precisely the same principles, either party is liberated from obligation, and his consent to the contract becomes null and void, if the other has concealed any material *advices* relating to the situation of ship or cargo, with respect to the accidents of the voyage. Such a suppression of facts either supposes fraud, or such negligence and

* See MAGENS, vol. ii. p. 7. Vol. i. p. 9. 10.

and fault as ought to have the same effect with fraud in annulling the contract.

The strongest case of concealment of advices, is that alluded to by Lord MANSFIELD, in the passage above quoted, where the merchant gets his ship insured, knowing it to be lost; or the underwriter insures, knowing the vessel to be arrived. There is an example quoted by Mr WESKET, the case of *Ratcliffe* versus *Shulbred*, where the fraudulent concealment and misrepresentation seems to fall very little short of that now mentioned.

1. But the principle may be illustrated in a variety of instances, from that degree of concealment which is scarcely distinguishable from fraud, down to that which originates merely in blameable inattention.

D'ACOSTA *v.* SCANDERET.

J. S. having a doubtful account of his ship that was at sea, *viz.* that a ship *like his* was taken, insured her, without any information to the insurers of what he had heard, either as to the hazard or circumstances which might induce them to believe that his ship was in great danger, if not actually lost. The insurers bring a bill for an injunction, and to be relieved; and Lord MACCLESFIELD decreed the policy to be delivered up with costs, but the premium to be paid back, and allowed out of the costs; and his Lordship said, That the insured had not dealt fairly

fairly with the infurers, that he ought to have difclofed to them what intelligence he had of the fhip's being in danger, and which might induce at leaft to fear that it was loft, though he had no certain account. For if this had been difcovered, it is impoffible to think that the infurers would have infured the fhip at fo fmall a premium as they had done, but either would not have infured it at all, or would have infifted on a larger premium. So that the concealment of the intelligence is a *fraud*. 2. *Eq. Abr.* 635. *Trin.* 1723. 2. *P. Will.* 170.

ROOK *v.* THURMOND.

Rook got infurance made on the fhip *Polly*, from *South Carolina* to *Cowes*. The fhip, on the 12th of July 1741, failed from *South Carolina* for *Cowes*, and on 18th July was taken as a prize by the Spaniards. The defence infifted on for the underwriter was, that the plaintiff had been informed by a letter from *Carolina*, by a fhip called the *Collet*, that the *Polly*, the fhip infured, had failed ten days or a fortnight before the fhip *Collet*; and that the fhip *Collet* had arrived in *England* feven days before the infurance was made; and that the plaintiff had not given the defendant information of this circumftance at the date of the policy.

The Chief Juftice declared his opinion, that the concealment infifted on was a fufficient circumftance to difcharge the defendant from the policy;

policy; for he said, that those contracts are made upon a mutual faith and credit; and that to *conceal such circumstances which may make any difference in the adventure is fraudulent;* for the insurer ought to have the advantage of judgment upon them; and that where there is such concealment, the insurance ought not to bind. But the defendant not being able to make out this fact to the satisfaction of the jury, the plaintiff had a verdict. 1. *Dict. Tr. and Com.* 148, *19th Dec.* 1743. *At Guildhall.*

Hodgson *v.* Richardson.

The defendant insured the plaintiff on a cargo of potash, verdigrise, cotton, and other perishable goods, " *at and from Genoa to Dublin; the* " *adventure to begin from the port of loading,* " *liable to average.*" The cargo had been put on board at *Leghorn,* August 10th; and the vessel had been originally bound for Dublin. Having lost her convoy, she had put into *Genoa,* where she had lain from the 13th August, to the 5th January, when she sailed. The insurance was made January 20th, when these facts, though known to the assured, were not communicated to the underwriter. The vessel was shattered and much damaged by a storm. A verdict having been found for the plaintiff, a new trial was moved for on the ground of material concealment.

L.

L. Mansfield. The fact here concealed is material; for who can say, that no risk was run, or no damage incurred during the five months stay at *Genoa*. The policy is founded on misrepresentation; for the expression used implies, that *Genoa* was the port of loading; and, at the trial, all the witnesses said, that, by usage, it was material to acquaint the underwriter whether the insurance was to be at the commencement, or in the middle of a voyage.

Wilmot J. Where the fact averred by the policy is *not true*, as here, that *Genoa* was the loading port, I will not speculate whether it be material or not. Although here the length of the stay at Genoa is very material, in the case of such perishable commodities.

Yates J. Material concealment vitiates all contracts, upon principles of natural law. And this concealment was material.—The rule for a new trial was made absolute. 1. *Blackst. Rep.* 463.

Stewart *against* Morison.

Andrew Morison, owner, and *James Morison*, freighter, of the ship *Three Brothers*, then loading with wheat at *Koningsberg*, for the Frith of *Forth*, received intelligence of their vessel from their correspondent, by a letter dated on the 6th September 1774, as follows: " The whole cargo,
" I expect, will be ready to ship to-morrow, so
" that you may take your measures with regard
" to

"to the insurance." And again, on the 30th September, by a letter dated on the 13th, in these words: " I have herewith the pleasure to cover " your bill of loading and invoice of 39 bolls " wheat, shipped for your account *per* the *Three* " *Brothers*, Captain *Maule*. Captain *Maule* is " *now ready to depart with the first fair wind.*"

On the 7th October, *James Morison* wrote to an insurance-broker in Edinburgh, to get L. 200 insured for *Andrew Morison* on the ship; and in his letter he added, " *The vessel was expected to* " *be loaded at Koningsberg, betwixt the 13th and* " *20th September.*" Insurance was done accordingly that same day, by *Stewart* and others, at 2½ *per cent.* " upon the Three Brothers, at and " from Koningsberg." And subjoined to the policy are the words of the letter, " said ship " expected to be loaded," &c.

On the 7th October, likewise, *Ellis Martine*, at the desire of *James Morison*, wrote to another insurance-broker, to get insured, on account of James, L. 150, on *goods* by the *Three Brothers*, " the ship warranted safe the 13th *ult. and no ad-* " *vice of her sailing.*" This policy was underwrote by the same people with the former, and contained the clause, " *warranted safe the* 13th " *ult.*" &c.

The vessel sailed from *Pilaw* on 13th September, but run ashore on the island of *Rugen*, and was totally lost. The insurers objected to paying the loss, upon the footing of *concealment*

by

by the affured. The Judge-admiral repelled the defence. But when the queftion came before the Court of Seffion, Lord GARDENSTON, *Lord Ordinary*, pronounced the following judgment:

" Is of opinion, That although the perfon
" who applies for infurance of a fhip or cargo in
" foreign parts, is not bound to produce or com-
" municate all his letters of intelligence concern-
" ing the voyage or adventure; yet he is bound
" fairly to communicate every material circum-
" ftance of his intelligence, from which any pro-
" bability of hazard may arife. The *Lord Ordi-*
" *nary* is alfo of opinion, That, in this cafe, the
" infured have either wilfully concealed, or in-
" advertently omitted very material circumftances
" of the hazard in their informations to the in-
" furers. In one of the policies, dated 8th Oc-
" tober, the " fhip is warranted fafe on 13th Sep-
" tember, and no accounts of her failing." But
" thefe material circumftances are fuppreffed or
" omitted, *viz.* that the fhip had been completely
" loaded between the 6th and 13th; that fhe
" was then ready to fail, and the bill of loading
" and invoices were tranfmitted. And the in-
" formation on the other policy is ftill more ex-
" ceptionable, as it intimates to the infurer, that
" the fhip was only *expected to be loaded* betwixt
" the 13th and 20th of September, though the
" infured had *pofitive intelligence that fhe was ac-*
" *tually loaded*, as above, betwixt the 6th and
" 13th; and that the mafter, after delivering
" his

" his bill of loading, and invoices, was then
" ready to fail with the firſt fair wind. Upon
" theſe grounds, the Lord Ordinary finds the in-
" furance void."

And to this interlocutor the Court, upon adviſing a *reclaiming petition*, with *anſwers*, adhered. *Fac. Collect. January* 19. 1779.

Kay *againſt* Young.

Kay, maſter of the brig *Robert*, wrote from *Elſineur*, on the 9*th Auguſt* 1780, to Mr *Pierſon*, merchant at *Borrowſtounneſs*—" I arrived here
" this morning, after a fine paſſage from *Riga* of
" five days. *I mean to leave this place this night,*
" *wind and weather permitting.* As there is no
" convoy home ſoon, it will be needleſs to be
" longer. It is reported the privateers are very
" plenty upon the coaſt of Norway; however, I
" mean to take my chance. Deſire *Mrs Kay* to
" inſure L. 36 Sterling."

This letter Mr Pierſon received *on the* 26*th. Auguſt ;* and by that day's poſt he wrote Meſſrs Kinnear and Son of Edinburgh, to get L. 100 inſured on the ſhip *Robert,* and informed them, that he had that day received a letter from Captain *Kay*, dated at *Elſineur*, on the 9th current, when he was clear to ſail.

Mr Pierſon's letter having been laid before the underwriters in Meſſrs Kinnear's office, on the 27th Auguſt, they all expreſsly refuſed to meddle with the policy on any terms.

Mr

Mr Pierson meantime had delivered *Kay's* letter to Mrs *Kay*, who, on the 27th August, wrote to a Mr *Grindlay* as follows: " Sir, The design of this is begging you would take the trouble to get insured L. 40, on account of Mr *Kay*, from *Elsineur* to the port of *Leith*, on wages and goods on board the brig *Robert*, himself master. I had a letter yesterday from *Elsineur*, wherein Mr Kay advised me he proposed to run it, as no convoy would sail from thence for some time *."

The ship having been taken, and an action brought for the insured values, the underwriter pleaded in defence, that the information given was defective in a material point. For had it been mentioned that the vessel was clear to sail on the 9th August, she must have, before the 27th, been reckoned a missing ship. And from the conduct of the underwriters in Messrs Kinnear's office, who had the real information before them, there is every reason to suppose that Mr *Young*, in the same circumstances, would not have meddled with the policy.

At first Lord ELLIOCK, *Lord Ordinary*, " assoil- zied the † defender, in respect proper information was not given." Afterwards his Lordship recalled

---

* The account here given of the decision *Kay against Young*, is taken from the original papers, the statement of this case in the Faculty Collection being somewhat incomplete.

† Acquitted the defendant.

recalled that judgment, and found the defender liable in the infured values, " in refpect there " was no fraudulent concealment of any circum- " ftance of hazard, in order to deceive the un- derwriter."

The latter reclaimed *; and the petition being followed with anfwers, the Lords " alter- " ed the Lord Ordinary's interlocutor," thus re- turning to the judgment firft given. *Fac. Coll.* 20*th Nov.* 1783.

SHIRLEY *againft* WILKINSON.

In this cafe, a letter from the captain, men- tioning, " That he was ready to fail, and that " he certainly would fail early in Auguft," was with-held from the underwriters. The regula- tion of the premium depended upon the time of failing, which determined whether the fhip was to be confidered as miffing. The queftion was, Whether the information with-held was mate- rial?

A verdict having been found for the plaintiff, the Court, on motion for a new trial, held, that the whole intelligence fhould have been com- municated to the underwriters, that they might have been enabled to exercife their judgment. *The rule made abfolute.* *Mich.* 22. *Geo. III.* —MS.

The

---

* Prefented a bill to the *Inner Houfe.*

The following case is one of those which depend on circumstances that may be viewed in different lights; but the general principle of it strongly supports the doctrine above stated.

Grieve *against* Young.*

On the 10th December 1779, *William Grieve*, merchant in *Eyemouth*, wrote to Messrs *Muat and Aitken*, his correspondents in *Edinburgh*, as follows: " Dear Sir, The *Jean* of *Dunbar*, Tho-
" mas *Neilson* master, sailed this afternoon's tide,
" with a fair wind, for *Alloa*. If you please you
" may get L. 160 done upon her with *Messrs*
" *Kinnear*, in case you should find the morning
" coarse, our mutual friend having left that for
" me as I found cause. You will do as you see
" prudent for our interest."

As *Eyemouth* is not a post-town, the method in which the merchants there carry on their correspondence with Edinburgh, is by sending their letters in the evening to the *Press*, or to *Ayton*, two stages upon the London road, where they are taken up by the post early next morning. The letter in question was sent to the *Press* on the evening of the 10th, and arrived in Edinburgh about six o'clock afternoon of the 11th. About eight o'clock afternoon of the 11th, Mr Grieve's correspondent got insurance done accordingly.

---

* This case has not been inserted in the Collection of Scots Decisions compiled by the Faculty of Advocates, but the Author has taken it from the printed papers in the cause.

The vessel, on the evening of the 10th, after the letter was dispatched to the *Press*, was driven back to *Coldingham Bay*, within two or three miles of *Eyemouth*; and *Mr Grieve* was informed of the disaster, in consequence of the crew having, about half an hour after eight in the morning of the 11th, been taken ashore in a fishing boat. The ship went to the bottom about ten o'clock, in sight of *Mr Grieve* himself.

The departure of the London post from the *Press* usually happens before seven in the morning; but, on many occasions, it is so late as nine, ten, or eleven o'clock; and sometimes, though seldom, not before one or two afternoon. On the 11th December, the day in question, the post did not leave the *Press* till near ten o'clock; so that the loss of the vessel not only happened, and was known to the assured before the insurance was made, but even before his letter had come into the hands of the post. *Ayton* is two, and the *Press* five miles distant from *Eyemouth*.

The underwriters having insisted, that it was *Mr Grieve*'s duty to have sent another letter to the *Press*, on the morning of the 11th December, countermanding his order, or to have got back his letter from the post-master there, the question came before the Judge-admiral, who found, " That it was incumbent on Mr
" Grieve, *by express*, to have informed his cor-
" respondents of the disaster, in order that the
" making of the insurance might have been
" stopt;

"ftopt; which *he had reason to think would have*
"*reached Edinburgh* time enough to have ftopt
" the infurance, and which *would have in fact*
"*reached Edinburgh* time enough for that pur-
" pofe."

The caufe having been removed into the Court of Seffion, the affured contended, That there was no obligation upon any merchant to convey intelligence with greater expedition than by the ordinary courfe of poft. That the fame reafon which made it neceffary to fend an exprefs from *Eyemouth* to *Edinburgh* in the prefent cafe, would make it equally incumbent to fend expreffes, though at greater diftances, from *Edinburgh* to *London*, or from *London* to the *West Indies*, wherever there was a bare poffibility of outftripping the ordinary poft or packet.

The underwriters, on the other hand, argued, That if the cafe had been reverfed, and *Mr Grieve* had wanted to fave infurance, by notifying the *arrival* of a veffel, he would have found no difficulty in accomplifhing this, and he would have made no fcruple of fending an exprefs to Edinburgh. On fuch occafions, the duties ought to be equal and reciprocal. But if it was not neceffary to fend an exprefs, it was furely incumbent on *Mr Grieve*, if he meant to act fairly, the moment he knew of the fhip's being driven back, to have difpatched a meffenger to the *Prefs*, or to *Ayton*, either to bring back his letter from the poft-office, or to put in another, explaining the circumftances cumſtances as they then ſtood. And in either of theſe caſes, no inſurance would have taken place.

The Court were of opinion, that it was not incumbent to ſend an expreſs to Edinburgh; but being ſatisfied that *Mr Grieve* had time to countermand the inſurance, in the ordinary courſe of poſt, and that it was his duty to have done ſo, gave judgment for the underwriters. *In Summer-ſeſſion* 1782.

The following caſe is nearly akin to that now ſtated. At the ſame time, it eſtabliſhes another very important point, that the aſſured is liable for the concealment or miſrepreſentation *of the agent* upon whoſe advices the inſurance is made.

FITSHERBERT *v.* MATHER.

On the 27th July 1782, *W. Bundock* of *Pool*, agent for *Fitſherbert*, the plaintiff, contracted with *Richard Thomas*, a corn-factor at *Hartland*, for the purchaſe of 500 quarters of oats, to be conſigned to *William Fuller* at *Portſmouth*, on the plaintiff's account; at the ſame time, he directed *Mr Thomas* to ſend him a bill of loading and invoice, and another to *Fitſherbert* himſelf, at *Cuthbert Fiſher's*, *Eſq*; *London*.

Mr Thomas ſhipped a part of the oats on board the *Joſeph*, which ſailed from *Hartland* on 16th September 1782. And ſame day he wrote to *Bundock* and *Fiſher*, covering invoice and bill of loading. His letter to *Bundock* mentions, that the

the ſhip had ſailed, ". but I am afraid the wind " is coming to the weſtward, and will force her " back. I have ſent a bill of loading and invoice " to *Mr Fiſher*, that he may inſure, if he likes, " as the equinox is near." That to *Mr Fiſher* mentions the ſhip having ſailed, and that " this " evening appears ſtormy."

About ſix or ſeven o'clock in the evening of the 16th September, (the ſame day on which the ſhip had ſailed) *Mr Thomas* heard a report that the ſhip was aground. And at ſix o'clock in the morning of the 17th, he knew that ſhe was loſt.

On the 19th September *Mr Fitſherbert* wrote to *Mr Fiſher*, deſiring him to inſure his intereſt, *as ſoon as the bills of loading ſhould arrive from Hartland*. This letter was received at London on the 20th.

The mode of ſending letters from *Hartland* to *London*, is as follows: The letters are collected by a private hand, who goes with them from *Hartland* to *Bideford*, about one or two of the clock on the day on which the poſt ſets out from *Bideford;* and the poſt leaves *Bideford* about nine o'clock in the evening. It happened that the 16th September was not a poſt-day, ſo that *Mr Thomas's* letter did not leave *Hartland* till one o'clock in the afternoon of the 17th; that is ſeven hours after that gentleman knew of the loſs of the veſſel. The letter to Mr Fiſher was received in London on the 20th; and on the 21ſt September, the defendant

fendant underwrote " L. 110 on a cargo of oats,
" on board the ship Joseph, at and from Hartland
" to Portsmouth," &c.

These were the material facts of a case submitted by the jury for the opinion of the Court.

The counsel for the plaintiff made two questions.

1*st*, Supposing *Thomas* to be the agent for the plaintiff, whether his negligence in not sending an account of the loss of the ship shall vacate the policy?

The whole that is required in making these kind of contracts, is, that they be made, *bona fide*, between the assured and insurer. If there be a real disclosure, as between *them*, the act of a third party is not material.

2*d*, Whether *Thomas* be the plaintiff's agent? All the orders which *Bundock* had given to *Thomas*, were to send such a quantity of oats on board a ship, and to send a bill of loading: The moment he had done so, his agency ceased.

For the defendant, it was contended, That *Thomas* was the plaintiff's agent. *Thomas* suffered a letter to go to *Fisher* several hours after he knew the ship to be lost; he himself knowing, (as appears by his letter to *Bundock*,) that an insurance might be made. It makes no difference, that the letter was *written* before the loss was known; because it was not *sent* till afterwards. Mr *Fitzherbert* refers to *Thomas's* letter; this connects the agent with the principal;

cipal; and, without such a reference, there would have been no insurance. Case of *Stewart v. Dunlop*, in H. of P. 1785 *.

Lord MANSFIELD C. J. " The policy has been effected by misrepresentation, because the insurer was warranted to suppose the vessel in safety on 17th September, at twelve or one o'clock, when *Thomas's* letter came away. This misrepresentation arises from the agent of the assured. It supposes either fraud or gross negligence in him. A misrepresentation founded on negligence, as well as on fraud, will vacate the policy."

WILLES J. " This is a gross misrepresentation upon the part of the assured's agent, for whom the assured must be liable."

ASHURST J. " The act of the agent must bind the principal; for the principal must be supposed to know whatever the agent knows. There is no hardship here; for if the fact had been known, the policy could not have been effected."

BULLER J. " The plaintiff expresly refers to *Thomas's* letter, and orders the insurance to be made,

* It does not appear, that this case, *Stewart* against *Dunlop*, establishes any principle whatever. It was a mere question of evidence, whether *Stewart*, the insured, had received intelligence of the loss of his vessel; and the circumstance, that a *Mr Boog*, who was much connected with *Stewart*, knew of the loss, and a *Mr Walkinshaw*, *Mr Stewart's* bookkeeper, had got *a hint*, was founded on among other presumptions. It seems to have no connection with this question.

made, "*when it shall arrive.*" It was therefore the foundation of the agreement."

"The principal, who builds information on that of his agent, must suffer for his agent's misrepresentation. When one of two innocent persons must suffer by the fault of a third, the question is, which of the two gave credit. Here it was the plaintiff who trusted *Thomas*, and he must take the consequences."

The *postea* to be delivered to the defendant. *Termly Reports, Mich.* 1785.

Upon an idea something similar, it seems to have been thought necessary, that the place where goods have been loaded, should, in certain cases, be expressed in the policy.

Case. If a ship was laden at *Aleppo,* and comes to *Messina,* to be insured, the adventure is to begin from *Messina*; but then it must be expressed, that she was laden at *Aleppo* (as PEMBERTON, C. J. said, though the opinion of some merchants was not so.) But if the insurance was of goods laden at *Aleppo,* and they were laden at *Messina,* it might make a difference. *Skin.* 54. *Trin.* 34. *Car.* 2.

"Insurance," says the ordinance of *Amsterdam,* "shall not be done on the ship's hull or
"goods, before the ship shall be at the place
"from whence one causes himself to be insured,
"without especially expressing in the policy,
"that the ship was not there arrived, under the
"pain of nullity."

Another

Another regulation of the same state requires, that the assured shall declare, whether the ship has sailed or not, at the date of the policy, or that he is ignorant upon that point, otherwise the insurance shall be null. *See Bynck. Quest. Jur. priv. l.* 4. *c.* 7.

2. It is here deserving of notice, that when the assured is guilty of concealing circumstances, by which the risk may be affected, the insurer is liberated, and the policy vacated, from whatever cause the loss may arise; and though it may be occasioned by an accident totally different from that of which the danger was concealed. This is a consequence of the fraud, or fault of the assured, which, for any thing that appears, may have *given rise to the contract;* and which therefore has the effect to destroy the policy *ab initio,* so far as respects the obligation of the insurer.

Seaman *v.* Fonnereau.

On the 24th of August 1740, the defendant underwrote a policy from *Carolina* to *Holland.* It appeared that the agent for the plaintiff had, on 23d August, received a letter from *Cowes,* dated 21st August, wherein it was said, "the 12th of this month I was in company with the ship *Davey* (the ship in question); at twelve in the night lost sight of her all at once; the Captain spoke to me the day before, that he was leaky, and the next day we had a hard gale."—The ship, however, continued her voyage till the 19th, when she was *taken* by the Spaniards; and there was no pretence of any knowledge of the actual loss at the time of the insurance; but it was in consequence of a letter received that day, dated 27th of June before. Several brokers were examined, who proved, that the agent ought to have *disclosed* the letter; for either the defendant would not have underwrote, or he would have insisted on a higher premium. And the C. J. was of that opinion, and declared, that as these are contracts on chance, each party ought to know all the circumstances; *and he thought it not material that the loss was not such a one as the letter imported;* for these things are to be considered in the situation of them at the time of the contract, and not to be judged of by subsequent events: He therefore thought it a strong case for the defendant, and the jury found accordingly. *Strange*, 1183. 16. *Geo.* II.

3. The danger of fraud upon the part of the assured, by concealing advices, and procuring insurance after he knows a loss to have happened, is so obvious and striking; at the same time, it is so difficult to detect dishonesty of this kind, by ascertaining the exact state of the assured's intelligence, that many foreign nations have, in certain situations, been led to adopt a *presumption of concealment* against him. If insurance is made after a loss has happened; and if it is *probable*, calculating intelligence to travel at a certain

tain rate, that the assured had been informed of the loss, they presume that such information was actually received, and they annul the policy on the score of concealment.

A great variety of suppositions have, in this view, been adopted with regard to the rate at which intelligence may travel. The *Spanish* Ordinance allows *a league* per *hour* on land; the *Genoese two miles* per *hour*, from the spot of land which the account first reached; that of *Middleburg* allows three miles to two hours, whether by sea or land; and so on *.

By some of those ordinances, as those of *Genoa, France*, and the towns of *Holland*, this is merely a *præsumptio juris*, which may be removed by evidence, or even by the oath of the suspected party. But one or two states, *Bilboa*, for example, have carried this matter the length of establishing a *præsumptio juris et de jure*; and it is provided, that the "insurance shall be null, "without liberty of hearing it in judgment, or "admitting any proof that the party may wish "to bring, that he had no advice, good or bad," &c.

All those regulations, however, allow parties to provide against the effect of this presumption, by an express stipulation, insuring "notwith- "standing *good or bad advices.*"

The Ordinances of *Antwerp* (in time of PHILIP II.) from a similar jealousy, prohibit all insurance

* For the regulations of different countries in this respect, see *Magens, vol.* 2.

surance after the risk has once commenced. The early regulations, it should seem, of mercantile nations, are often marked by an extreme suspicion of fraud. The reason is obvious. Merchandise, in an early period of society, is not sufficiently understood, to satisfy those who practise it, of the advantage of fair dealing; and among people addicted to a military life, it is not attended with that respectability which produces an attention to character. The Jews, who were the first traders of Europe, were despised for being so; and were therefore in all probability less scrupulous in their dealings.

In England, no such presumption of concealment, as that above mentioned is admitted, and every policy continues valid, although made after a loss has happened, unless the sufferer produces evidence of actual fraud and concealment by the other party. At the same time, from the difficulty, in many instances, of adducing a direct proof upon this subject, our courts have been satisfied with presumptive evidence; as was the case in the late decree of the Court of Session, in the question *Stewart against Dunlop*, affirmed by the House of Peers in 1785.

4. A question may here arise, to what length this necessity of information extends. It cannot be meant that parties are to give each other information of every circumstance they know respecting the vessel or cargo; this would be a labour without end; and, were it required,
would

would afford a ground for vacating every infurance whatever. From the principles above stated, it must readily occur, that the circumstances which, in order to avoid the imputation of fraudulent concealment, it is necessary to communicate, are only those that *vary the risk*, and, at the same time, are *not supposed to be already known to both parties.*

" Either party," says Lord MANSFIELD, (in the case of *Carter v. Boehm*) " may be innocently
" silent, upon grounds which are open to both
" for the exercise of their judgment; *aliud est*
" *celare, aliud tacere ; neque enim id est celare,*
" *quicquid reticeas ; sed cum quod tu scias, id ig-*
" *norare, emolumenti tui causa, velis eos, quorum*
" *interfit id scire.*—There are many matters as
" to which the assured may be innocently silent.
" He need not mention what the underwriter
" knows ; *scientia utrimque par, pares contrahentes*
" *facit.*—The assured need not mention what
" the underwriter *ought* to know ; what he *takes*
" *upon himself the* knowledge of ; or what he
" *waves* being informed of."

This may be illustrated by the following cases:

CARTER *v.* BOEHM.

George Carter, Governor of *Fort Marlborough*, (or *Bencoolen*) procured an infurance upon that settlement, against capture by a foreign enemy, " for one year, from the 16th of October 1759,
" till

" till the 16th of October 1760, interest or no
" interest." The fort was taken by *Count
D'Estaing* within the year. A verdict was found
for the plaintiff by a special jury, and a new
trial moved for, on the objection, that circumstances were not sufficiently disclosed.

1*mo*, Because the state and condition of the
fort was not disclosed; 2*do*, Because the Governor did not disclose that the French, not being in a condition to relieve their friends upon
the coast, were more likely to make an attack
upon this settlement than to remain idle; 3*tio*,
That he had not disclosed his having received
a letter of the 4th of February 1759, from which
it appeared, that the French had a design to take
this settlement *the year before.*

Lord MANSFIELD, in stating the opinion of
the Court, observed, that, as to the first, the underwriter knew the Governor to be acquainted
with the state of the place, and that he could
not disclose it, consistent with his duty; and he
knew, by the Governor's insuring, that the possibility, at least, of an attack, was apprehended:
Knowing this, he underwrote without asking
any questions; by so doing, he took the knowledge of the state of the place upon himself.

The second concealment relates to a mere matter of speculation or opinion; with regard to
which the underwriter was as able to judge as
the Governor.

As to the third concealment, of a letter relating to a defign, which the French are fuppofed to have entertained *at a former period,* that does not appear materially to vary the *rifk at the date of the infurance. The Rule difcharged.* 3. *Burr.* 1905. *Eaft.* 6. *Geo.* III.

THOMSON *againft* BUCHANAN and *others.*

In fummer 1778, *Thomfon* had freighted a fhip, the *Grizzy,* with a cargo to *Gibraltar,* from which fhe was to proceed to *Malaga,* and then, with a new cargo, to return home to *Leith.*

The mafter of the fhip, on his arrival at *Gibraltar,* wrote to his owner the following letter, dated 28th September 1778. " Sir, This is to ac-
" quaint you of my arrival here yesterday, after
" a long hard paffage, and to acquaint you,
" that *there is as much danger going from here to*
" *Malaga, as coming from England here.* I hear,
" that the merchants at *Malaga* wont fhip any
" goods on board *Englifh fhips, before they hear of*
" *a convoy to take them from there.* I am going to
" write *Mr Ferrie* to-morrow by poft, to hear
" what he thinks of it; for there is a great num-
" ber of fhips at *Malaga* that is chartered, and
" *the merchants wont fhip aboard of them.* They
" are fhipping aboard of *Spanifh* fhips for *London.*"

After receiving this letter, the purfuer got the fhip infured at *Glafgow,* by the defender, to the extent of L. 600, at the rate of 25 guineas *per cent.;*

cent.; and there was a note subjoined to the policy, in these words: "The last advice from *Gi-*
"*braltar*, was of 28th September 1778, and the
"vessel arrived only the day before, and had a
"cargo to discharge. If said ship sails with
"convoy from *Malaga* or *Gibraltar*, bound for
"*England*, and arrives safe, L. 5 *per cent.* shall
"be returned."

The ship was taken the same day she sailed from *Gibraltar*, and carried into *Almeria*; and intelligence of the capture was received on the morning after the policy was underwritten.

The underwriter defended himself on this ground, that the policy was vacated by the concealment of the letter of advice from *Gibraltar*. The Judge-admiral in Scotland "repelled the defence." But the cause being brought into the Court of Session, the Lords "suspended the let-
"ters, sustained the defences, and assoilzied."

The question being carried by appeal to the House of Peers, it was pleaded by the assured, That although it is incumbent upon every person who offers a policy to an underwriter, to communicate all facts which may vary the risk, and of which the insurer must be supposed to be ignorant; yet it is not necessary for him to communicate his own or his correspondents *speculations* upon the risk of the voyage. That the letter in question contained nothing but certain opinions of the Captain, founded upon circumstances that ought to have been equally well known

known to the underwriters themselves; and they appear to have been aware of a confiderable degree of danger, by the high premium they took, of 25 *per cent.*

The Court " ordered and adjudged, that the in-
" terlocutors complained of be reverfed; and the
" decree of the Judge-admiral in Scotland affirm-
" ed." *Fac. Coll. June* 20. 1781. *Coll. of appealed Cafes, March* 13. 1782.

This decifion feems to be well founded. There is a clear diftinction between a general danger attending the trade, and a rifk to which the veffel affured may in particular be expofed. The former ought to be known to the underwriter as well as to the affured.

MAYNE *v.* WALTER.

The fhip infured was warranted Portuguefe property. She had an Englifh fupercargo on board, which was known to the affured plaintiff, but had not been communicated to the defendant underwriter. By a commercial ordinance of France, " If the fupercargo of any trading veffel
" be a fubject of a ftate at war with France, the
" veffel fhall be lawful prize."

Lord MANSFIELD. It is not faid that the plaintiff knew of this ordinance, which is directly contrary to the law of nations. The court never heard of it before: Probably it was unknown to both parties. But it was a circumftance refpecting the hazard of the adventure, which the underwriters themselves ought to have known. They took the risk therefore, and must be the sufferers. Judgment for the plaintiff. *M.* 23. *G.* III. *MS.*

Court *against* Martineau.

The *Essex* of *Liverpool* captured a ship and brig off the coast of *Ireland*, bound from *St Eustatia* to *Amsterdam*. The owners of the *Essex*, residing at *Liverpool*, ordered insurance upon the prizes to be made in *London*. The policy was, " At and " from sea to Liverpool, on the *Zee Fortune*, " warranted well the 28th January 1781."

On Sunday, 4th February, the assured, who was also a part owner, sent an express to his broker, with an account of the brig, but expressing great surprise about the ship, and ordering farther insurance on her, adding, that if she arrived on Monday morning, he would send another express. This express reached the broker on Tuesday the 6th. On Wednesday, not having received the other express, the broker got the policy underwrote at 50 guineas *per cent*. The non-arrival on Sunday could not have been known *by post* in *London*, till Wednesday after the policy was underwritten. But, on Tuesday 6th February, an entry in *Llyod's* books, coming from the assured, was put up before the post came in, mentioning the capture by the *Essex*, that the brig was at *Crookhaven*, the *Essex* at *Liverpool*, and the ship not arrived. The loss of the

the ſhip was known at Liverpool, time enough to have prevented the inſurance *by an expreſs*.

Court, the inſurer, brought an action, upon the footing of material concealment, to recover the inſurance-money which he had paid. BULLER J. before whom the cauſe was firſt tried, directed the jury to find for the plaintiff, on an opinion that the concealment was material: Lord MANSFIELD was of a different opinion. A verdict was found for the defendant. There were ſimilar verdicts in ſeveral cauſes tried at Lancaſter. Upon motion for a new trial, they came all on together.

Lord MANSFIELD (after the argument), obſerved that " this was an inſurance *from ſea to* " *Liverpool*. Would not this policy be void, if " underwritten after the arrival?"

It was anſwered for the defendant, that it would not, unleſs one of the parties knew of the arrival. In moſt caſes of policies on ſhips abroad, the event muſt be over before the inſurance is made.

After the Court had taken time to adviſe, Lord MANSFIELD ſaid,——Nothing is clearer than that a policy is good, though the ſhip be arrived.

This action is grounded on the letter ſent expreſs, on the Sunday after the poſt went out, ſtating that the " ſhip was not arrived, and he fear" ed was loſt;" from which the entry had been made in Lloyd's books. The promiſe to ſend an expreſs

express did not affect the broker's knowledge; it was not executed; and besides, it communicated nothing but what the broker knew otherwise, that every assured, in the defendant's situation, would undoubtedly send an express to prevent the insurance, if the ship arrived; and this the underwriters themselves must have known. The broker knew on Tuesday that the ship was not arrived; and he had emphatically told this to the underwriters, by offering so high a premium as 50 *guineas*. The insurers must have supposed that the entry in *Lloyd's* and the broker's intelligence did not come by post. But, the assured is only bound to communicate the whole result of his intelligence, not the ground or means of it. If the underwriter wished for farther information how the accounts came, he should have enquired farther; the broker said nothing to mislead him. By not asking how they came, the plaintiff waved the enquiry. *The rule discharged. Mich. 23. Geo. III. 21st Nov.*—MS.

III. The same general reasoning is applicable where the assured, instead of concealing the truth, actually *misrepresents* the situation of the subject insured.

If the assured is guilty of a *wilful* misrepresentation, the contract will be void, upon the head of fraud; if the erroneous information is not the effect of intention, the question must be, whether the mistake into which the underwriter is led, be *material* or not; that is, whether he has been induced

induced to form a conception of the rifk, as different from what it is in reality.

It is impoffible to fix, by a general rule, what degree of mifreprefentation is held to be material, and what not. This muft vary according to the circumftances of each cafe; according as the miftake produced by it occafions a fenfible difference between the hazard undertaken, and that underftood. This may be illuftrated by examples.

Before proceeding to thefe, it is to be obferved, that a *reprefentation* of facts, made to one underwriter, is conftrued to have been made to all that fubfcribed after him; becaufe the latter are fuppofed to have been, in fome degree, induced to fign, from the authority and example of thofe that preceded.

M'DOWALL *againſt* FRAZER.

This was an action upon a policy of infurance on the " fhip the *Mary and Hannah*, from New " York to Philadelphia." At the time when the infurance was made, which was in London, on 30th January, the broker reprefented the fituation of the fhip to the underwriter, as follows: " *The Mary and Hannah, a tight veſſel, ſailed with* " *ſeveral armed ſhips, and was ſeen ſafe in the* " *Delaware on the* 11*th December, by a ſhip which* " *arrived at New York.*" In fact, the veffel was loft on the 9*th December*, by running againft a chevaux de frife, placed acrofs the river. On a trial before Lord MANSFIELD at Guildhall, a defence was founded on the mifreprefentation as to the time the fhip was feen; and the jury found for the defendant.—Motion for a new trial.

On the part of the plaintiff, it was admitted, that a reprefentation, if fraudulent, or erroneous in a material point, annuls the contract. But it was contended, that the reprefentation in the prefent cafe, was not alleged to be fraudulent; and that, although it was erroneous, the miftake was not in a material point: That the meaning of the reprefentation was to inform the underwriter that the fhip had got fafe through two-thirds of her voyage from New York, and beyond the reach of capture; and fo far as related to this material part, the reprefentation was perfectly true.

The court were unanimous, that the mifreprefentation, as to the time in which the veffel had been feen in fafety, was *material*, and that the verdict was right. *Douglas Reports*, 16th November 1779.

BARBOUR *againft* FLETCHER.

Two underwriters, *Shulbred* and *Fletcher*, had underwritten on the fhip the *True Blue*, at different times; *Shulbred* firft, *Fletcher* afterwards.

It appeared, that when *Shulbred* figned the policy, in March 1778, the broker was getting feveral others, on other fhips, fubfcribed at the fame time, all belonging to the fame owner, and faid, said, speaking of them all,—" Which vessels *are* " *expected* to leave the coast of Africa in No-" vember or December 1777." In fact, the vessel in question had sailed in May 1777, and *Shulbred* swore that if he had known that circumstance, he would not have signed.—Verdict for the plaintiff.

On motion for a new trial, it was insisted, in behalf of the defendant, that a representation to the first underwriter is considered as made to all who sign after him; and that the present representation was material.

Lord MANSFIELD admitted, that a representation to the first underwriter extends to the others; but this is not material: It related only to what was *expected*, and the underwriters did not enquire into the ground of the expectation. This was lying by till after a trial, in order to make an objection, if the verdict should be for the plaintiff.—The rule for a new trial discharged. *Dougl. Rep. 29th November* 1779.

Upon the same principle with this decision, if it is stated that a vessel is *believed* to be in a certain situation, the representation is not material: The underwriter ought to enquire into the grounds of the belief. See *Cooper's Rep. Pawson v. Watson.*

STACKPOLE *v.* SIMON.

This was an insurance on the life of Mr *Sheppey*, for a year; he died within the term of

the

the policy. The broker who effected the insurance told the underwriter, that the gentleman for whom he acted would not warrant, but from all accounts, he (the broker) *believed it to be a good life.* It appeared that Mr *Sheppey* had, before his death, gone to the south of France, for the benefit of his health, or to avoid his creditors.

Lord MANSFIELD. There is here no warranty; the underwriter therefore takes the risk of its being a good life upon himself. If, no doubt, there be a concealment of what is known, with regard to the state of health, it must vacate the policy as a fraud. But here, the broker does not pretend to any knowledge of his own, but speaks according to his best information. Verdict for the plaintiff. *At Guildh. Hil. Vac.* 1779. See *Park's System of Marine Insurance*, p. 497. *.

It

---

* The author takes this opportunity of acknowledging the use he has made of a late very full and ingenious treatise on insurances, which has appeared since a part of his MS. went to the press. With the greatest part of the cases adjudged by the English courts, not formerly published, he had been furnished, previously to the appearance of Mr *Park's System*, by a friend in London, upon whose accuracy he could rely; and he has now obtained additional satisfaction upon that point, by comparing his own MS. notes with the statement of such cases given by Mr Park. He has, however, used the freedom, in a few instances, where he had not been furnished with the adjudged case, to insert such an abridgment of it, upon Mr Park's authority, as might illustrate sufficiently the principle in question; and in these instances, he has referred the reader to that Gentleman's publication.

It seems here necessary to anticipate the subject of a future chapter, so far as to observe that a *representation of facts*, which is intended only to convey information, differs considerably from a *warranty, or condition* of the contract. That the latter must be strictly adhered to, but the former need only be true in general, so as not to produce, in any sensible degree, a false conception of the risk in the mind of the underwriter. It may farther be noticed, that all verbal stipulations, and all communications written upon a *different paper* from the policy, are held to be merely *representations of facts*; but that whatever is written on the *same paper* with the policy, is held to be *a condition*, which must be literally complied with.

There are one or two clauses, however, *in the body of the policy*, which seem only intended for the information of the insurer, and have not the effect of strict warranties. Consequently, it is not of importance, although a mistake should be committed in these particulars, unless that mistake be *material;* that is, unless it has affected the insurer's conception of the risk.

The clause in every policy, specifying the *name of the vessel* and *of the master*, seems to be of this kind. The assured, in these clauses, means only to communicate a piece of information to the underwriter; he does not intend to warrant that the ship shall have this or that name; that one man or another shall go as master; and

M he

he accordingly subjoins an explanation, in these words :—" Or by whatever other name the ship " shall be called."—And, " or whoever else " shall go for master in the said ship."

If a mistake, therefore, should be committed, in the name of the ship or of the master, the same rule will hold, as in other cases of misrepresentation. If, notwithstanding the error, parties were sufficiently agreed about the nature of the adventure, or of the subject insured, the bargain will subsist: But if the underwriter can show that he had been *misled* by the erroneous designation or description in the policy, and that he has *actually suffered loss*, in this case the false designation appears to be *material*, and will vacate the agreement.

Upon this principle, we may perhaps reconcile two or three decisions in different countries, apparently inconsistent, in cases where the broker had mistaken *the name of the ship*.

A merchant at Amsterdam got insurance on his ship " *Le Thomas, Capitaine Pierre* " *Guion.*" A loss being incurred, the insurer defended himself upon this ground, That the ship's name was not *Le Thomas*, but *La Dauphine Galere*: That she bore the insignia of *La Dauphine Galere*, and that name inscribed on her stern.

It appeared that this last had been the old name of the vessel; but the owner not having a passport for her, and having one filled up with the

the name *Le Thomas*, had got liberty from the officer of the marine department to change her name, and had got all the clearances in the name of *Le Thomas*. The inferior courts in Holland decided for the infurer; but the Senate, by a majority, altered that judgment. 1722. *Bynckerſh. Qu. Jur. Priv. l.* 4. *c.* 11.

This deciſion, as far as appears, muſt have proceeded upon the principle, that there was no evidence of the inſurer having really been miſled, as to the ſubject inſured, at the time of ſubſcribing. The inſurer intended to underwrite the ſhip, belonging to a particular perſon, upon a particular voyage, by whatever name that ſhip might be called.

In the following caſe, a miſtake, both as to the name of the *ſhip* and of the *Captain*, was rectified, where the underwriters could ſhew no detriment.

Bates *v.* Graham, et al.

Mr *Criſp*, in the Weſt Indies, inſtructed his correſpondent Mr *Bates*, to inſure goods on the *Mary Galley* of St Chriſtopher's, *Captain A. Hill commander*. Bates carried the letter to *Stubbs* a broker, who, by miſtake, procured inſurance from the defendant, " on the *Mary, Captain* " *Hazlewood.*" The *Mary Galley* was loſt; after which, the inſurers agreed to alter the policy, and rectify the miſtake. It was objected at the trial, that the *Mary* was a ſtouter ſhip than the

Mary Galley; and therefore the infurers ought to have an increafe of premium for the alteration: But it was held by HOLT, C. J. that the miftake might be made right; and he cited a cafe which happened when PEMBERTON was C. J.: An infurance was made from *Archangel to the Downs, and from the Downs to Leghorn;* but there was a *parole agreement*, that the policy fhould not commence till the fhip came to fuch a place. It was held the parole agreement fhould not avoid the writing. 2. *Salkeld*, 444. December 3. 1703.

In this cafe it is evident, from the infurers agreeing to rectify the policy, that they confidered themfelves as not hurt by the miftake.

In the following cafe, however, there is evidence that the infurer, in confequence of a miftake in the name, had *actually formed a miftake with regard to the fubject;* it appeared that he had been led, contrary to the ufage of thofe who are experienced in fuch matters, to accumulate rifks upon one bottom; and confequently, *quod non fatis conftitit de re*, that parties were not agreed about the fubject of their bargain.

WATT *againft* RITCHIE.

Ritchie underwrote an infurance on a fhip, which belonged to *Watt*, by the name of the *Martha of Saltcoats*, for a voyage from Chriftiana in Norway to the frith of Clyde. Though this name

name was mentioned to the insurance-broker, by the person commissioned to make the insurance, and had been formerly borne by the vessel, yet another appellation was given to her, prior to the insurance, that of the *Elizabeth and Peggy of Saltcoats;* under which new and proper denomination, the owners of the cargo, a few days after, got insurance made from the same Mr Ritchie. The vessel having been captured by a French privateer, *Watt* sued *Ritchie* before the Court of Session in an action for the insured values.

For the defender it was pleaded, That the law requires the strictest interpretation of contracts of insurance, in favour of the underwriter. Even the smallest deviation from the terms of the contract will prove fatal to the insurance, although producing no apparent prejudice to the insurer, *Buchanan v. Hunter-Blair**. The risk run must be exactly the same with that understood. Although then the mistake should have had no tendency to injure the defender, the contract would nevertheless be void, as its terms really respected a nonentity, and ought not to be extended, by interpretation, to any adventitious meaning. In fact, however, it *had* a tendency to hurt the underwriter, as it led him, in opposition to a maxim founded in the experience of all those who are versant in the business

---

* This case of *Buchanan v. Hunter-Blair*, was reversed on appeal, after the decision had taken place, *Watt v. Ritchie*.

business of insurance, to accumulate different risks on the same bottom. Besides, such a proceeding might often become an engine of fraud; for suppose another vessel, the true name of which was the *Martha*, to have sailed along with the *Elizabeth and Peggy*; in that case, the pursuer might have claimed his insurance on either of the two vessels upon which the loss should have happened, though the premium had been paid for one only.

It was answered for the assured, That no concealment or inaccuracy is regarded as of importance in this contract, unless either fraudulent, or materially varying the object of the policy, or changing the risk understood to be run. *Bur. Rep. vol.* iii. *Carter v. Boehm*. Nor is an error, merely as to the name of a ship, which is otherwise sufficiently distinguished, of that important kind. Accordingly, in all policies respecting ships, and in the present one, these words, " by whatever name the said ship shall " be called," are to be found. A decision was likewise produced much in point, from the *Quæstiones juris privati of Bynkerschoek, lib.* iv. *cap.* 11. *p.* 610.

The Lords, however, were of opinion, that a sacred strictness ought to be preserved in the interpretation of contracts relative to insurance; and therefore adhered to the judgment of the Lord BRAXFIELD, *Lord Ordinary*, which was in these words: " In respect it is acknowledged by the
" pursuers,

"pursuers, that their ship was registered by the
"name of the *Elizabeth and Peggy of Saltcoats*,
"finds, they have no claim against the defender,
"upon the insurance made by him on the ship
"*Martha of Saltcoats*, there being no such ship,
"at least the true name being concealed or mis-
"represented, by which the underwriter might
"have been deceived; therefore sustains the
"defences, and assoilzies the defender, and de-
"cerns." *Fac. Coll.* 23*d January* 1782.

In the following case, where the adventure
had been *erroneously described*, it does not appear
that parties were really under any mistake.
They had made their agreement according to
certain jottings, or a *label*, as it is called; and
the policy had not been drawn out corresponding to that label. Here, undoubtedly, the erroneous description falls to be corrected, and the
bargain sustained, according to the original intention of parties.

Motteux *v.* Lond. Ass. Co.

A had insured for B and plaintiff, his assignees,
on the ship *Eules*, with the cargo; and the entry in
the Company's book of the contract, was in short
items, called a label, which was thus: "*At and
"from* Fort St George to London, lost or not
"lost;" and the policy was soon after made
out, and taken in the following words: "That
"the adventure was to commence from *the ship's
"departing*

" *departing* from Fort St George to London."
Before the infurance was made, the fhip was loft in Bengal river, whither fhe had been fent from Fort St George to refit. The bill was brought to have the infurance-money paid, being L. 500, as a lofs, &c. and founded the *equity* that the policy was not made agreeable to the *label*, according to which the rifk is to commence from the fhip's *coming firft* to Fort St George; and the going to Bengal to refit, being a thing of neceffity for performing the voyage, was no deviation; and the lofs being during that time, was within the intent of the contract for the infuring. Lord Chancellor HARDWICKE faid, this was not proper to determine here. The 1*ft* queftion is as to the agreement; 2*d*, as to the breach; and doubted as to the agreement. The memorandum is not a printed form, as to the material points; and the policy muft be governed by that, if not varied. The words in the memorandum or label (*at* Fort St George) include the flay of the fhip there; and the policy follows the words, but adds thus, *viz.* " The beginning " of the adventure to be from the fhip's de- " parting from Fort St George for London ;" which excludes the rifk whilft the fhip ftaid there; and this feems an inconfiftency in the policy, firft to defcribe the voyage *at and from, &c.* and then to exclude the rifk, &c. This feems a *miftake* in writing the policy, and is to be rectified, as in the cafe of articles, or a settlement;

And

and decreed the words to be added in the policy, for the adventure to commence *at and from* Fort St George. *Viner. Abr. tit. Bottomry-bonds,* Dec. 6. 1739. *Atkyns, t.* 545*.

Sect. III. *Of mutual Error and Mistake.*

Hitherto of the effect of *fraud*, and of error arising from the *negligence and fault* of one of the contracting parties. The effect of *mutual error*, without the intervention of misrepresentation or concealment, remains to be considered. It was formerly observed, that, in this case, a *substantial* error, or such a mistake, as, if corrected in time, would have *totally prevented the bargain*, is necessary in order to invalidate the consent of parties.

1. Let it be supposed, therefore, in the *first* place, that a mistake has happened with regard to the nature and qualities of the ship and cargo; that this error is *mutual*, the assured lying under the same misconception with the underwriter; and that the former has said or done nothing to mislead the latter. Suppose, for example, that, from causes unknown to either party, the vessel has contracted a weakness in her hull, in consequence of which, she is considerably exposed to the

---

* In the case, *Henkle versus R. Exch. Ass. Co.* collected by *Vezey*, I. 317, the underwriter failed in proving the policy to be erroneously made out.

the danger of leaking, or of foundering. How far will such a mistake vacate the policy?

There is here one point abundantly obvious: That the insurer never can be liable for the consequences of the ship's *absolute incapacity*, from the beginning, to perform the voyage. When a ship, in the maritime phrase, is not *seaworthy;* that is, where, from age, or natural defect, she is *insufficient for the voyage*, no person would knowingly insure upon her, because it would be subjecting himself to a certain loss. Every insurance, therefore, must proceed upon this idea, that the vessel, (barring *accidents*, and beside the ordinary tear and wear,) is able to accomplish her part of the adventure. An owner or freighter must be supposed to *warrant* the ship's sufficiency, and every insurer to contract upon that faith and belief. The mistake here is of a capital nature; it is an *error in substantialibus*, which, if it had been corrected, would have prevented parties from even entering upon terms*. The obligation of parties must be limited to those risks

---

* It does not appear, that the foreign authorities are, in general, explicit upon this point. They fail to distinguish between two things which are very different, *viz.* the *pre-existent defect or insufficiency* of the subject, and its *perishable nature*. The former destroys the policy from the effect of *error*, the defect being *latent* at the time of the agreement. But the *perishable nature* may be *foreseen and expected*, and the insurer will be liberated, upon a totally different principle.

The

risks which can be supposed to have been in their view when they made the bargain.

MILLS v. ROEBUCK.

Messrs *John* and *Thomas Mills* purchased, in the year 1757, a French built ship, which they called the *Mills Frigate*; and they employed her in the Leeward-island trade. The first cost of the ship was L. 900; beside this sum, her repairs and outfit amounted to L. 1649, for the first voyage. She was constantly decked and repaired for every voyage in the river Thames, in the best manner possible, it being left to the Captain and ship-builder, to do every thing they thought proper.

On the arrival of the *Mills Frigate* at *St Kitt's*, in the year 1764, Messrs *John* and *Thomas Mills* received

The French Ordinance says, "The loss, diminution, or "waste, that may happen from the *perishable quality* of any "thing, shall not fall on the insurer." *Magens, v.* ii. *p.* 173. The *Guidon, ch.* v. *art.* 8. states the same rule, but without any farther discrimination. See also *Valines*, 1. 164.—2. 80. The insufficiency of a ship is, no doubt, an *effect* of its perishable quality. But this circumstance, the *perishable nature* of a subject, may appear in two ways; 1*st*, The subject, in consequence of its *perishable nature*, may have acquired a *total incapacity* to accomplish the adventure; and this fact may be *latent* at the date of the policy. In this case, the contract is null, as founded on *substantial error*. 2*dly*, The precise state of the subject at the time of the policy, and the effects which must arise from its *perishable nature*, may be known, or foreseen and expected, and yet the insurer may not be liable for these consequences; but this arises from different principles, which shall be considered under the doctrine of *wear and tear* of ship or cargo.

received a letter from the Captain, dated *St Chriſtopher's, April* 23. 1764, informing them, that he "arrived at *Nevis*, after a moſt diſmal "paſſage, and violent gales of wind; that the "ſhip ſtrained ſo much, by the preſſure of ſail, "they were obliged to carry on her in that great "ſea, that it was with the utmoſt difficulty they "could keep her free; that ſhe had ſo looſened, "that they could not carry ſail on the wind, and "ſeeing no probability of the wind's ſhifting, or "abating enough, to give a chance of beating "up, bore away for *Nevis*, in a weak, leaky and "diſtreſſed condition."

The broker, Mr *Towgood*, ſhewed the whole of this letter to *George Hayley*, Eſq; who had before underwrote this ſhip to him ſeveral times, particularly L. 400 the laſt outward-bound voyage; alſo to the other underwriters. Mr Hayley, although he expreſſed doubts ariſing from it, began to write L. 300 at the common premium; but the broker telling him, that, conſidering the Captain's letter, he was too bold, he altered it to L. 200. Mr *Hayley*, therefore, knew every circumſtance relating to the ſhip, which was known to Meſſrs *Mills;* he knew alſo, that ſhe was a *French built* ſhip, and conſequently liable to all the accidents, to which ſhips of that conſtruction are peculiarly ſubject.

The ſhip was warranted to ſail, and did ſail, the 26th of July. On the 27th, in the evening, ſhe ſprung a leak, in fair weather; and being in danger

danger of foundering, returned to *St Kitt's*, and was condemned. The infured made a demand on the underwriters, for the lofs of L. 50, 19 s. *per cent.* on the fhip, and a total lofs on freight. The underwriters pleaded that the fhip was *infufficient for the voyage.*

The cafe was firft tried in the Court of Common Pleas, before Lord CAMDEN, who directed a verdict for the affured; but afterwards, on motion for a new trial, his Lordfhip declared he had changed his opinion, and the Court unanimoufly made the rule abfolute. The affured then tried the queftion, againft another infurer, in Exchequer, before Lord C. B. PARKER, when it appeared that, after the *Mills Frigate* arrived at *Nevis*, (fome people objecting to fhip their fugars in her, on account of the damage referred to in the above mentioned letter), the Captain, to remove this fufpicion, if a falfe one, or to prevent further ill confequences, fhould it prove well grounded, requefted all the Captains then loading in the ifland to furvey her; who reported, " That the fhip's
" making more water than ufual, on her voyage
" from *London* to *Nevis*, was occafioned by fome
" neglects in calking: That fhe otherwife appears to be ftrong and found, and, when calked, fully fufficient to carry a cargo of fugar to
" *London*." The fhip was calked, agreeable to thefe directions. In the evening of the day on which he failed, the Captain found the fhip had fprung a dangerous leak, and was obliged

to

to put back. On her being lightened, it appeared that she had started a plank; and the plank thus started, discovered that which could never have been known previous to such an accident, *viz.* that *the iron-bolts by which the planks were fastened to the timbers, were entirely decayed and eat out by rust,* and several of her planks started, one of them more than an inch from the timbers, all the way fore and aft; and in the report made by the surveyors appointed by the judge of the Vice-admiralty court in *Nevis*, it was declared, " that the ship is in a bad condition, and entire-" ly unfit to proceed on her voyage, without " being first thoroughly repaired; and it is their " opinion, that the ship cannot be thoroughly " repaired at that place, without more expence " than the value of the ship and freight will a-" mount to."

The Court of Exchequer gave judgment for the underwriter. A writ of error was afterwards brought in the Court of Exchequer Chamber, which was referred to Lord MANSFIELD and *Lord C. J.* WILMOT, who, after argument, likewise reported their opinions to be in favour of the underwriter; and judgment was pronounced accordingly. See *Park's System of Insurances, p.* 252., where that author states this case at much greater length, and observes, that, although the report in these cases is usually made in private, and the reasons upon which it is founded are not publicly given, yet, from the full disclosure of circumstances, cumftances, it is impoffible to fuppofe the decifion to have proceeded on any other principle than that of *feaworthinefs* *.

The fame principle is illuftrated by the reafonings in the following cafe, in which the jury feem to have confidered the infufficiency as not proved.

ARNOLD *v.* GODIN.

The *Tyger*, Captain *Harrifon*, being bound from London to Gibraltar, the plaintiff got an infurance made on her, " intereft or no intereft, " free of average, and without benefit of falvage " to the infurers," and at the foot of the policy there was a warranty, that the fhip fhould depart with convoy from fome port in the Channel. The faid fhip proceeded on her voyage as far as the Downs, and failed from thence under convoy, as warranted ; but, foon after her departure, fhe received a very confiderable damage, which obliged her to return to Dover pier to refit ; and, after the neceffary repairs were finifhed, fhe failed again, in profecution of her voyage ; and for her fecurity therein, to join the convoy at Spithead ; but having got as far as the Ifle of Wight, fhe proved fo leaky, as obliged her to a fecond return, and fhe once more arrived at Dover, to fearch

---

* This decifion was the fubject of much difcuffion, at the time it was pronounced. Pamphlets even were publifhed on the queftion. It is to be found at great length in *Wefket's Digeft*.

search for leaks. Her owners, on this, thought it advisable to have her surveyed by men of skill and judgment; and therefore, two ship-carpenters, and two masters of ships, having examined her, declared, that they had surveyed both sides from stem to stern above the wales, and the transom, after the planks were ripped off, " and " found the *timbers* to be very *rotten*, and in so " bad a condition, that except all her upper " works were pulled down and new-built, they " did not judge her in a fit condition to proceed " on her intended voyage; and that if she was " so repaired, the charges would come to more " than she would be worth, with all belonging " to her." The plaintiff insists, that she was a very good ship, when she set out on her voyage, and she was only rendered otherwise by the bad weather she had met with, which at last not only made her unfit for her voyage, but occasioned her proving a total loss to her owners; that she would have weathered the storm in all probability unhurt, had not the *Swift* privateer drove foul of her; that when her first hurt was repaired, the builder supposed her stronger than before the storm. Mr Burton, who fitted her out in the Thames, declared, she was in very good condition, and fit for any voyage, though he did not examine her, but only calked her, and mended her outside and floor-timbers; but it is natural to suppose, that if her timbers were found in October (when these repairs were done) they

could

could not have been rotten in January, when she received her damage. And the defendant grounds his reasons for not paying the said insurance, on that part of the policy's contents, which asserts the ship to be " tight, staunch and strong," and, barring future accidents, able to go through the voyage; whereas he supposes this vessel not to have been so, as he thinks it clear from the preceding affidavit, and from the verbal evidence of one of the surveyors; to which he adds, in order to make the proof of her defects the stronger, that, on her first setting out, she belonged to two Jews, who, on her return to Dover pier the first time, sold her to Mr Richard Glover, a considerable merchant of this city, who ordered her to be repaired, and actually laid out upon her L. 150, which, as it appears, was in a manner thrown away, as, on her second return, she was condemned, broke up, and sold in parcels; and her incapacity to proceed on her voyage having been so apparent, from the foregoing survey, as to induce Mr Glover to desire the shippers to take their goods out; and though he had got L. 300 insured on her, he seemed so sensible of the deceitful bargain with the Jews, in selling him an old rotten ship, that he never demanded one farthing of the said insurance from the underwriters. Verdict for the plaintiff. *Lex Merc. Red.* 281. *At Guildhall Trin.* 1747.

2. It might, perhaps, be supposed, that a material error with regard to the situation of the ship,

ship, in respect of the accidents of the voyage, might likewise be sufficient to vacate a policy. For example, it might be said that an insurance should be null, if the vessel shall appear to have been *lost* or *arrived*, at the date of the policy. There is here, it might be argued, a material error on one side or other, which, if corrected, would have totally prevented the contract.

From an idea of this kind, it was long customary in Britain, to insert a clause, "*lost or not lost*," which seemed to imply, that, without such a stipulation, the underwriter was understood to be only liable from the date of the policy; and that any *previous loss* was not considered as in the view of parties. But a little reflection must show that this idea is entirely without foundation. For the insurer undertakes the risk *from* a port, or *at and from* a port, both of which imply, in the construction of merchants, certain precise points of time, at which he understands the risk to commence, totally unconnected with the date of the contract; in some cases they may be prior, in others posterior. As the insurer, therefore, fixes upon a different period for the commencement of risk than the date of the policy, he must mean to undertake all risks from that period, whatever may be the state of matters at the date of his subscription. There is here no *error* upon the part of the underwriter; he expresly insures the vessel from the time of its *sailing from*, or *arrival at* a particular port; he he is aware, that it may be loft or arrived at the date of the policy; and he fubjects himfelf to that rifk.

Notwithftanding the claufe, accordingly, "*loft or not loft,*" it is believed the *practice* of England was always confonant to the principles now ftated. There was never a claufe, *arrived or not arrived*; yet, if it appeared that the veffel had been arrived at the date of the policy, it never was difputed that the premium was due. And the principle is now fo well afcertained, that the claufe, *loft or not loft*, is never inferted in Scotch policies, though, from cuftom, it continues in Englifh *.

More doubt may be entertained, in contracts with regard to a future rifk, where there is no fuch claufe as *at and from* in policies of infurance, to afcertain the precife time from which the obligation of parties fhall commence. A remarkable decifion was lately given by Lord MANSFIELD upon this point, in the following cafe of a wager.

Earl MARCH v. PIGOT.

Mr *Pigot* and Mr *Codrington* agreed, (in the Newmarket phrafe,) to *run* their fathers againft each other. Each of them wagered upon his own father's furvivance. It appeared, that Mr *Pigot's*

---

* See, upon this point, the cafe *Court againſt Martineau*, quoted under the head of *Miſtake occaſioned by Fault, p.* 1. ch. ii. § 2.

Pigot's father had died early on the morning of that very day, on which, after dinner, the wager was laid. Was this within the bet?

It was argued for the affirmative, that this was like an insurance, where nothing depends on the date of the policy, but where there is a retrospect implied. And, if the possibility of the event which happened had occurred, it would have been expressly included in the wager, making no difference on the risk.

It was answered, that the clause, *lost or not*, is necessary in our policies, before they can have a retrospect; and that no event is included in the wager, which was *not in the view of parties*. If a person lays upon a horse which is dead at the date of the wager, the bet will not hold.

The court, however, thought, that parties would have included the past, as well as the future, had the case been thought of; and that they meant merely a wager, " *which should come first to his estate*;" and unanimously found for the pursuer. 5. *Burr.* 2804. *Trin.* 11. *Geo.* III.

Although we entertain the highest deference for the respectable authority which pronounced this decision, we cannot help feeling some doubt with regard to it. The principle that holds in cases of insurance, evidently does not apply here; for there is no clause, such as that (*at* and *from*) in policies of insurance, to fix the commencement of risk, independent of the date of the policy. It must certainly appear doubtful, how far a man is liable for the risk of adventures which he *did not undertake*, but which he merely *would have undertaken*. If, in any insurance, the period of commencement should be forgot to be specified, would it, in that event, have any retrospect, previous to the date of the contract? *Roccus* states a case exactly in point: " The Senate," says he, " determined, that a wager, *who should be elected Pope*, was ineffectual, because, at the time of the wager, *the Pope had been already chosen*, although that was a circumstance of which the contracting parties were ignorant*."

3. It remains to be considered, how far the same principle of error in contracts, will apply, so as to vacate a policy, when the mistake is not such as, if corrected in time, would have totally put a stop to the bargain, but merely such as would have altered the premium. Suppose there should be smaller peculiarities in the construction of a ship, unknown to the owner; or suppose that a merchant insures his *returns*, without knowing the exact commodities he is to receive:

in

---

* *Roccus, Not.* 73. This distinction between an insurance and a common wager, has not escaped *Casa-Regis*. After quoting certain commentators, who are of opinion, that insurance is not valid after a loss has happened, he says, " Hi doctores intelligi debent loqui voluisse in contractu *sponsionis*, qui post casum sinistrum factus sustineri, non potest, &c. licet in hoc male dissentiat *Scaccia*, &c. ubi negat hanc differentiam inter sponsionem et assecurationem." *Casa-Regis, Disc.* 1. § 13.—24.

In these cases, it should seem, where there is no concealment, the policy shall not be vacated, because the ship is a little stronger or a little weaker; that the cargo should be a little more or a little less perishable. The owner is supposed to *warrant* the vessel and cargo to be of such a nature, as will lay an *ordinary degree* of risk on the insurer; but this admits of considerable latitude: Unless we confine the implied warranty to such qualities as are *essential to the contract*, there is no other accurate line at which we can stop*.

It may only farther be observed, that there are very few cases which admit of considerable peculiarities of ship or cargo, unknown to the assured; for the owner or freighter must be supposed to know, in general, the nature of his own ship and cargo. And the want of information, as to these particulars, is generally imputable to direct fraud.

CHAP. III.

Of the right of parties to retract from their engagements, in a Policy of Insurance.

SO much with regard to the form of this agreement, and the nature of that consent which is requisite to its validity; it remains to take notice of a considerable peculiarity which occurs

---

* This shews the position laid down by the foreign ordinances, "That the insurer is not responsible for the effects of "the *perishable nature* of the subject," not to be true in its whole

occurs in insurance; That neither a formal written deed, nor legal consent, is sufficient to render the bargain complete. It is farther necessary, that *a performance* should have taken place on either side, in order to bind the other party, and to prevent him from retracting.

In the Roman law we have examples of contracts, which had a considerable analogy with that of insurance, where a particular *future* payment or performance was promised for a consideration in hand. Those bargains, "do ut des," and "do ut facias," were not completely supported by the judge. The fullest consent was not sufficient to render them a ground of action at common law; but if a partial performance had been made on either side, there was room for a claim upon the contract, from views of equity.

Similar ideas appear to have been entertained with regard to insurances. Each party must make some performance, before the other be completely bound; and in this respect the principle seems to have been carried farther than in the Roman contracts above mentioned: For, in those bargains, *do ut des*, and *do ut facias*, the performance of one party established a valid obligation on both: But, in insurance, the performance of either does not prevent *himself* from receding, but

whole extent. Every *latent defect* arises from the *perishable nature* of the subject; and yet the underwriter must be liable for *latent defects*, unless they are so great, as that, if discovered in time, they would have totally prevented the contract.

but only *the other party, to whom the performance was made*.

Thus, in order to render the contract complete, so as not to admit of *repentance* on the part of the underwriter, the older regulations agree it is necessary the premium should be paid to him by advance*.

And by the more modern notions on this subject, the underwriter, though he may not actually receive the premium, must *acknowledge the receipt of it* in the contract †.

This practice must undoubtedly have originated from an idea that the contract was not complete, nor binding upon the underwriter, unless there had been a *rei interventus*, a performance by the other party to him.

On the other hand, the insurer undertakes *a risk*. Before the voyage is commenced, *while the risk is yet entire*, the underwriter cannot be considered as having performed any part of his bargain; and while this is the case, it is universally agreed that the assured has it in his power to recede, by breaking up the voyage, or abandoning the adventure. While no risk has been run by the insurer, matters are entire as to him; and the assured may retract, and recover the premium. In order to render the contract complete, it is necessary the adventure insured should have

---

* *Roccus de assec.* 83. *Consolato del Mare of Barcelona. Ord. Copenh.*

† *Ord. France*, No. 668. *Ord. Koningsb.* No. 775. Practice *of Britain; of Hamburgh,* &c.

have commenced, and the underwriter have run some part of the risk; the *commencement of risk* constitutes a performance on the part of the underwriter.

Those contracts among the Romans, which had no particular *name*, and which, by lawyers, are said to be comprehended under the words, *do ut des*, and *do ut facias*, occurred but seldom in society; and this was the reason why judges did not think it worth while to support them, unless they were accompanied by a *rei interventus*. The same reasoning was, at an early period, applicable to insurance, then a rare and unusual contract; and this was no doubt the *original* source of the peculiarity now mentioned.

But, with respect to one of the parties, there occurs an additional reason why he should have the liberty of retracting, so long as, with respect to him, matters remain entire. If two persons make a bargain, the performance of which, from a change of circumstances, becomes infinitely more hurtful to the one than beneficial to the other, it would be hard that the latter should insist upon specific performance. It is enough, in that case, if the party who must be the greatest sufferer by performance, should indemnify the other for his *positive loss*, or, at most, allow him a consideration for the profit he might have reaped, for his *lucrum cessans*, as far as that is capable of being ascertained.

In an insurance, the loss incurred by the assured, in prosecuting the adventure insured, might,

might, in many cases, infinitely exceed the advantage reaped by the underwriter. While matters are entire, therefore, it appears equitable, that the assured should have it in his power to recede from his agreement, by breaking up the adventure; and that the underwriter should be satisfied with receiving the *damage and interest*.

It does not, however, appear possible to ascertain the probable gain which the insurer might have acquired by the subsistence of the policy. It is uncertain whether he might have reaped gain or incurred loss. No consideration has been thought due, therefore, in respect of his *lucrum cessans*. And, with regard to *damage*, he incurs none by the breach of the policy, as he has run no risk, farther than what may be thought to proceed from the trouble of keeping an account of the transaction.

From this last consideration, he is, upon the retracting of the assured, allowed to retain a certain small proportion of the premium. This sum differs a little, in different countries. In Amsterdam, it is *one per cent.*; in Britain, and most other commercial states, it is *one-half per cent.* of the sum insured.

From this peculiarity of the contract of insurance, that it is incomplete until a performance has taken place on both sides, a variety of curious questions arise, which shall be the subject of particular discussion hereafter.

E L E-

ELEMENTS

OF

INSURANCE.

PART II.

Of the Nature of an Insurance-contract, and the Obligations arising from it.

INSURANCE was formerly explained to be a contract, by which one man, for a consideration received, becomes liable for the loss arising to another, from any specified contingency.

The one party, it was observed, the insurer, is supposed to receive the premium in hand, at the date of the policy; for which he promises to indemnify the assured, in case the latter shall sustain damage from some future event.

The performance requisite upon the part of the assured is therefore at an end, previous to the execution of the agreement, by his payment, real or supposed, of the *premium*. It is the underwriter

derwriter who is laid under *future obligation* by the policy; and that deed is accordingly subscribed by him alone.

The infurer undertakes *a risk;* he comes under an obligation, in favour of the assured, to a certain amount, upon the existence of a specified event. It here, therefore, occurs to consider three points:

1*st*, The *duration* of the insurer's risk:

2*d*, The *nature* of his risk; or, in other words, the nature of the *event* against which provision is made, by insurance:

3*d*, The *extent* of the insurer's *obligation*, or the *amount* to which he is liable, when the event happens.

CHAP. I.

Of the Duration of the Insurer's Risk.

THE duration of the risk undertaken by an insurer, is a matter that requires to be fixed by express agreement in every particular case, and must become an essential clause in every policy. The expressions which are commonly used for this purpose, have acquired a precise meaning by the usage of merchants.

The observations that occur upon this part of the subject, consist principally of mere matter of fact with relation to the practice of different mercantile nations. In order to state the variations

tions in this respect with more distinctness, it may be proper to consider separately, 1*st*, The *commencement* of risk; and, 2*dly*, Its *termination*.

Sect. I. *Of the Commencement of Risk.*

Insurance is generally made in two ways, "*from a port*," or "*at* and *from*." It is likewise on *ship*, or *cargo*, or *freight*.

Insurance *from* a port, whether on ship or goods, is, by the practice of England, understood to mean, " from the time the vessel *breaks ground*, " in sailing from that port."

At and from, when applied to *a ship*, includes the period of her stay in that port, from the time of her arrival there *.

At and from, when applied to *goods*, means, from the time those goods are put aboard the vessel.

Thus it is observed, that " if a ship be insured " *from the port of London* to Cadiz, and, before " she breaks ground, takes fire and is burnt, the " insurers on such ship shall not answer; for " the adventure began not till the ship was gone " from the port of *London*. But if the words " had been *at and from* the port of London, they " would have been made liable. If such an in- " surance be made *from London to Cadiz*, and " the ship *had broke ground*, and afterwards
" been

* See the case, *Motteux v. L. Ass. Co.* quoted under the head of *Mutual Error*, P. i. ch. 2. § 3.

"been driven by storm to the port of London, "and there had taken fire, the insurers must "have answered; for the breaking ground was "an inception of the voyage *."

The risk on *freight*, or upon that profit which the ship shall gain by the carriage of goods from one port to another, must likewise commence from the time those goods are shipped.

Tongue *v.* Watts.

The plaintiff insured " on ship and *freight, at* "*and from Jamaica to Bristol.*" A cargo was ready to be put on board; but while the ship was careening, in order to the voyage, a sudden tempest arose, and she and many others were lost. The rigging and parts of her were recovered and sold; and the defendant paid into court, as much as, upon an average, he was liable to for the loss of the *ship*. The plaintiff farther insisted to be allowed L. 600 for the freight the ship would have earned in her voyage, if the accident had not happened; but as the goods were not actually on board, so as to make the insurer's right to freight commence, the Chief Justice held he could not be allowed it. 19*th Geo.* II. *Strange,* 1251.

The rules now mentioned with regard to the commencement of risk, are very generally adopted, and, indeed, with few or no variations, in the different countries of Europe. At Amsterdam

* Molloy, *l.* 2. *ch.* 7. § 9.

sterdam and Stockholm, however, the risk on ship commences " from the time she begins " to take aboard her ballast for the voyage." At Bilboa, the *hour* of commencement must be expressed in the policy.

At the same time, there may occur some variations, arising from the nature of different adventures.

A ship being insured from the Greenland seas, or *Davis'* straits, the risk homeward commences from the time the fishing ends *.

It is determined by the ordinances of Stockholm, that " where the insurance for the out- " ward bound voyage of a ship, and that for its " return, are underwritten by two different per- " sons, the risk and obligation of the latter com- " mences from the day and hour when the " master *begins to take in ballast or goods.*"

Sect. II. *Of the Termination of Risk.*

The period at which the risk of the insurer is understood to terminate, both in relation to ship and goods, admits of considerable variety, by the practice of different nations. As to the insurance on freight, there are some cases in which freights are due the moment the ship sails; these

---

* " Turba 18 mercatorum Amsterd. affirmabat reditum " incipere postquam finita erat piscatio, et de ea satis inter " partes conveniebat." *Bynkersh. Quæst. Jur. priv. l.* 14. *c.* 17.

these are not proper objects of insurance. But, in general, the insurance on freight must terminate when the ship is understood to have earned her freight; that is, when discharged of her cargo.—And, *first*, as to the termination of risk *upon ship*.

By the practice of Britain, the risk on ship ends, when she has been 24 *hours moored* in harbour, in good safety. The same is the rule at Bilboa.

It is to be understood, however, that by the vessel *being moored*, is meant, her being moored in such a situation as that she can *deliver her cargo*.

Waples *v.* Eames.

The ship *Success* was insured, "at and from "Leghorn to the port of London, and *till* "there moored 24 hours in good safety*.*" She arrived the 8th July, at Fresh Wharf, and moored, but was the same day served with an order to go back to the *Hope*, to perform a fourteen days *quarantine*. The men upon this deserted her; and upon the 12th, the Captain applied to be excused going back, which petition was adjourned to the 28th, when the Regency ordered her back; and on the 30th she went back, performed the quarantine, and then sent up for orders to air the goods: But before she returned, the ship was burnt on the 30th of August.—Question, Whether the insurer was liable?

For

For the defendant it was infifted, that the fhip arriving and being moored on the 3d July, and remaining fo till the 30th, here was a performance of what he had undertaken; and his rifk ought not to be extended to fo long a time as the 8th July, and the burning on the 23d of Auguft. But it was ruled, that though the fhip was fo long at her moorings, yet fhe could not be faid to be there *in good fafety*, which muft mean the opportunity of unloading and difcharging; whereas, here fhe was *arrefted within the 24 hours;* and the hands having deferted, and the Regency taking time to confider the petition, there was no default in the mafter or owners: And it was proved, that, till the 14 days were expired, there could be no application to air the goods; wherefore the jury found for the plaintiff.—— *Strange's Reports,* 1243. 19. *Geo.* II.

In order to a veffel's being *moored in good fafety,* no more appears neceffary than that fhe fhould be lying in fuch a fituation as is proper for delivering her cargo, according to the cuftom of the port.

In two feparate infurances on the fhip Ceres, " from Clyde to a market in the Weft Indies, " and with liberty to proceed to Jamaica." The veffel having difpofed of the greateft part of her cargo in the Weft Indies, proceeded to Morantbay in Jamaica, and was there lying at anchor for feveral days, and had landed a fmall part of her cargo, before fhe was loft in a hurricane.

Among a great many questions that occurred in this case, before the Court of Session, it was maintained by the assured, that the vessel, although she had been lying at anchor for several days, had not been *moored to a wharf or quay;* but had been lying merely in an open road. It was answered, That this was according to the custom of the port, and that the vessel both could have delivered her cargo, and did deliver a part of it in that situation. The Court of Session paid no regard to the objection. In 1786. *Marshall, Hamilton and Co. against Crawford, Barns, and others.*

So much with regard to the practice of Britain. In many places, however, at *Hamburgh* for example, the risk continues till the ship is discharged; and in others, as at *Copenhagen*, it continues for a certain number of days, unless the vessel be discharged sooner *.

Secondly, As to the termination of risk *on goods*. At *London* it terminates " when the goods are *discharged* and *safely landed*," at the port of delivery specified in the policy.

There is a great variety, however, in this particular, in the practice of different states. The ordinances of Antwerp, Amsterdam, and Stockholm, fix *fifteen days* after the arrival; that of Rotterdam, *fourteen;* that of Coningsberg, *six, ten,* or *fourteen,* according to the size of the ship. And the policies of many countries fix a certain

* *Magens*, vol. i. 47, 48.

tain time, " unless the ship shall be delivered
" sooner."

It may here be questioned, whether the insurer is liable until the goods are delivered upon land, or only until they be removed by the proprietor out of the ship.

By the ordinances, as well as the expression of policies, in most foreign nations, the insurer is understood to bear the risk of all carriage in lighters or boats, both in loading and unloading *.

British policies differ here from all foreign ones, and make use of the following clause: " Beginning the adventure *from the loading* " *thereof* aboard the said ship, until the same " shall arrive at   and there be safely landed." In consequence of the expression of this clause, although goods are not at the insurer's risk while in boats and lighters *carrying aboard*, yet, what appears a little inconsistent, they seem to be at his risk while *carrying ashore*. And MAGENS mentions a case, in which Sir JOHN STRANGE and Mr HUME CAMPBELL delivered an opinion to this purpose.

Perhaps an idea may be adopted, that will be of more extensive application: That the termination of the insurance does not depend merely upon the circumstance of the goods being *landed*

or

---

* Ord. of Antwerp, of Amsterdam, of Rotterdam, of Spain, of France, of Coningsberg, of Hamburgh, of Stockholm, of Copenhagen. *See Magens*, i. 45.

or not; but upon their being put, whether at sea or on shore, into the custody of the person to whom they are consigned.

Sparrow v. Carruthers.

The defendant insured goods " to *London*, " and until the same shall be safely *landed* there." The ship arrived in the port of *London*, and the owner of the goods sent his lighter and received the goods out of the ship; but before they reached land, an accident happened, whereby they were damaged, for which this action was brought against the insurer.

For the defendant it was insisted, that, as the accident had happened after the owner had taken the goods into his own possession, it was a loss after the insurance was ended. To which it was answered, that if this had been an action against the master or owners of the ship, it might have been a good answer, for they were certainly discharged; but in this action it could be no answer: For, during all the voyage, it might be said the goods were in the possession of the assured, who took the ship to freight, and whose servant the master was, to this purpose, as much as the lighterman: And these words are put into policies, to guard against all loss, till there is an actual landing; because, in the case of ships of great burden, that are forced to lie off, there may be carriage for many miles in boats
or

or lighters; and it was in the course of trade for the owner of the goods to send his lighter.

But the *Chief Justice* held that the insurer was discharged. He said, it would have been otherwise, had the goods been sent by the *ship's boat*, which is considered as a part of the ship and voyage; and the jury, (which was of merchants,) expressing they thought it turned upon that distinction, brought in a verdict as to this point against the plaintiff. *Strange's Reports*, 1236. 12. *Geo.* II.

Hitherto we have considered the *usual* termination of risk on ship and goods; but there are many cases, where the nature of the voyage or cargo may produce a variation from the general rule.

Thus, insurance on *privateers* is generally done for an exact period from the date of the insurance, as for a certain number of weeks or months. The same rule, it is obvious, must be observed in insurances *from fire*, and *on lives*.

A similar variation takes place where the cargo is sold on board, in which case it need not be landed at all to free the insurer. Of this the following examples are given by MOLLOY:

" A merchant insures his goods from *London to*
" *Sallee, and there to be landed*. The factor,
" after arrival, having opportunity, sells the
" cargo aboard the same ship, without ever un-
" lading her; and the buyer agrees for the
" freight

"freight of those goods for the port of *Venice*;
before she breaks ground the ship takes fire.
The assured and buyer are absolutely without
remedy; for the property of the goods becoming changed, and freight being contracted
de novo, the same was as much as if the goods
had been landed. And so it is, if the factor,
after her arrival, had contracted for freight
to another port, and the ship had happened to
take fire, the assurers are hereby absolutely discharged for ever *."

"It has been adjudged, that on voyages to the
coast of Africa, the Missisippi, and such other
places, where the ships go to trade, and dispose
of their cargoes by barter, and the like, and
not to land and deliver them to consignees and
factors, the risk on the goods outwards ends
on *breaking bulk*." *Wesket, p.* 11.

The following is another instance of variety in this respect, arising from the nature of the adventure.

The *Perseverance*, Captain *Hope*, was, in March 1775, insured in the usual manner "*at and from Liverpool* to the *Greenland seas*, during her fishing there, and back to *Liverpool*." Meeting with damage in those seas, she returned to *Liverpool* sooner than she otherwise might have done, and being repaired, was sent a second time the same season to the fishery. The same underwriters

---

* *Molloy, l.* ii. *c.* 7. § 13. *Locen. l.* ii. *c.* 5. § 9. See also *Malynes Lex Merc.* 112.

underwriters assured her again, and it was agreed to refer to the decision of arbitrators, Whether the first policy included the *whole* risk, (the ship having come back by necessity to repair,) and consequently, whether a return of premium should be made on the second policy? or, whether the insurers should keep both premiums, and the two voyages be considered as distinct?

The case being submitted to arbitrators, it was urged for the insurers, That insurance on a Greenland ship was supposed to have a respect to the *Stat.* 11. *Geo.* III. *c.* 38. requiring her to stay in the Greenland seas till the 10th August, unless she departs with the blubbers and fins of one whale, or unless she shall be forced by necessity to leave them sooner. That the *Perseverance* having caught some fish, and being obliged to return by necessity, had been found entitled to the bounty. That the same rule which ended the voyage as to government, ought to regulate it as to the insurance; for otherwise the insurers might be made liable, on pretence of returning to repair, for innumerable voyages, and for an indefinite time. That therefore a ship's returning, and being entitled to the bounty, ought to terminate the risk of the insurers. The arbiters determined in conformity with this opinion*.

In voyages to Newfoundland and Labrador, it is customary to carry on the fishing all the time the outward cargo is unloading. Consequently,

an

* See *Weskett*, 264. where the case is stated at great length.

an infurance on cargo outward, with the ordinary claufe " until fafely landed," is underftood to continue till the goods are entirely landed, notwithftanding the delay that takes place upon the part of the affured in this particular. See Douglas' *Reports, Cafe of Noble v. Kennoway.*

Thefe differences in the nature of the voyage often occafion a variety of *claufes* in the policy with refpect to the termination of the rifk.

One of the moft remarkable of thefe claufes occurs in the cafe of infurance *to a market*, or *to ports of difcharge.* In confequence of fuch a claufe, the infurer's rifk muft be fuppofed to continue, not only until a market is found for the goods, and the veffel there fafely moored, but till the cargo is difpofed of.

Cafe. If the policy of infurance run, " until " the fhip fhall have ended, and be difcharged " of her voyage," arrival at the port to which fhe is bound, is not a difcharge until fhe be unloaded. *Per tot curiam* on a demurrer, *Skinner,* 243. *Mich.* 1. *Jac.* II. *B. R. anon.*

CHAP.

CHAP. II.

Of the nature of the Insurer's Risk, or of the event against which provision is made by the Policy *.

THE clause in a maritime policy, specifying the risks undertaken by the insurer, is as follows:

"As to the perils which the assurers are contented to bear in the course of this adventure, they are, of the seas, men of war, fire, enemies, pirates, rovers, thieves, jetsons, letters of mark and reprisal, surprisals, takings at sea, arrests, restraints and detainments of all kings, princes, or people, barratry of the master and mariners, and all other losses, perils, and misfortunes, which have or shall come to the hurt, detriment, or damage of the said ship, &c. or any part thereof†".

R   1. From

---

* In considering the *nature of the insurer's risk*, there are two points which deserve attention;—the nature of the event provided against; and the degree of connection between the extent and the loss. These cannot easily be treated of separately.

† In a policy on lives, or from fire, it is not usual to insert any such enumeration; and the nature of the case scarcely admits of it. These policies, however, as well as mercantile insurance, often contain a variety of exceptions from, and limitations upon the risk, suited to the circumstances of different cases, as will be mentioned more particularly in another place.

1. From the enumeration here given, and from the nature of the contract of insurance in general, it seems to follow, that the insurer means to subject himself to the consequence of all perilous *accident*, or *unforeseen* misfortune, which may happen to the subject in the course of the adventure *.

It is for *accident* that he is liable, and for accident only; that is, such unfortunate events, the amount of which cannot be foreseen, but depend upon the issue of the voyage. Were it otherwise, the contract would not be an "agree-" ment for indemnity on an *uncertain event*," which is understood by an insurance; but it would be for a determinate and ascertained performance.

The nature of insurance supposes a *risk* undertaken, and not an ascertained performance; because the intention of the merchant is to secure himself from a loss, the amount of which cannot be calculated, and which therefore might be ruinous to him.

2. Hence it has become an established rule, that an underwriter is not liable for damage arising from the *natural decay*, or the *perishable nature* of the subject insured. These are not *accidents*. They either are foreseen, or they may have been foreseen; and their amount may be exactly ascertained. They depend not upon the issue of the voyage, but arise from a pre-existing cause,

---

* 2 *Val. Com.* 12. 14. 74. 79.

cause, totally unconnected with it. A bargain, by which a man should subject himself to loss arising from these sources, would not contain that risk or hazard, which appears essential to the contract of insurance.

The French Ordinance says, " that the loss, " diminution, or waste, that may happen from " the perishable quality of any thing, shall not " fall on the insurers*."

" In grain, wine, salt, figs, raisins, oranges, " distilled liquors, herrings, olives, and other " vivers," says the *Guidon*, " because it happens " sometimes, that they are spoiled in the un- " loading, or, while in the ship, are subject to be " heated, turn sour, become wet, putrefy, leak, " or damage one another, the insurer is in no " degree liable for such partial losses †."

Upon this principle, an insurer is not liable for the natural *tear and wear* of the ship, or her furniture; nor for the ordinary waste and corruption incident to the cargo. These are particulars, the amount of which does not depend at all upon the event of the voyage, and which admit of calculation, as well *before* as *after* the adventure. A bargain may no doubt be made, with a view to provide against such damage; *but the bargain would change its nature.* If a person makes an agreement, by which his life is warranted for ten or twenty years, it is an insurance. But if

---

* *Mag.* vol. ii. 173. † Guidon, ch. v. § 8.

if for 200 or 300, it becomes, from the certainty of the event, a different contract.

Upon the same principle, that the insurer is not answerable for the ordinary tear and wear of the ship, neither is he responsible for the ordinary waste and deterioration of commodities, nor that *leakage* of liquors, which was to be expected, and unavoidable.

It is said, " If the party insured can prove, " that the prejudice or leakage was occasioned by " unfortunate accidents, as *bad weather*, *arrest*, " or the like, the insurer must bear *these* losses." Ord. of *Koningsberg*.

It is observed by Mr *Wesket*, who, in a matter of practice, is certainly of great authority, " that " in England there is seldom any particular sti- " pulation in the policy with regard to leakage. " It is understood, the insurers are liable for such " loss as happens from storms and other un- " avoidable *accidents, deducting the ordinary or* " *common leakage* *."

By the ordinances of *Hamburgh*, " when pe- " rishable commodities spoil, or receive damage " of themselves, by reason of their natural quality; " as, for example, when wines turn sour, or leak " out; Seville or China oranges, lemons, apples, " &c. perish; chesnuts and corn are heated; and " so forth; as likewise, when *rats and mice* eat " and destroy any thing. In all such cases, the " assurer is not liable to make good the damage, but

---

* Voce, (*Leakage*.)

" but the same remains to account of every one
" to whom the goods belong; unless such damage
" arose from hence, that the ship was prevented
" from pursuing its way, by reason of restraints,
" &c. by external violence, &c." Those losses,
it seems, above enumerated, are considered as
consequences of the perishable nature of the subject*.

On the same footing are the provisions and
stores on board a vessel, which are intended to
be consumed, and ought not to be accounted for
by the insurer, so far as they are applied to the
purpose expected; their consumption being so
far imputable to design, and not to unforeseen
accident.

Thus by the ordinances of *Rotterdam* and
Middleburgh, " nothing that serves for the ordi-
" nary consumption of the voyage can be insu-
" red." By those of *Koningsberg* and *Amsterdam*,
they may; but it must be " *along with the ship,
and not alone, or separately.*" The insurer likewise, by these last mentioned regulations, is not
liable for such ordinary consumption, if the *adventure arrives*; because, in that case, these expences are calculated on, so as to be refunded
with profit; he is liable for them, however, if
the *adventure is lost*. This seems rather to be a
variation from general maxims, as the loss arising
from the ordinary consumption of provisions and
stores, admits of previous calculation.

In

* To the same effect, see *Ord. of France, Stypman. ad Jus Marit. par.* iv. c. 7. p. 320.

In consequence of this principle, that insurance protects against *accidents* only, various regulations have been adopted in different countries, to prevent the insurer from being subjected to that damage which arises from *tear and wear*, or *natural decay*.

By the ordinance of Amsterdam, it is provided, " That whereas ships often sail in good condition, and are insured as such; but in the course of long voyages are much deteriorated, and the insurers are cast to pay the original value; although these ships, if they had made a safe voyage, would not have sold for one third; therefore it is left to the Commissioners of Insurance to determine, in such cases, according to their discretion."

There is a contrivance, (probably adopted principally with a different view), which prevails in many countries, that may operate in favour of the insurer, in the respect now mentioned. This is to prohibit the owner from insuring the full value of his adventure. The principal object of such a prohibition was, no doubt, to prevent fraudulent losses; at the same time, it obliges the assured to bear a share of loss, which may correspond, in some degree, to the supposed natural and expected deterioration of the ship and cargo.

These limitations, it must be observed, with regard to the extent to which insurance may be made, cannot be effectual for the purpose alluded ed to, unless over-valuations are checked by an examination of the vessel, previous to the voyage. This measure has been adopted in France, where, in pursuance of an edict, 17th of August 1779, all ships are prohibited to sail, until a survey has been made. And it is believed the merchants of London have of late adopted the measure of a register, for a similar purpose, though not under public authority *.

It was, for a long time, the practice in Britain, that the insurer was considered as entitled to a retention of 2 *per cent.* on every loss incurred; a practice which seems to have originated from an idea of the propriety of an abatement, in consideration of natural decay of ship and cargo. This practice, however, has of late been going gradually into desuetude, and, it is believed, is now become rather uncommon both in England and Scotland.

Upon the principles above stated, therefore, it seems to follow, that no loss and damage which can be foreseen and estimated, no natural and expected deterioration falls under the risk undertaken by the insurer. On the other hand, whatever does not admit of previous ascertainment, the damage of a storm at sea, the peril of capture, of depredation by thieves or pirates, forms the proper object of an insurance-contract. The general danger of these may, no doubt, be foreseen;

* This is likewise the case at Leith, but it is believed has not been fully adopted on the west coast of Scotland.

foreseen; but the precise amount of loss can only be estimated from the event*.

3. From the account that has been given of the perils undertaken by the insurer, it is obvious, they do not include those misfortunes which arise from the fault or voluntary deed of the other party.

The fault or deed of a party, it may be observed, is not accident. It *might* and *ought* to have been foreseen and prevented. Neither will any

---

* It is deserving of notice, that writers on this subject have generally confounded two things that are very different; the *natural and expected* deterioration of the subject, and its *pre-existent*, though *latent* defect. "Insurers," says the *Guidon*, "are not liable for the *defective, insufficient,* or *perishable* nature of the thing insured." But the freedom of the underwriter from risk, in these cases, is founded on very different principles.

He is not, on the one hand, liable for the ordinary effects of the *perishable nature* of ship or cargo; because these effects are not a matter of accident, they are *foreseen* and *expected*.

The *pre-existent defect* or *insufficiency*, on the other hand, of either ship or cargo, may be latent; in which case, the discovery of such defect, within any given time, or in the course of any particular adventure, will be unforeseen and unexpected, and might therefore become the proper object of insurance: But the insurer is freed from the effects of latent *pre-existent defect*, from the principle that error in contracts destroys the consent of parties. He is in no degree responsible for the perishable nature, but he is for pre-existent defect, unless it goes so far as to make the ship *not seaworthy*. See Part i. ch. 2.

any man be allowed to secure himself against the consequences of his own fraud or negligence. The principle is perhaps obvious; it admits, however, of some striking illustrations in the law of insurance.

Thus, in cases of damage arising from *restraint or embargo*, it is said, " where a policy " of insurance is against restraint of Princes, " that extends not where the *insured* navigate " against the laws of countries, or where there " shall be a seizure for not paying custom, or " the like." *Per Hutchins, L. Commiss.* 2. *Vern.* 176.

By the ordinance of Hamburgh, " all the da- " mages which happen to ship or goods, by " means of any arrests or restraints, and which " the insurer is to bear, are to be understood of " those cases, when the arrest is to be laid by " the sovereign authority of Kings, &c.; but " not, indiscriminately, when private persons, for " any particular demand they may have upon " the skippers, owners, or the ship, shall cause " the ship or goods to be arrested or molested " by the Magistrate; in which case the insurer " is not liable, *so far as relates to those that gave " occasion to the arrest*, but *otherwise, and in case " there was no foundation or lawful cause* for it, " then the assurer remains liable to the suffer- " ing party; and so likewise all others concern- " ed, *on whose account the arrest was not laid,* " shall remain entitled to their demands upon

"the insurers, whether the arrest was well
"founded or not."

We have already noticed several considerations which destroy an insurance upon illicit trade. The principle now mentioned, affords a farther reason why the underwriter should not be liable for detention or confiscation on account of a *contraband cargo*, because this must be owing to the fault and misdemeanour of the owner or freighter *.

" An accident," says VALINES, " is not that
" which happens through the defect, or perish-
" able nature of the thing insured, nor through
" the *act or fault of the proprietor* †."

4. The point is by no means so clear, when it is enquired, " How far the insurer is free
" from damage occasioned by the fraud or negli-
" gence of the shipmaster or crew ?"

It will throw light upon this question to attend to the distinction between an insured who is owner of the ship, and one who is only a freighter of goods.

It requires no illustration, that when a person commits his goods, *for hire*, to any common carrier, he is entitled to expect honesty and diligence

---

* See *l.* 3. *Cod. De naut. fænore.* " Qui suscipit in se periculum navigationis, suscipit periculum fortunæ, non culpæ," is the observation of the commentators upon this law.

† 2. *Val. Com.* 12. 14. 74. 79.

diligence from the perfon to whom his property is thus entrufted. And if it fuffers damage, either from want of ordinary care, or from embezzlement, in the hands of a fervant, the mafter, who reaps the benefit of the hire, and to whom the proprietor is fuppofed to have trufted, muft be accountable. This ftate of obligation is reafonable in itfelf, and highly expedient; and it has been fettled by repeated decifions.

In the cafe of goods put on board a fhip, it is the mafter of the fhip to whom the proprietor of thefe goods muft look for indemnification in regard to any lofs he may fuftain from the negligence or knavery of the failors. " The reafon," fays Molloy, " why the mafter ought to be li-
" able, is, becaufe the mariners are of his own
" chufing, and under his correction and go-
" vernment. If they are faulty, he may punifh
" them; and, if they are guilty of embezzle-
" ment, he may reimburfe himfelf out of their
" wages."

The fame argument holds from the mafter to the fhip owners. The owner of a fhip appoints the mafter; and it is to him that the freighter trufts for the mafter's good conduct, as he has the ultimate management and direction of every thing on board; he likewife reaps the advantage arifing from the freight. It has been found, therefore, by repeated decifions, that the owners of fhip are refponfible for the captain whom
they

they employ, and the extent of this obligation has been regulated by statute *.

So far as the *owner of ship*, therefore, is the assured, an underwriter cannot, *without an express bargain*, be supposed liable *to him* for the misbehaviour of master and crew. For them, the assured owner is ultimately responsible; and their deeds are his. To subject the underwriter in such a case, would be to relieve the assured from all consequences arising from the carelessness or dishonesty of his own appointments, and to give *him* a claim against the insurer, from that very carelessness or dishonesty. A bargain of this nature must appear very singular; and although it has prevailed in the practice of insurance, it is certainly not consequent upon the natural state of obligation arising from that contract, but must have been introduced by express stipulation.

In fact, such an interpretation of the policy, could have no other effect than to make the money change hands; for *naturally*, and independent of express provision, the ship-owner is liable for the act and deed of his servants; and the merchant who suffers in his property by the misbehaviour of

---

* This point with regard to the obligation and responsibility, between master and owner, does not appear to be strictly connected with the present subject; and it is therefore sufficient upon this head to refer to the following authorities,— *Boson v. Sandford. Salk.* 440.   *Lane v. Cotton. Salk.* 18. *Digest de exerc: actione. Dig. Nautæ, Caupones, Stabularii,* &c.

of master and crew, has, at common law, an action for indemnification, both against the delinquent, and his employers. Unless this be removed by express bargain, the claim of the ship-owner upon the policy would be met by a counter-claim of damages arising to the underwriter, from the master's delinquency.

Where the assured is merely a *shipper of goods*, the situation of parties is somewhat different; though not so different, as to lead upon the whole, to an opposite conclusion.

The assured *shipper of goods* has not the direction of the adventure; he does not appoint the master or crew; they are not his servants; his connection with their proceedings is a great deal more remote than that of the *ship-owner*.

Neither, as in the former case, will the assured's action upon the policy be met by any counter-claim upon the part of the underwriter. For although, upon the insurer's paying the loss, he acquires right to the merchants claim of damages against the delinquent master, and the owners of the ship his employers; yet he is here liable to the *shipper of goods* in the first instance, and is left to seek his redress as he best can.

But, even in this case, there appears sufficient reason to conclude that, *naturally*, and *without express provision*, the underwriter could not be subjected to loss arising from the misdemeanour of master or crew.

It

It appears a very unfavourable conftruction of any bargain, to infer, by implication, that one perfon means to take upon himfelf the confequences of another's delinquency to the commiffion of which he has had no acceffion; befides, there feems to be lefs occafion for the remedy of infurance in cafes of damage by fraud and negligence, than in thofe loffes which arife from the operation of unintelligent caufes. When a merchant fuffers by winds or waves, he has no means of redrefs againft thofe minifters of adverfe fortune; and he muft of neceffity feek to fecure himfelf againft fuch contingencies, by having recourfe to thofe who are willing to undertake a great future rifk, for a fmall prefent emolument. But when damage refults from fraud or negligence, the injured party has his recourfe againft the delinquent, or his employers.

But farther, although the affured *fhipper of goods* does not appoint the mafter or crew, he, neverthelefs, appears to be infinitely more connected with them than the underwriter is. He looks round for a proper veffel to tranfport his merchandife, and he fingles out one belonging to owners, upon whofe honefty he thinks he can depend, with regard to her future deftination, and to whofe attention and fkill he can truft, with regard to the appointment of proper navigators. But the underwriter muft be, in a thoufand cafes, totally unacquainted with the character and circumftances of the fhip-owners; and with
regard

regard to the ship's destination, he must depend entirely on the information of his assured. If, therefore, the *shipper of goods* makes choice of a vessel belonging to owners who shall be either disingenuous with regard to the plan of the adventure, or careless in the appointment of masters and crew, he seems to have, in a very great degree, himself to blame; and he ought naturally to bear the consequences of his own misconduct and improper choice. "When one of two in- "nocent persons," said Mr *Just.* BULLER, (in *Fitzherbert v. Mather*) "must suffer by the fault "of a third, the question is, who gave credit; "and the one who trusted must take the conse- "quences."

And this leads to a consideration that appears conclusive. The underwriter must be supposed to depend upon his assured, for the whole of his information with respect to the plan and conduct of the adventure. He undertakes a risk, precisely such as it is represented to him, and as it appears *ex facie* of the policy. But if, in consequence of a *breach of contract* on the part of the *ship-owner*, or, what is the same thing, a *breach of orders* on the part of the owner's servant, the plan or conduct of the adventure should be varied from the policy; this is a different risk from what the insurer meant to undertake; and he will not, by construction, be subjected to a loss which is not within the terms of his bargain. In short, to place this matter in a simple point of view, let the *ship-owner* be considered as the same person with the *master*, for whom he is responsible; and it will be evident that the underwriter never can, *without an express bargain*, be subjected for the *owner's* faulty or fraudulent breach of contract. This is, in fact, one aspect of a general doctrine, which shall be afterwards more fully illustrated; that the insurer is not naturally liable for *any* variation from the terms of the policy.

Upon the whole, it appears, that, unless there be an express clause to that effect in the contract, the insurer cannot be understood to subject himself to the consequences of fault or fraud of the *ship-owner*, nor, what is perfectly synonimous, of fault or fraud of *master or crew*.

This idea seems to have been received among those states in which insurance first introduced itself; probably from the tendency there is to limit, rather than extend, the interpretation of a contract which is new and unusual.

By the practice of the *Italian States*, malversation, or *barratry*, as it is called, of master and crew, is held to be at the risk of the assured, unless the contrary be expressly provided*.

It was held, in the same manner, in the kingdom of *Castile*, that " the indemnification which " is at the risk of the insurer, is understood to " extend to *accident*, but not to what happens
" from

* *Decis. Rotæ Genoæ*, 3. § 15. *Ord. Gen.* No. 154. Policy at *Florence*. *Magens*, vol. 2.

"from the fault of the assured, nor through the "*fault of the master of the ship**."

Roccus, an Italian writer of some note, seems to adopt a consequence of the same principle. He thinks, that, if robbery be committed on the seas by pirates, this is the act of third parties, and the insurer is liable; but if theft or embezzlement happen within the ship, the underwriter is not responsible; for, says he, " this is not the ef- " fect of *accident*, but bad management, and for " such embezzlements the master himself is li- " able." This is maintaining, that the insurer is not liable to an assured *shipper of goods*, for damage arising from the master's fault, or crime †.

T   Similar

---

* " El seguro que es à cargo del assegurador, se entien- " de sucediendo por caso fortuito; mas no si sucede por " culpa del s'assegurado, ny por culpa del maestre de la " nave." *Cleirac*, p. 296. quotes *El Laberinto del Comercio*, of *Jo. de Evia*.

† " Primus casus est, si furtum committatur in mari, per " piratas, et tunc inter casus fortuitos connumeratur, et as- " securator, suscipiens in se casus fortuitos, tenetur in casu " furti, *Not*. 41. Secundus casus est, si furtum fuit commissum " *in navi*, et aliquæ *merces* subripiantur;" (that is, an embezzlement to the prejudice of an assured *shipper of goods*,) " et tunc, pro hoc furto, *assecuratores non tenentur*; tum quia " dominus tenetur eas custodire, et, si furatæ sint in nave, " non videtur hoc ex casu fortuito evenisse, sed ex negligen- " tia non bene custodientium;" (this seems to imply, either that the proprietor of merchandises was understood to accompany his goods in person, and was bound to guard them from embezzlement; or else, that he was himself answerable for the shipmaster to whom he entrusted them,)
" tum

Similar views have been adopted by authors of a more modern date. "In general," says *Denisart*, "the insurer is liable for accidents of the sea; but not for losses which happen through the act of the assured, nor from the *fault of master or crew* *."

And we find an express provision to this purpose, in so modern a code as that of Lewis XIV. which can only be imputed to improved notions upon the subject: "The insurer shall not be obliged to bear the losses and damages arising to the ship and goods, through the master's and mariners fault, *unless, by the contract, he be engaged for the master's misdemeanours* †."

As commerce advanced, that suspicion of fraud, which prevails in the infancy of trade, gradually wore off; insurance became more common, and its advantages were more felt; and in some countries

"tum etiam, quia pro furto in navi commisso, tenetur magister navis, quia per receptionem mercium, tacite videtur pacisci ut salvæ restituantur." (That is to say, the insurer is not liable, because the proprietor of goods may indemnify himself, independent of insurance, by an action against the faulty person.) *Roccus, Not.* 42. *De Assecur.* Among all the older commentators, it is a matter of disquisition, Whether damage by *theft* is to be reckoned as one of those *accidents* that are provided against by an insurance-policy. Loss arising from the act of an intelligent agent does not figure to the mind so strongly in the light of *accident*. But the point is too clear to bear argument.

* *Denisart. Collect. de Jurispr.* (voce *Assurance.*)

† *Ord. Fr. des Assur.* § 28. *Magens* 2. 172.

countries the old form of this contract by degrees received a more extensive construction, while, in others, it was rendered applicable to a greater variety of cases by the introduction of express clauses and stipulations.

And here a distinction, formerly alluded to, naturally presented itself; the distinction between an assured *owner of ship*, and *shipper of goods*. We find it held by several writers, and inculcated by the regulations of mercantile states of no mean rank, that the underwriter is liable for the misdemeanours of the captain and crew, to the *shipper of goods*, though not to the *ship-owner*.

That ancient and curious French treatise, the *Guidon*, gives an explanation of *barratry*, which seems rather applicable to fraud in relation to *goods*, than to the *ship*. " And of this," it adds, " the insurer runs the risk; only the assured " *shipper of goods*, (*marchand chargeur*,) is bound " to prosecute the master himself in the first in- " stance *."

The same book treats of insurance on *the body of the ship*, in a separate chapter, as a subject totally unconnected with that barratry, for which the insurer is liable †. And lays it down, that, " if insurance be made upon the *hull of a ship*, " the underwriter is not liable for the malver- " sation, fraud, or deceit of the master, be-
" cause

---

* *Cleiracs Guidon, c.* 9. § 1. *De barat, baraterie.*
† *Ch.* 14. *Des Assurances sur Corps de Nef.* § 4.

"cause the assured *owner*, (*bourgeois*,) has cho-
"sen him, and approved of his skill and ho-
"nesty, and may depose him, if he proves un-
"worthy."

Cleirac, in his commentary on this last passage observes, that " it applies to the special case
" of an *owner, who insures his ship*, conducted
" by a master of his own chusing, which is dif-
" ferent from that of a *merchant who insures his
" goods*, loaded in such a ship as he can find, and
" who has no authority over the master *."

Roccus, an author formerly quoted, mentions
this as a point about which doubt had been
entertained; " For," says he, " to the assured
" *who has shipped goods on board*, nothing can be
" imputed so as to make the fault of master or
" crew any thing else than mere *accident* as to
" him; unless the *shipper of goods* be at the same
" time *owner of the ship*, for then he will be liable
" for the master's fraud †."

The

---

* *Cleiracs Guidon*, p. 319.

† " Nam assecurato, qui bona fide posuit merces in electa
" navi, nec tantam notitiam et fidem de magistro navis ha-
" bebat, non potest aliquid imputari quin dicatur casus
" fortuitus et sub assecuratione comprehensus; nisi domi-
" nus mercium esset etiam dominus navis, quia tunc ad
" eum spectaret fraus navarchi." *Rocc. de Assec.* Not. 44.
The reader will find it very difficult, or rather impossible,
to reconcile the opinions of the different commentators with
one another upon this point, or even to make them consistent
with themselves. See *Santerna*, p. 3. § 68. *Roccus*, num. 40.
et seq.:—and above all, *Casa-regis, disc.* 1. § 71. *et seq.* with
the authorities there quoted.

The regulations of the great cities of *Holland*, explicitly adopt the same distinction. These shall be stated more fully afterwards.

5. But whatever may be the *natural* obligation of the insurer with regard to loss occasioned by the misdemeanour of master and crew; whether, as seems most reasonable, the underwriter is, in no case, liable for such loss, without an express bargain; or whether, according to the distinction above stated, he is naturally liable to an assured *shipper of goods*, though not to an assured *owner* of ship; the greater part of modern nations have not left this point to depend upon *construction* merely, but, impressed with the advantages of insurance, they have carried it to a length that is absurd and dangerous. They have very generally adopted an express stipulation, by which the underwriter becomes responsible for the *fault*, and even for the *fraud* of the master and crew.

The effect of a clause of this nature in favour of an assured *shipper*, must be to preclude the underwriter from founding a defence on any variation from the plan of the adventure, which has originated with the master or crew. Its effect, in favour of an assured *ship-owner*, must be, farther, to transfer the responsibility of the owner for his servants, and to cut off any claim of damages which the underwriter might have against him from the delinquency of master and crew. The dangerous

ous tendency of such a bargain is very obvious. In the former case, it destroys a great motive to fidelity in the shipmaster, by removing the interest which the merchants, his employers, have, in that fidelity. But, in the latter case, it is a contrivance by which a man may secure himself against the consequences of his own negligence or dishonesty, in the appointment of improper persons to offices of trust. It is not surprising, therefore, we find several states reprobating altogether the idea of such a contract.

" No insurance," says the Ordinance of *Antwerp*, " shall hereafter be allowed against the " *barratry*, roguery, or other misbehaviour of " the master or ship's crew; all usages and " customs to the contrary are hereby abolished; " and all such contracts are declared void, and " of no effect *."

By the regulations of Spain, as well as by the expression of their policies, whether on *ship* or on *goods*,—" insurance is to be un" derstood against the sea, wind, fire, enemies, " friends, and any other accident that can hap" pen, *except barratry of the master*, or a defici" ency of the merchandise †."

With regard to the propriety or legality, however, of such a bargain, there must appear, from what has been already stated, a considerable difference between the situation of an assured *shipper*

---

* Ord. Antw. No. 54. See *Magens, v. 2. p. 25.*
† *Ord. Spain*, No. 42. Forms of Span. policies.

shipper of goods, and *owner* of ship. It is to the last of these Lord MANSFIELD alludes, (in the case of *Nutt v. Bourdieu*), when he says, " The " provision against *barratry* is a very extraordi- " nary one. It is strange it should have crept " into our policies, and more so, that it should " have continued in them so long. That the " underwriter should insure the conduct of the " captain, whom he does not appoint, and can- " not dismiss, to the owner who can do either."

From such views as these, the great towns of Holland have adopted a distinction which seems to be well founded. By *Ord. Rotterd.* § 43. if the master has been appointed by the assured owners, there can be no provision against his barratry; but if he has risen to that station in the course of the adventure, and without their interference, such an assurance is permitted.

It appears to be the universal practice of Holland[*], to distinguish between an assured *owner of ship*, and *shipper of goods*. The form of a policy *upon ship* being in favour of the *owners*, contains no provision against the fraud of the *master*, but only that of the *crew*, with whom the connection of the owners is not so immediate. The policy *on goods*, in favour of the merchant, contains a provision against the fraud of both *crew* and *master*.

The *Copenhagen* form of a policy on ship insures against " *negligence* of the master, and
" ship's

---

[*] See *Magens*, vol. 2. Forms of Policies at *Amst.* and *Middleb.*—*Bynk. Q. Jur. priv. p.* 553.

"ship's company, *barratry* of the ship's company only, and not of the master." That on goods provides for "*barratry* and *negligence* of the master, and ship's company *."

It must, however, be acknowledged, that the appointment of servants to a difficult trust, and remote from the eye of their employer, is a matter, in which the greatest attention and honesty cannot always command success. It is a matter which depends as much upon good fortune as good management. The regulations of the greater part of mercantile states have entered strongly into this view. In England, the legislature has provided, by special statute, that merchants who may suffer by the embezzlements of master or crew, shall not have recourse against the ship-owners, farther than to the value of ship and freight †. Such considerations have overbalanced the danger of fraud from an insurance on the behaviour of master and crew.

If therefore any person chuses to undertake the risk of warranting to another, the honesty and diligence of his servant, it has not, by most nations, been thought just or expedient to prevent the ship-owner from obtaining such security. And the underwriter may, by an express clause, subject himself, even to the owner of ship, for the misdemeanours of master or crew, always supposing, there is no proof of accession upon the

---

* *Magens* II. *p.* 323, 324.
† See *Stat.* 7. *Geo.* II. *c.* 15. (1734.)

the part of the assured himself. From the tendency of mercantile nations to extend the practice and application of the contract of insurance, such provisions against the misbehaviour of master and crew have become very general in Europe.

6. In Britain, all policies, without discrimination, provide against *barratry of the master and mariners*. Barratry, say all our authorities, means fraud, deceit, dishonest intention. It comes from the Italian, *baratrare* to cheat. The application of the term seems to be perfectly general, to every species of knavery.

There is some reason, however, to believe, that the idea of an insurance against the fraud of the master and ship's company, first introduced itself where they were fraudulent, by *running away with the ship;* that being the case, in which the assured, by the absence of the master, was deprived of his natural recourse against the delinquent himself.

Upon this supposition, we may account for a distinction adopted by the earlier writers, and mercantile ordinances, between *barratry* and *embezzlement*. By the *Florentine* policy, " insurers " are to be liable for all misfortunes, *&c.* not ex-" cepting the barratry of the master, *&c.* ;" " the insurers, at the same time, declare, they " will not be liable for what the master of the " ship *steals or embezzles* *." The reasonings in

---

* *Ord. of Flor.* No. 9, 10. See *Roccus,* who makes the same distinction.

in several adjudged cases, to be stated in the sequel, confirm the same hypothesis.

The clause of insurance against barratry, however, has long been interpreted as extending to every species of *fraudulent* malversation.

Perhaps the same hypothesis may afford a probable reason, why it has become common to insure against *fraud*, and not against *negligence*. The original view of insuring against master and crew, was to provide a security from those malversations only, which, by the flight of the master, deprived the owner of his recourse against the culprit himself.

Some nations, however, provide against *negligence*. The policies of the great Dutch cities, which in respect to the whole doctrine of barratry, seem to be considerably systematic, and those of *Copenhagen*, contain a stipulation of this kind. In a policy on *ship*, the assured *owner* provides " against fraud or barratry of the crew only; and " *negligence*, both of master and crew." In a policy on *goods*, the assured *merchant*, provides " against frauds or *negligences* of either master " or sailors*."

The practice of *Hamburgh* subjects the insurer to the " *mistake, neglect*, or *malice* of the master, " or his mariners †."

In

---

* On ship. " Onaghtsamheid van schippers en Bootsgesellen, ook schelmerye van de voorste Bootsgesellen." On goods. " Schelmeryen en onaghtsamheiden van schippers en Bootsgesellen."

† *Magens. v.* 2. *p.* 244.

In some countries, the stipulation with regard to *barratry* is understood to comprehend *gross fault*. The *Guidon* explains *barratry* as nearly synonimous with breach of contract; and as extending not only to fraud, and to *negligence*, but likewise to all *deviations* made by the Captain, without the knowledge of the assured*. The French Ordinances say, that " insurers shall not " be answerable for the loss or damage that may " happen to ship or goods, through the *fault* " of masters or mariners, *unless*, by the policy, " they be liable for *barratry*†.

But, in British policies, there is no express provision with regard to negligence, or mere fault, in opposition to dishonest intention; and it has been settled by repeated decisions, that *barratry* is applicable to *fraud* only, and implies something of a criminal nature.

It remains to illustrate, by adjudged cases, these two positions last stated.

Case.

---

* " Barat, ou baraterie de changement de patron, est le " changement qui se fait des maistres de navires, voyages, " escales, restes, havres; malversations, roberies, larcins, " alterations, deguisemens des marchandizes, *le tout pro-* " *cedant du patron du navire*, equipage, *et negligence d'iceux.*" *Guidon, c.* 9. § 1. It is difficult to see how a " changement " des maistres du navire," can come under the chapter of accidents, " procedant du patron," which, however, is necessary to constitute *barratry*.

† *Magens, v.* 2. 172.

Case. Where a ship was insured against the barratry of the master, in an action brought thereupon, the jury found, that the ship was lost by the *fraud* and *negligence* of the master. The Court held, that if the master ran away with the ship, or embezzled the goods, the merchant may have an action against him; for it is reasonable, that merchants, who hazard their stocks in foreign traffic, should secure themselves in what manner they think proper, against barratry of the master, and all other frauds. And this must be intended fraud of the master, and not a bare neglect; and they all agreed, that *fraud* is *barratry*, though not named in the contract; but *negligence might not*. 1. Modern Rep. 230, 231.

Knight v. Cambridge.

Cambridge brought a writ of error upon a judgment given against him in the common pleas, in an action brought by the plaintiff upon a policy of insurance of the ship, *Riga Merchant*, " at and from Port Mahon to London." And Serjeant Braithwaite, for the plaintiff in error, insisted, that the judgment was erroneous, because the breach was ill assigned. For the policy was, that the defendant *Cambridge* should insure the said ship, among other things, against the *barratry* of the master, and all other dangers, damages, and misfortunes, which should happen to prejudice of the said ship; and the breach assigned figned was, that the ſhip in the ſaid voyage, *per fraudem et negligentiam magiſtri navis prædictæ, depreſſa et ſubmerſa fuit, et totaliter perdita et amiſ-ſa fuit, et nullius valoris devenit.* This, he infiſted, was not within the meaning of the word *barratry*; but the breach ſhould have been expreſs, that the ſhip was loſt by the barratry of the maſter; befides the owner of the goods has a remedy againſt the owners of the ſhip, for any prejudice he receives by the fraud or neglect of the maſter; and, therefore, there is the leſs reaſon the inſurers ſhould be liable; befides, if the word barratry, import fraud, ſtill it does not import neglect, and the fact alleged here is, that the ſhip was loſt by the *fraud and neglect* of the maſter. But the court was unanimouſly of opinion, that there was no occaſion to aver the fact, in the very words of the policy; but if the fact alleged came within the meaning of the words in the policy, it is ſufficient. Now barratry imports *fraud.* (*Du Frene, Gloſſ. v. Barataria, fraus, dolus,*) and he that commits a fraud may properly be ſaid to be guilty of a neglect, *viz.* of his duty. Barratry of a maſter is not confined to his running away with the ſhip; and the general words of the policy ought to be conſtrued to extend to loſſes of the like nature, as thoſe mentioned before. Now loſſes ariſing from the fraud of the maſter, are of the like nature as if he had run away with the ſhip, (ſuppoſing bar-

ratry

ratry to be confined to that, which it is not,) because it imports *any fraud*. And the judgment was affirmed. *April* 27. 1724. *Raym.* 1349. *Strange's Reports*, 581.

It must here be observed, that, without a clause against barratry in the policy, there are several species of malversation of the master, or breaches of contract, which, instead of subjecting the insurer, would have the effect to free him entirely from risk. For example, all *variations from the line of voyage* stipulated, though made with a criminal intent, instead of subjecting, would liberate the insurer, without this express clause; and notwithstanding this clause, *all deviations that are not fraudulent*, (as will be afterwards shown,) destroy the obligation upon the part of the insurer.

It becomes, therefore, of importance to define accurately what circumstances constitute *fraud* in the master, and distinguish a breach of the contract *by barratry* from any other. And here, it should seem, that a master must always be supposed in *mala fide*, and guilty of *fraud*, when he commits any act that is clearly *illegal* and *criminal*.

Three circumstances seem, in most cases, essential to constitute *barratry*. That the master should act *contrary to his instructions; with a view to his own private advantage; and to the evident detriment of some party concerned*.

The

The master cannot, in general, be considered as fraudulent, while he acts agreeable to his instructions. For he is the servant of the owner of the ship; is appointed by him, and must take his directions accordingly. He is not presumed to know the bargains and insurances which may have taken place as to the voyage. If his owner chuses to subject himself to the consequences of breaking those bargains, or forfeiting those insurances, it is a matter in which the master is nowise concerned.

Neither is he guilty of fraud, if, while he does break through his instructions, it is done not for his own advantage, but for the benefit of the adventure. It is unnecessary to enquire at present how far the master is vested with discretionary powers in this respect. It will probably be allowed, that there are certain cases in which the master may desert the line of voyage marked out in the policy, and vacate the owners insurance, without the imputation of impropriety or misconduct. But there can be no doubt, that many situations exist, in which he may do this from a sincere desire to consult the interest of his employers, and, consequently, without being *fraudulent*. And where the breach of orders in the master, though with a view to his own advantage, does not appear capable of hurting third parties, although the master may be rash and *faulty*, he does not deserve to be considered as *criminal*.

" To

" To make it barratry, there muſt be ſomething of a *criminal* nature, as well as a *breach of contract. Strange*, 1173. As when a ſhip goes out of its proper courſe by a tortious act of the maſter or mariners, *for their own benefit*, which is of the ſame nature as a piracy or robbery at ſea."

Stamma v. Brown.

The ſhip the Gothic Lion being advertiſed to be going to Marſeilles, goods were ſhipped on board her on behalf of the plaintiff, and a bill of loading ſigned by the maſter, whereby he undertakes to go a *droite route* to Marſeilles, and the defendant underwrote a policy from Falmouth, (where the goods were taken in), to Marſeilles. Before the ſhip departed from the port of London, another advertiſement was publiſhed for goods to Genoa, Leghorn, and Naples; and the plaintiff's agent was told, it was intended to go to theſe ports firſt, and then come back to Marſeilles; but he inſiſted, that his bargain was to go firſt or directly to Marſeilles, and he would not conſent to let her paſs by Marſeilles, or alter his inſurance. The ſhip, however, did paſs by Marſeilles; and after delivering her cargo at the other ports, ſet out on her return to Marſeilles with the plaintiff's goods. But in her voyage thither was blown up in an engagement with a Spaniſh ſhip.

And

And in an action upon the policy, the breach was assigned, as a loss by the *barratry* of the master. And the plaintiff insisted, that any fraud or malversation of the master was within the meaning of the word *barratry*.—*Du Fresne* terms it, "*Dolus qui fit in contractibus;*" and so do all the Dictionaries, as *Florio's Italian Dict. verbo, barateria; Minshew, Furetier*, &c.; and that in the cases, *Knight* and *Cambridge*, and *Knight v. Dod*, where the loss was laid to be *per fraudem* of the master, the court held it to be a good assignment of a breach, there being the word *barratry* in the policy. The defendant's counsel said, this was no more than a *deviation*, in which case the insurer is discharged, and the plaintiff's remedy is against the owner or master; that this cannot be called a *crime* in the master, while he is acting all the time for the benefit of his owners. The *Chief Justice*, in his direction to the jury, told them, that this being against the express agreement to go first to Marseilles, seemed to be more than a common deviation, being a formed design to deceive the contractor; and compared it to the case of sailing out of port, without paying duties, whereby the ship was subject to forfeiture, and which has been held to be *barratry*. The jury staid out for some time, and, upon their return, asked the *Chief Justice*, " Whether, if the master was to have no bene-
" fit to himself by passing by Marseilles, and went
" only for the benefit of his owners, that would
" be

"be a barratry?" and the *Chief Justice* answering, "No," they found for the defendant. And upon a new trial being moved for, the case was argued, and all the court was of opinion that the verdict was right; for the master has acted *consistent with his duty to his owners,* and the plaintiff's agent knew of the intended alteration before the goods were put on board, and might have refused to ship them, or have altered the insurance. " To make it barratry, there must be " something of a *criminal* nature, as well as a " breach of contract;" and that here the breach being assigned only on the barratry, was not supported by the evidence: So the defendant had judgment. *Strange,* 1173. 16. *Geo.* II.*.

ELTON *v.* BROGDEN.

The ship *Mediterranean,* went out in the merchant service with a letter of mark, and being bound from Bristol to Liverpool, was insured by the defendant.

In her voyage, she took a prize, returned with it to Bristol, and received back a proportional part of the premium. Then another policy was made; and the ship set out with express

---

* It must probably occur with regard to this case, that though it certainly was not barratry, yet there was some truth in the observation, " that it was more than a common deviation," for it was, properly speaking, not a *deviation,* but an *alteration of the voyage;* the effect of which shall be afterwards considered.

press orders from the owners, that if they took another prize, they should put some hands aboard such prize, and send her to Bristol; but the ship in question should proceed with the merchant goods. Another prize was taken in the due course of the voyage; and the captain gave orders to some of the crew to carry the prize to Bristol, and designed to go on to Newfoundland; but the crew opposed him, and insisted he should go back, though he acquainted them with the orders; upon which he was *forced* to submit, and, in his return, his own ship was taken, but the prize got in safe.

And, now, in an action against the insurers, it was insisted that this was such a deviation as discharged them. But the Court and jury held that this was excused by the force upon the master, which he could not resist; and therefore fell within the excuse of necessity, which had always been allowed. The plaintiff's counsel would have made *barratry* of it; but the Chief Justice thought it did not amount to that, as the ship was not run away with in order to defraud the owners. So the plaintiff had a verdict for the sum insured. *Strange,* 1264. 20. *Geo.* II.

This decision requires an explanation; and the best that can be given, is Lord MANSFIELD's commentary upon it, delivered in deciding the case *Valleio v. Wheeler,* to be afterwards stated. " I think," says his Lordship, " the most pro-
" bable

" bable ground is, that, as this was a veffel up-
" on a privateering voyage, it was neceffary
" they fhould take care of the prize when they
" had taken it; and the crew exercifed their
" judgment *for the benefit of the fhip.*" It is difficult to fee, on any other fuppofition, how to
get rid of the idea of barratry of the *mariners*,
in the tranfaction in queftion, which is equally
provided againft with barratry of the *mafter*.

8. It was formerly obferved, that, in general, a
mafter cannot be guilty of barratry, while he acts
according to inftructions from his owner. And
this pofition was illuftrated by the cafe *Stamma
v. Brown*, in which the captain had *altered the
voyage*, in confequence of fuch inftructions.

It is, however a matter of fome hefitation,
whether this pofition be well founded in its utmoft extent. Are there no cafes in which the
captain muft be held guilty of barratry, even
in obeying his inftructions? And who are the
perfons whofe concurrence may juftify him from
a charge of this nature? Is it the owners of
the fhip, or the merchants who have fhipped
goods on board?

It is clear, in the firft place, that there can
be no barratry in relation to the fhip, if the
fhip-owners are advifers of the meafure, in confequence of which the damage has been fuftained. For example, if the mafter, by order
of his owners, has attempted to fmuggle, and
a confifcation is the confequence, thefe *owners*
cannot

cannot purfue the infurers on the claufe of barratry. The fame holds as to fhippers of goods, where, in confequence of fome illegal proceeding of the captain, *to which they are acceffory*, a lofs arifes to the *cargo*.

But fhall the inftructions of one of the parties concerned in an adventure, liberate the captain from the imputation of barratry, fo as to free the infurers from lofs fuftained by the *other parties?* For example, if the captain be inftructed, by the *owners of the fhip*, to commit piracy, and a confequent lofs be fuftained by the *goods on board;* will not the claim of the *fhippers of goods*, upon the policy, be effectual, although that of the *owners* might not? Or, fuppofe the captain has received inftructions to commit fome act that may infer barratry, from *one part owner*, without the acceffion of the reft; how far will the fraudulent commands of the owner, in fuch a cafe, wipe off the barraterious acceffion of the mafter and crew?

And here there feems to be room for a difference of opinion.

It may, on the one hand, be faid, that barratry appears, from a variety of adjudged cafes, to extend to every meafure of the captain that is criminal. *Barratry* is *fraud*, or *difhoneft intention*, to the prejudice of the affured. But every *crime* implies *difhoneft intention*. If, therefore, it infers *a crime* in the mafter to obey the inftructions of his owners, the infurers muft, notwithftanding withstanding these instructions, be liable for barratry.

To illustrate this, let two cases be distinguished. In the *first* place, the owner of a ship may, without the concurrence of the proprietors of cargo, instruct his captain to alter the *course* or *destination* of the voyage, or some other circumstance of less moment with regard to it. This certainly implies some degree of fraud, or breach of contract, against the shippers of cargo. It is a fraud, however, of the *owner*, and not of the *master*. The master may obey these instructions, without supposing that any thing improper is intended; and he is bound to obey his owners in such matters. Here, therefore, although a loss should arise to the cargo, in consequence of the improper instructions of the *ship-owners*, still, however, the proprietors of goods can have no relief against the insurers *on the score of barratry.*—The captain is not necessarily *criminal* in obeying such orders. On the contrary, the insurers shall be liberated from risk, on account of the vessel having varied from the terms of the insurance; and there will remain, to the injured shippers of goods, only an action of recourse against the *owners of ship*, for damages arising from breach of contract.

It seems accordingly to have been established by the case *Stamma v. Brown*, that in an *alteration of the voyage*, or any such matter, the instructions of the owner, although calculated to procure

procure an undue advantage over the shippers of cargo, shall liberate the captain from the charge of barratry; and confequently free the infurers.

But, in the *fecond* place, the owner may inftruct the mafter to do fomething that is *clearly illegal;* for example, to fmuggle, to fink the the fhip, to embezzle the cargo, to evade port-duties. The cafe here is very different. The mafter himfelf muft be held to be fraudulent; for the criminality of thefe acts, and the neceffary damage which muft refult to the fhippers, are matters of which he cannot be ignorant. Neither can he here be juftified by the commands of his employer; for the orders of a fuperior will not juftify the commiffion of a crime. In all fuch inftances, therefore, where the fact alleged is, *ex facie, illegal and criminal,* the mafter who executes the fraudulent commiffion, is himfelf guilty of fraud, and he feems to fall under the charge of barratry, according to the conftruction which a variety of adjudged cafes have put upon that term.

However plaufible thefe reafonings may appear, a contrary opinion has been adopted by the firft law authorities in Britain. And it feems to be eftablifhed, by two folemn decifions, that, in all cafes, the captain is freed by the inftructions of his *owners,* from the imputation of barratry, and, confequently, no action lies

againft

against the underwriters upon that clause of the policy.

9. Before stating these decisions now mentioned, however, it is deserving of notice, that a distinction may be made between an assured who is merely a *shipper of goods*, and one who is *freighter* of the ship. The former is a person who, along with other merchants, entrusts his merchandises on board a particular ship, and pays a freight to the owner for their carriage. When a vessel is, in this manner, loaded by a number of different merchants, she is called a *general ship*. But a *freighter* is a person who hires, by charter-party, the whole ship, for any particular adventure, and either fills it entirely with his own goods, or takes in a cargo on freight from different merchants. The *freighter* appoints, or at least approves of the captain, and superintends the whole adventure; and he may not improperly be considered as a temporary owner of the ship.

10. In cases of barratry it is not necessary for the assured to show that the barratry actually was the cause of the ship's loss. It is sufficient, if there have been a barratry and a subsequent loss; and that the one *might have been* the cause of the other. For when one party is guilty of a breach of agreement, and a damage ensues, the burden of proof, that the failure was not the cause of the loss, must lie on him who is in the fault.

Having

Having premised these observation, it remains to state two cases which illustrate the whole subject of barratry.

VALLEIO and ECHALAI *v.* WHEELER.

On a trial at Guildhall, before Mr *Justice* ASHURST, and a special jury, the material facts of the case appeared to be as follows.

The ship *Thomas and Matthew*, Brown master, was insured " from London to Seville," and the policy undertook against barratry. She was a general ship from London to Seville; belonged to *Willes*, as owner of the hulk, but was *chartered by Darwin* for the voyage.

She sailed to Guernsey, out of the road to Seville, and there took in brandy, in evasion of the duties. Afterwards fell into a storm, was much damaged, and driven back to Dartmouth. Then was refitted; but, in sailing, was so much farther damaged as to be incapable of continuing her course, and put in at Helford. The ship was not confiscated on account of the contraband goods; but in consequence of the damage she had suffered, the goods were spoiled.

The plaintiffs, who were *shippers of goods*, brought their action to recover against the underwriters; and the jury found a verdict for the plaintiffs agreeably to the direction of the Court; they found, " that the voyage to Guernsey was *with the knowledge of Willes, but without the knowledge of Darwin.*"

Motion for a new trial, on two grounds, that *Willes* was accessory to the voyage to Guernsey, and *there can be no barratry with consent of the owner;* and that the barratry was not the cause of the loss.

Lord MANSFIELD. Of the common law cases with respect to barratry, that of *Stamma v. Brown,* is in point; where it was found there was no barratry in the master changing the line of voyage, not for his own benefit, but that of his owners.

Undoubtedly where the assured owner or freighter is accessory to the barratry, he cannot complain of it. But here *Willes,* though owner of the hulk, who was accessory, is not concerned. It is *Darwin,* who having freighted the whole ship for his sole use, is to be considered as the owner; and the question must be with regard to the accession of *Darwin;* or whether there was a fraud to *his* prejudice.

The master goes upon an iniquitous voyage, which is a fraud upon *Darwin.* And whether the loss happened *during* the fraudulent voyage or *after,* is immaterial. But it certainly happened *in consequence* of the barratry. If there had been no insurance against *barratry,* this *consequential* loss would have liberated the insurers, as a *deviation.*

ASTON J. Barratry means *fraud* by the foreign ordinances. Doubtless where the master is acting *not for his own advantage,* but the benefit

nefit of his owners, or with *their consent*, he is not guilty of barratry. But here though *Willes* is the *nominal*, *Darwin* is the *real owner*, *pro hac vice*; and this is barratry, being for *an illegal purpose*, without the consent of the temporary owner; and being *a criminal act*. There is no saying here at what time the mischief was occasioned; and the insurers are liable for the *consequential* loss, although not directly or necessarily consequent on the deviation.

WILLES J. This is barratry; because *Darwin* was the *freighter*; and a deviation like the present, for a bad purpose, if without the knowledge of the *freighter*, is the same as if done without the knowledge of the *owner*. The only question here is, Whether this was a loss by the act of barratry? It might not have happened but for the barratry.

ASHURST J. was of the same opinion. Compare *Cooper's Reports, p.* 143. with *Loftus's Reports,* 631.

NUTT and *others, Assignees, &c. of Hague, a bankrupt, against* BOURDIEU.

THIS was an action on a policy of insurance, made by *Hague* before he became a bankrupt, on goods laden, or to be laden in the ship *Rachette,* (or *Bellona*) for a voyage from *London* to *Rochelle*; subscribed by the defendant on 27th October 1769.

The

The jury found a verdict subject to the opinion of the Court, of which the following are the material facts.

In October 1769, *Joseph Le Grand*, one of the partners of a mercantile house at Rochelle, being in London, with the ship *Bellona*, and in want of money to make up a cargo, applied to Messrs *Hague*; who supplied him with goods to the amount of L. 1800. But as the Messrs *Hague* were not sufficiently acquainted with the house of *Le Grand*, to entrust them with merchandizes to such an extent without a security, a contract was therefore entered into, between the *Hagues*, and *Joseph Le Grand*, and *René Guiné* the captain, whereby it was agreed that the bills of loading should not be delivered at *London* but at *Rochelle*, upon payment of the price in good bills, and of all charges and expences. And, in default, it was expressly agreed, that the said merchandizes were to be received for account of the Messrs *Hague*, by the bearer of their orders, free of freight and charges, for which Captain *René Guiné* was to have recourse against the *Le Grands* only.

Captain *René Guiné* accordingly delivered the bills of loading to *Hague*, who forwarded them, with the contract, and instructions to Mr *Rodrique* his correspondent at *Rochelle*.

When *Guiné* arrived at *Rochelle* harbour, instead of entering the port, he cast anchor before *St Martin du Rhé*; and *Le Grand* being put on shore,

shore, got privately into the city; and having consulted with his partners how to render Mr *Hague's* precautions ineffectual, he got *René Guiné* the captain to sign new and fraudulent bills of loading, by which, instead of being confined to land the goods at *Rochelle*, he was allowed a liberty of going either to *Rochelle* or *Bourdeaux*. The ship was accordingly carried to *Bourdeaux*, and there *René Guiné* contrived to land the goods, in the hands of *Le Grand's* agents.

It is unnecessary to mention the steps taken by *Rodrique*, to procure indemnification to *Hague*, his correspondent. At last, upon a petition stating the facts, presented to the Lieutenant of the Admiralty of *Guienne*, Captain *René Guiné* was found " guilty of *barratry of the master*, for " having signed false bills of loading," and *Le Grand* " of having been an instigator and accom- " plice of the captain ;" and besides being found liable in indemnification to *Hague*, they were both condemned to the galleys.

The jury particularly found, " That the cap- " tain, *by the instigation and direction of Messrs* " *Le Grand, the owners of the ship*, went with the " ship and cargo to *Bourdeaux* instead of *Ro-* " *chelle*, where the cargo was sold by the agent " of *Le Grand*."

For the plaintiffs it was contended, That the fraud of the master here amounted to barratry. Barratry is defined, *fraus, dolus*. MOLLOY considers

siders malpractices against the cargo as barratry. " It is where the master or mariners cheat the owners or insurers, by running away with the ship, or *embezzling the cargo.*" *Postlethw.* Lord MANSFIELD, in *Valleio v. Wheeler,* said, " Whatsoever by the master is *a cheat, a fraud, a cozening, a trick,* is barratry in him."—" Nothing could be so general."

It makes no difference here, that *Le Grand* was on board. For he had, by the contract, parted with his interest in the ship for that voyage. No express charter-party is necessary to transfer the *ownership* of a vessel, so far as respects the insurance; it is sufficient, that she be not a *general* ship, but *let to a single person* only. In *Valleio v. Wheeler,* it was found sufficient that the freighter was sole occupier of the vessel for the voyage.

The Court of Admiralty in *Guienne* had found this to be " barratry of the master;" and the circumstance of the owner being accessory, does not diminish the master's criminality.

For the defendant, it was urged, The construction of barratry in *France* is very different from what it is in *England.* In *France,* any *neglect* of the master is barratry; but in *England,* there must be something *criminal.* Valines* states two cases, in which the assured cannot recover

---
* *Valines,* ii. 80.

cover for barratry; where the owner himself acts as master; and where the master himself is the assured.

According to the English signification of *barratry*, it must be committed *against the owners*. It is said, that *Hague* is owner *pro hac vice;* but the last words of the agreement are decisive against such a construction; for it was a conditional sale of the cargo to the *Le Grands*, and, in default of their paying for it, in the stipulated manner, *Hague* was to pay no freight or charges, but the captain was to have his remedy against *Le Grand* alone. So that *Hague* had merely the *use* of the ship, and not the *direction* of her. In *Valleio v. Wheeler*, the vessel was *chartered to a single person*, who was therefore owner for the voyage; but this was merely an undertaking to carry *Hague's* goods to *Rochelle*.

According to the doctrine in *Stamma and Brown*, when a merchant has shipped goods on board *a general ship*, and the captain has deviated with the consent of the owners of the ship, that was held not to be barratry, so as to entitle the owner of the goods to recover against the underwriter. In 2. *Chan. cas.* 238. it is held, that the owner of the ship is not liable for the barratry of the master; for which reason barratry is insured against, but deviation is not. In barratry the captain must commit a fraud upon *his owner;* but if the owner be guilty, it then

ceases

ceases to be barratry, and becomes some other crime, for which he is answerable to the party injured. There was no relation between the master and the shipper. The former acted under the direction of the *owner of the vessel*, and therefore cannot be said to be guilty of a fraud against *him*; in which case only an insurer can be liable as for barratry. For all species of embezzlements by the master or mariners to a certain amount, the owner of the ship is liable, by 7. Geo. II. c. 15. *a fortiori*, if he himself is consenting to them; and the underwriter is only answerable for *those acts* of fraud for which the *owner is not;* but where goods are lost or spoiled by the default of the master, the owner is liable in respect of the freight, *Boson v. Sandford* and others, *Salk.* 440. In the case of *Lewen and Suasso*, Lord Hardwicke said, " Barratry " is an act of wrong done by the master against " *the ship* and goods."

Lord Mansfield said,—the judgment of the Court in *Guienne* is entirely out of the question. Their notions of barratry are evidently different from ours; for they find the *owner* himself guilty of barratry.

The provision against barratry is a very extraordinary one. It is strange that it should have crept into our policies, and much more so, that it should have continued in them so long; that the underwriter should insure the conduct of the

the captain, (whom he does not appoint and cannot difmifs,) to the owner who can do either.

Barratry, in the Englifh fenfe, can only be committed againft the owners of the fhip: For barratry is fomething contrary to the duty of the *mafter* and *mariners*; the very terms of which imply that it muft be in the relation in which they ftand to the *owners of the fhip*. The words ufed are "*mafter* and *mariners*," which are very particular. An *owner cannot commit barratry;* he may make himfelf liable by his *fraudulent conduct* to the owner of the goods, but not as for *barratry*. And, befides, *barratry* cannot be committed againft the owner *with his confent*: For though the owner may, if he confents, become liable for a civil lofs, by the mifbehaviour of the captain, yet that is not *barratry*. Barratry muft partake of fomething *criminal*, and muft be committed *againft the owner*, by the mafter or mariners. In the cafe of *Valleio v. Wheeler*, the Court took it for granted that *barratry* could only be committed againft the owner of the fhip. The point is clear.

Judgment unanimoufly for the defendant. *Termly Reports. Trin.* 1786*.

---

* It is imagined the doctrine delivered in thefe two cafes, muft appear folid. For *fraud with the owner's confent* or *barratry of the owner*, if the phrafe may be allowed, implies not only a *deviation*, but an *alteration* of the voyage. The *rifk undertaken never commences*, but the adventure is different from the beginning. This phafis of the queftion fhall be confidered more fully afterwards.

The facts of the following case are not calculated to illustrate any principle, except this, which requires no illustration, that a man cannot take advantage of his own fraud; and that if the captain of a ship procures insurance, neither he nor his assigns can have action against the underwriters, on the clause of *barratry*. The expression and reasoning of the case, however, support the same position with *Nutt v. Bourdieu*.

Lewen *v.* Swasso.

The plaintiff *Lewen* being sued at law upon a policy of insurance " on a *ship*, and against the " barratry of the master," brought his bill in Chancery to be relieved, and for an injunction, charging that one *Matthews* the *master, and also owner* of the ship, had, before the voyage, entered into a bottomry bond to *Swasso*, the defendant, for L. 200; and that afterwards, by bill of sale, he assigned over his interest in the ship to the defendant as a security for this L. 200; and the plaintiff insisted that *Matthews* was nevertheless, in equity, to be considered as owner of the ship, though in law the ownership and property would be looked upon to be in the defendant; and that the owner of a ship could not either in law or equity, be guilty of a barratry concerning the ship, and therefore prayed an injunction, and that the policy might be delivered up. The voyage insured was from London to Marseilles, and from

from thence to some port in Holland. The case was, that the master sailed with the ship to Marseilles, and then, instead of pursuing his voyage, sailed to the West Indies, and there sold the ship, and died insolvent. These matters being confessed by the answer, an injunction was moved for on the principle, that a mortgager is to be considered in equity as owner of the thing mortgaged; and that *Matthews, the master, being owner, could not be guilty of barratry.* Lord Hardwick Chancellor, granted the injunction. *Dict. Tr. and Com.* 147. 16. *Geo.* II.

This judgment, it should seem, must have been well founded, although *Matthews*, the master, had not been owner. It was enough that he was the *assured*. For it is evident a shipmaster cannot insure against his own barratry; and the policy being so far void with respect to the original party, could not acquire validity by any assignment of the interest to *Swasso* the defendant.

11. Before leaving the different provisions that have been adopted to secure the assured against the misdemeanour of master and crew, one point yet remains deserving consideration. It has been shewn, that the clause against *barratry* implies something *criminal*; it therefore does not include mere *fault, negligence, ignorance,* or any thing that does not suppose *dishonest intention.* Is there, in a *British* policy, any provision whatever against mere *fault*; and is the underwriter liable

liable for loss arising from the *negligence* of master and crew?

The following case occurred lately in Scotland. A mercantile house in *Greenock* got insurance on their vessel bound to *Charlestown*. In an action on the policy, among a variety of defences, the underwriters stated the following; That from the assured *owners* having overloaded their vessel, or, from her naturally drawing too much water, the captain had found it impossible to clear a *bar* at the entrance of *Charlestown* harbour. That the agents of the assured at Charlestown had made application to the captain, to unload the cargo, in order to lighten the ship; but he refused, and persisted unreasonably in waiting for a spring tide; he continued without the harbour, exposed to accidental storms; in one of which, and while attempting to clear the *bar*, the vessel was overset and lost. That the loss here was occasioned by the obstinacy and *gross fault* of the captain, for which the underwriters are not responsible.

It must have depended on the evidence, whether, in this case, the captain had been guilty of misconduct or not; and in what degree. But the question never went to proof, having been settled by private agreement before the point of law was decided.

Whether or not the underwriter be in Britain, liable for *mere negligence*, is a question, upon which there do not appear to be any express decisions;

cifions; and, although, from the whole general reafonings hitherto ftated, a negative conclufion feems to follow, yet there is fo little uniformity of opinion upon the point, either among lawyers, or merchants, that it will not be confidered in the light of a digreffion to ftate a few reflections that have occurred on both fides, and which were principally fuggefted by the pleadings in the cafe above quoted.

Upon the part of the affured, it might be contended:

" Underwriters muft undoubtedly be held to fubject themfelves to the confequences of the mafter's *fault* or *negligence*; for they exprefsly take upon themfelves his *fraud* or *barratry*. But the obligation to be liable for another man's *fraud*, is a greater and more extraordinary obligation, than to be fubjected to the confequences of his *fault* or *negligence*. Moft men would feel more reluctance to come under the former obligation than the latter. When a perfon, therefore, has exprefsly fubjected himfelf to the confequences of *fraud*, he may be conftrued as intending to bear alfo the confequences of *negligence*. In the greater obligation, the fmaller is implied *."

" But, in ordinary policies, the underwriter exprefsly takes upon himfelf, not only barratry, but

* In *Knight v. Cambridge*, the act of barratry was *failing without paying port-duties*. In *Valleio v. Wheeler*, (as ftated in *Cooper*,) this is imputed to *craffa negligentia*. But it rather affords a prefumption of *fraud*.

but certain kinds of faulty negligence. It is usually expressed, that he becomes liable for the perils of "fire," and of "surprizal." The accident of *fire* supposes fault somewhere; and there could be no *surprizal* without negligence. Besides the enumeration of particular perils, every policy contains a general clause, by which the underwriter subjects himself to " *all other perils, losses, and misfortunes, which can any way happen*" to the subject insured. This clause, which is expressed as comprehensively as possible, must at least include all *perils of the same kind* with those specially enumerated. And as *fire* and *surprizal* are mentioned, the general clause must include all other species of *faulty negligence.*"

" But to what endless cavils and litigation would it open a door, if the master's neglects should be sustained to liberate the insurer! In the conduct of a maritime adventure, it is often impossible to distinguish the degrees of fault, or to draw the line between fault and mere accident. How many instances may be figured! In the case of a *shipwreck*, it might be said, that the crew should have followed this or that measure; lain upon one tack or another; furled this or that sail; thrown out this or that anchor; and used every precaution but what was taken. In the case of *capture*; the crew and master should have been more active; they should have fought a longer battle, or run away sooner. And the difficulty of forming a judgment of these matters, is apparent from the variety of opposite opinions

opinions that were formed in the courſe of the late war, with regard to the conduct of naval officers; and the oppoſite, and inconſiſtent evidence which was produced on different ſides. The point, what *degree* of fault ſhall be ſufficient, does not admit of general rules; and cavils with regard to it muſt become perfectly endleſs. No inſtance of loſs could occur, where there might not be room for diſpute and litigation, upon the pretence of *faulty negligence* in the maſter or crew; and the proof, in ſuch caſes, would be inextricable."

" Accordingly, mercantile people ſeem to be agreed in rejecting a defence of this nature againſt the claim of the aſſured. How many inſtances of ſuch negligence muſt be daily occurring, and yet there is no example of this defence having been ever ſtated to the claim of the aſſured. In the courſe of the laſt war, a captain, from inattention, ignorance, or drunkenneſs, was ſo out in his bearings, as to miſtake the coaſt of France for that of England, and was captured accordingly; and the underwriters in Scotland, paid the loſs."

On the other hand, it may be argued in behalf of the underwriter:

" Very little doubt can be entertained, that an inſurer is not reſponſible for any miſdemeanour whatever, of maſter or crew, without ſome expreſs clauſe to that effect. For every miſdemeanour carries along with it a breach of the expreſs

or

or implied terms of the agreement; and to say, that an insurer is not naturally liable for misdemeanours, is saying no more than that he is not liable beyond the terms of his contract. It is clear from a variety of adjudged cases, that the express clause of *barratry* does not include *negligence or fault;* for " in order to *barratry*, " there must be something *criminal.*" *Strange's Reports*, 1173. There is no provision, therefore, express or implied, against mere *fault*, in a British policy."

" It is a great mistake to suppose, that the defence of mere *fault* of the master, has not often been resorted to against an action upon the policy. On the contrary, it is every day sustained, wherever the insurer pleads *deviation*. A *deviation* from the line of voyage marked out by the contract, contrary to instructions, must imply either *fault* or *fraud* in the master and crew. For if a change of measures be necessary or expedient for the concern, it is, as shall be afterwards shewn, no *deviation*. But a *fraudulent* departure from the policy is *barratry*, and subjects the insurers; a *faulty* departure, or a *deviation*, is daily sustained to free them from obligation. What renders this argument perfectly conclusive, is, that in *Holland*, where the insurer expressly undertakes both *fraud* and *negligence* of the master and crew, a *deviation* by the master, without the accession of his owners, is no defence against an action on the policy; and the underwriter must bear the consequences
of

of a *faulty* as well as of a *criminal* breach of inftructions *."

" There is another cafe, in which it is univerfally admitted, that the infurer is not liable for lofs arifing from faulty negligence, *viz.* where the mafter is guilty of fault in the *ftowage of the cargo* †. Now it will be difficult to fhow how negligence with refpect to the ftowage of goods differs from any other fpecies of neglect."

" There are feveral cafes adjudged, which, though not exprefs upon the point, are highly favourable to the fame opinion."

" In the cafe, *Waples v. Eames*, formerly ftated, a lofs had arifen from the veffel being obliged to perform quarantine. Among other reafons for finding a verdict in favour of the affured, it was ftated by LEE, *C. J.* that " there " was no default in mafter or owners."

" In

---

* See *Bynkerfh. Q. Jur. Priv. l.* 4. *c.* 8. *et paffim.*

† " Si le maiftre du navire," fays the *Guidon*, ch. 5. § 9. " charge marchandizes incompatibles; comme fi, au bas, " fous le premier tillac, il y avoit raifins, alum, figues, ris, " grains, fel, ou autres femblables denrées: et entre deux " tillacs, au deffous du premier, il charge vins, huiles, " olives, ou autre marchandizes qui coule, et que, par lef- " dits coulages, la marchandize bas fut gaftée, appretiation " fera fait du damage, lequel tombera fur le maiftre, fans " que l'affureur y contribue." See to the fame effect, Ord. of *Antwerp.*—*Wefket* (*v.* commodity.) And the foreign commentators, *paffim*.

" In the case, *Mills v. Fletcher*, where the question was, whether the assured were entitled to claim for a *total loss*, the defendant pleaded, that the loss had become total by the improper conduct of the captain; and Lord MANSFIELD, in directing a verdict for the plaintiff, was at pains to refute this charge."

But the following recent case seems to be more in point than any we have yet seen.

GREGSON *v.* GILBERT.

Gilbert insured *Gregson* upon slaves, from Guinea to Jamaica. The ship, in the course of her voyage, had missed the Island of Jamaica, and being reduced to great distress for water, it was found necessary to throw some of the slaves overboard. When this resolution was taken by the captain and crew, there remained but one day's allowance of water, at two quarts *per* man.

Gregson brought an action for the loss; and his declaration stated, " That by perils of the
" sea, contrary winds, currents, and other mis-
" fortunes, the voyage was so much retarded,
" that a sufficient quantity of water did not re-
" main for the support of the slaves, and other
" people on board, and that certain of the
" slaves, mentioned in the declaration, perished
" for want of water." The jury found a verdict for the plaintiff.

Motion

Motion for a new trial, upon the footing that this was not a loss by perils of the sea, as stated in the declaration, but by the captain's mistake.

The Court were unanimous, that the declaration ought to set forth truly the peril which was the cause of the loss: And they made the rule for a new trial absolute; from which it seems to follow, that they considered a loss by the *mistake* of the captain, as not included under the general provision against *perils of the sea*. B. R. *Easter* 23. *Geo*. III.———M. S.

It is impossible to dispute, that *fault* is a matter of degree, and that it cannot easily be reduced to general rules, but must, in every particular case, rest in the breast of a jury. But the same thing holds with regard to every action of damages *ob damnum culpa datum*; yet there is no doubt, that an action will lie on account of damages sustained by a certain degree of gross negligence. The same degree of fault, which is sustained to subject a shipmaster, or his employer, in *damages* to the party who suffers by his misconduct, ought, perhaps, to liberate the underwriter from loss; and the principles which serve to fix the one, appear sufficiently accurate to determine the other.

" It is, no doubt, the want of general rules, joined to the difficulty of proof, that have prevented this defence from being more frequently started. *Gross fault* depends, in general,

ral, upon complicated circumstances, of difficult investigation; and the amount of which, when proved, in the breast of a judge or jury, is fluctuating and precarious. As to the two perils of *fire* and *surprisal*, which are expressly undertaken, they do not necessarily imply such a degree of *fault* as deserves notice; and they do not seem intended to mark out any particular *class* of dangers, different from the ordinary perils of seas or capture."

12. There is another question with regard to the *nature of the insurer's risk*, a good deal different from any that has hitherto been stated. It relates to the degree of connection, which must take place between the *accident* and the *loss*, whether considered as cause and effect of each other, or in respect of nearness of time. The *loss* must be a *direct* not a *remote consequence* of the accident provided for; it must be an immediate effect of the cause; and it must happen within a *certain period of time*.

As to the first of these points, the connection which must subsist between the accident and the loss as *cause and effect*, it admits of no accurate rule. The one must be a *direct consequence* of the other: But in what degree, must rest in the breast of a jury in every particular case. Instead, therefore, of attempting any general rules, it will be more useful to show, by examples, what losses have been held to be *remote*, and what *immediate*.

JONES

Jones *against* Schmoll.

This was an action on a policy of insurance, "At and from Bristol to the coast of Africa, during the stay and trade there, and from thence to ports of discharge in the West Indies." There was a memorandum on the policy. "The assurers are not to pay any loss that may happen in boats during the voyage, (mortality of negroes by natural death excepted,) and *not to pay for mortality by mutiny, unless the same amount to 10 per cent.* to be computed on the first cost of the ship, outfit and cargo, valuing negroes so lost at L. 35 *per* head."

The demand upon the policy was for the loss of a great many slaves by mutiny.

The evidence of the captain was, that he had shipped 225 prime slaves on board: That on the 3d May, before he sailed from the coast of Africa, an insurrection was attempted; the women had seized him on the quarter-deck, and attempted to throw him overboard; but he was rescued by the crew; upon which the women and some men threw themselves down the hatchway, and were much bruised. That he sent the ringleader on shore; that twelve men and a woman afterwards died of those bruises, and from abstinence. On the 22d May there was a general insurrection; it was a case of imminent necessity, and the crew were forced to fire upon the slaves, and attack them with weapons. Several slaves took to the ship's sides, and hung down in the water by the chains and ropes, some for about a quarter of an hour; three were killed by firing, and three were drowned, the rest were taken in, but they were too far gone to be recovered; many of them were desperately bruised; many died in consequence of the wounds they had received from the firing during the mutiny, some from swallowing salt water, some from chagrin at their disappointment, and from abstinence; several of fluxes and fevers; in all to the number of 55.

The underwriters had paid for nineteen, who were either killed in the mutiny, or died of their wounds.

For the plaintiff, it was contended, that though the rest did not actually die in the mutiny, or from any wounds received at that time, yet they had all died *in consequence* of the mutiny; for if there had been no mutiny, nothing of the kind would have happened; and on this ground the insurer ought to be liable.

Another consequential loss was stated, that the very circumstance of there having been a mutiny amongst the remaining slaves, had so far lessened their value in the estimation of the planters, that they were sold at L. 17 a-head less than they would otherwise have done; and on this circumstance also, the plaintiff ought to recover.

Lord MANSFIELD.—I think not.—The underwriter is not answerable for the loss of the market, nor the price of it. That is a *remote consequence*

consequence, and not within any peril insured by the policy.

It is a question for the jury, how many of the negroes that died are within the provision of the policy, with respect to " mortality by mutiny :" They may be classed as follows :

1st, The first class certainly comes within the meaning of the policy, of mortality by mutiny. Such as were killed in the fray.

2d, So do those who died of their wounds.

3d, Another class as clearly do not. Such as being baffled in their attempts, in despair, chose a mode of death by fasting, or died by despondency. That is not a mortality by mutiny, but by failure of mutiny.

4th, The great class are such as received some hurt by the mutiny, but not mortal, and died afterwards of other causes, as those who swallowed water, jumped overboard, *&c. &c.* This is the great point.

Verdict. That all the slaves who died of their wounds, were to be paid for.

That all who had died of their bruises, or wounds which they had received in the mutiny, though accompanied with other causes, were to be paid for.

That all who had swallowed salt water, or leaped into the sea, and hung upon the sides of the ship, without being otherwise bruised, or who died of chagrin, were not to be paid for. *Sitt. after Trin.* 1785, *at Guildh. Termly Reports,*
(collected

(collected in the note to *Robertson v. Ewer, Hil.* 1786.)

ROBERTSON *against* EWER.

The ship *Dumfries* was insured by the defendant "from London to the coast of Africa; during her stay and trade there, and at and from thence, to her port or ports of discharge in the British West India Islands."—" Free of average under 3 *per cent.*"

She sailed on her voyage to the coast of Africa, there took in a cargo of slaves, and proceeded to the Island of Barbadoes, where she arrived on the 18th December 1781. An embargo had previously been laid on all shipping by Lord *Hood*, the commander in chief upon that station. Notwithstanding this, the captain of the *Dumfries* attempted to sail on 21st December 1781, but was prevented. He applied for permission to sail, which being refused, he, a few days after, sailed without leave, and was pursued and brought back by a sloop of war, after a slight engagement, in which the damage was less than 3 *per cent.*

Upon her return, Lord *Hood* ordered all her men to be dispersed among his Majesty's ships of war. The embargo continued till the 7th January 1782. On the 22d of the same month, the small-pox broke out among the negroes, who were all obliged to be put ashore. In consequence of which, and for want of mariners, she

was

was detained at Barbadoes above two months after the embargo was taken off.

This action was brought to recover the amount of wages and provisions, in confequence of the detention under the embargo at Barbadoes. Mr J. BULLER, before whom it was tried, was of opinion, that this policy being on the *body of the ſhip,* and the average loſs thereon being leſs than 3 *per cent.* the plaintiff could not recover, and he was nonſuited.

In ſupport of a rule for a new trial, it was argued,

1ſt, That this was a loſs by " arreſt, reſtraint, and detainment." Suppoſe the embargo had laſted longer, till the ſhip was worm-eaten, the aſſured could have *abandoned* her, and recovered a total loſs. In *Goſs v. Withers,* Lord MANSFIELD ſaid, " by the general law, the " inſured may abandon in the caſe merely of an " arreſt or embargo by a Prince, who is not an " enemy." Upon the ſame principles, he may recover here, where the loſs is partial.

2dly, This is a loſs by *barratry of the maſter.* The barratry of the maſter, in refiſting a lawful embargo, had occaſioned the diſperſion of the crew, and the conſequent delay.

The damage need not be an *immediate* one to the ſhip. It is ſufficient to charge the underwriter, if it is *a conſequence* of the peril inſured againſt. Where the aſſured incurs a *ranſom* or a *ſalvage,* the loſs is a ſum of money, and yet the insurer is liable, although the body of the ship may have sustained no actual injury.

In this case, all the damage arose from the dispersion of the crew, and was therefore a consequence of the master's barratry. The small-pox did not break out till some time posterior to the removal of the embargo; so that the vessel might have sailed in the interval, but for the want of sailors.

For the defendant it was maintained, that this was an insurance on the *body of the ship*, which had received no damage. Such an insurance did not comprehend a *loss upon the voyage*, where the body of the ship was not injured. For such a loss the freight must answer.

The master's conduct was not barratry, as he acted for the benefit of his owners. Besides, the loss is *too remote a consequence* of the barratry, whereas it ought to be direct and immediate. *Jones v. Schmoll*.

In the case *Fletcher v. Pole*[*], the ship *Tartar* was insured " at and from London to Newcastle " and Marseilles, and at and from Marseilles to " her ports of discharge in the West Indies." Having met with a storm, she was obliged to put into Port Mahon; and the captain obtained leave of the Vice-admiralty Court to have the ship surveyed, in consequence of which she was detained there for a considerable time. Part of the demand upon the underwriter was founded on

---

[*] Before Lord *Mansfield* at *Guildhall* after Easter 1769.

on the expence of wages and provisions incurred during the detention, as part of the damage occasioned by the storm. But Lord MANSFIELD ordered these articles to be struck out of the account. That loss was as immediate a consequence of the storm, as this is of the barratry.

The Court considered it as a settled point in practice, that sailors wages and provisions are not recoverable in consequence of a policy on the body of the ship. In the case of a *ransom* or *salvage*, there is a damage done to the body of the ship. The rule discharged. *Termly Reports, Feb.* 4. 1736.

Upon precisely the same principles, the underwriter is not liable for the rise or fall of markets, nor for the failure of the assured's speculations in trade. Such an insurance as this, that goods shall bear a certain price, is no doubt sometimes entered into. But it is not implied in a common maritime policy.

It may no doubt frequently happen, when the assured meets with an *accident* in the transportation of his merchandise from place to place, that the damage he sustains arises not so much from any deterioration of the commodities themselves, as from the effect of circumstances with regard to their market value. But this loss appears too *remote a consequence* of the accident to affect the insurer. It has accordingly been often decided, and is a point perfectly settled, that the underwriter

underwriter is not liable for the change of markets.

* *Rucker* infured *Lewis*, on fugars, by the fhip the *Vrow Martha*, from St Thomas's to Hamburgh. In courfe of the voyage, the fugar was *damaged* by the fea-water; in confequence of which accident, the proprietor not only fuffered a lofs by the actual diminution of the value of the fugars below the prime coft, but he likewife fuftained a lofs, by being obliged to fell them immediately at what they would bring; whereas, if he had kept them for fome time, as he had intended, he would have brought them to a rifing inftead of a falling market.

And he infifted, that he was entitled to be indemnified of both thefe loffes.

Lord MANSFIELD faid, " Infurance is a con-
" tract of indemnity againft the perils of the
" voyage; the infured engages, that the thing
" fhall come fafe; he has nothing to do with
" the market; he has no concern in any pro-
" fit or lofs which may arife to the merchant
" from the goods."—" The affured here acted
" upon fpeculation, and had ordered the goods
" to be kept up till the price fhould rife. But
" no private fcheme or project of trade of the in-
" fured can affect the infurer, who knows no-
" thing of it. He does not mean to infure, that
" the

---

* This cafe is fo complicated, and touches upon fo many points not yet explained, that it feems proper to referve a full ftatement of it to a fubfequent chapter. See *Part* II. *ch*. 3. § 2. *on Partial Lofs*.

"the price of fugars shall rise to any particular
"amount. If speculative destinations of the
"merchant, and the success of such specula-
"tions are to be regarded, it would introduce
"the greatest injustice and inconvenience."

It was found, that the assured was only entitled to the diminution of value which the sugars had sustained below the prime cost, without regard to the loss occasioned, by their having come to an unfavourable market. 2. *Burr.* 1167.

The following Scotch case serves to illustrate the same position.

RICHARDSON *and Co. against* STODART *&c.*

In the year 1776, *Richardson and Co.* of *Perth*, opened a policy of insurance on a cargo of salmon for *Venice*, where it was intended the salmon should arrive during the season of Lent. Having met with unfavourable and tempestuous weather, which obliged him to throw overboard a part of the cargo, the shipmaster put into the port of St *Lucar*, on the coast of Spain, in order to refit the vessel.

At that place, he was persuaded by certain merchants, that it would be more for the interest of all concerned, to dispose of the cargo there, even at an undervalue, than to proceed to the place of his destination, which he would not probably reach before the end of Lent; when, besides the necessary fall of the market, the salmon would probably

probably be spoiled with keeping. The cargo was sold accordingly at an undervalue.

In an action, at the instance of *Richardson and Co.* against *Mess. Stoner Hunter and Ker*, the St *Lucar* merchants, although no suspicion of fraud was thrown upon these gentlemen in the transaction; yet the Court of Session considered their conduct as so rash and faulty, that they subjected them in the damage sustained, in consequence of the sale at St Lucar, by the owners of the salmon.

Mess. Richardson and Co. also raised an action against the underwriters, with a view of increasing their security of payment; and it was pleaded for the assured, that the damage sustained at St Lucar was within the risk of "*perils of the sea;*" as it was a storm at sea that had ultimately been the cause of the imprudent sale; that it was immediately owing to "*arrest, restraint, and detainment,*" though not of "*kings and princes,*" yet of "*people,*" whose condition or quality is not excepted in the policy. But what they principally rested upon was, that the master was guilty of *barratry*, in the present very imprudent departure from his instructions, which was a breach of his contract with the owners.

It was answered, the only loss which arose here from "perils of the sea," that of part of the salmon thrown overboard, the insurers are willing to repair. As for the going into the harbour

bour of St Lucar, it was no lofs in itfelf; nor did any other confequence follow from it, than a *fcheme of trade*, concerted for the benefit of the owners, which is ftrangely compared to *detention by kings, princes, or people*. With regard to barratry, it is a criminal act, and cannot exift without *a fraudulent defign*; whereas, although the conduct of the captain might be injudicious, and imprudent, ftill there was nothing in it which betrayed the want of honeft intention.

The Court found, " That the underwriters " were not liable for any lofs that might have " arifen from the fale of the falmon at St Lu- " car." *Fac. Coll.* Nov. 20. 1783, and *Dec.* 22. 1784*.

In this cafe, it is clear there was no barratry. The decifion may be fuppofed to have proceeded on one of two grounds: Either that the mafter was guilty of *grofs mifconduct*, which ought to free the infurer; or elfe, what is more probable, that the lofs here did not arife from *fea-damage*, but from an imprudent *fcheme of trade*, in which the mafter had acted in his capacity of fupercargo.

13. So much for the connection that muft fubfift between the *accident* and the *lofs*, as caufe and

------

* There was a feparate point in this cafe, which was alone decifive of the queftion. There was a N. B. in the policy, " Corn, fifh, fruit, &c. warranted free of average, except general," &c. But, according to the Reporter, the Court did not reft their judgment on this ground.

and effect of each other. In the same manner there must be a connection *in point of time.*

Here, however, the terms of the policy suggest a precise rule, which judges have wisely laid hold of. An underwriter, it has been decided, is not liable for the consequences of any accident, unless these consequences are felt during the currency of the risk. It is not enough that the *accident* happens, the *loss* must actually be sustained during the subsistence of the contract. The expiration of the policy forms a precise line, after which the insurer cannot be subjected to *consequential* losses.

Lockyer *against* Offley.

The defendant, on 19th August 1785, underwrote L. 200 on the ship *Hope*, from Hamburgh to London.

In the course of the voyage, the master committed *barratry*, by smuggling on his own account, by hovering, and running brandy. On the 1st September 1785, the ship arrived safe at her moorings in the river Thames, and remained there in safety till the 27th of the said month of September, when she was seized by the revenue-officers for the smuggling before stated.

These were the material facts of a verdict submitted by a jury for the judgment of the Court, upon this point, Whether the *seizure of a ship,* AFTER *the completion of her voyage*, for a *cause* *of forfeiture* DURING *the voyage,* is within the policy*.

For the plaintiff, it was argued, that this was evidently a loss arising from barratry, which had subjected the ship to forfeiture. The *Hovering act*, 24. Geo. III. c. 47. declares, that vessels acting like the ship in question, *shall be forfeited:* and as no particular time is expressed, the forfeiture attaches that moment the cause of seizure arises.

This is different from the case of a ship receiving a wound, which does not cause her immediate death, and where it may be uncertain when the loss shall be complete: for here the loss has actually taken place: the ship was forfeited the moment of the smuggling, even although she had afterwards come into the hands of a *bona fide purchaser*; and an insurer cannot stand in a better situation than a *bona fide purchaser*.

In the case of a capture and ransom, the assured receive no actual injury during the voyage; but merely become liable, at a subsequent period, to a claim on the ransom-bill; the event of which may be contingent at the termination of the policy. So that the insurer is not only liable

---

* There was another point in this cause, Whether the loss was *total*, and the assured had a right to abandon? to which a great part of the jury's verdict related. But as that point does not appear to have been decided, it is unnecessary to state here, either the facts found by the jury, or the reasonings with regard to it.

liable for loss happening during the voyage, but for *future damage* arising from any *act done during* the voyage. This is, at least, a consequence of damage done during the voyage, and Lord MANSFIELD, in *Valleio v. Wheeler*, said,—" Whe-
" ther the loss happened by the act of barratry;
" that is, *during* the fraudulent voyage, or *af-*
" *ter*, is immaterial."

If the assured cannot recover in this case, underwriters can never be liable for this species of barratry by smuggling; for the seizure can scarcely be ever made, till the vessel has been in port 24 hours.

For the defendant, it was observed, That although the seizure, for smuggling, of a ship, after she had been 24 hours in port, was a thing that happened frequently; yet this was the first instance of an attempt to subject the insurers in such a case.

It is a mistake to say, that the peril insured against is the *act of barratry*; it is *a loss by barratry*. This loss must happen before the termination of the insurance. In *Valleio* and *Wheeler*, not only the *act of barratry*, but the *loss by barratry*, was completed during the voyage insured; here the loss by the seizure is subsequent. To subject the insurers here, would be a great extension of their supposed obligations, and would stir unexpected claims; as the condemnation might take place at any distance of time, after all accounts had been settled between the parties.

parties, averages paid, and even the policy cancelled.

No change of property takes place in confequence of the act of fmuggling, till condemnation of the veffel. The affured muft be deprived of the *poffeffion* of the fubject. If the property were changed by the *forfeiture* merely, the Crown would be entitled to the profits of any voyage between the forfeiture and condemnation.

WILLES J. delivered the unanimous opinion of the Court.

The queftion feems to be new,—and fome rule is neceffary. But it is more important, that the rule be *accurate and certain*, than that it be eftablifhed one way or other.

The infurance is for a limited time, and the lofs was not fuftained till near a month after that time was expired. That, under the excife-laws, the forfeiture attaches the moment the act is done, may be true as to fome purpofes; for example, to prevent intermediate alienations or incumbrances. But the *actual property is not altered till after the feizure*. If the veffel, before the feizure, had gone another voyage, the Crown would not be entitled to her earnings. Till the feizure, it is not certain whether the barratry fhall be taken notice of, and be the caufe of a *lofs*.

It would be dangerous to fubject the infurer in *remote* confequential damages. In the cafe

Meretony

Meretony v. Dunlop [*], a ship was insured for six months, and three days before the expiration of the time, she received her death's wound, but was kept afloat by pumping till three days after the time. There, a verdict was given for the insurer, and confirmed by the Court. Suppose a man, whose life is insured, receives a mortal wound some short time before the expiration of the term, but lingers till it is elapsed, the insurer would not be liable. In *Valleio and Wheeler*, the ship was *lost during the voyage*.

It has been argued, that this ship would have been liable to the forfeiture, even in the hands of a fair purchaser. I do not know that it has been so decided;—may depend on circumstances. But it does not thence follow, that *the insurer is, at any distance of time, answerable for the loss, under a limited undertaking*.

This leads to the view which weighs most with the Court. The custom-house officers may *seize* at any time within three years; and the attorney general may file an information, as long as the ship is in being. Is the insurer all this time to continue liable? Suppose the ship had gone several voyages afterwards; suppose a partial loss paid, and the underwriter's name struck off, shall an action be brought afterwards? His accounts could never be settled while the ship is in existence. There must be some limitation therefore on the duration of the risk; and the subject

[*] East. 23d Geo. III.

subject admits of none which is accurate, except that pointed out by the policy, *viz.* "the ship's mooring 24 hours in good safety."

Judgment for the defendant. *Termly Reports*, *May* 26. 1786.

The following case is so parallel, that we cannot forbear inserting it, upon the authority of *Mr Wesket*.

ROCHE *v.* THOMPSON.

The *Margaret, Captain Burke* was insured from Limerick to Havre de Grace. She arrived there after having suffered damage during the voyage; and whilst the repair of those damages was performing, being some weeks after her arrival, she was seized in the port of Havre, an *embargo* having been laid on all British ships, and hostilities commenced between France and England.

The owner of the ship brought actions against the insurers, not only for the *repairs*, but also for the loss occasioned by the seizure and embargo, which he stated as a *consequence* of the necessity of continuing at Havre to repair. The defendants paid into Court an average loss for the repairs of the damage incurred during the voyage. But for any *remote* consequences of that damage, consequences which had appeared after the expiration of the policy, and the ship "had "been 24 hours safely moored," they denied that they were accountable.—Verdict for the
defendant

defendant. At *Guildh. Trin.* 1779. See *Wesket's Digest.*

CHAP. III.

Of the Nature and Extent of the Insurer's Obligation, when a loss is incurred in terms of the Policy.

WE have hitherto considered what is the nature of that *event* against which provision is made by insurance; in other words, what is the *nature*, and *duration*, of the insurer's risk. It remains to be examined, what is the *extent of his obligation*, when the event happens, against which it was meant by the contract to provide. This leads into a very extensive field, and renders a division of the subject necessary.

There are two great circumstances which affect the insurer's obligation upon loss being incurred. These are, in the *first* place, the particular *nature of the policy*, or the *interest* which the assured has in the subject; and, in the *second* place, the *nature and extent of the loss*.

With regard to the first of these, the particular nature of different policies, it may be observed, that contracts of insurance differ materially from each other with respect to the *pecuniary interest* which the assured possesses in the subject of the bargain. This circumstance, of the assured having a pecuniary interest, regulates the
effect

effect of the agreement, so as to determine whether or not the insurance shall be held as a contract of indemnity, and how far the obligation of the one party shall be measured by the other's loss.

The other circumstance affecting the amount of the underwriter's obligation, is the *extent of loss*. It is sufficiently obvious in what manner the obligation of the underwriter must be encreased or diminished according to the extent of damage incurred. At the same time, there occur considerable varieties in this respect, arising from the application of different policies to different kinds and degrees of loss.

SECT. I. *How the extent of the underwriter's obligation is affected by the assured's interest in the subject.*

With respect to the interest which the assured may have in the subject of the bargain, three different sorts of policies ought to be distinguished.

1*st*, *Insurances*, properly so called; or *open policies upon interest*. That is, policies in which the amount of the insurance is limited by the pecuniary interest which the assured has in the risk; and the extent of that interest is left to be ascertained by a proof.

2*dly*, *Wager* policies; in which the assured has no interest in the subject; and

3*dly*, *Valued* policies; which partake of the nature of both the former. Of these in their order.

1. In-

1. Insurance has been explained "a contract "of indemnity, from loss arising upon an un- "certain event." An insurance, it has been observed, is not a bargain for a certain ascertained payment or performance; but with regard to a *risk* undertaken by one of the parties. The claim of the assured must depend upon an event that is uncertain, either as to its existence, or its extent. From this consideration, that insurance is an agreement for a *conditional* payment or performance, it must appear to possess something of the nature of a *wager*. A wager has been defined "any thing pledged "upon a chance*." According to this explanation, an insurance, which is "an indemnity "from loss pledged upon a chance," becomes a species of wager.

It should seem, however, that this is using the term *wager* in rather too extensive a sense. In strict language, a *wager* is an agreement with regard to a subject in which neither party has, independent of the bett, a pecuniary interest. But an insurance supposes that the one party has such an ascertainable interest in that subject, the safety of which is warranted by the other. If one man, for example, undertakes to pay a sum of money to another, in case the lottery ticket of this last should turn up a blank, the contract is properly an insurance; but if such payment depends upon the comparative success

* Johnson's Dict.

succefs of two tickets, in neither of which the contracting parties are interefted, it is a mere wager.

There feems to be ftill another difference; the object of infurance, ftrictly fpeaking, is not to make a *pofitive gain*, but to avoid *actual damage* and harm, from the event provided againft. The affured muft not only have an intereft in the fubject, but he muft be feeking *indemnification*, in cafe that fubject, in which he is fo interefted, fhould be loft or impaired. To ufe the phrafe of the civil law, infurance relates to a *damnum emergens*, and not to a mere *lucrum ceffans*. Not to the failure of an expected profit, but to an actual lofs incurred.

It muft, however, be acknowledged, that although an infurance, ftrictly and accurately fpeaking, feems to relate to *pofitive lofs* merely, in oppofition to *expected profit*, yet this diftinction is not generally attended to. The failure of an advantage, of which we have formed a ftrong expectation, does not appear very different from actual damage fuftained. Between a wager, therefore, and an infurance, the material difference feems to be, the affured having a pecuniary intereft in the fubject. It is only where there is fuch an intereft, that there can be room for the proper object of an infurance contract, an indemnification from lofs.

2. Numerous are the contrivances which men have fallen upon for the gratification of their

propensity to gaming. And it is easy to see, that the uncertain event of a maritime adventure, affords a very obvious and extensive field for the calculation of chances, or the interposition of fortune. In most of the foreign mercantile states, indeed, the practice of gaming in insurance, seems to have been nipt in the bud by the wisdom of the Legislature. But, in Britain, (where little attention, comparatively, has been paid by the public, to the regulation of this contract) as soon as commerce became extensive, and insurance generally understood, the practice of wagering on mercantile adventures became extremely common.

It was customary to carry on those mercantile wagers, by clothing the bargain with the forms of a real insurance-contract, and by supposing an *interest* in the assured, into the fictitious nature of which the underwriter precluded himself from enquiring. They were conceived in the terms, " Interest, or no interest ;" or, " without farther proof of interest than the policy." In those agreements, as the assured is not supposed to have any real interest in the subject, there can be no real loss which shall regulate the obligation of the underwriter. They want the essential requisite of an insurance ; they are not obligations of indemnity ; but are to be considered, though in the form of an insurance, as mere wagers, and the view of parties in the bett, must be gathered from other circumstances.

As a confequence of the affured having no intereft in the fubject, it followed, that the underwriter could have no concern with *partial loſſes*. A partial loſs was not an event fufficiently accurate, to be the criterion of a wager. Thefe policies were, therefore, expreffed " free of *ave-*" *rage*," and " without benefit of *falvage* to the " infurer." That is, the underwriter was not to be liable for *partial* (or *average*) loffes ; and, if the veffel was once captured or wrecked, during the currency of rifk, and the infurer had paid the loſs, he was not to claim the advantage of any partial recovery that might be made.

3. There are, however, many cafes, in which the affured has an intereft in the fubject to be fecured, but in which it may be difficult or impoffible to afcertain the exact amount of that intereft. For example, in a policy upon *returns* from a diftant country, the exact value and even the nature of which are in many cafes uncertain ; in the cafe of infurance on *prizes*, where the real value is difficult to difcover, until the veffel is brought into port, and fold ; and, in every inftance, where the owners have been prevented, by accident, from receiving regular or fatisfactory advices.

In thefe, and fimilar circumftances, it feems proper, and has become cuftomary, to infert a claufe of valuation in the policy ; by which the underwriters agree to eftimate the affured's intereft at a certain fixed amount, without the neceffity of
farther

farther proof upon the subject; to receive a corresponding premium; and to indemnify the assured to that extent, in case of loss. The clause for this purpose, either specifies a particular sum as equivalent to the assured's interest; thus, "In "case of loss, the said ship shall be valued at "L. 1000, and the said cargo at L. 1500;" or it estimates the value as equal to the sums underwritten; "the said ship, &c. valued at the sums "underwritten."

A *valued policy* evidently partakes of the nature, both of a policy on interest, and of a wager. It supposes, on the one hand, a *bona fide* interest in the assured. On the other, this interest does not altogether regulate the amount of the underwriter's obligation. There must be a real interest; but a contrivance is fallen upon to supersede the necessity of proving the exact amount.

4. The bad consequences of every species of gaming, whether by way of wager or otherwise, need not be insisted on. The practice of gaming, by the agreeable exercise which it affords to the mind, tends to engross the attention, and to withdraw the exertion of men from useful pursuits. At the same time, by pointing out a speedy, tho' hazardous mode of accumulating wealth, it produces a contempt for the moderate profits of honest industry. These are not its worst consequences. Not only does it pervert the activity of the mind, but deprave the affections. By the frequent and great reverses of fortune to which

it

it gives occasion, it becomes the source of much private misery; and it is detrimental to the public, by suggesting constant temptations to fraud, and to atrocious crimes.

There are few well regulated governments, accordingly, in which gaming has not been laid under considerable restrictions. And by the ordinances of almost all the commercial states of Europe, *wagers upon mercantile adventures* are totally prohibited. No support is given, in any extent whatever, to a gaming contract, if it be executed in the form of an insurance*; and every insurance upon *expected profit*, even in opposition to *positive loss*, is considered in a very unfavourable point of view.

" The owners and masters of ships," says a French regulation, " shall not have insurance " made on the freight their vessels shall earn; " nor merchants on an expected profit of their " goods; nor seafaring men on their hire †." " All insurances," says the ordinance of *Coningsberg*, " on expected gain, wagers, or such like " inventions, future freight-moneys, seamens " wages, are universally forbid, and declared of " no force ‡."

In Britain ideas less strict have been entertained. In particular, the distinction between an insurance against *positive loss*, and upon *expected profit*,

---

* Ord. of *Amsterdam* and *Rotterdam*; of *Coningsberg*, *Genoa*, *Stockholm* and *France*.

† Ord. Fr. No. 677.   ‡ No. 780. as collected by *Magens*.

profit, is totally overlooked; a variety of bargains of this kind are in daily practice, and meet with full support from the law. Such is the speculation sometimes entered into, that goods shall bring a particular price; the insurance on *freights*; and the agreement by which a factor, to whom a cargo is consigned, insures his expected commission on the sale of it.

It does not indeed appear, that a direct wager, however contrary it may be to utility, can be considered as invalid at common law. In fact, it will perhaps be found difficult to draw the line between wagers, and other bargains for a conditional payment or performance. From the English Courts they have accordingly received complete support, unless where prohibited by statute, contrary to morality or decency, or calculated to create a prejudice to third parties.

Independent of the effect that is given, at common law, to a wagering contract, it may be observed that policies of insurance with the clause "Interest or no interest," were not necessarily wagers. The assured might have an interest, although, by the contract, the underwriter precluded himself from enquiring into it.

From about the time of the Revolution, accordingly, wager-policies became common; and being made effectual by judges, they increased rapidly, along with the advancement of trade, and the practice of real insurance. Those fictitious insurances, from the situation of mutual

tual trust and confidence which subsists between assured and underwriter, connected, in a peculiar manner, the power with the temptation to fraud; and were therefore, more dangerous than common wagers.

Besides this, and the general mischievous consequences attending them in common with all other species of gaming, mercantile wagers had another particular inconvenience; that, by increasing the demand for insurance, they augmented the rate of premium, and consequently the expence attending the transportation of goods to the real trader. These evils called at last for the interference of the Legislature; and a stop was, in some measure, put to the practice by a British statute, 19. *Geo.* II. *c.* 37.

The preamble states the pernicious consequences arising from policies, without interest; the fraudulent loss of ships and cargoes; the encouragement of prohibited trade; and the encouragement of gaming. Therefore the statute provides, "That no assurance on ships or goods
"shall be made after the 1st August 1746, by
"any British subject, *interest or no interest*, or
"*without farther proof of value than the poli-*
"*cy*, or by way of gaming or wagering;—or
"without benefit of salvage to the insurer;—
"and every such insurance shall be void." § 1.

"Provided always, that assurance on private
"ships of war, fitted out by any of his Maje-
"sty's subjects, solely to cruise against any of
"his

" his Majesty's enemies, may be made by or for
" the owners thereof, interest or no interest,
" free of average, and without benefit of salvage
" to the assurer; any thing herein contained to
" the contrary notwithstanding." § 2.

" Provided also, that any merchandise or ef-
" fects from any ports or places in Europe or
" America, in the possession of the Crowns of
" *Spain* or *Portugal*, may be assured in such way
" and manner as if this act had not been made."
§ 3.

" And be it enacted, that it shall not be law-
" ful to make *reassurance*, unless the assurer
" shall be insolvent, become a bankrupt, or
" die; in either of which cases, such assurer,
" his executors, administrators, or assigns, may
" make reassurance to the amount before by
" him assured, provided it shall be expressed in
" the policy to be a *reassurance*." § 4.

By the next section of the statute, it is enacted, that " every sum of money to be lent on
" bottomry, or at *respondentia*, upon any Bri-
" tish ship bound to the *East Indies*, shall be
" lent only on the ship, or on the cargo of such
" ship, and shall be so expressed in the bond;
" and the benefit of salvage shall be allowed to the
" *lender*, his agents and assigns, who alone shall
" have a right to make assurance on the money
" so lent. No *borrower* of money on bottomry
" as aforesaid, shall recover more by an assu-
" rance,

" rance, than his real intereſt, excluſive of the
" money borrowed."

The exception in this ſtatute with regard to private ſhips of war, is obviouſly to encourage privateering adventurers. The other exception, permitting inſurance, without further proof of intereſt than the policy, on *Spaniſh* and *Portugueſe* ſhips, is founded on a regulation of thoſe countries, by which no foreigner is permitted to trade between Spain or Portugal, and their colonies in South America; ſo that all ſuch trade muſt be carried on under fictitious names.

As a farther exception to this ſtatute, it deſerves notice, that the prohibition is not underſtood to extend to inſurances on *foreign ſhips*. Theſe are not within the words, and ſcarcely within the evils to be guarded againſt. This point was decided in the following caſe.

Thelluson *againſt* Fletcher.

A policy of inſurance was made " on all
" goods loaden, or to be loaden, aboard the
" ſhips *Le Soigneux, la Pucelle, & le Vainqueur,*
" all or any of them. The ſaid goods and mer-
" chandiſes, by agreement, are valued at ——
" on 25 caſks of clayed ſugar, and 12 hogſ-
" heads of Muſcovados. The policy to be deem-
" ed ſufficient proof of intereſt in caſe of loſs."
The ſhips were *French* property.

Two of the ſhips were captured, and the other loſt. The defendant had underwritten L. 300, and the jury had valued the damages at the ſum inſured, without any evidence of the aſſured's intereſt, except the defendant's ſubſcription to the policy.

On motion for a new trial, it was urged for the defendant, that it was incumbent on the aſſured to ſhew ſome further intereſt; and an affidavit was produced, tending to prove, that in fact the aſſured had no intereſt. It was contended for the purſuer, that the preſent inſurance being on foreign ſhips and property, did not fall within the ſtatute *Geo.* II. prohibiting wager-policies.

The Court ſaid, that this was not a policy within the ſtatute; foreign ſhips not having been included in that act, on account of the difficulty of bringing witneſſes from abroad to prove the intereſt. The rule diſcharged. *Douglas's Reports,* 7th February 1780.

It was not till ſome time after the ſtatute 19. *Geo.* II. formerly mentioned, that the ſame prohibition was extended to all other wagers in the form of inſurance. Wagering policies, particularly on lives, had, it is believed, become extremely common, and were attended with the general inconvenience of being a mode of gaming. Such inſurances on lives are reprobated altogether by many of the foreign mercantile ſtates,

as

as dangerous to the person whose life is insured. But it is not imagined, that apprehensions of this kind could have much weight under the government of England.

With the view, principally, it should seem, of preventing gaming, all *wagers in the form of an insurance*, whether on *lives*, or on *any other event*, are prohibited by a statute, 14. *Geo.* III. cap. 48.

The preamble states, " That inconveniencies " had arisen from wagering insurances on lives." It is therefore provided, " that no *insurance* shall " be made on the *life* of any person, nor on " any other *event or events whatever*, wherein the " assured has no interest, or by way of gaming or " wagering. And every insurance contrary to " the meaning hereof, shall be null." § 1.

" It shall not be lawful to make any policy " *on lives*, or on *any other event*, without insert- " ing the name of the person interested, or for " whose use, benefit, or on whose account, such " policy is so made or underwritten." § 2.

" In no case shall a greater sum be recovered " than the amount or value of the interest." § 3.

" Nothing, however, in this act, shall extend " to insurances on shipping and merchandise, " which may continue to be insured as former- " ly." § 4.

This statute has received a general interpretation, and is understood as applicable to every wager

wager in the form of a policy of insurance, except with relation to shipping and merchandise, which had been formerly restricted by *statute* 19. *Geo.* II.

ROEBUCK *v.* HAMMERTON.

This was an action upon a wager in the form of a policy, on the sex of the *Chevalier D'Eon*. It was made subsequent to the *statute* 14. *Geo.* III. *cap.* 48.

The counsel for the plaintiff insisted, that the statute did not extend to this case; that it was not only not a policy, but the subject-matter itself was incapable of insurance; and that the nature of the act, not the form of the instrument, ought to decide. But this was a *mere wager* reduced into writing, not upon any *future* contingency, but upon a fact *then existing*; and therefore to construe it a policy, within the meaning of the statute, would be to extend the act to all wagers, when the parties, for greater security, might think proper to reduce them into writing.

Lord MANSFIELD stopped the counsel for the defendants, saying it was too clear to give themselves the trouble. The parties themselves have called it a policy, it is indorsed a policy, opened as a policy, and any number of persons might have subscribed it as such. Therefore it is clearly within the act.—*Per. Cur.* Let a nonsuit be be entered.—*Cowper's Rep. Hil.* 18. *Geo.* III. B. R.

Another cafe, *Mollifon v. Staples*, is ftated by Mr *Park*, of a policy " on the event of there " being an open trade between *Great Britain* " and the province of *Maryland*, on or before " 6th July 1778." Lord MANSFIELD faid the plaintiff could not recover; 1*ft*, Becaufe, having no other intereft than the general concern which every man has in the events of war and peace, it feemed doubtful whether this was an intereft in terms of the act; 2*dly*, The policy was void, not having the name inferted according to the 2d § of the ftatute. *Park's Syftem, p.* 491. *Note.*

It does not appear, that this liberty of wagering had ever been allowed with regard to infurance from fire. Nay, in thefe infurances, it has not only been requifite in all cafes, that the affured fhould have an intereft in the fubject, correfponding to the fum infured, but it has been cuftomary to provide, by a fpecial claufe in the policy, that the infurance fhall not admit of affignment. So that, although the affured fhould transfer his right in the fubject, yet the infurance does not become ufeful to his affignee, until the transference is made known to the underwriters, and the policy indorfed by them.

LYNCH *v.* DALZELL.

On the 28th July 1721, *Richard Ireland* took out a policy of infurance from the *Sun-fire office*, upon

upon his house the *Angel Inn at Gravesend*, which was continued from year to year. After his death, his son and sole executor *Anthony Ireland*, brought the policy to the office, about Christmas 1726, and had an indorsement made thereon, that the policy belonged to him; and he paid the premium for the succeeding year.

On the 24th August 1727, a fire happened at Gravesend, which burnt the house, and the appellants, *Roger and John Lynch*, appeared and claimed the insurance as purchasers from *Anthony Ireland*. The usual affidavits were produced, that the *Lynches* had sustained a loss; but there was no evidence, that *Ireland* had suffered any damage by the fire; indeed it appeared, that although the sale of the subjects had been previous to the fire, yet the conveyance of the policy had taken place after it, and had been perfectly voluntary on his part.

Upon these facts, a bill in Chancery, exhibited by the *Lynches*, was dismissed by *Lord Chancellor* KING. In consequence of which they brought an appeal.

It was argued for the assurers, that these policies are not conveyed with the subject, as incident thereto, but are only special agreements with the persons insuring, against such loss or damage as those persons should sustain. And the appeal was dismissed, and the decree affirmed, 13th March 1729. 3. *Brown's Cases in Parliament*, No. 71.

SADDLERS'

SADDLERS' COMPANY *v.* BADCOCK.

Mrs Strode, lessee of a house, insured the same for seven years from fire, to the value of L. 400: her term therein expired before the policy, *viz.* at Midsummer 1740; on the 6th January following, the house was burnt down; on the 23d February following, *Mrs Strode* assigned the policy to the plaintiffs, who are ground landlords, and now a bill is brought against the insurance-office for the L. 400. *Lord Chancellor* said, the question is, Whether by the assignment the plaintiffs are entitled to recover the L. 400? And I am of opinion, that the party insured ought to have a property in the thing insured at the time of the insurance made, and at the time of the loss by fire, or he cannot be relieved. *Mrs Strode* had no property at the time of the fire, consequently there was no loss to her; and if she had no interest, nothing could pass to the plaintiffs by the assignment. If the insured was not to have a property at the time of the insurance or loss, any one might insure upon another's house, which might have a bad tendency to burning houses; insuring the *thing* from damage, is not the meaning of the policy, it must mean insuring *Mrs Strode* from damage, and she has suffered none.—Bill dismissed without costs.— *East.* 1745. 1. *Wilson* 10.

5. From the nature of insurance, as a contract of indemnity, as well as from the statute that has been quoted, it appears very material to settle

settle what is such an interest as the assured is entitled to cover from risk, by an agreement of this nature; so that he may not pay a greater premium than is sufficient for his security; nor be deprived, in any degree, of that safety which he is permitted to derive from insurance.

In the *first* place, it is clear, that the assured may cover his *real property*; the ship with her furniture, and the cargo. And under this head fall to be included, not merely the original cost of either of these, but all expence incurred with a view to the adventure. The whole *outfit* of the ship, and the whole expence attending the cargo, form an addition to their respective values; and, in case of the adventure failing, are a positive loss to the owners.

The principle, that a person is entitled to secure himself against *all positive loss*, extends not only to the real property on board, and the expence of outfit, but to the *premium* given for the insurance in question. There can be no doubt, that a person who insures himself, loses the premium he gives for that security; and there is no reason why he should not be indemnified of this, as well as of any other damage. In fact, the *expence of insurance* is not materially different from the value of *ship and cargo*. It is a part of the cost attending the adventure; a part of the outfit; and it becomes a part of the value of the goods at the next market.—The premium of insurance, in fact, especially in time of war, may

may be a very great proportion of the affured's intereft, fometimes 25, 30, nay 60 guineas *per cent.*; if he was not entitled to cover it, he would frequently be under a neceffity of rifking more than he could afford to lofe.

The right of the merchant, accordingly, to infure his *premium*, has, it is believed, been acknowledged by all the mercantile ftates of Europe. There are, indeed, one or two of the regulations of Spain (under Philip II.) which prohibit " to infure the *coft of infurance*, upon gold, " pearls, &c. and merchandife from the Indies." But it feems hard to fay, whether this regulation has arifen from early and imperfect views, or from an intention of checking the extent of infurances upon importations from the Indies.

At prefent, it is univerfally eftablifhed, that an owner may cover his premium, as well as his fhip or cargo, with commiffion, brokerage, and all other expences attending the policy. Thus, by the ordinances of Amfterdam, it is provided, " that goods may be infured with all charges till " on board, the premium of infurance included."

If L. 100, therefore, is to be infured, at 10 *per cent.* premium, the owner muft, for his own entire fafety, infure not only L. 100, but likewife L. 10, which he gives to be fecure as to the former fum; and one pound, which is the premium of infurance for the L. 10. The whole fum to be infured, muft be L. 111, or, more accurately, L. $111\frac{1}{9}$.

Not only may a merchant infure his real property, but, in Britain, alfo the profit which he is entitled to expect; taking always proper precautions to prevent miftakes as to the nature of the intereft covered. Thus a merchant who has a cargo configned to him, may infure his *commiffion* upon the fales. This is a profit which he has good ground to expect, if the adventure arrives. In fuch a cafe, however, it is underftood in practice that he muft exprefs the infurance to be "on commiffion."

The general point is well illuftrated by the following decifion.

Le Cras *againft* Hughes.

The policy underwritten by the defendant, was "from *St Ferdinando de Omoa* to *London;* "on goods, &c. and on the fhip *St Domingo,* "prize to the fquadron under Captain *Luttrel.*"

Verdict for the plaintiff, fubject to the opinion of the Court on the following cafe. That Captain *Luttrel* commanding a fquadron, and Colonel *Dalrymple* the land forces, proceeded to take two regifter fhips, one of which, the *St Domingo,* was lying a-float under the protection of *Fort Omoa*; the fort, fhip and cargoes, became a joint prize to the land forces and fquadron. That the fhip was loft, with great part of the property on board. That the intereft intended to be covered was that of the officers and crews of the fquadron, in the prize. The queftion was, Whether this be an infurable intereft?

Lord

Lord Mansfield.—The assured certainly did not consider this as an evasion of the statute 19. Geo. II. And the insurers knew the whole circumstances at the time they underwrote. They had been in the Gazette.

There are here two questions; 1*st*, Whether the sea-officers had an interest vested in them; 2*dly*, Whether they might insure upon the *contingency* of their afterwards obtaining such an interest.

The prize-act and proclamation produce an actionable interest; they give the navy " all the " ships they shall take." There can be no difference between a sole and a joint capture. The expression, " All they shall take," must equally apply in the one case as in the other, to " all " they shall be found entitled to by the cap-" ture."

But besides, the Crown has long been in use to grant captures to the taker; here the assured have *possession*, with *expectation founded on universal practice*. In order to render insurance a contract of indemnity, an interest on the part of the assured is necessary; but no particular form of interest. It is sufficient, if the contingency be of such consequence, that I *may* be a loser if it does not happen. Mr *Holford* insured Lady *Lade's* not having a son; the event deprived him of the chance of an estate; and this was an insurable, though no legal interest. In *Grant v. Parkinson*, it was held that the profits of a voyage were insurable; an
agent

agent of prizes may infure his chance of profit; yet in neither of thefe cafes, is there an intereft vefted in the affured. The infurance is good on both grounds*. Judgement for the plaintiff. *Eaſt.* 22. *Geo.* III. B. R. MS.

The fame point is illuftrated by the cafe of *Grant v. Parkinſon,* (to be afterwards ftated †,) where the affured, who had a contract to fupply the army with fpruce beer, had procured infurance on molaffes,—to the extent of L. 1000, " being profits expected to arife from the cargo, " in the event of arriving."

This doctrine, however, as was formerly mentioned, is not univerfally received abroad. And hence arifes the prohibition, in fome of the foreign ordinances of infurance on freights.

An infurance *on freight,* is obvioufly in fome degree an infurance of *expected profit,* and not *from poſitive loſs.* No doubt, the freight may be confidered as partly correfponding to the outfit of the veffel; for the expences incurred in fitting her out, and in laying in provifions and ftores for the adventure, may be confidered as incurred for the fake of the freight. At the end of the voyage the fhip's ftores may be fuppofed to be confumed, and the repairs made, with a view to the voyage, to be worn out; and the owner receives indemnification for them

---

* This cafe likewife included a queftion with regard to the effect of average lofs, on a valued policy. See below, Part 2. ch. 3. § 2.

† See below, *ejuſd.* §

them by the freight. These expences, with the interest that falls due upon them during the course of the adventure, may be insured either as a part of the *value of the ship*, or under the separate denomination of *freight*. And so far the policy will still be a contract providing against a positive loss. But, as there is included under the idea of *freight*, something which the ship may earn beyond an equivalent for the actual outlay, the bargain becomes an insurance upon an expected profit.

The ordinances of France and Coningsberg prohibiting all insurance " on the freight which " vessels shall earn, and on expected profits," were formerly quoted.—Those regulations, it must be observed, do not prevent the owner or freighter from securing himself completely from positive loss, because he may still insure his outfit, and the interest of his money, under the names of ship and cargo. And they appear calculated to have one good effect, in preventing the expence of outfit from being doubly insured. For by the name of *freight*, is sometimes meant the *gross sum* which the owner receives for the service performed by the ship; and which contains an indemnification to him for his outlaid expences, and for the interest of money, besides the *clear profit* he draws from the adventure. In this manner the outfit may be doubly insured, once under the name of freight, (meaning *gross freight*), and another time

time under the name of ship and cargo. An impropriety which is effectually prevented by the French ordinance.

In England, where the idea of an insurance on expected profit is admitted in every extent, a distinction is made between *gross and nett freight*, which has the same effect of preventing a double insurance on the outfit.

By *nett freight*, is meant the clear profit arising from the voyage to the ship-owner; what remains from the ship's earnings, after deduction of all charges in the course of the adventure. This seems to be alluded to by the ordinance of Amsterdam, when it says, " Freight, and the " ordinary charges, usually called common ave- " rage, (*deducting men's wages, and other charges* " *that must have been paid out of it if the ship* " *had arrived*), may be insured and recovered " so far as it can be proved to what the gain or " overplus from the voyage would have amount- " ed."

Suppose the gross freight of a ship from Jamaica to London, that is, the sum which the owners will receive on the delivery of the cargo, to be, - - - L. 1000 0 0
The provisions and outfit, with the master and crew's wages due to them for the voyage, but which they would lose if the ship never arrived, may be - - 300 0 0

L. 700 0 0

L. 700

L. 700 appears, therefore, to be the *nett freight*, being the sum which the owners would put in their pocket, in the event of the ship's arrival.

Agreeably to this distinction, it should seem that a person may insure all the actual expence, with the interest of money, in relation to his ship, by an insurance *on ship*; but not the expected profit he is to derive from the ship's earnings. He may secure the expected profit to be drawn from his ship, by an insurance *on freight*, being understood in England by that expression, to insure his *nett freight*, that is, his *positive gain*, as distinct from his expence incurred.

In the same manner, he may insure the whole charges attending his goods, by an insurance *on cargo*. And he may secure an expected profit on his merchandises by a provision to that effect; the most common mode of executing this, is by specifying the cargo, and *valuing* it in the policy at so much a pipe, hogshead or ton.

A *reinsurance*, though it seems to suppose a solid interest in the assured, is prohibited expressly by § 3. of the statute 19. *Geo.* II. above quoted.

By *reinsurance*, is meant, when the underwriter withdraws himself from risk by procuring an insurance in his own favour. It corresponds to *hedging* in other contracts upon a future chance. A *reinsurance* is carefully to be distinguished from a *double insurance*. The latter takes place where the *assured* is twice secured in the same subject;

the former, where the underwriter in one policy becomes the assured in another, upon the same subject, with the view of withdrawing himself from hazard.

The clause in statute 19. *Geo.* II. above quoted, had been intended to prevent a mode of gaming by reinsurance, then in vogue in London. Mr *Magens* considers the remedy as a hard one, by depriving merchants of the power of withdrawing themselves from insurance business, when their circumstances may render it highly expedient.

But surely of all the species of gaming in insurance, that now under consideration is the worst. For as *reinsurance* is a measure supposed to be fallen upon after the commencement of the voyage, or after the vessel has been long at sea, there is more danger of its being suggested by private grounds of knowledge, with respect to the hazardous situation of the subject insured. Such a bargain, by which a man endeavours to get clear of his former engagements, seems to convey some suspicion of a concealed motive. For this reason, reinsurances suppose a higher *premium* than any other kind of policy; and if they were commonly practised, would tend more than any other, to increase the *expence of insurance* to the real trader. The limitations, therefore, made by the statute upon this practice, seem not inexpedient, and as they were intended to prevent a concealed mode

of

of wagering, had probably become neceſſary. At the ſame time the exceptions as to death and inſolvency, ſeem ſufficiently well calculated to prevent hardſhips from ſuch a prohibition.

The intereſt of an underwriter to be relieved from the hazard of his own contract, is univerſally ſuſtained abroad, as a proper ſubject of inſurance; and moſt of the foreign mercantile ſtates authoriſe *reinſurance* by an expreſs regulation *.

There is another intereſt which muſt be diſtinguiſhed, and which is in reality very different from this, although they have ſometimes been confounded; an intereſt in the *ſolvency of the underwriter*. Indeed this appears ſo totally diſtinct from the *reinſurance* laſt mentioned, that it does not deſerve to be called by the ſame name, much leſs to be conſidered as regulated by the ſame principles, or as falling equally under the ſtatutory prohibition of wager-policies.

A *reinſurance* is a *hedging* contract, by which the underwriter withdraws himſelf from all riſk. An *inſurance againſt inſolvency* is a contrivance by which the aſſured ſtrengthens his former ſecurity. It is difficult to conceive a fairer intereſt, or one more clearly actionable than that which a creditor has to recover payment of his juſt debt. Such a ſecurity is univerſally permitted among the foreign mercantile ſtates. And it is not prohibited in Britain; for it cannot be with-

---

* See *Magens*, and the commentators, *paſſim*.

in the meaning of the word *reinsurance* in the statute 19. *Geo.* II.; neither from what has been formerly stated upon that subject, does it appear to be within the mischief of a wagering contract. It is accordingly believed to be a frequent practice, both in England and Scotland, for the merchant to insure the solvency of his underwriters; and it meets with full support from the law.

Where the assured has lent money on the security of the ship's bottom, this appears a sufficient interest to give validity to the policy. Thus, by the Ordinance of Hamburgh, " when " any person lends money upon bottomry, he " may make his assurance to the full, for prin- " cipal, interest, and premium *."

France seems to vary from the other states of Europe in this particular, so far as to restrict an insurance on a bottomry interest, to the *principal sum and premium*. This proceeds upon their notion of preventing an insurance on expected profit. " The lenders on bottomry shall not in- " sure *the profit* on the sum lent, under the pe- " nalty of the policy being invalid, and of cor- " poral punishment †."

A doubt has been started by Mr MAGENS, of which it may perhaps be difficult to find a satisfactory solution, Whether an insurance on a bottomry interest does not fall under the statute 19.

* See *Ord. Hamb.* No. 930. *Ord.* of *Flor.* No. 11. of *Amsterd.* No. 531, 532, &c.
† *Ord. Fr.* No. 676, 677.

19. *Geo.* II. as a *reinsurance?* For the borrower agrees to pay a high interest for the sum advanced. The lender agrees to lose the principal, if the ship be lost, and looks to the ship only for security; so that the lender, in consideration of the high interest or profit which his money is to bear, undertakes the sea-risk, and *insures* the borrower to a certain extent. And if the *lender* gets himself insured, is not the contract a *reinsurance?*

However ingenious this idea of Mr Magens may appear, it has met with no attention; an insurance on a bottomry or *respondentia* interest being universally admitted in England. The limitations to prevent gaming in this species of insurance, by the statute *Geo.* II. were formerly quoted.

It only remains to be observed, that when insurance is made upon such an interest, this circumstance must be expressed.

In the case *Glover v. Black*, where an insurance had been made " *on goods and merchandise,*" and the interest appeared to be a *respondentia* bond over the cargo, it was found, that the plaintiff could not recover. 3. *Burr.* 1394. In a subsequent case, however, it has been found, that a *respondentia* interest may be covered by an insurance " *on goods, specie, and effects;*" such being the usage. *Park's System, p.* 13. *Gregory v. Christie.*

In

In Scotland no inftance has yet occurred, in which an infurance on a bottomry intereft has been made the fubject of legal difcuffion.

It only remains to ftate a few cafes, in which there appeared to be no fufficient intereft in the affured.

Kent v. Bird.

The plaintiff, a furgeon on board an Eaft Indiaman, agreed to pay to the defendant, a paffenger on board the fame fhip, the fum of L. 20 Sterling, at the next port the fhip fhould arrive at, provided the defendant undertook, that the fhip fhould fave her paffage to China that feafon; and in cafe fhe did not, then that he would pay to the plaintiff the fum of L. 1000 at the end of one month after the arrival of the faid fhip in the river Thames. Lord Mansfield and the Court of King's Bench, found this to be a wager-policy within the ftat. 19. *Geo.* II. *c.* 37. and therefore void. *Cowper's Reports,* 22d *April* 1777.

Lawry, *and another, againft* Bourdieu.

The plaintiffs had lent to *Lawfon*, captain of the *Holland Eaft Indiaman,* L. 26,000, for which he had given them a common bond in the penal fum of L. 52,000. While he was with his fhip at China, the plaintiffs got a policy of infurance underwritten by the defendant, and others, which was in the following terms: " At and " from *China* to *London,* beginning the adventure
" upon

" upon the goods from the loading thereof on
" board the said ship at *Canton* in *China*, &c.
" upon the said ship, &c. from and immediately
" following her arrival at *Canton* in *China*, valued
" at L. 26,000, being the amount of Captain
" *Patrick Lawson's* common bond, payable to
" the parties, as shall be described on the back
" of this policy;"—" and in case of loss,
" no other proof of interest to be required
" than the exhibition of the said bond; warrant-
" ed free from average, and without benefit
" of salvage to the insurer." At the head of
the subscription was written, " *on a bond as
" above expressed.*"—Captain *Lawson* sailed from
China, and arrived safe with his privilege, (as
it is called,) or adventure, in London, on the 1st
of July 1777, none of the events insured against
having happened. The receipt of the premium
was acknowledged on the back of the policy. In
1780, the insured brought this action for a *return* of the premium, on the ground, that the policy being without interest, the contract was void.

Upon the trial at Guildhall, Lord MANSFIELD
directed a verdict for the defendant, on this
footing, that *in pari delicto, melior est conditio possidentis*; which was found accordingly.
But his Lordship having afterwards entertained
some doubt, allowed a motion for a new trial,
when he returned to his first opinion. The
present, he observed, was strictly a *gaming policy;*

cy; the plaintiffs say, " we mean to game, but " we give our reason for it; Captain *Lawson* " owes us a sum of money, and we want to be " secure, in case he should not be in a situation " to pay us." It was a *hedge*. But they had no interest; for if the ship had been lost, and the underwriters had paid, still the plaintiffs would have been entitled to recover the amount of the bond from *Lawson*. The policy therefore was illegal, and the Court will not interfere to assist either party. *In pari delicto, &c.* The Court, by a majority, discharged the rule. *Doug. Rep.* 18*th Nov.* 1780.

Kulen Kemp, *and others, against* Vigne.

Upon a motion by the plaintiff, to set aside a non-suit, the following facts were reported by *Justice* Buller:—That the insurance was upon goods on board the ship *Emanuel*, at and from *Falmouth* to *Marseilles*, warranted a *Danish* ship; and on the policy was this memorandum: " The " following insurance is declared to be on mo- " ney expended for reclaiming the ship and " cargo, valued at the sum, which shall be de- " clared hereafter. The loss to be paid in case " the *ship* does not arrive at Marseilles, and " without farther proof of interest than this " policy; warranted free from all average, and " without the benefit of salvage."

It appeared that the plaintiffs were proprietors of the *cargo* but not of the *ship*. That the ship
originally

originally failed with the cargo on board from *Riga* on a voyage to *Marseilles*, and that an infurance had been effected at *Bremen* upon the cargo for that voyage; in the courfe of which fhe was taken, and brought into *Falmouth* by an *Englifh* privateer. That fentence of condemnation had been there obtained, which was afterwards reverfed, upon the prize having been proved to be a neutral fhip; but the expences of procuring that reverfal were ordered by the Admiralty Court to be a charge upon the cargo. The plaintiffs agent accordingly paid the fum of L. 1031, 14 s. for the expences of reclaiming the fhip and cargo, and immediately got the policy in queftion effected.

In the February following, the fhip fet fail from *Falmouth* with the original cargo on board, in the profecution of her voyage to *Marseilles*; but on the 26th of the fame month, before her arrival there, fhe was captured by a *Spanifh* fhip, and carried into *Ceuta* in *Spain*, where fhe was again condemned. An appeal was brought in the fuperior court of *Madrid*, which promifing to be of long continuance, the cargo was ordered to be fold, and the proceeds to be brought into court, to wait the event of the fuit.—In May 1783, the veffel was reftored by fentence of the court, and the furplus of the proceeds, which arofe from the fale of the cargo, was paid to the owners, deducting the expences incurred in

Spain

Spain in prosecuting the appeal. After all the charges paid, there only remained twenty-six rix-dollars. As soon as the ship was liberated, she sailed from *Ceuta* to *Malaga*, in order to refit, and having there made the necessary repairs, set sail for *Bremen*, and in that voyage was lost.

The insurance made upon the cargo at *Bremen* has been paid.

The declaration averred, that "*whilst the ship was proceeding in her said voyage from* Falmouth *to* Marseilles, *and before she could arrive at* Marseilles, *she was* CAPTURED *by the* Spaniards, *and thereby the said ship, and also the goods and merchandises on board her, were totally lost to the plaintiffs.*"

Mr J. BULLER proceeded to observe, that at the trial it was objected for the defendant, 1*st*, That this was not an insurable interest; and, 2*dly*, That the plaintiffs could not recover upon the policy in this form of declaring, for they had stated the loss to have happened by *capture*; whereas, though the vessel was captured, yet having been afterwards restored, she might have reached her destined port notwithstanding the capture, in which case the underwriters would have been discharged by the terms of the memorandum: And that he being of that opinion, had non-suited the plaintiffs.— After argument by counsel, Lord MANSFIELD said, the answers to this case are decisive:

This

This is a wagering policy.—The intereſt of the plaintiff was money laid out in reclaiming the *cargo*. The event inſured was the ſafe arrival, not of the *cargo*, but of the *ſhip* at Marſeilles. It is the ſame as if the event inſured had been the arrival of any other ſhip at Marſeilles.—As this is a wager, the aſſured cannot abandon their intereſt, although the object of the voyage ſhould be defeated by any accident in the courſe of it. After the capture, they might ſtill have purſued their voyage to Marſeilles; but did not.

WILLES, J.—Doubted whether the plaintiffs had not an inſurable intereſt, but was clear upon the other points. There was a deviation in the veſſel not following out her voyage to Marſeilles. And the plaintiff has declared for a loſs by *capture*, whereas the policy might have been complied with by the ſhip's going to Marſeilles, notwithſtanding the capture.

ASHURST, J.—This is a wagering policy; in which caſe, the party inſured takes upon himſelf to do every thing which the owners of the ſhip might have done; and they might have directed the ſhip to Marſeilles.—It is alſo certain, that the party inſuring a ſhip to any place muſt uſe all due diligence to further her voyage thither.

BULLER, J.—It would be a ſufficient objection, that the loſs is averred to be by capture.—But upon the merits, although the parties seem to have had it in view to insure a real interest, they have not expressed these intentions in the policy.—The Court is bound to look to the instrument, and cannot help them. The policy is not adapted to the real truth of the case.—Rule discharged. *Termly Reports. Trin.* 1786.

6. In order to render effectual the different statutory provisions that have been mentioned, for the prevention of gaming insurances, it is absolutely necessary, that the policy should, in some way or other, point out the person for whose benefit the security is taken.

To this branch of the subject, therefore, belongs the consideration of that clause in the policy which specifies the *name of the assured*. "A B, C D, and Co. as well in their own name, "as in the name of every one to whom the same "shall belong, do make insurance, and cause "themselves to be assured, &c."

It is of great moment, in order to prevent fraudulent dealing with respect to the assured's interest, that his name should be expressed in the policy, and not left blank, to be filled up at a subsequent period. By the foreign ordinances, accordingly, it is in general provided, That "no assurance shall be made, if the name of "the person that causes the same to be done, "shall not be clearly and expressly mentioned "in the policy, before any assurer underwrites "it.

" it. Nor shall a blank space be left in poli-
" cies, to fill up the name; for in that case, the
" same shall not be valid, nor the assurance of
" any effect*."

The *Amsterdam* regulation requires, that the insurers should be made acquainted with the name of the person who gave the order to insure. At *Stockholm*, " the name of the assured
" must be inserted in the policy; but any one
" insuring by commission, may either have his
" own name inserted, or that of his constituent."
Ord. Stockh. No. 1031.

Hamburgh is believed to be the only state that has expressly allowed " the name of the assured
" to be left out, and the policies to be filled up
" to the bearer only." *Ord. Hamb*. No. 875.

In *Britain*, where there have been very few positive statutes upon insurance, it was understood, in practice, that a policy, in which the name of the assured had been left blank, was nevertheless a valid agreement in favour of the person who could show an interest at the date of the contract. Such policies, however, were unusual; but it was extremely common for the broker to insert his own name only in the policy, leaving it to be ascertained *aliunde*, on whose account the insurance was made.

This

* *Ord. Gen*. No. 146.; of *France*, No. 665.; of *Koningsberg*, No. 773.; *Copenh*. No. 1264.

This practice, however, muſt naturally have given riſe to frequent diſputes with regard to the perſon who had the intereſt at the date of the contract; and it was calculated to favour colluſive dealing between the broker and aſſured.

By the ſtatute 14. *Geo.* III. *c.* 48. § 2., it had been provided, that " it ſhould not be lawful " to make any policy on *lives*, or on *any other* " *event whatever*, without inſerting the name of " the perſon for whoſe uſe, benefit, or on whoſe " account, ſuch policy is made."

This ſtatute did not extend to policies on ſhipping and merchandiſe; and a further enactment therefore took place, ſo lately as the 1785.

The preamble ſets forth, that the making inſurances on ſhips and effects, without ſpecifying the names of the perſons on whoſe account they are effected, hath been miſchievous, and productive of great inconveniencies; it is therefore enacted, that " after 5th July 1785, no perſon " reſiding in *Great Britain*, ſhall make policies " of aſſurance upon his intereſt in any ſhips or " goods, without inſerting therein his own name, " as the perſon intereſted, or the name of his " agent, effecting the ſame, *as agent*. And per- " ſons, not reſiding in *Great Britain*, ſhall not " make ſuch policies of aſſurance, without in- " ſerting therein the names of their agents; and " every policy underwrote contrary to the true " meaning hereof, ſhall be void." 25. *Geo.* III. *cap.* 44.

This

This ſtatute is explained by the following deciſion.

PRAY *and others, againſt* EDIE.

The plaintiffs, who lived in *Georgia*, had formerly been owners of the veſſel inſured, but, before May 1785, had transferred their property in her to one *Pierce*, who reſided in the ſame country. The names of the plaintiffs were at the head of the policy, which was underwritten by the defendant in September 1785; and the declaration ſtated, that they made it for the benefit of *Pierce*, in whom the intereſt was averred to be.

Upon theſe facts, two queſtions aroſe, *firſt*, Whether, when an agent effects a policy for his principal reſiding abroad, the act of the 25. Geo. III. *cap.* 44. requires, that ſuch agent's name ſhould be inſerted *eo nomine*, as agent?

2*dly*, Whether, under the ſame act, it is neceſſary that ſuch agent, who effects the policy for his principal reſiding abroad, ſhould himſelf reſide in England?—

For the plaintiffs it was argued, that the act being rigorous againſt foreigners, is unfavourable. That with reſpect to the preſent plaintiffs, it has the effect of an *ex poſt facto* law, as they could not be appriſed of it. With regard to the firſt objection, it does not appear by the words of the act, that in caſe the principal reſides abroad, the agent's name muſt be inſerted *eo nomine*, as agent. The ſecond clauſe

of

of the statute declares, that the *name of the agent* shall be inserted, but that is only descriptive of the person, not of his character. From the preamble, the act seems intended merely to guard against the effecting policies in *blank*. As to the second objection, there are no words in the statute which require, that the agent should live in England. Besides, by signing the contract, the underwriter has precluded himself from taking advantage of the law.

The counsel on the other side was stopt by the Court.

Lord MANSFIELD, C. J.—There is no doubt as to the construction of the act. It is intended to remedy inconveniencies which had arisen from omitting to insert the names of the persons for whom policies are effected. This is done by enacting, that the name of the principal himself, or that of his agent, must be inserted. If the agent were not to be named in the policy, *eo nomine*, as agent, the public would still be left ignorant who the insured was, and the principal intention of the act would be defeated. The same must hold in the case of the insured living abroad, who cannot insure in his own name.

I am also inclined to think the other objection good, as to the residence of the agent; but it is unnecessary to give an opinion upon this point.

BULLER, J.—The word *agent* must be taken in both clauses in the same sense.—The view of of the Legiflature requires it. No doubt, that he fhould, by the act, alfo refide in *Britain*.

Per Cur. Judgment for the defendant. *Termly Reports. Trin.* 1786.

7. Having confidered the reftrictions which the Legiflature has thought proper to impofe in relation to wager-policies, and the precautions it has adopted, to render thofe reftrictions effectual, we may now return to examine the nature of an infurance contract, when conftituted upon a legal intereft.

And here a confideration of importance may be recalled to mind; that a policy upon intereft is a contract of indemnity; confequently, the amount of the affured's intereft muft regulate the extent of the infurer's obligation. But how is the amount of intereft to be verified? This leads to examine more particularly the difference between *an open* and a *valued* policy.

Where, in the firft place, the policy is *open*, that is, where the value of the fubject infured is not fixed by previous eftimate, the extent of the underwriter's obligation muft, obvioufly, be proportioned to what the amount of that intereft fhall appear to be, from evidence. And here, it is the actual damage on fhip, goods and freight, that muft be paid; the probable value of the fhip at the date of the lofs, with expence of outfit; the *prime coft* of the cargo, appearing by the invoices and bill of loading, with charges; and the actual *nett freight*, if freight was infured.

But

But where the amount of the interest is fixed by a *valuing clause*, the intention of such previous estimate is to supersede all proof upon this subject; and the *prime cost*, or actual loss, must be held as ascertained by the express agreement of parties.

Much difference of opinion seems to have arisen, about the construction, and effect, of clauses of this nature, whenever it appears that the subject has been estimated above its real value.

On the one hand it has been observed, that the consequence of an *overvaluation*, if it shall be sustained to the whole extent, is to give the assured an interest to destroy the ship and cargo; that such an interpretation, therefore, might be exceedingly dangerous, and might open a door to many frauds, to the prejudice of underwriters: And that, even supposing the overvaluation to have taken place innocently, there is an absurdity in allowing the assured to derive an advantage from his own error and mistake. It has been therefore urged, with no small plausibility, that valuing clauses should receive a strict interpretation: That they ought to be allowed no farther effect than merely to establish a *presumption of value*, until the contrary be proved. But when the underwriter does produce evidence that the valuation is erroneous;—that an overvaluation has taken place;—the mistake ought to be corrected. If the overvaluation appears to have taken place *bona fide*, the insurance ought

ought to be reduced to the real intereſt; if *fraudulently*, the policy ought to be annulled altogether.

In ſupport of this opinion, ſeveral foreign regulations are produced. Thus, by ordinance of *France:* " If the inſured ſues for payment of
" the ſum inſured, *above the value of his effects*
" *or intereſt*, he ſhall be puniſhed.—We forbid
" the making any inſurance or reinſurance on
" goods or effects above their real value, in one
" or more policies, under the penalty of ſuch inſurance being invalid, and confiſcation of the
" goods."

By the ordinance of *Coningſberg*, " No perſon
" is to offer any thing to be inſured above *the*
" *legal and conſtituted value*. If any one, from
" an eager deſire of gain, ſhall run the riſk of
" inſuring a ſhip or goods *to a greater ſum than*
" *their equitable value*, he ſhall be ſeverely puniſhed according to the circumſtances; the
" inſurance ſhall be void, and the premium fall
" to the inſurer; but if, by accident, and without any evil deſign of the party inſured, the
" value inſured exceeds the uſual and equitable
" worth of the ſhip or goods, the inſurance ſhall
" indeed remain in its full force; but the inſurers, in caſe of loſs or damage of the goods
" inſured, ſhall not be bound to pay more than
" their actual worth, and in proportion to the
" ſum for which they reſpectively bound themſelves; likewiſe what overplus they receiv'd
" in

"in the premium on account of this abatement, "after deduction of a half *per cent.* they are to "return to the parties infuring."

And by the regulations of *Amfterdam,* " no "valuation in the policy fhall take place, of thofe "goods and effects, whereof the real value can "be produced *."

From the fame conviction of the danger of fraud, in allowing overvaluations to be effectual, we find other nations impofing reftraints in this refpect, and eftablifhing a prefumption of fraud, when the *eftimated* fhall be found to exceed, in a certain degree, the *real* values. Thus the ordinance of *Rotterdam* (in 1721) fays, " That in "cafe goods be fent in return for others, and "the true value of the returns cannot be afcer- "tained, then the Chamber fhall fet a value on "them, *not exceeding* 50 *per cent. above the capi-* "*tal fent out.*" By ordinance of *Middleburg* and *Copenhagen* alfo, " Returns from the *Eaft Indies* "cannot be valued higher than *double* of the "capital fent out."

In England it feems alfo to have been at one time intended to fubject this matter to fome regulation; and with a view to prevent fraudulent overvaluation, it was propofed, among the refolutions of the Commons, in 1747, to enact, that in order to a valuation being confidered

---

See *Magens, vol.* ii. *p.* 136. To the fame effect we have the opinion of *Roccus* ;—and of that ancient Code, the *Confolato del Mare of Barcelona.*

fidered as the meafure of a lofs, *goods* ought to be valued, not in general, but particularly, by weight, meafure or package, and each fort valued apart. It was propofed, that no valuation *on ſhip* fhould be valid, if it exceeded a certain proportion of the fhip's real worth.—Thefe regulations were never carried into effect; they fhow, however, the fenfe of mercantile people as to the danger of overvaluations.

But, it may be afked, do not thefe valued policies fall within the ftatute 19. *Geo*. II. at leaft fo far as refpects the *overvaluation?* For although they are not wagers altogether, yet are they not wagers fo far as the infurance exceeds the intereft?

It may readily be allowed, that every *fraudulent* overvaluation ought to be attended with the penal confequence of vacating the policy entirely. But it cannot be admitted that fuch a circumftance, if happening by innocent miftake, fhould reduce the underwriter's obligation to the real value. By fuch an interpretation, the great object and advantage of thefe valuing claufes, that of precluding a difficult and troublefome proof, would be entirely cut off. Every valued policy would afford room for endlefs cavils and inextricable litigation; and it would be neceffary that fuch infurances fhould be entirely laid afide. The policy, therefore, is in practice fupported to the whole extent,

tent, although there should appear to have been an overvaluation.

At the same time it must be supposed, that the assured has actually *some interest*, and does not appear to have made use of the valuation as a cloak to a wager; otherwise the policy will fall under the statute 19. *Geo*. II. against gaming insurances. We must likewise suppose there is no proof of fraud in the overvaluation in question.

But these things being taken for granted, it does not seem necessary for the assured, in a valued policy, to prove the amount of his interest, but merely that he had such an interest on board, as might, in his situation, be naturally estimated at the sum valued; nor is it of any consequence, although the underwriters should prove such overvaluation.

It is pretty remarkable, that this opinion, with regard to the import and effect of a valued policy, which is at present entertained in Britain, seems to have been held very long ago, among the mercantile states in Italy.

Case. Vincentio de Medicis procured insurance upon " grain, by the ship *La N. S. del Carmine*, " valued at 8000 ducats." The vessel, in the course of her voyage, was pillaged by the French.

Upon an action at the instance of the assured before the maritime court of the city of *Messina* in Sicily, besides some other defences of
less

less moment, it was pleaded for the underwriters, That the vessel had not been loaded to her usual extent; in consequence of which, the cargo actually on board was at 8000 ducats much overvalued: And that if they were liable at all on such a policy, they could only be subjected to the real proven cost of the cargo at the port of loading.

It was answered for *Vincentio*, that if the original cost of the gain, the expences of outfit, and the interest of his money, or, what was the same thing, the price which the cargo would bring at the port of discharge, were considered, there would not appear to be any overvaluation; that he was entitled to insure his expected profits, as well as his positive loss; or if such policy was not properly an insurance, it was valid as a *wager:* That the insurers had precluded themselves from the objection stated, by the express clause of valuation in the policy, and by receiving a premium corresponding to the whole sum insured.

The Court of *Messina* decided in favour of the assured. See *Roccus. Resp.* 31. *Anno* 1628.

In England, the courts of law seem, at first, to have been inclined to open up a valued policy where there was an overvaluation.

LE PYPRE *v.* FARR.

On a policy on goods, by agreement " *valued*
" at L. 600, and the assured not to be obliged to
" prove

"prove any interest." The *Lord Chancellor* ordered the defendant to discover what goods he put on board. For although the defendant offered to renounce all interest to the insurers, yet his Lordship referred it to a master to examine the value of the goods saved, and to deduct it out of the value or sum of L. 600, at which the goods were valued by the agreement. 2. *Vern.* 715. *Mich.* 1716.

An opposite rule, however, upon this point, is now considered as established, both by the general opinion of merchants, and in consequence of the doctrine delivered by Lord MANSFIELD in the case *Lewis v. Rucker* *.

" A valued policy," says his Lordship, " is
" not to be considered as a *wager* policy, or like
" *interest or no interest;* if it was, it would be
" void by the act of 19. Geo. II. The only
" effect of the valuation is, *fixing the amount of*
" *the prime cost*, just as if the parties admitted it
" at the trial. But for every other purpose, it
" must be taken, that the value was fixed in such
" a manner, as that the insured meant only to
" have an indemnity. If it be much *undervalued*,
" the merchant himself stands insurer of the sur-
" plus; if it be *much overvalued*, it must be
" done with a bad view, either to gain, contrary
" to 19. *Geo.* II. or with some view to a fraudulent
" loss;

---

* This case relates more properly to another branch of the subject, and will be found under the head of *Partial Loss.* Part 2. ch. 3. § 2. art. 2.

"loss; therefore the insured never can be allow-
"ed in a court of justice to plead, that he has
"greatly overvalued, or that his interest was a
"trifle only. It is settled, that upon valued po-
"licies, the merchant need only prove *some in-
"terest*, to take it out of 19. Geo. II. because the
"adverse party has admitted the value; and if
"more was required, the agreed valuation
"would signify nothing. But if it should come
"out in proof, that a man had insured L. 2000,
"and had interest on board to the value of a
"*cable* only, there never has been, and there
"never will be a determination, that by such an
"evasion the act of Parliament may be defeated.
"There are many conveniencies from allowing
"valued policies; but where they are used
"merely as a cover to a wager, they would be
"considered as an evasion. The effect of the
"valuation is only fixing conclusively the prime
"cost; if it be an *open* policy, the prime cost
"must be *proved*; in a *valued* policy it is *agreed*."
2. *Burr.* 1167. *May* 2. 1761.

M'NAIR *v.* COULTER *and others.*

Robert M'Nair, at *Glasgow*, had a vessel employed in the West India trade, commanded by his son *James M'Nair*. After several successful voyages among the West India islands, *James M'Nair* sent information to his father, that he was about to sail from *Barbadoes* for *Virginia*, with a cargo, the value of which, along with the ship, would amount to about L. 1200 currency.

Robert M'Nair got L. 1000 Sterling insured at *Glasgow* upon this voyage. The policy was " on the ship *Jane*, and all and whatsoever kind " of goods laden or to be laden on board of her. " The said goods, body, tackle, &c. *valued at* " L. 1000 *Sterling, without farther account.*" The vessel was lost off *Bermudas*.

It afterwards appeared, that the information given by *James M'Nair*, with regard to the value of his cargo, was false. But there was no evidence that his father *Robert* was accessory to the fraud.—*James* was afterwards prosecuted for having *wilfully sunk the ship;* but the jury acquitted him of that charge; and found him " only guilty of having sent fraudulent advices, " with a view to the insurance."

The underwriters defended themselves against a demand of the L. 1000 insured, upon a variety of grounds. Two of which were, that this was a *wager-insurance*; and that there had been a *wilful deviation*. But after some fluctuation in the decisions of the Courts of Scotland upon these defences, they were both ultimately repelled *upon appeal* in 1770.

Another plea of the insurers was, that as there was here an *admitted overvaluation*, they could only be found liable *to the extent of the real loss*. Upon this point, the Lords of Session pronounced the following judgment: " Find the policy of
" insurance

infurance " does not, in this cafe, oblige the in-
" furers to pay the fums at which the fhip and
" cargo were infured, but only the real value
" of the fhip and cargo; and find the value of
" the fhip to be L. 450 *Virginia* currency."

Robert M'Nair brought a fecond appeal of this, among other points, in 1773; and it was argued in his behalf, That this is a *valued policy* of both fhip and cargo, where not only the fhip, but a confiderable intereft on board are admitted to have exifted.—That under fuch a policy, the affured muft recover the whole fum in the infurance, as he could not have any claim for a return of premium for fhort intereft, if the fhip had arrived fafe.—That in all valued policies, the affured having fuch an intereft on board, as to take it out of the meaning of the ftatute 19. *Geo.* II., the conftant rule has been to take the *quantum* of that intereft from the value expreffed in the policy, without any other proof of the quantity or value of the goods.

The Houfe of Peers " ordered and adjudged
" that fo much of the interlocutors of the 8th
" February, and 21ft June 1765, as find that the
" policy of infurance does not, in this cafe, ob-
" lige the infurers to pay the fum at which the
" fhip and cargo were infured, and fo much of
" the interlocutor of the 13th February 1772,
" as finds the appellant is not entitled to recover
" from the refpondents the L. 1000 Sterling,
" fpecified in the policy, but only a fum equal
" to

" to the damages he sustained by the loss of the
" ship *Jane*, and her cargo, be reversed*." *Appealed Cases.* Feb. 12. 1773.

WILSON *against* WORDIE.

Wilson, and others, owners of a private ship of war, having got notice that she had captured a Spanish merchantman, made insurance upon the prize; which, in the policy subscribed by *Wordie*, and others, the underwriters, was valued at L. 20,000, including 20,700 dollars in specie. The vessel, while lying in *Lowlandman's Bay*, in the isle of *Jura*, was retaken by a *French* privateer, but not before the captors had sent ashore 4200 dollars, which indeed appear to have been nearly the amount of the specie found on board of the prize.

When the cause came from the Court of Admiralty in Scotland, before the Court of Session, it was pleaded for the insurers: It is an established maxim respecting insurances, that the concealment or misrepresentation, even by mistake, of any such important fact or circumstance, as makes " the risk run different from that un-
" derstood at the time of the agreement," renders the policy void. The overvaluation in this case,

---

* There seems to be another ground of defence on this case, which was not started. The insurance was made upon *fraudulent* information given by *James M'Nair*, his father's *agent*; (See the case of *Fitzherbert v. Mather.*) An assured is responsible for the fraud or negligence of the agent, to whose advices he trusts in making the insurance.

case, so undeniable, especially as to the dollars, evidently increased the disadvantage of the insurer's situation, or the risk which they run, and ought therefore to prove fatal to the claim of the owners.

But though the policy should not thus be annulled *in totum*, it ought, at least, in consideration of its object, to be restricted to the loss truly sustained. Insurance is a contract of indemnity; and where no damage can possibly arise, or so far as no subject exists on which it may be incurred, there is no room for any obligation. Hence the defenders are liable according to the true extent only of the loss in question, notwithstanding the overvaluation in the policy. " For no man " should be allowed to avail himself of having " overvalued." If the error has arisen, not by misapprehension, but by fraudulent design, then is the contract totally vitiated in respect of the insured, whose crime falls under the cognisance of the law, while the insurer continues entitled to his full premium. Even wager-policies, as they are styled, are expressly prohibited by act 19. *Geo.* II. The valuing of policies, nevertheless, is by no means useless, as it imports an admission on the part of the underwriter, which *supersedes the necessity of proof* by the assured; yet it is evident, that the insurer is *not thereby precluded from detecting an erroneous valuation, by a proof to be adduced by himself.*

Answered:

Answered: The very purpose of *valued policies*, is to remedy the uncertainty of real amount, which, on many occasions, is unavoidable, and almost always when a prize is insured before arrival. It behoves the insurer indeed, in specifying the value, to be free from any fraudulent design. But though an overvaluation should happen, if *bona fide* made, it will stand good. The statute of *Geo.* II. was directed only against those insurances, in which the insured has no true interest; but enacts nothing with respect to cases in which he holds a substantial property, though of less value than that rated in the policy.

The Lord *Hailes, Ordinary*, having reported the cause, some of the judges were of opinion, that the sole effect of the valuation, was to create a presumption, which, however, might be overcome by proof; but the majority adopted the argument of the owners.

"The Lords found the underwriters liable in "terms of the policy of insurance underwritten "by them."

In a reclaiming petition, the underwriters argued thus: Suppose the full specified number of dollars, *viz.* 20,700, to have been on board and all saved, then surely to that extent, no claim could lie against the underwriters. Now, in fact, the whole specie really on board, *viz.* 4200 dollars, was saved; and what difference could it make, that an additional number which

never

never at all exifted, had been ftated by miftake? Did that create any lofs?

On advifing this petition, with anfwers, in which the former argument of *bona fides* fupporting the valuation, was again urged, the Lords " adhered to their former judgment." *Fac. Coll. Dec.* 2. 1783.—The infurers having confulted very eminent Englifh counfel upon this cafe, were advifed to acquiefce in the judgment of the Court.

A valued policy has, in every inftance of overvaluation, fome degree of connection with a wager. In the following cafes, where there is a real intereft, but befides the *valuing claufe* there is a provifion *that the policy fhall be fufficient proof of intereft*, it may become a matter of confiderable hefitation, whether the legal or illegal circumftances of the contract fhall be held to predominate. The queftion in fuch a cafe muft depend upon the *actum et tractatum* between parties, at the time of the agreement, and whether they meant to evade the ftatute of Geo. II.

GRANT *againft* PARKINSON.

A policy was underwritten " at and from *Surinam* to *Quebec*, upon any kind of goods, *&c.* and on the body, *&c.* of the fhip;—*the goods valued at L.* 1000, being profits expected to arife on the cargo in the event of arriving at Quebec; and *in cafe of lofs, the infurers agree to pay*

pay the same without any other vouchers than this policy."

A verdict was found for the plaintiff; but, upon the ground that this policy was within statute 19. *Geo.* II. leave was given to move that the verdict should be set aside, and a nonsuit entered.

Lord MANSFIELD.—I have changed my opinion from that I entertained at *Guildhall*, and now think that the policy is not void.

Before the statute, valued policies were common, and no proof was necessary, either of the value or the interest, whether the words "without farther proof than the policy" were added or not. After the act passed, it was held necessary, in a valued policy, to prove *some interest;* and it was competent to the other side to show that it was an evasion. But a small interest was easily shown.

What is this case? An insurance by a person who supplied the army with spruce beer, on profits to arise from a cargo of molasses, and the profits insured appear to be certain. The policy was not meant to conceal the nature of the interest, but to get rid of the necessity of proving the *quantum:* I cannot take it out of the common case of a valued policy. The words of the statute are strong, and they struck me so at Guildhall. If it had been a new question, as to the effect of a valued policy, the words might have occasioned difficulty; but all judges have construed them as I have stated.

BULLER,

BULLER, J.—The words of the policy are capable of either of the two conftructions; the queftion is, which is the fair one? To come at that, all the policy muft be taken together, and it is clear, that a real intereft was meant. Therefore the parties were not wagering, and the policy not within the act.——The Rule difcharged. *Mich.* 22. *Geo.* III. MS.

The cafe of *Da Cofta v. Firth* *, was fimilar; in which the goods and merchandifes had been " *valued at the fum infured, without farther proof* " *of intereft than the policy.*" And the Court faid, it was a policy of a peculiar fort, and of a mixed nature, being partly a wager-policy, partly on intereft. But they confidered it as affording a ground of action.

8. An *overvaluation*, therefore, unlefs fraudulent, is not fufficient to deftroy the effect of a *valuing claufe*, or to cut down the eftimate which parties have previoufly agreed to make of the *prime coft*.

But in every policy on intereft, whether *open* or *valued*, it may happen that the fubject fhall be *overinfured*. The merchant, fearing for his fhip or cargo, and anxious to be fecured from hazard, has tranfmitted an order of infurance to different places; and it is unexpectedly filled up, at both, to the whole amount of the *valued* intereft. Or, in an *open* policy, the owner of fhip or

---

* 4 Burr. 1966.

or cargo may, from miftake, have eftimated his property at an overvalue, and obtained infurance accordingly. In all fuch cafes, throwing fufpicion of fraud out of the queftion, the obligation of the underwriter muft be reduced below the terms of the contract, and made to correfpond with the actual amount of intereft, and the real or agreed values of fhip or cargo.

A queftion here arifes, whether, for this purpofe, a deduction fhall be made from all the different underwriters, in one or more policies, proportionally to their fums fubfcribed, without refpect to the dates of their feveral fubfcriptions? or whether the firft policy fhall be allowed to ftand, and thofe of a pofterior date fet afide?

The foreign ordinances have enforced the latter rule, and the prefent practice of Britain has adopted the former.

Thus it is provided by the ordinance of *Spain*, " In all policies that fhall be made on fhips go-
" ing to the Indies, if more is infured than the
" cargo is worth, the laft underwriters fhall be
" ftruck out, and neither gain nor lofe more
" than the half *per cent.* for cancelling the rifk;
" which fhall be run by all the remaining infu-
" rers proportionably; and thofe who have laft
" figned the policy fhall be deemed the pofterior
" underwriters, although others have figned it
" the fame day *."

To

---

* Ord. Spain, No. 85.

To the fame effect are the regulations of Antwerp, Florence, Hamburgh, Middleburg, France, Stockholm, and Genoa.

Some of the foreign ftates adopt a diftinction between the cafes where there have been two feparate policies, and that where there is an over-infurance in one policy. "In return of pre-" miums," fays the regulation of *Amfterdam*, " as alfo in averages and loffes, the infurers who " have underwritten one and the fame policy, " although it be with difference of dates, fhall " fhare equally :—but if more than one policy " is employed and underwritten for one and the " fame parcel of goods, or the fame intereft, " then the *firft* policy in date, without regard-" ing that which is fubfequent, fhall fubfift to " the amount of the fum infured for the value " of the goods and effects; and the reduction " fhall fall upon the policy of latter date, as " well in the cafe of returns of premium, as of " averages and loffes *."

The law of *Bilboa* feems to enter into the fame diftinction. There is, in fact, fomething plaufible to be faid in favour of the practice of annulling thofe infurances that are *pofterior*, and fupporting thofe that are *prior in date*. It may be argued, that if the bargain turns out advantageous, thofe who are firft in date, have a *jus quæfitum* to the full benefit of their contract, of which they cannot be deprived by any fubfe-

---

* Ord. Amft. No. 535.

quent act of the assured. And upon the same principle they must be liable for the loss, if the bargain be unfortunate. Besides, a contrary rule may open a door to much collusive dealing upon the part of the assured; enabling them to *hedge*, and to withdraw themselves from their first bargains, by subsequent policies of a fraudulent nature.

The same rule seems anciently to have been established in England. *Gerard Malynes* tells us, that "when merchants cause a greater sum "to be assured than the goods are worth, or "amount unto, when they are laden into any "ship which is expected homeward, making ac- "count that their factors will send them great- "er returns than they do; in this case, the "*custom* is, that those assurers that have *last* "subscribed to the policy of assurance, bear not "any adventure at all, and must make restitu- "tion of the premium by them received, abating "one half in the hundred for their subscription; "and this is duly observed; and so a law not "observed is inferior to a custom well observed."

Of this rule, the author now mentioned, expresses great approbation, by calling it, in the language of the period when he wrote, "a *rare* "custom of insurances *."

By the modern practice of Britain, however, it is perfectly established, that in cases of *double* or *over-insurance*, every underwriter, first and last,

---

* *Lex Merc.* 112. See also *Molloy*.

laſt, ſhall be reduced proportionably, without regard to the order of their ſubſcriptions, or the dates of the policies; they being always allowed to retain one half *per cent.* on the deficiency of intereſt, as a conſideration for the trouble of keeping an account of the tranſaction, and cancelling the riſk *.

In Mr MAGEN's eſſay, we meet with ſome very judicious exceptions, which that intelligent author propoſes to make, from the Britiſh rule now laid down. Theſe are of ſufficient importance to deſerve notice, and they cannot be better ſtated than in the author's own words.

"When a ſpace has intervened between ſhipping and ſhipping, inſuring and inſuring, the inſurer who ſtood *alone*, for a while, expoſed to a riſk, upon the goods *firſt ſhipped*, ſhould not afterwards be put on a level with thoſe who underwrote later, and for whoſe riſk goods were later ſent aboard, or not ſent at all. At *London*, it is commonly inſiſted, that all who have inſured on goods expected for one and the ſame perſon's account, without particulariſing them, whether they be comprehended in one or more policies, and underwrote ſooner or later, ſhall contribute equally to any loſs, or receive a return of premium, if over-inſured; which would be juſt and right, if all the ſeveral policies had been ſigned before any goods went on board, but not otherwiſe."

"For

---

* To the ſame effect, ſee the Ordinance of *Rotterdam* No. 267.—In *Magens*, v. 2.

"For a proof of this affertion, let us fuppofe, that a perfon who expected goods from *Cadiz* in the fhip B, to the value of L. 5000, infured L. 2000 provifionally at the *London* Infurance-office, under the general term of *goods*, before he knew of any goods being fhipped; on his receiving advice, fome time after, that the value of L. 2000 was gone on board, he got L. 3000 more infured by the Royal Exchange Infurance-company: Now we maintain, that L. 2000 value of the goods *firft* fhipped, ought to be applied to the London Infurance-company, and not mixed with the goods loaded *laft*; for it is poffible, that the fhip B might have perifhed in the bay of *Cadiz*, with only the firft fhipped goods on board, and before the refolution was taken in *London* to increafe the infurance; confequently the Royal Exchange Company would not have been comprehended in the faid lofs *."

"When an infurance is intended to be done both *abroad and at home*, an explanation in the policies on both fides, *which* fhall have the preference, or ftand good firft, is a very material circumftance, becaufe this cannot be decided by the dates alone; for inftance,"—

"A perfon refiding at *Hamburgh*, had the value of 10,000 rixdollars, or L. 2400 Sterling to fhip for *Lifbon*, and had actually loaded, on the 1ft of *July*, to the value of L. 4000 rixdollars; whereupon he gave an order that day to his correfpondent

* *Magens*, 91.

OF DOUBLE AND OVER-INSURANCES.

respondent in *London*, to get insurance done for L. 1000 Sterling, without any limitation, either in premium or circumstances; and on the 4th of July, he got insured at *Hamburgh* the remaining L. 1400, or 17,500 marks, though he had not then shipped more than the first mentioned 4000 rixdollars, or 12000 marks; and the 5th of *July*, some circumstances occurred, that induced him to alter his design, and to resolve on shipping no more:—Now, the query is, Who ought to make a return of premium according to the sense of the *Hamburgh* ordinance?—To which we reply, That notwithstanding the underwriting of the *London* insurers must be of a later date than that of those in *Hamburgh*, who underwrote the 5th of July, because the order sent to *London* on the 1st of July, could not possibly arrive there before the 7th, and therefore the underwriting in *London* could not be before that or the next day; yet we are very clear, that the insurance in *London*, though later in date, ought to stand good before that made at *Hamburgh*; for, if *between* the 1st of July, when the order for insurance was sent to *London*, and the 4th of the same month, when it was made at *Hamburgh*, the ship had been burnt, this last mentioned insurance would not have taken place; and consequently that done in *London*, on the order given the 1st of July, must have borne the entire loss of these *first shipped goods*: Therefore we think it is evident, that the *return* of premium

mium ought to be made by the *Hamburgh* infurers*."

In Britain, as has been obferved, it is eftablifhed by modern practice, that a deduction fhall be made from the fubfcription of every different underwriter on the fubject infured ; and this, whether the error as to the amount of intereft has taken place in one, or in different policies; and whether in a *double*, or an *over-infurance*. But although it is clear that the affured ought to be prevented from receiving more than a juft fatisfaction for his lofs, yet it may be a queftion whether he can only fue each underwriter for his rateable proportion of the actual lofs; or whether he may, in the firft inftance, fue upon either policy, or any of the underwriters, to the whole extent of their fubfcription, leaving it to them to procure recourfe againft their fellows. And here we may diftinguifh between an *over-infurance* and *double* infurance.

An *over-infurance* takes place in every inftance where the affured procures infurance to a greater extent than his real intereft ; as when he is not aware of the precife value of his fhip or cargo ; when, after a policy is underwritten, the goods are *fhort-fhipped*, or a part of them, before the commencement of rifk, relanded : or where the merchant, afraid of not procuring, at one place, infurance equivalent to his whole property.

---

* *Magens*, 91.

property, fends an order to more places than one: It may happen either in one or more policies.

A *double infurance* is where the affured not thinking his fecurity fufficient from one policy, opens another on the very fame fubject. It occurs principally in two cafes; where an affured is doubtful of the *refponfibility* of his firft underwriters; or where he is doubtful whether the hazard undertaken in the firft policy be fufficiently extenfive.

The former is intended as a fingle fecurity for a number of fubjects, a part of which are difcovered not to exift. The latter is meant as a double or additional fecurity for one fubject. A merchant procures infurance on 40 *hhds* tobacco; it appears he had only 20 *hhds*; the infurance upon the other 20 is null, as upon a fubject that does not exift; this is an *over-infurance*. But fuppofe a merchant to have got infurance from A. B. on his cargo, which he knows to confift of only 20 *hhds*, he is afraid of A. B.'s infolvency; he therefore goes to C. D. and infures the very fame 20 *hhds*. Or fuppofe he has infured them, "warranted from capture," a war breaks out, and he wifhes to be more fully fecured; he therefore procures a fecond infurance on the fame merchandifes, without any fuch warranty; this is a *double infurance*.

A double infurance is a valid contract, to the effect of procuring an *additional fecurity* to the affured. It is meant, however, to conftitute *a fecurity*

curity only; there is but one subject lost, and therefore the assured can recover only one satisfaction. But it is a question, whether either set of underwriters shall be subjected to, or able to pay the loss; therefore each set *eventually runs the whole risk;* they are both therefore entitled to keep the whole premium.

Hence it follows, that, in a *double insurance,* the assured is entitled to exert his option, upon which of the policies he shall insist for indemnification, to the extent of the sums underwritten in either. And when the assured has recovered an entire satisfaction upon the one policy, the underwriters, who have paid more than their share of the real loss, have an equitable action against their fellow-insurers, to recover, according to their several proportions, in the same manner as if they had all been sued in the same action.

Newby *against* Reid.

It was ruled by Lord Mansfield, C. J. and agreed to be the course of practice, that, upon a double insurance, though the assured is not entitled to two satisfactions, yet, upon the first action he may recover the whole sum insured, and may leave the defendant therein to recover a rateable satisfaction. *Blackst. Reports,* p. 416. *After Easter,* 3. Geo. III. B. R.

In two cases, *Rogers v. Davis* [*], and *Davis v. Gildart* [†], (reported by Mr Park,)—*Rogers* had procured insurance first at *Liverpool*, and afterwards at *London*, in two separate policies from Newfoundland to certain ports in the West Indies. The defendant, *Davis*, an underwriter in the *London* policy, to the extent of L. 200, refused to pay above L. 124, upon the ground that the *Liverpool* insurers ought to bear a share of the loss. The plaintiff insisted that the defendant must pay the whole of his subscription, because the voyage had been altered on the other policy; and therefore the *Liverpool* underwriters could be subjected to no part. There was a verdict for the plaintiff, with liberty for the defendant to sue the Liverpool underwriters, if he thought fit.

Davis accordingly did so. *Gildart*, an insurer on the first policy, pleaded that the London insurance was a *reassurance*, and illegal, and that the plaintiff, having formerly neglected to state this defence, could not recover against him.

Lord MANSFIELD said, If there be here two securities for the loss, there can be no doubt that the assured may bring his action against either. And, if the whole money be recovered from the one, *he* may seek recourse for a proportion against the other. This is not a *reinsurance*, but a *double insurance*. The plaintiff had a verdict.

---

[*] *Mich. Vac.* 17. *Geo.* III.
[†] *East. Vac.* 17. *Geo.* III.   *At Guildhall.*

In *over-insurance*, however, the case is very different. There are not two securities for one subject; but an insurance on different subjects, a part of which are discovered to be nonentities. So far as respects the overplus, therefore, the contract is null; the insurer never runs *any* risk; and cannot retain the surplus premium. Above the extent of interest, he is under no obligation whatever. In cases of *over-insurance*, therefore, whether in one or in different policies, a deduction must, in the first place, be made, from different subscriptions; and then each underwriter may be sued for his proportionable share of the loss.

Although no man can recover more than once for the thing lost, nor more than its *real* or *estimated* value, yet the same, or different persons may secure a variety of different interests in the same thing. The following case relates to this point, and serves to illustrate the whole subject of double insurances.

Godin *v.* the London Assurance Company.

The material facts of this case, as stated by Lord Mansfield, in delivering the opinion of the Court, were as follows.

Mr *Meybohm* of *St Petersburgh*, had dealings with Mr *Amyand and Co.* of *London*, and was indebted, on the balance of accounts, to that Company. *Amyand and Co.* sent a ship to Mr *Meybohm* at St Petersburgh, to fetch certain goods.—*Meybohm* shipped

shipped the goods, and promised to send the bill of lading by the next post, but never did. Afterwards, in August 1756, *Amyand and Co.* got insurance from private underwriters, for L. 1100, on the ship, tackle and goods, " at and from " London to St Petersburgh, and back again to " London;" and of this sum L. 500 was declared to be on *eleven sixteenth parts of the ship*, and the remaining L. 600 to be *on goods*. Between the 26th August and 28th September 1756, Mr *Amyand* had insured L. 800 more with other private insurers, *upon goods only,* " at and from St " Petersburgh to London."

About the 27th of October, he received a letter from *Meybohm,* dated at *St Petersburgh,* 2d September 1756, mentioning what goods he meant to send them, directing them to get insurance thereon, and to place the goods and insurance to a particular account; specifying also some iron, which was for Mr *Amyand's* own account. On the 28th, 29th and 30th October, Mr *Amyand* accordingly got insured L. 900 more, with other private insurers, *on goods only,* " at " and from the *Sound* to *London.*"

Meantime, *Meybohm* having shipped the goods, indorsed the bills of lading to one Mr *John Tamez* in *Moscow,* who, on the 7th of October 1756, wrote to his correspondent, Mr *Uhthoff,* in *London,* to insure these goods: In this letter, he desires Mr *Uhthoff* to insure the whole, " that he, *Tamez,* might be sure in all events; " for he suspected, that these goods were intend-
" ed

"ed to be confligned by *Meybohm* to fomebody
"elfe, and perhaps might be infured by fome
"other perfon;" and he fays, they were tranf-
ferred to him in confideration of his being in
advance to *Meybohm* more than their amount.

This letter from Mr *Tamez*, with thefe directions to infure, was received by Mr *Uhthoff* on
15th November 1756; he accordingly applied,
through the medium of *Godin*, the plaintiff, to
the defendants, the *London Affurance Company*,
who, on the 16th November 1756, being appri-
fed that there might be another infurance, neverthelefs made that in queftion for L. 2316 *on the
goods*, "at and from the *Sound* to *London*." The
goods were loft in the voyage.

The queftion is, Whether the plaintiff is entitled to recover the *whole* lofs from the prefent
defendants, or only the *half* from them, and the
remainder from the underwriters of Mr *Amyand's*
policy?—A verdict has been found for the whole,
fubject to the opinion of the Court.

Firft, To confider it as between the infurer
and infured, the infurer fhould pay the whole,
having received a premium for the whole rifk.

But as infurance is a contract of indemnity
merely, a man cannot recover doubly for the
fame lofs; and if he infures the fame fubject
twice, either in his own name, or by the intervention of any other perfon, and recovers the
whole from one infurer, this infurer ought to
ftand

stand in the place of the insured, to receive contribution from the other who was equally liable.

It has been said, that the indorsement of the bills of lading transferred *Meybohm's* interest in all policies by which the cargo assigned was insured; and therefore *Tamez*, as the assignee of *Meybohm*, has a right to Mr *Amyand's* policy, and may recover the money insured; and even, he may bring *trover or detinue* for the policy itself; and hence it is urged, that he may have a double satisfaction.

But different people may insure different interests on the same bottom.—And here Mr *Amyand* had an interest of his own, distinct from that of *Meybohm*.—He had the ship; and he had a *lien* upon the goods, as a factor to whom a balance is due; and he had insured L. 1900 on both, *before he got any instructions from Meybohm*.—It does not appear, that even his last insurance in October was made *as agent for Meybohm*.

But supposing *Amyand* had made his insurance as factor for *Meybohm*; yet, even then, *Tamez* can never come against the underwriters upon *Amyand's* policy, for his own benefit; for Mr *Amyand*, as factor for *Meybohm*, is a creditor of *Meybohm's*, upon a balance of accounts between them; he is in possession of the policy, and has a *lien* upon all goods of his principal, so long as they remain in his possession. *Kruser et al. v. Wilcox et al.*

Besides,

Besides, the defendants underwrote, knowing that there might be another prior insurance, and took a premium for the whole risk.—It would be hard to make the plaintiff seek his redress from *Amyand's* underwriters, against whom it is doubtful, if he would recover at all, or, at least, without expence.—This is not, therefore, a *double insurance*, although there are two insurances; for these are not upon the same subject.

Mr *Tamez* is entitled to receive the whole from the defendants upon their policy; and they will have a right, in case he can claim any thing under Mr *Amyand's* policy, to stand in his place for a contribution to be paid by the underwriters to them; but still they are obliged, in the first place, to pay the whole to *Tamez*. Judgment for the plaintiff. 1. *Burr.* 490. *Feb.* 9. 1758.

So much with regard to the difference between policies, in respect of the assured's interest in the subject;—the distinction between wagers and proper insurances;—the restriction of gaming policies, with the means adopted to render those restrictions effectual;—the circumstances that constitute an insurable interest;—the mode of ascertaining the amount of this interest, by subsequent evidence, or by previous estimate:—and the effect of double and over-insurance.

Sect.

SECT. II. *In what Manner the Obligation of the Underwriter is affected by the Nature and Extent of the Loss.*

The amount to which the underwriter is liable, must obviously depend not only upon the extent of the *assured's interest*, but also on the amount of *damage and loss* sustained in the adventure.

And here two different kinds and degrees of loss may be distinguished: A *total* and a *partial* one. Concerning each of these, there arise several questions of considerable difficulty and importance.

ART. I. *Of total Loss and its Effects.*

Every insurance policy contains a clause, by which the assured are entitled "to labour for "the preservation of ship and cargo." But without any such express stipulation, there seems to lie an *implied* obligation upon the assured, to exert themselves, in every reasonable way, to the utmost of their power, in prosecuting and promoting the adventure insured. Insurance may be considered, in one view, as a sort of copartnership between the contracting parties, in which the underwriter entrusts to the assured the sole management of their common concern. The assured has the interest of others as well as himself, to manage; and it is an interest which the underwriter purchases for a valuable consideration. The assured is therefore bound to
strict

strict diligence: "Inactivity in such a case," says Valines*, " would be fraudulent."

But this obligation upon the assured, extends only a particular length. After damage has been sustained to a certain amount, there may be reason to conclude, that the adventure ought to be laid aside; that any farther prosecution of it would be productive of disadvantage to all concerned; that the expence attending it would go beyond the profit. In such a case, the assured must have it in his option to lay aside the voyage.

While he exerts himself in counteracting the effects of unfortunate accident, and incurs extraordinary expence, by endeavouring, with any reasonable prospect of success, to carry on the adventure, he has, undoubtedly, from natural equity, a claim for such expence against the insurer, *cujus in rem versum est*. There is not only room for a presumption of *tacit consent*, on their side, to such measures, but, in many cases, they may reap actual benefit by the assured's disbursements.

Several states have anxiously wished to strengthen and extend this claim. In the old Hamburgh policy, there was a clause empowering and desiring the assured to act for the insurers, " Be it with profit or loss." The Amsterdam and Stockholm policies give still more power: " That it shall be lawful for the assured to act " according to their judgment, to sell the goods
" saved

---

* 2. Comm. 99.

" faved, and diftribute the produce, without the
" infurers confent. The infurer fhall pay all
" charges, whether any thing be faved or not,
" and fhall not be allowed to object to the affur-
" ed's accounts, given upon oath." There is
perhaps danger in vefting the affured with a
power fo extenfive.

But after, from loffes and misfortunes, it is
reafonable to confider the voyage as defeated;
there appears no equity or common fenfe in fub-
jecting the infurers to any farther expence, to
which, if upon the fpot, they would not have
confented, and which can no longer be incurred
for their advantage. If the owner perfifts in the
adventure beyond a certain point, he feems to
be cut off from any claim for the additional expences fuch obftinacy may occafion. And it has
been doubted how far a court of law ought to
fuftain his action againft the infurers, to a greater
extent than the value of fhip and cargo.

It is held by *Valines*, that, although what the
affured doth for the recovery of fhip and goods,
is fuppofed to be done in name of the infurers,
and for their account; yet his reimburfement of
charges ought to be limited to the *value* of the
effects recovered, unlefs the infurers fhould give
him fpecial authority. 2. *Val. Com.* 99. This
appears a hard limitation: Perhaps it ought not
fo much to be confidered, what is the actual value recovered, as what there was a reafonable
profpect of recovering.

On the other hand, the assured, in such circumstances, when the continuance of the voyage would no longer be for his own interest; when it might, in all probability, be detrimental to the insurers themselves, may refuse to make any farther useless exertions in the prosecution of the adventure, and he may come upon the underwriters for the whole insured values, and for the expences already *usefully* incurred.

At the same time, as the insurers may perhaps entertain a better opinion of the adventure, and as there may still remain some part of the value of ship and cargo, he cannot retain these in his own hands, while he obtains complete indemnification, by his action upon the policy. He must make a *cession* or *abandonment* of his interest, to the underwriters.

As this power to *abandon*, in order to have recourse against the underwriters for a total loss, is calculated to favour the assured, who are, by that means, secured from the risks of a doubtful or unprosperous adventure; if the assured shall chuse to relinquish this advantage, they have it in their power to persevere in the voyage. It is in the option of the assured whether to abandon or not *.

It would be in the highest degree dangerous, however, and absurd, if the assured could abandon, without assigning the failure of the voyage as a reason for such conduct. It would be relieving him entirely from the obligation to diligence

* Foreign Ord.—*passim.*

gence and activity, and would put it in his power, whenever he chose, to convert into a total loss, what might otherwise be a partial one, perhaps of a trifling nature: Neither can he abandon in part; for a partial abandonment implies a partial, not a total loss.

The underwriter, it has been observed, cannot oblige the assured to abandon: But, surely, by offering to pay a total loss, he can prevent any further expences from being incurred, above the amount insured. I know not of any authorities, by which this point is clearly established; but the rule seems highly expedient, and highly equitable; as it puts the assured and underwriter on an equal footing.

Whatever entitles the assured to *abandon*, constitutes a *total loss*, with respect to the obligation of the underwriters. And here, as *damage* is a matter which admits of various degrees, it seems difficult to lay down a general rule, what precise degree of loss shall, in all cases, entitle the assured to relinquish the adventure. Upon this subject, *insurances upon interest, wager policies,* and insurances *on privateers*, or on a cruising expedition, may deserve a separate examination.

I. And, *first,* In common policies upon interest, whether valued or not, it seems to be established, that a *total loss*, or what shall entitle the assured to abandon, does not require the total wreck, capture, or destruction, in any other way, of the hulk of the ship, or of the cargo, in a literal sense. Were this the case, it would be impossible that a loss could ever be total; for scarce any wreck is so complete, but some piece of the ship, or some remnant of the cargo may be saved. But as the ship is insured with a view to the execution of a particular adventure, every loss may be considered as total, which completely disappoints the object of parties;—every loss which is so great as to *defeat the voyage*. In the words of Lord MANSFIELD, "If the voyage be lost, and not worth "pursuing,—If farther expences be necessary, "and the insurer will not, at all events, undertake to pay that expence, the assured may abandon*."

This principle may, in policies on interest, be illustrated in a great variety of cases, which, in England and Scotland, have been decided with uniformity, in favour of the assured's right to abandon, wherever such a damage occurs as is sufficient to *defeat the voyage*.

1. Suppose, for example, a ship has suffered *sea-damage*, and has incurred a *salvage* in order to preserve her from entire shipwreck; if the necessary *salvage* exceeds the value of the thing saved, the loss is total, and the assured may abandon and recover from the underwriters.

2. In the same manner, if the *freight* shall exceed the value of the goods saved, the loss is total: As may be illustrated by the following case:

BOYFIELD

* In *Goss v. Withers*. See below.

BOYFIELD v. BROWN.

Upon the execution of a writ of enquiry before Lord HARDWICKE *Chief Juſtice*, it appeared that the defendant was an inſurer to the extent of L. 200 upon corn, the value of which was L. 217; that the corn was ſo damaged in the voyage, that it ſold only for L. 67, and the freight came to L. 80. And upon this the queſtion was, whether as the freight which the plaintiff was obliged to pay exceeded the ſalvage, this was not to be conſidered as a total loſs.

And for the plaintiff it was inſiſted, that he ought not to be in a worſe condition, than if his corn had gone to the bottom of the ſea; for then he would have had no freight to pay; and now that the voyage has been performed, whereby the freight is become due, he has a right to apply the goods ſaved to diſcharge that. It was proved to be the uſage, where the goods ſaved exceed the freight, to deduct the freight out of goods ſaved, and make up the loſs upon the difference.

For the defendant it was inſiſted, that as his inſurance was upon the corn, and the whole did not periſh, he ought, in making up the loſs, to deduct the goods ſaved: But no inſtance could be ſhewn on either ſide, of an adjuſtment where the freight exceeded the goods ſaved.

The *Chief Juſtice* was of opinion, that, within the reaſon of deducting the freight, when the goods

goods saved exceed it, the plaintiff was, in this case, wherein they fell short, entitled to have it considered as a total loss. And the jury found for the plaintiff accordingly. 2. *Strange* 1065. *Mich.* 10. *Geo.* II. *

3. In the same manner, where there has been a *capture* and *ransom,* and the value of the subject recovered has fallen below the ransom, the assured may abandon.

Lane *and* Caswell *v.* Collier.

The ship *Reprisal* sailed from *Cape Fear*, with a cargo of pitch, tar, &c. for *Bristol,* and had got within an hundred and fifty leagues to the westward of *Cape Clear* in Ireland, when she was attacked and taken by three French ships bound for Newfoundland. They carried her thither, to a French port, called *Carpoon,* after having taken out all her men, and dispersed them aboard their own ships.

On their arrival at *Carpoon,* the captors took out all her pitch, (being two hundred and three barrels) some tar, what rice was aboard, &c.; and after detaining her about three or four weeks, they offered *Captain Gowen* his ship and remaining cargo, for 9500 livres, (about L. 425 Sterling)

---

* We shall afterwards have occasion to observe, that a different rule now takes place with regard to corn and similar commodities, in consequence of the N. B. introduced into policies since the date of this decision.

Sterling) which he accepted, and he left his son as an hostage for the payment of the ransom.

The ship departed from *Carpoon* for *Bristol*, and on her voyage met with very bad weather, which broke her rudder, and was forced to put into *Appledore* in Devonshire, (the first port they could make in safety) where the captain applied to *Mr Perkins* of Bristol, to whom he was consigned by *Jones* the owner; but *Perkins* refused to pay the ransom-money, or to have any thing to do with the ship or cargo. Upon which the captain came upon the insurers; and those who had insured on the goods empowered and desired him to sell the cargo for what he could, in order that if it produced more than the ransom, they might have the benefit; but the insurers on the ship would not intermeddle, or give any directions about it.

The captain returned to the ship, and sold that and the cargo jointly, for above L. 100 less than the redemption-money, after deducting charges, and he has been obliged to pay or give security for the remainder, to procure his son's liberty.

The plaintiff claimed a *total loss*; but the defendant pretended, that as part both of the ship and goods were saved, he is only subject to an average. The jury found a verdict for the plaintiffs. See *Lex Mercat. Red.* 282. *At Guildhall, Hil.* 1745.

4. In the same manner, where, in a policy upon interest, the voyage is defeated by a seizure

or detention, the assured may claim as for a total loss.

Storey v. Brown*.

Insurance on the *Sarah Galley*, " at and from " *London* to *Gibraltar*, and from thence to *London*, valued at the sum insured." The ship was chartered from *London* to *Gibraltar*, and thence to the *Nore*, to receive orders from the freighter; and the plaintiff was the sole owner of the ship. The ship arrived in *Gibraltar* in *June*, and was loaded with wines by the freighters correspondent for her return-voyage. At *Gibraltar*, the ship was seized by the *Salisbury* and *Solebay* men of war. The master was turned out of possession, and several of the sailors impressed. The captors proceed against the ship and cargo, as forfeited.—The ship was ordered to be restored, and was sent by the freighters correspondent, with a cargo for Dunkirk, where she was afterwards overset and lost. An action was brought by the insured; and though it was relied on for the defendant, that the ship was not totally lost, but had been delivered after the capture to the agent of the freighter, and by him sent another voyage; yet as the taking at *Gibraltar* was a breach of the policy in the voyage, *whereby the return-voyage was prevented*, a special jury gave the

---

* We cannot help observing, that the circumstances of this case seem to be very imperfectly handed down to us. It scarcely appears a well-founded decision.

the plaintiff a verdict for a total loss; and he had judgment accordingly. *Trin.* 18. and 19. *Geo.* II. 1746. *B. R.* Stated in the case of *Fitzgerald against Pole*, before the House of Peers.

5. In cases of *capture and recapture*, the cases in which we see the operation of the maxim, " that " a loss is total when the voyage is defeated," are still more numerous.

In the *first* place, in policies upon interest, the capture undoubtedly occasions a total loss, so long as it continues; but where a recapture takes place, it is to be considered, *whether, in the circumstances of the case,* the capture has had the effect to *defeat the voyage*: And the assured has it in his power or not accordingly to abandon.

Goss *v.* Withers.

There were two policies of insurance; one " on the ship *David and Rebecca*;" the other " on " *goods* aboard the said ship,"—" from *New-* " *foundland* to the *Straits*, or *Lisbon*." On the 23d December 1756, she was taken by the French; the master, mates and all the sailors, excepting an apprentice and landman, were taken out; and the ship was carried to France. She remained in the hands of the enemy eight days; and was then retaken by a British privateer, and brought into *Milfordhaven*. It was proved, that immediate notice was given by the assured to the underwriters, accompanied with an offer to abandon the ship to their care. It was also proved,

ved, that before the capture by the enemy, a violent ſtorm aroſe at ſea, which firſt ſeparated the ſhip from her convoy, and afterwards diſabled her ſo far, as to render her incapable of proceeding on her deſtined voyage, without going into port to refit.

It was alſo proved, that part of the cargo was thrown overboard in the ſtorm, and the reſt of it was ſpoiled, while the ſhip lay at *Mildfordhaven*, after the offer to abandon, and before ſhe could be refitted. And the aſſured proved their intereſt in the ſhip and cargo to the value inſured.

It was argued for the aſſured, 1*mo*, That this was a *total loſs*: For the ſhip was ſo long in poſſeſſion of the enemy, that the owners muſt be ſuppoſed to have loſt the hope of recovering it. *Grotius*, *l.* iii. *c.* 6. § 814. *De Jure Bell. et Pac.* And the owner was therefore diveſted of the property. *Dean v. Dicker*, 2. *Strange*, 1250.

2*do*, That here the aſſured have a right to abandon to the inſurers. That the cargo was periſhable, and part of it thrown overboard. The ſhip was in port in England, the hands all in France in priſon; and that the coſt of ſalvage would exceed the value of the thing ſaved.

For the inſurers, it was maintained, that this was only an average-loſs. That the owners were not *diveſted* of the property; for the veſſel had not been carried *infra præſidia hoſtium*. And that the circumſtances of the caſe were not ſuch as ſhould entitle the aſſured to abandon; particularly, ly, as, by the prize-act, 17. *Geo.* II. *c.* 6. the owner was entitled to recover his ship from the recaptor on paying falvage.

Lord MANSFIELD, in delivering the unanimous refolution of the Court, faid, That the *firſt* point, whether the owner was divefted of the property, was immaterial in this queftion between the infurer and affured. That queftion can occur in two cafes only; namely, *firſt*, between the owner and a neutral perfon, who has bought the prize from the enemy; 2*dly*, between the owner and a recaptor. In an action againſt the Hundred for a robbery, it is quite immaterial, whether the robbery *changed the property* of the goods or *not*. And the effect of a capture, with regard to the property of the ſhip, was a parallel cafe.

That, as to the *fecond* point, whether the infured had a right to abandon upon the 18th January 1757;—there was not a ſingle authority which did not fay, that the infured might abandon in cafe of the ſhip being *taken*. He may even abandon in the cafe merely of an *arreſt* or *embargo*. At one period, therefore, and during eight days, the affured was entitled to demand as for a total lofs. And the fubfequent recapture of the ſhip, *difabled to purſue her voyage*, cannot take away a right which the infured has acquired at the time of the capture. That there might be circumftances, in which the capture might be but a trifling hindrance to the voyage, and where it would be fraudulent in the owner to turn an average into a total loss, by abandoning. But *here the voyage was completely defeated by the capture.*

It was found, that the loss was total, in consequence of the voyage being defeated by the capture; and that the owner might abandon, to the insurers, the claim which he had against the recaptors, to have the ship and cargo restored to him. 2. *Burr.* 683. *Nov.* 1758.

HAMILTON *v.* MENDES.

It appeared in this case, that the ship *Selby*, in which the plaintiff had interest, was insured from Virginia or Maryland to London, by the defendant, to the extent of L. 100.—The ship valued at L. 1200 Sterling. That, after taking on board 192 hogsheads of tobacco, to be delivered at London, she sailed from Virginia on the 28th March, and, on 6th May, was captured by a French privateer, who took out six men of the nine on board, besides the captain, leaving only the mate and one man, and putting some French men on board. But the ship sustained no damage by the capture.

That on the way to a French port, the *Selby* was retaken by an English man of war on the 23d May, and arrived at Plymouth the 6th June following; when the plaintiff, in due course, intimated an intention of abandoning; to which the defender refused to accede, but offered to pay

pay the salvage and whole expence incurred. The whole cargo was afterwards delivered safe to the freighters.

The question, therefore, (submitted to the opinion of the Court) was, " Whether the plain- " tiff, on the 26th June, when he made the offer, " had a right to abandon, and can recover as for " a total loss."

Lord MANSFIELD, in stating the judgment of the Court, said, that the debate had turned upon the four following points.

First, Whether, by this capture, the *property was divested*, and the loss total for ever? But this question was immaterial between insurer and assured.

2*dly*, Whether, if the property was not changed, still a capture was a total loss? And here his Lordship agreed with the plaintiff, that a capture, *while it lasted*, inferred a total loss.

3*dly*, Whether the recovery of the ship, in the circumstances of the case, was not such as to change a *total* into an *average* loss? And here every case stood upon its own circumstances. That where the voyage was lost, or where the insurer would not undertake for all further expence incurred in the pursuit of it, the assured might abandon. But here the capture had occasioned only a slight temporary interruption to the voyage, and when the offer to abandon was made, the defendant had offered to bear the additional expence it occasioned.

4*thly*,

4*thly*, Whether the loſs having once been total, and a *right veſted* in the inſured to recover the whole upon abandoning;—that right could be *diveſted*, or taken from him by any ſubſequent event?

Every claim for *indemnity* (like the preſent) muſt, by the common law, be proportioned to the loſs at the time when the claim is brought. Whatever takes away the loſs, muſt deſtroy the claim in whole or in part.—Parallel caſe of a tenant who has *done waſte*, but *repaired* it before action.—Of a ſurety ſued to judgment, who has no need of an action for indemnity, if, before an action brought, his principal ſatisfies the debt. There can be no claim for indemnity without a *ſubſiſting loſs* at the date of the action.

Beſides, there was no right to abandon here *veſted in the plaintiff*. For the aſſured is never obliged to abandon. He has an election, and no right can veſt as for a total loſs, till he has made that election. He cannot elect before advice be received of the loſs; and if that advice ſhews the peril to be over, and the loſs removed, he cannot elect at all. *Roccus, not.* 204. *not.* 50. *Spencer v. Franco;—Pole v. Fitzgerald.*—The caſe of *Goſs v. Withers* had been miſunderſtood. It was there delivered, " That in caſe of the " ſhip being taken, the inſured might demand " as for a total loſs."—But it was in the circumſtances of that caſe," where a total loſs occaſioned
" by

" by the capture, continued till the time of a-
" bandoning or bringing the action."

The consequences of the plaintiff's doctrine were dangerous. The only reasons for abandoning in such circumstance must be, to load the underwriter with the fall of the market, or to take advantage of an over-valuation.—Both of which were unfair.

Therefore " the plaintiff can only recover ac-
" cording to the nature of his case at the time
" of the action brought, or (at most) of the offer
" to abandon."—The plaintiff here can only recover for an average loss. 2. *Burrow*, 1198. 8*th June* 1761.

Milles *against* Fletcher.

The ship *Hope*, and her freight, were insured from Montserrat to London. The ship, when proceeding on her voyage, was captured on 23d May, by two American privateers, who took the captain, all the crew, and part of the cargo out of her. The rigging was also taken away. She was afterwards retaken and carried into New York, where the captain arrived on 23d June, and taking possession of her, found that part of what had been left of the cargo (which was sugar) was washed overboard, that 57 hogsheads of what remained was damaged, and that the ship was leaky, and in such a state that she could not be repaired without unloading her entirely. The owners had no storehouses at New York, where

where the sugars could have been put while the ship was repairing, nor any agent there to advise and direct the captain. No sailors were to be had. The only method he had of paying the salvage, which amounted to the value of 40 hogsheads of sugar, was by sale of part of the cargo, or the ship. The captain did not know of the insurance. If he had repaired the ship, his expences would have exceeded the freight by more than L. 100. There was an embargo on all vessels at New York, till the 27th of December, and by the destination of his ship, she was to have arrived at London in July. Under these circumstances he consulted with his friends at New York, and resolved, upon their opinion, and his own, to sell the ship and cargo, as the most prudent step for the interest of his employers. The cargo was accordingly sold and paid for. The ship was also contracted for, but the person who had agreed to buy her, run away, and the captain left her in a creek near New York, and returned to England, where he arrived in the February following, and gave the plaintiff notice of what had been done, which was the first information he received of it, and the plaintiff immediately claimed as for a total loss, and offered to abandon.

The jury found a verdict for a total loss; and upon motion for a new trial, Lord MANSFIELD stated the law in cases of recapture as established by the two decisions, *Hamilton against Mendes*, and

and *Goss against Withers;* " that if the voyage is lost, and not worth pursuing, if the salvage is high, if farther expence is necessary, if the insurer will not, at all events, undertake to pay that expence, &c. the insured may abandon, notwithstanding a recapture." His Lordship applied these principles to the circumstances of the present case; and likewise shewed that the loss was not imputable to the captain, who had acted usefully and for the best. And the Court unanimously discharged the rule. *Douglas Reports.* 23d *June* 1779*.

EDMONSTON *against* JACKSON.

In September 1776, the ship *Duntreath*, belonging to *James Edmonston* was, by *William Jackson*, insured at L. 1300 " from Grenada to Florida, and from Florida to Grenada."

At the date of this policy, the ship had, in prosecution of the adventure, arrived at Florida. In returning, it was, on the 29th November, *taken* by an American privateer; *retaken* about five weeks after, and carried to Rhode Island. From Rhode Island it was carried to New York, and there underwent a thorough repair; the expence of which, with the salvage, amounted to L. 658. It remained at New York till January 1778, when it proceeded on its voyage to Grenada; but was *taken again* by the enemy, *retaken and carried into Grenada.* From the second

---

* See a different and malignant account of this decision in *Weskett.* p. 4.

second capture it had received no damage; but no person appearing at Grenada in behalf of the owners, it was appraised and sold, by order from the court of Admiralty there, and the proceeds, which amounted to L. 1045, deposited, after payment of the salvage and other charges, in the hands of the keeper of the Admiralty-register.

Mr *Edmondston* sued the underwriters before the Court of Admiralty in Scotland; 1*st*, for L. 658, as the amount of salvage and repairs at New York; and, 2*dly*, for L. 1300, being the whole sum underwritten on the policy, upon the supposition that the second capture, with the subsequent proceedings at Grenada, were to be considered as a *total loss*; and the assured offered to *abandon* the proceeds of the ship, lodged in the Admiralty-register of Grenada.

To the first conclusion no objection was made; but in answer to the second, it was objected, that the insured was entitled only to the salvage paid to the recaptors, and the other charges incurred in bringing the ship to Grenada. The Admiralty sustained the insurer's defence; and when the case came under the review of the Court of Session, it was pleaded by the insurer:

That as the first capture had been settled by parties, upon the footing of an *average* loss, the question at issue must depend on the events subsequent to the ship's departure from New York.

That

That where, notwithstanding a capture, a ship had arrived at her destined port, without any material damage, before action brought, or offer to abandon, the insured were only entitled to an *average* loss. That here there was no other damage incurred by the capture than the salvage due to the recaptors, which amounted only to an eighth of the value, and was no such loss as could entitle the assured to abandon. As for the subsequent appraisement and sale, these arose from the negligence of the owners themselves, who ought to have claimed the ship from the recaptors, upon its arrival at Grenada.

The Court laid out of view the events preceding the ship's departure from New York; and found,—" That in this case the assured was " not entitled to abandon on account of the se-" cond capture; and that the insurer was only " liable for a partial loss." *Fac. Coll. Feb.* 1. 1780.

The following cases, which are of a more miscellaneous nature, afford farther illustration of the same general principle.

Dacosta v. Firth.

A policy was underwritten by *Dacosta* the plaintiff, " upon any of the packet-boats that " should sail from Lisbon to Falmouth, or such " other port in England as his Majesty should " direct his packets appointed between Lisbon " and England, for one whole year, commen-
" cing

" cing 1st October 1764 inclusive, upon any
" kind of goods and merchandises whatsoever."
And it was agreed that the goods and merchandises should be " valued at the sum in-
" sured on such packet-boat, without further
" proof of interest than the policy; and to make
" no return of premium for want of interest;
" the policy being on bullion or goods."

The defendant Mr *Firth*, who was one of the assured, had an interest in bullion on board the *Hanover packet*, being one of the King's packets between Lisbon and Falmouth.

On the 2d of December 1763, this packet was totally lost off Falmouth, in a voyage between Lisbon and Falmouth : And the loss was adjusted in writing, under the policy, in the words following.

" Adjusted a loss on this policy, at L. 100
" *per cent.* the *Hanover packet, Captain Sherborn*,
" being totally lost at Falmouth.—Should any
" salvage hereafter be recovered, the insured
" promises to refund to the insurers whatever
" he may so recover, *in such proportion as the sum
" insured bears with the whole interest.* London,
" 23d October 1764, for *Richard Seward,—*
" *Michael Firth.*"

Da Costa accordingly had paid the total loss. In April 1765, the iron-trunk, which contained all the bullion, was fished up, and thereby all the bullion recovered, without any loss or prejudice whatever, and delivered to the defendant.

And

And now the underwriter purſues the defendant to recover back what he had paid him, upon this ground, that there has been no loſs incurred except the ſalvage.

The aſſured defends principally, that the queſtion had been already adjuſted as a *total loſs*. By the adjuſtment, he was only to repay for the goods recovered, " in the proportion of the ſum " inſured to the whole intereſt." It had happened, by accident, that his particular property had been recovered ; but that did not entitle the underwriter to retract his agreement. As the ſum inſured was not equal to the whole intereſt, he was not bound to refund the whole bullion recovered, but a certain proportion, equal to L. 48, 4 s. Sterling, which he paid into Court accordingly.

The Court agreed, that this was a policy of a peculiar ſort ; it was partly a wager policy, tho' within the exception of Stat. 19. *Geo.* II. *c.* 37. partly a valued policy, and fairly ſo ; and the inſurer having agreed to a total loſs, cannot now diſpute it.

The caſe of *Lewis v. Rucker ; Hamilton v. Mendez*; and *Goſs v. Withers*, were only, " that " where the *average* loſs appears *before ad-* " *juſtment*, the underwriter ſhall pay only the " *real* damage." Here there was a *total* loſs at the time of the adjuſtment. *Per Cur.* Judgment for the defendant. 4. *Burr.* 1. *Nov.* 1766.

CAZALET

Cazalet and others against St Barbe.

This cause was tried at the sittings after Hillary Term, 1786, when the following case was reserved for the opinion of the Court:—That the defendant underwrote the policy upon the ship *Friendship*, from *Wyberg* to *Lynn*, to the amount of L. 100. That the damages sustained by the ship in the voyage insured, do not exceed L. 48 *per cent.* which sum the defendant hath paid into Court.—That when the ship arrived at the port of *Lynn*, she was not worth repairing.

The question for the opinion of the Court is, whether the plaintiffs have a right to demand for a total loss.

WILLES, J.—The finding of the jury in this case, is decisive, that the damage did not exceed L. 48 *per cent.*—The case states, that the ship was not worth repairing; but no mention is made of what was her real worth; so that the remaining materials of the ship, if sold, may make up the difference between L. 48 and L. 100 *per cent.* There has been no loss, either of the ship, or of the voyage; but being an old ship, she suffered so much, that she was not worth repairing.

ASHURST, J.—It does not appear, that the vessel's not being worth repairing, arose from damage sustained in the voyage. The jury have found the loss to be partial.

BULLER, J.—There can be no abandonment without a total loss, either of the ship, or of the voyage;

voyage; but here neither is loft.—Judgment for the defendant. *Termly Rep.—Easter* 1786.

Manning *against* Newnham.

A Dutch ship, which had been loaded at *Surinam*, was brought into *Tortola* as a prize; and was insured with her cargo and freight " at " and from *Tortola* to *London*."—The insurer, to be free from particular average, valued at the sum insured, though particular parts of the cargo were likewise valued separately.

Soon after sailing, the ship sprung a dangerous leak, which obliged her to return to *Tortola*, and unload. It was found, that she was, in her present situation, unfit for a long voyage, and she could not be repaired, either at *Tortola*, or *St Thomas*.—She was therefore condemned, and sold for L. 1500 currency. There was no proof of any special damage to the cargo; but no ship could be had large enough to carry the whole of it. It was therefore sold at *Tortola* for a sum within L. 700 of the value in the policy. If it had arrived in *London*, the assured would have made a profit of many thousand pounds. He purchased two thirds of it, which, at the time of this action, were still on the sea, in other ships under insurance.

The defendant proved, That some of the damages were old, some recent. He contended, there could be no total loss, while so large a proportion

portion of the cargo remained, and was coming, under insurance, to Britain. And he endeavoured to excite a suspicion that the assured, who had taken the average loss on themselves, had converted a partial into a total loss; especially, as the insurers had no agents at *Tortola*, but the assured.—The jury found a verdict for the plaintiff, as for a total loss.—Motion for a new trial.

Lord MANSFIELD, after stating the evidence, said, This case had been left with the jury as an average loss, but they had found a total one. The Court had considered it much, and are all of opinion, that the jury are right, and that there is no bringing this case out of the general rule, which is, " if the *voyage*, in consequence of pe-" rils within the policy, be totally defeated, or " not worth pursuing, there is a total loss; but " if the voyage can still be pursued, the assured " shall not abandon." There are three subjects of the insurance; ship, freight, and cargo. The ship is totally unfit for the voyage, and irreparable; no other ships are to be found; must the assured wait till there are? It did not appear likely to happen soon. The same arguments apply to the cargo as to the ship. The voyage does not continue, because a part of the cargo is still at sea, on insurance, in other ships. If the voyage continued on these other ships, freight would be due *pro rata*. But it is admitted, the freight is totally gone. On all these grounds, we are of opinion, the voyage is totally lost; it is consonant

nant with all the cafes; and it is better to adhere to general rules than to introduce nice diftinctions.—Rule difcharged. *Trin.* 22. *Geo.* III. MS.

GAVIN KEMPT and Co. *againſt* GLEN.

Certain goods belonging to *Gavin Kempt and Company*, were infured, by *William Glen*, and others, on a voyage from *Clyde* to *Antigua*. The ſhip failed from *Greenock* on 18th Nov. 1782. On 7th December, ſhe was overſet in a gale of wind, but was foon brought to rights, and proceeded in the voyage.

On 24th January following, ſhe was *captured* by the enemy, was *retaken* on 26th; and, on 29th, arrived at the place of deſtination in *Antigua*.

Afterwards, in confequence of an application in behalf of the owners, the goods were fold by authority of the Admiralty. No regular appretiation was made; and from the account of fales, a very few articles appeared to have been damaged. But the prices fell more than 50 *per cent.* below the infured values.

The owners brought their action againſt the underwriters, before the Court of Seſſion, for a *total loſs*.

The underwriters urged, that the damage occafioned in the courfe of the voyage appears to have been very trifling, and not fuch as to entitle the aſſured to abandon. As to the fall of the prices below the values fpecified in the policy, that muſt have been the effect, either of fraudulent over-valuation, or a fall of the market, for neither of which the inſurers are reſponſible.—The aſſured were found not entitled to claim as for a total loſs. *Fac. Coll. June* 16. 1786.

6. When a voyage is defeated in this manner, it is no objection to the aſſured's right of abandoning, that he can recover a part of the value of the adventure, nor is that to be deducted from his claim againſt the inſurers. When the voyage is once defeated, he may come upon the underwriters in the firſt place, leaving them to recover what they can, at their own labour and charges.

Pringle *againſt* Hartley.

A bill in chancery was brought for relief againſt a verdict and judgment given in the Court of Common Pleas, upon a policy of inſurance, and to have an injunction to ſtay execution upon the judgment: The caſe appeared to be, that the ſhip inſured was taken by a Spaniſh privateer; and that after it had been carried *infra hoſtium præſidia*, it was retaken by an Engliſh privateer.—It was argued for the now plaintiff, who was the defendant at law, that although by the law of nations, the firſt capture of the ſhip, and its being *infra hoſtium præſidia*, had abſolutely diveſted the right of the original proprietors, yet that now, by the ſtatute made in the year 1740, it is otherwiſe, being thereby provided, that if the ſhips of our Engliſh merchants ſhould

should be taken by an enemy, and afterwards retaken by any of his Majesty's subjects, the right of the original proprietors in such ships should be reserved, on their paying one moiety of the value to the recaptors for salvage: Upon this it was argued, that the verdict and judgment are unjust, in regard that the whole insurance money is given in damages, when it appears that the plaintiff at law, upon payment of one half of the value of the ship, might recover it back, and therefore that one half of the insurance money ought only to have been given in damages; upon which the injunction prayed by the bill was moved for. On the other side, it was insisted that this was a right verdict, and that the insured was not to be put to the delay, expence and trouble, of ascertaining the value of the ship, in order to recover it back, upon payment of one moiety of the value to the captors: That for recovery thereof, the insurers might stand in the place of the insured, and make use of their names, as had been offered: That they did not pretend to oppose so much of the bill as sought this; but insisted that this could be no ground for granting the injunction prayed: That this point had been debated before Lord Chief Justice WILLES, upon trial of the issue at *nisi prius*, who had declared his opinion, " that " this right of *salvage* ought not to preclude the " insured from their recovery upon the insur- " ance, till the salvage should be settled; that
" the

"the defendants, the infurers, would be entitled "to ftand in the place of the infured, to make "what advantage they could of the falvage."

Lord HARDWICKE, Chancellor, being of the fame opinion, refufed to grant the injunction; and faid, that the damage in recovering the falvage, is as much a part of the infurance as the fhip itfelf. *Dict. Tr. and Com.* 148. *Mich.* 18. *Geo.* II. 3. *Atkyns*, 195.

II. With regard to *wager* policies upon a common mercantile voyage, there cannot, it may be obferved, be any *abandonment;* becaufe the owner has no intereft which he can cede to the underwriters. It is exceedingly material, however, in thofe infurances, to afcertain what is to be held as a total lofs; for they neceffarily contain a claufe "free of average, and without "benefit of falvage to the infurer." That is, the underwriter fhall be liable for no *partial lofs*, and fhall reap no benefit from any part of the fhip or cargo that fhall be faved: So that it is neceffary to fix what fhall be held a *total lofs*, in order to fettle what fhall be the criterion of the bett.

From this claufe, "free of average," in a wager policy, when taken literally, it may feem to follow, that no lofs can fall upon the infurer, except fuch a one as implies the total deftruction of the fubject infured; for example, the demolition

lition of the hulk of the veffel by fire, her foundering, or her being captured.

It does not, however, appear agreeable to the fpirit of the policy in fuch cafes, to confine the wager to the mere prefervation of the hulk of the fhip. It feems to be *the voyage* that is the fubject of the bett; and if the voyage is defeated from any of the dangers fpecified in the policy, it has been generally underftood that the wager is gained by the affured.

The Englifh decifions upon this fubject are extremely voluminous; particularly if we may be allowed to confider as authentic thofe which were produced and appealed to in the remarkable cafe *Fitzgerald v. Pole* before the Houfe of Peers. And we are the more difpofed to lay hold of thefe decifions now mentioned, becaufe the other adjudged cafes upon the fame point, are delivered with very little perfpicuity. The queftion itfelf may perhaps appear, fince the ftatute 19. *Geo.* II. againft wager infurances, rather a matter of curiofity than practical utility. But as wager policies are ftill legal upon *privateers, foreign fhips,* and *Spanifh trade,* it cannot with propriety be omitted. The decifions upon it may be laid down under fome arrangement.

1. And firft, where the *failure of the voyage* has arifen from feizure, detention, embargo, or circumftances of a like nature; the lofs is total, and the condition of the wager is incurred.

HANBURY

Hanbury *and* King.

Insurance on the *Anna*, at and from any port or place, or degree of latitude, wheresoever the ship might be on the 7th May 1741, till her arrival at London, *interest or no interest, free of average,* &c. This ship was a tender to the fleet sent to the South Sea under the command of Lord Anson, and proceeded to Juan Fernandez, where she was discharged the King's service: But being in want of stores to return to England, she was sold for the use of the fleet by the captain for L. 300, for which he received a bill on the commissioners of the navy, afterwards paid to the plaintiff, the sole owner, together with the freight, and all the sailors wages, to the time of the sale of the ship. The plaintiff and owner also received L. 6410 for the freight of the outward bound voyage, and L. 2590 as seven months freight, being the time computed the ship would have taken to return home. An action was brought on the policy; and although it was insisted for the defendant, that the ship had not been destroyed by any peril in the policy, but sold by the owner for the use of government; and that the insured had actually received a price and freight for her, as having performed her homeward bound voyage; so that if there was any loss in point of value, it would only be a partial and average loss, which was expresly not to charge the insurers: Yet upon all

all the above facts, (agreed between the parties) as the ship had been rendered incapable of performing the service for which she was fitted out, *viz.* attending the fleet in the South Seas, and home, the plaintiff recovered a verdict for a total loss, by a special jury, agreeable to the directions of the Court. *Mich.* 19. *Geo.* II. *B. R.* 1746 *.

Barclay *and* Collier.

Insurance on the *Ludlow Castle* man of war, from Jamaica to England, *interest or no interest, free of average,* &c. This ship was, in her voyage, compelled, by a storm at sea, to put into Antigua, where *Admiral Knowles*, being in want of a hulk for his Majesty's service, thought proper to convert the *Ludlow Castle* to that use.—The treasure on board her was brought home in the *Scarborough*.—The insured brought his action; and though it appeared in evidence that the ship was existing, it was determined, and by a special jury a verdict given accordingly, that the voyage from Jamaica being lost, the plaintiff was entitled to recover, which he did. *Mich.* 17. *Geo.* II. *B. R.* See *Fitzgerald v. Pole*.

In the following case, however, an opposite decision seems to have been given.

Spencer

---

* Appealed to in the case of *Fitzgerald v. Pole*, before the House of Peers.

Spencer v. Franco.

The plaintiff caused himself to be insured on the *Prince Frederick*, "from Vera Cruz to Lon-"don, *interest or no interest, free of average, and* "*without benefit of salvage.*"

There was a war between England and Spain, and Gibraltar actually besieged by the Spaniards. The ship was seized, by order of the Viceroy of Mexico, and turned into a man of war, called the *St Philip*, and sent as Commodore, with a squadron of Spanish men of war, to the Havanna. The defendants proved the signing of preliminary articles of peace before the seizure of the ship; and therefore insisted, that this seizure did not alter the property, and consequently the defendants were not liable; for if the property was not altered, this insurance made by the plaintiff, who had no interest, cannot bind, as nothing comes within the policy but a total loss; and though there be these general words in the policy, *restraint* or *detainment* by Princes, Hardwicke, *Chief Justice*, declared, 1*st*, That a *war* might begin without an actual declaration by proclamation; as, in this case, by laying siege to Gibraltar, a garrison town; 2*dly*, As a war may begin by hostilities only, so it may end by a cessation of arms; and these preliminary articles being signed before the seizure of the ship, and there being a cessation of arms, he
thought

thought the ship being taken afterwards, not to be a taking by enemies, unless the jury took the capture to begin from the time the arms were seized, which was before the articles, and that was left to the jury: 3*dly*, Supposing the ship not taken by enemies, *quære*, Whether this detention, for near the space of a year, was, in those sorts of policies, *interest or no interest*, a detention within the policy; or whether in such policies, the insurers are ever liable, but in case of total loss? And if so, this ship being afterwards restored, then he directed the jury to find for the defendant: This, he said, depended on the *custom* or usage among merchants.—The jury gave a verdict for the defendant, but did not declare upon what point; but they must be of opinion, she was not seized in time of war, and that, therefore, the policy being, *interest or no interest*, the assurers were not liable, because there was *no total loss*.—Lex Merc. Red. 287. At *Guildhall*, 15th Dec. 1736.

In the same manner, the rule holds, where a voyage has been defeated *by a capture*. There seems to have prevailed an idea, that a *capture*, by *changing the property of the subject*, inferred a total loss, although the vessel should be afterwards retaken: At least, it seems to have been considered as enough, that the vessel was *once lost*, to bring the case within the intendment of the wager; and it does not appear that so much attention was paid to the circumstance,

whether

whether the *voyage was defeated* by the capture, or not. In every case that occurred of capture and recapture, there seems to have been an elaborate argument, with regard to what constituted a capture, by the civil law, and by the customs of modern Europe; until Lord Mansfield, in the case of *Goss and Withers*, formerly stated, shewed, that the enquiry was of no consequence.

Dean v. Dicker.

This was an insurance on goods by the *Dursley* galley, *interest or no interest*, at and from *Jamaica* to *Bristol*. In her passage, she was taken by a *Spanish* privateer, and carried into *Mores*, a port in *Spain*; kept eight days, and then cut out by an *English* ship. And the plaintiff insisting, that this, though on goods, was to be considered as a wager on the bottom of the ship, brought his action as upon a total loss. The defendant insisted, that, by the statutes 13. *Geo.* II. *c.* 4. and 17. *Geo.* II. *c.* 34. this ship is to be restored to the owners, paying salvage, and consequently, this is only an average loss, and the plaintiff can only recover upon a total one. But the *Chief Justice* held, that, in this case, the plaintiff ought to recover; for this is a wager upon a total loss in the voyage, and here has happened one; for the being carried into port, and detained eight days makes one. And where a policy is *interest or no interest*, the provisions of the acts in the case of valued policies cannot take

take place. The act does not declare the property is not gone by such a capture, but only provides for restoring the ship to whom it belonged. He said it might be otherwise, where the recapture was before the ship was carried *infra præsidia,* or in the case of goods actually on board, and upon a valued policy. *Strange* 1250. 19. *Geo.* II.

WHITEHEAD *and* BANCE.

Insurance, " on the *Dispatch* galley, *interest or "no interest, free of average, &c.* from Jamaica " to Hull." In her voyage she was taken by a French privateer, and carried to Hamburgh; and after being twelve days in the hands of the enemy, she was taken by *Hurst,* master of an English ship, and brought to London, where she was adjudged to be restored to the owner, paying salvage. The owner sold the ship and paid the salvage. An action being brought on the policy, notwithstanding the ship had not been lost, but was sold by the owner, it was held to have been a loss of the voyage; and the special jury gave a verdict accordingly. *Mich.* 23. *Geo.* II. 1749. In *Fitzgerald v. Pole.*

DE PAIBA *v.* LUDLOW.

Action upon a policy of insurance, where the defendant insured the plaintiff, " *interest or no* " *interest,* against all enemies, pirates, takings at " sea, and all other damages whatsoever."—It appeared, that the ship was taken by a pirate of Sweden,

Sweden, and was in his possession for nine days, and then was retaken by an English man of war, and, after the suit commenced, brought into Harwich. The question was, whether in such case, the defendant was responsible,—And it was referred by the Chief Justice for the opinion of the Court; and after argument by *Serjeant Whitaker*, for the plaintiff, and by *Dr Henchman* for the defendant, it was determined for the plaintiff.—For though it was objected, that the insurer was only responsible where the plaintiff had a property, and that the custom of insuring *interest or no interest*, was introduced since the Revolution; yet it was said that such insurance was good: And the import of it is, that the plaintiff has no occasion to *prove* his interest, and that the defendant cannot controvert that. —And though the ship was here retaken, yet the plaintiff received a damage, for his voyage was interrupted; and the question is not, whether the plaintiff had his ship, and did not lose his property; but what damage he sustained.— *Comyns* 360. *Mich.* 7. *Geo.* I.

The reasonings in the following case are not supported by the verdict.

Daubony *v.* Read.

The *Broomfield* was insured by the defendant "at and from the Leeward Islands to Bristol, "*interest or no interest, free of average loss, and* "*without benefit of salvage.*"—The ship on her passage home was captured by a Spaniard; but after

after having been in possession of the enemy thirty-nine hours, she was retaken by the *Terrible* privateer belonging to Liverpool, and carried into Waterford, and afterwards to Liverpool; where, after a commission of appraisement from the Admiralty, she and her cargo were sold to pay the salvage due to the recaptors.— One of her former owners now bought the whole, and afterwards parcelled her out among several gentlemen at Bristol, to which place she was again ordered, and where she arrived. The plaintiff maintains this could not be an arrival agreeable to the meaning of the policy in question, under the circumstances above stated of her capture, recapture, appraisement, and sale, and with an entire new set of owners; he therefore thinks he is entitled to a total loss.

The defendant, on the contrary, argues, that this was no more than a bare capture and recapture, which, he says, has never been deemed a total loss. In reply to which, the plaintiff affirms, that this was still more; for the ship, after being retaken, was carried into Waterford by the privateer, kept some considerable time there, afterwards was carried into Liverpool, and there, with the cargo, appraised and sold to pay the salvage, and a new set of owners engaged, before she set out for Bristol, by which the whole voyage was altered and lost. Verdict for the defendant. *Lex Merc. Red. At Guildh. after Mich.* 1750.

Assievedo

Assievedo v. Cambridge.

Upon a special verdict, it appeared, that *Assievedo* had insured a sum of money, upon a ship called the *Ruth*, for a particular voyage, without having been at all concerned in point of interest. The ship was taken by the enemy, and kept in their possession for nine days, and then, before it was carried *infra præsidia*, it was retaken by an English man of war. The question was, Whether this was such a taking as should entitle the plaintiff to recover the sum insured against *Cambridge?*

It was argued for the plaintiff, that this was rather a wager than an insurance. That it is of no consequence, whether this is such a taking as will divest the property out of the owners, but whether the ship is taken. The case was compared to a man laying a *wager*, that he should not be robbed in going to such a place; he is robbed; but taking some persons along with him, pursues the robber, and recovers what he lost: here, though the money is recovered, yet the wager is lost. So if the wager had been, that such persons should not be married together; they are married, and afterwards divorced *præcontractus causa*; yet the wager is lost. It was said farther, that, without this exposition, *Cambridge* would have two chances, *viz.* that it is not taken, or that it is retaken; but *Assievedo* would have but one, *viz.* the taking. It was likewise argued, that, by the law of modern nations,

tions, such a capture as the present would divest the property; the vessel having been in the enemies possession for more than 24 hours.

For the defendant, it was maintained, that no taking but what divested the property could be supposed to entitle a person who had insured upon real interest, to recover against the insurer; and surely a wagerer, or one who procured himself to be assured without real interest, ought not to be put in a better situation. And as to what divested the property, the rule of the Roman law was resorted to, which required the vessel to be carried *infra præsidia;* as well as the practice of the Court of Admiralty in England *.

The Court seemed to be of opinion for the defendant. They thought that the plaintiff being found to have no interest in the ship insured, could make no difference in his favour; and, that the property was not divested by the capture, they held to be clear.

The case was not decided. *Lucas* 77. *Hill.* 10. *Ann. B. R.*

III. It remains to consider that peculiar species of insurance, which takes place upon *privateers*, or upon *cruising expeditions*, in which the ship generally is not insured for a certain specified course, but for a certain limited time. This, it has been seen, is the only kind of wager-policy at present permitted in this country, upon British ships.

By

---

* Terremoulin v. Sands. 1. *Raym.* 271.

By former practice, insurances on privateers were generally executed as wager-policies, "in-"tereſt or no intereſt,"—whether the aſſured had intereſt or not.

In theſe the ſame queſtion occurred, as with regard to common wager-policies; whether the underwriter is liable, in conſequence of the *cruiſe* (that is the adventure) *being defeated*, or merely in conſequence of the demolition of the hulk of the veſſel?

At a former period, the idea ſeems to have been, that, in theſe wager privateer inſurances, *the cruiſe* was the adventure; and whatever defeated the cruiſe within the date of the inſurance; whatever prevented the privateer from being in a ſituation to cruiſe at the expiration of the policy, implied a total loſs, and ſubjected the underwriters for the bett.

POND *v.* KING.

Upon a ſpecial verdict, it appeared, that the plaintiff had made inſurance upon the *Salamander* privateer, " intereſt or no intereſt, free of " average, and without benefit of ſalvage to the " inſurer." The defendant underwrote two ſeparate 100 pounds at different times on the policy. The ſhip ſailed on the 24th of December, and was taken by the French on the 2d of February following, after an engagement of more than an hour, with a much ſuperior force; and ſeveral of her men had been killed and wounded. Afterwards, 117 of her men, including the captain and

and all the officers, moſt of her ſmall arms, and the commiſſions, were removed into the enemy's ſhip, and carried into France; only 17 Engliſh being left on board the *Salamander*, of whom five ſoon after died of their wounds. The ſhip was in the enemy's poſſeſſion for three days, when ſhe was retaken by the *Hunter* privateer, Captain *Veale*, who put ſome men aboard, and kept her cruiſing with him for eight days. Afterwards, being prevented by wind and weather, from reaching a Britiſh port, Captain *Veale* carried her to *Liſbon*, where he took out of her two carriage-guns, and a quantity of proviſions for his ſhip's uſe. The captain of another privateer in company, likewiſe took out two other carriage-guns. By all theſe circumſtances, the cruiſe was totally diſappointed.

It was argued for the defendant, that a policy made *free of average*, cannot affect the inſurer but by a total loſs. And that a total loſs was prevented by the recapture.

For the plaintiff, it was argued, in the *firſt* place, that the property was diveſted by the capture; and, independent of this, that there had happened ſuch a damage as had diſappointed the adventure. The Court were unanimous in giving judgment for the plaintiff. *Lex Merc. Red.* 272. 21. *Geo.* II. 1. *Wilſon*, 191.

JENKINS *v.* MACKENZIE.

The plaintiff made an inſurance in London on the *Tryal* privateer, fitted out at Briſtol, " for
" two

"two calendar months, wherever the ship might
"then be, on a cruise, or in any port or place
"whatsoever or wheresoever; the said ship to be
"valued at—, *interest or no interest, free of ave-
"rage, and without benefit of salvage.*"

The privateer sailed from Bristol on the 29th May 1746, and, some days after, she was met by a French privateer of superior force, who attacked, and, after a brave defence, took her.

She had been in the enemies hands about eight hours, without their removing any of her men or stores, when Admiral *Martin*, with his whole fleet, appearing, retook the *Tryal*, and hearing of the gallant behaviour both of Captain *Jenkins* and his crew, they unanimously agreed to give up their salvage to them. The Admiral ordered the ship to be furnished with all necessaries, and sent a man of war sloop to see her safe into Bristol, where she arrived the latter end of June, between three and four weeks before the insurance expired.

These circumstances, the plaintiff thinks, entitle him to a total loss, as the voyage was overset, and the policy being *interest or not*, will admit of no average.

The defendant agrees to the last assertion; but for that very reason insists he has no loss to pay, as he is free from a partial one; and there can be no total one, where the ship is arrived, and (as he insists) might have been fitted out again before the limited term of two months expired, had the owners not determined the contrary:

And

And besides, though the ship was taken, yet as she was never carried *infra præsidia* of the enemy, or was so taken as to be beyond a possibility of a recapture, and hath returned to Bristol, so long time the two months expired as was sufficient to refit her in, the defendant supposes that the neglect of the owners ought not to be imputed to the underwriter; more especially as several ship-builders and merchants attended to prove there was time enough for the repair. Verdict for the plaintiff. *Lex Merc. Red.* 283. At Guildhall, *Mich. Term* 1749.

Jalabert *and* Nevill *v.* Collier.

The *Dartmouth* galley being fitted out as a privateer in October 1744, sailed on a cruise; and the plaintiffs being concerned in her, got insurance made on their part for one calendar month, of which the defendant underwrote L. 200. After being out two days, she fell in with two French men of war, and, after a very gallant defence, was taken. A part of her crew, however, taking advantage of circumstances, contrived to escape with the vessel from the Frenchmen, and, in two days after, got safe into *Dartmouth*. Upon her arrival there, she was refitted by the owners, and sailed on another cruise. After this the ship was kept insured from month to month, and the defendant underwrote several subsequent policies on her, without any demand having been made upon the first; although he

settled

settled a loss upon her, in relation to a policy, six months after.

The plaintiffs, however, have now claimed the loss, as the taking of the ship entirely overset the cruise; for she could not be refitted and sail on another, before the expiration of the month for which she was insured.

But in support of the contrary, it is alleged by the defendant, and confirmed by the opinion of several very considerable merchants, that this could not be counted a total loss, more especially as it is not on a cruise; the words of the policy being, "to be insured lost or not lost to *any ports or places* for one calendar month." And besides, the ship was so far from being a total loss to the owners on the first risk, that she afterwards met with very great success, by taking a rich prize. And if this doctrine, offered by the plaintiffs, had taken place with respect to insurances made for a time, every coalier might bring this as a plea; as they are always insured on these terms; though it was never apprehended that every little accident which happened within the time, and obliged them to refit, was deemed a total loss.—The plaintiffs were nonsuited, because unprepared to shew the impossibility of her being fitted out again before the expiration of the insurance. *Lex Mercat. Rediv.* 270. *Trin.* 1749. *At Guildhall.*

There appears, however, something unreasonable, not to say absurd, in considering a privateering

teering expedition in the same light as any other adventure. It is impossible to say, that a *cruise* has been defeated, merely because, at the termination of the term specified in the policy, the privateer is not in cruising trim.

Suppose two or three days before the term expires, she takes a very rich prize, after an engagement; and she finds it necessary to go into port to refit. But the damage she has sustained is very inconsiderable, compared to the value of her prize: Will it be said, that her adventure has been unsuccessful, or that her cruise has failed, merely because she happens to be repairing when a particular day arrives? This would carry the absurdity along with it, of allowing the assured to abandon, in consequence of success, and not of ill fortune. Had the privateer met with no prize, no repair would have been necessary. But it is a very strange interpretation to call that a failure, the obtaining of which was the very object of her voyage.

In fact, there can be no means of ascertaining with accuracy, what defeats a cruising expedition, except the demolition of the hulk of the vessel.—For her being confined to port affords no rule whatever.

This has been found accordingly in the following remarkable case.

FITZGERALD *v.* POLE.

Peter Joyce being a part owner of one moiety of a ship, called the *Goodfellow* privateer, together

ther with the other owners, fitted her out to cruise. Mr *Joyce* being himself the master of the ship, and abroad, employed Messrs *Fitzgerald* to get insurance done for his interest and use, in which *Pole* the defendant underwrote for L. 100.

The purpose for which the *Goodfellow* privateer was fitted out and employed, was totally defeated by a mutiny of the sailors on board, their desertion from her, and carrying off the fire-arms belonging to the ship, within the term of four months, for which the insurance was made.

In an action upon the policy, it was argued for the plaintiff, that the original nature of insurance was, no doubt, a contract of indemnity, by which the assured was only to be reimbursed to the extent of his real loss. But that in the subsequent invention of *valued policies, free from average*, and those, *interest or no interest*, it is the performance of the voyage or adventure, in a reasonable time and manner, and not the bare existence of the ship and cargo, that is the object of the insurance, and so it had often been adjudged. That, in an insurance on a ship, as a " privateer, to cruise during a limited time," the cruise is the adventure; and the ship's capacity to cruise, notwithstanding the perils of the sea, is the subject-matter of the insurance; and this had been found by several decisions.

It was answered for the defendant,

1*st*, That the insurer being, by the terms of the policy, free from all average, the plaintiff could

could not be entitled to recover, but in case of a total loss; and the ship being found by the special verdict to be in good safety, at her proper port, at and after the end of the four months, for which the insurance was made, there could be no such loss.

2*dly*, The ship is alone insured, and not the cruise. It is the ship alone that is repeatedly *expressed* in the policy, to be the thing insured. Besides, it must be the subject itself expressed, and not any consequential benefit arising from it, that is *meant* to be insured; for such consequential benefit is uncertain, and incapable of being estimated. But,

3*dly*, Supposing the cruise to be the thing insured, yet there is here no loss of the cruise, the vessel having cruised till within a fortnight of the whole time, and taken a very rich prize, of the value of L. 4200 Sterling. And,

4*thly*, Supposing the cruise to be the thing insured, it is neither averred in the declaration, nor found by the verdict, that *Peter Joyce* had an interest in the *cruise*, but only that he had an interest in the *ship*.

The Court of King's Bench gave judgment for the plaintiff; upon which a writ of error was brought in the *Exchequer Chamber*; and after twice arguing the case, the judgment was unanimously reversed. The plaintiff brought his appeal in the *House of Peers*; but the House of Peers affirmed the sentence of the Exchequer Chamber.—5. *Brown's Par. Cases.*—131.

Since

Since this decision, in every case where insurance on privateers is made *free of average*, it is understood, that nothing can be recovered, unless the ship be *taken,* or *totally wrecked or lost,* or *adjudged irreparable, i. e.* not *sea-worthy,* or *not worth the expence of repairs.*

Hitherto of privateers insured "*free of average.*" But of late it has become usual, at least in Scotland, and it is believed likewise in England, to insure them on a common policy, expressing, in the description, that the vessel is a private ship of war, *with liberty to cruise against the enemy.* And this last expression is the chief peculiarity in those insurances.

In this case every kind of damage is provided against; and the loss is never reckoned total, unless the ship be adjudged *not sea-worthy,* or not *worthy of the expence of repairs.* In short, a privateer is in the same situation with any other vessel insured by a policy upon interest.

It is obvious, that the insurance " interest or " no interest," which has, at a former period, given rise to so many intricate cases, is a very improper one, and that it affords much temptation to fraudulent losses. It has been confined by the Legislature to privateers only. But there is room to hope, that, even with regard to them, it will, in a short time, from the inconveniencies attending it, be entirely laid aside.

ART.

ART. II. *Of partial Loſs, and its Effects.*

The effect of a total loſs is, as has been ſtated, to put it in the option of the aſſured, whether he ſhall perſevere in the adventure, or abandon the ſhip and cargo to the underwriters, and ſue them for the whole amount of their ſubſcriptions, ſo far as theſe do not exceed the intereſt. A partial loſs is attended with no ſuch conſequences. In this caſe the aſſured is bound, with induſtry and attention, to perſiſt in the voyage; and he is entitled to claim indemnification of the ſpecial damage only, which has actually been ſuſtained.

What conſtitutes a *partial loſs*, is not a matter of any doubt; but in what caſes the inſurer ſhall be ſubjected to it. And this depends not only on the ſtate of obligation between the aſſured and underwriter, but upon the mutual relations ſubſiſting between the different part-owners of ſhip and cargo, who are intereſted in the preſervation of one common ſubject, and in the promotion of a joint adventure. On ſome occaſions, every individual owner muſt bear the damage incident to his own property. In other inſtances, equity points out that the loſs ſuſtained by individuals ought to be repaired by a general contribution of all concerned. In the former caſe there is nothing ſingular. But, in the latter, the circumstances which give rise to such a contribution,—the situations in which it takes place,—and the principles by which it is regulated, open a very curious and important field of enquiry. The regulations and practice with regard to this subject, form accordingly a very considerable branch of the law of mercantile nations.

This enquiry, it is true, does not strictly belong to insurance. It is an investigation with regard to the obligations between joint owners, or those who are concerned in a common adventure; and affects the insurers in a consequential manner only, so far as they may have undertaken to indemnify this or that particular proprietor, who may be subjected to, or relieved by a contribution. The whole observations that occur, however, upon the branch of the subject now under consideration, depend so much on the doctrine of contribution, or AVERAGE, that it here becomes necessary, however digressive it may appear, to examine the principles and rules which regulate the distribution of partial loss among the different parties concerned in one common adventure.

* * * * *

DIGRESSION, *concerning* AVERAGE; *or the Division of partial Loss among the different parties concerned in a common adventure.*

1. The laws of society do not, in general, attempt to correct the inequalities of accidental situation. The ruinous loss, which one man has incurred, may be the subject of pity and sympathy; and the success of another, when disproportioned to the exertions which have produced it, may excite discontent; but the public will not consider itself as entitled to interfere; or, by restoring them to the level of their different merits, to remedy the caprice or injustice of fortune. But this observation does not hold universally. There are certain cases in which the feelings of mankind are interested to afford not only pity and sympathy, but redress to the sufferer; and in which the judge is disposed to reduce parties to their proper equality of situation. This happens wherever, from mistake, or by accident, *the loss of one man has been converted to the gain of another.* The great equitable maxim of the Civil law is, " *Nemo debet* " *locupletari aliena jactura.*—No person should be " allowed to reap advantage by another's loss *."

The operation of this principle may be exemplified in a variety of situations which are daily calling

---

* *Kames' Pr. Equity.*

calling for the intervention of courts of equity. Thus, where a person possessing a house or lands *bona fide*, lays out money in the reparation or melioration of the subject, which is afterwards recovered by the true proprietor;—the latter is bound to indemnify the *bona fide* possessor for his improvements; otherwise he should be benefited by the other's loss.

In order to found a claim of *restitution*, however, to the suffering party, two circumstances are necessary;—that his loss has been *directly converted to the other's gain*;—and that this *gain admits of a precise estimate*. It is not every loss upon one part, productive of consequential advantage to others, that can be the foundation of an equitable claim of this nature. The loss of one man's goods by shipwreck, increases the demand for those of his neighbour, and enhances their market value; yet the sufferer has no claim for indemnity. The connection between the loss and gain is not sufficiently immediate; the one is too remote a consequence of the other; and the amount of advantage which the damage may have occasioned, cannot be ascertained with sufficient accuracy.

Unless there be an *actual subsisting gain* upon the one hand, as well as a loss upon the other, there can be no room for *restitution*. Where, therefore, one man's money has been directly converted to another's emolument, but the advantage has, before action brought, been intercepted

cepted by accident, the suffering party cannot recover upon the maxim above stated. Altho' the one is a loser, the other is not enriched; and to sustain action, would be only transferring, not removing the situation of hardship.

2. But there is another principle upon which one man who has acted usefully for another, and has thereby incurred a loss, is entitled to indemnification, although the benefit intended should be afterwards intercepted by accident. Every man who acts *usefully, with a view to the advantage of another, and with the view of remuneration,* has a right to a *recompence* for his labour bestowed, and expence incurred.

Thus, where a man's house is in danger of falling or becoming ruinous, and, in his absence, his neighbour interferes, and incurs expence in repairing or supporting it; the person who has acted in this friendly manner, is entitled to indemnification for his expence and his labour, altho', before the owner could reap any benefit by it, the house should be demolished by fire or earthquake.

The same holds in every case where one person acts properly as a *negotiorum gestor* for another. Here a man takes upon himself the office of a factor, though without an express commission, in a case where there is no opportunity of applying for that commission; and, if there were, where nobody in his senses would refuse to grant it. He trusts, that the person for whom he acts will

will not refuse that remuneration, or *recompence*, which, if he could have been applied to, he certainly would have promised.

3. To one or other of the principles now mentioned, all those cases may be reduced, in which the owners of ship, or of cargo, are not singly subjected to the damage sustained by their own property, but in which the loss of individuals must be made up by a rateable contribution of their fellow-adventurers. Such a distribution of loss is, in mercantile language, denominated *average*, and the situation which admits of it, *an average loss**.

The great and leading illustration of *average loss*, occurs in the case of a *jettison*. When, in a storm, a part of the goods are thrown overboard, to save the ship, or the rest of the cargo, the proprietors of the subject preserved must contribute to make up the loss. The one set are gainers by the preservation of their property, which, but for the jettison, would, in all probability, have gone to the bottom. Equity therefore seems to require, that when two parties are so intimately connected in a common adventure, the one should not be allowed to derive a gain from the other's misfortune.

The

---

* The English word HALF corresponds to a word of a similar sound in all the *Teutonic* languages, pronounced with the *l* mute. (See *Johnson's Dictionary*.) Hence the word HALVERS, *partners*, (q. *Halfers*,) and HALVERAGE, *partnership*.—HALVERAGE, or AVERAGE LOSS, therefore, means a *partnership loss*.

The application of the principle in this inſtance was very well underſtood in ancient times; and the regulations of *Rhodes* with regard to it, were adopted into the *Roman* law, and make a diſtinguiſhed figure in *Juſtinian's* compilations.

" By the law of *Rhodes* it was provided, that if, to lighten a ſhip, a jettiſon is made, that which is thrown away for the general ſafety, ſhall be refunded by a general contribution." *l.* 1. *Dig. ad Leg. Rhod.*

On the other hand, where thoſe principles above ſtated, are not applicable, no contribution takes place; where the loſs, upon one ſide, is not directly converted to the gain of the other party, there can be no claim of *reſtitution;* and where the expence or trouble has not been incurred uſefully, with a view to another's benefit, and in the expectation of remuneration from him, there can be no title to a *recompence.*

" If, in order to lighten the ſhip, a part of the goods are unloaded into a boat, and are thereby loſt, while the ſhip is preſerved;—the value of the goods in the boat ſhall be refunded by contribution. On the other hand, if the boat is preſerved, and the ſhip loſt, the goods in the boat ſhall not contribute: For, in the former caſe, the goods were hazarded in the boat, in order to ſave the ſhip; but in the latter caſe, the loſs of the ſhip had no effect upon the ſaving of the boat*."

Caſe.

* *Ad Leg. Rhod. l.* 4. Foreign Ord. *paſſim.*

Case.—The plaintiff being one of the owners of a ship, loaded on board her 210 tons of oil, and the defendant, 80 bales of silk, upon freight. The ship was pursued by enemies, and forced into a harbour, and the master ordered the silk on shore, being the most valuable commodity, (tho' they lay under the oils, and it required a great deal of time to get at them.) The ship and oils were afterwards taken, and the owner of the oils brought his bill to have contribution from the owner of the silks; and although it was admitted, that if goods were thrown overboard, in stress of weather, or in danger, or just fear of enemies, in order to save the ship and the rest of the cargo, that which is saved shall contribute to a reparation of that which is lost; and the owners of the ship shall contribute in proportion; yet, in this case, the loss of the oils did not save the silks; neither did the saving the silks lose the oils; and the bill was dismissed accordingly; which was confirmed in the House of Peers. *Shower, P. C.* 18. 19.*

The same holds, if a part of the ship has been cut away, and thrown overboard with a view to the preservation of the cargo. "If the mast is "cut, that the ship with the cargo, may be free "from

---

* This judgment may perhaps be objected to, upon the ground, that the master had lost the oils by a partial attention to save the silks. But, in all probability, the oils were too bulky to be carried ashore; therefore, "the saving of "the silks did not lose the oils."

" from danger, the principle of contribution shall
" operate." *L.* 5. § 1. *ej. tit.* ; *l.* 2. *ej. tit.*

But jetson is not the only case in which there is room for a contribution. Whenever one party incurs a loss, which is directly productive of another's gain, or where labour and expence is usefully incurred, with a view to another's advantage, and from the prospect of remuneration, the same rule holds.

" If, to avoid or escape an enemy," says *Magens*, " a ship anchors in an open road, under
" the protection of some castle, and there parts
" her cable, it undoubtedly ought to be considered as a gross average."

At the same time, the furniture and appurtenances of a ship are supposed to be sufficient to stand out against the ordinary run of accident at sea; and if, from a failure in this respect, or from the mere violence of a storm, the ship suffers damage in her hards and rigging,—or from the fault of any party concerned;—such damage having been incurred with no view to the preservation of the rest of the concern, will fall upon the individual proprietor *.

In the same manner, where a loss is incurred by advance of money to *ransom* a ship or cargo. " If
" a ship is *ransomed* from pirates, *Servius, Ofilius,*
" *Labeo*, all think that contribution is due. But
" what a robber carries away is lost to the *pro-*
" *prietor ;*

---

* See *Magens pass. l. Si faber incudem. ff. ad Leg. Rhod.*
Ord. Spain. No. 80. *Of Antwerp*, No. 27.

"*prietor;* nor is contribution due to him who ransoms merely his own property." *L.* 2. § 3. *D. ad Leg. Rhod.*

Holt, *C. J.* said, "That it seemed just and reasonable, that the owners of goods ransomed, ought to pay the redemption. If a *pirate* should take the ship and goods, and the master redeem them, the owners shall make him satisfaction; and much more when taken by an enemy." In the case, *Tranter v. Watson*, Raymond, 931.

"If a pirate takes part of the goods *to save the rest*, contribution is due." *Sir F. Moore, fol.* 297, *Hicks v. Pilkington**.

The same thing ought to hold as to the redemption of a *ransomer*, who has bound himself as an hostage for the ransom of ship and cargo.

A similar rule must undoubtedly be enforced, where a *salvage* has been paid in consequence of a capture and recapture. The cases are perhaps few, in which a *salvage* incurred for the recovery of goods *from shipwreck*, can be for the benefit of the adventure at large; or, indeed, of any other person than the individual proprietor of the effects saved. Yet, in any such instances, there can be no doubt that the same equitable principles are applicable; and that all those who have reaped an advantage by the *salvage* paid, or to whose benefit, with the view to a recompence, it

---

* *Ord. of Bilboa,* § 9.

it was directed, must be liable in contribution accordingly.

Another instance may sometimes occur, in what is called *demurrage*; where, in consequence of *seizure, detention, embargo,* extraordinary expence of mens victualling and wages has been incurred; and this appears to have been done for the general emolument. Such expences, however, are in most cases understood to be for the sole benefit of the ship-owner.

It seems unnecessary to multiply examples upon a point so clear. In consulting the foreign ordinances, cases may be found in which the principles may be misapplied; but no dispute can arise with regard to the principles themselves. And it seems to be fully understood, among all mercantile nations, that the rule of law, which enforces *average*-contributions, shall be equally comprehensive with the general maxims of equity on which it is founded.

4. It should seem, in most cases of partial loss, that both the principles above mentioned concur in founding a contribution. If the loss of one is productive of actual advantage to the rest, they are liable to him in *restitution*, because they have *reaped a gain*. If that gain has been intercepted by subsequent accident, they are liable in a *recompence*, because their advantage was the object and view of their neighbour's expence or labour, and he had trusted to them for indemnification. Thus, in cases of *ransom*, of *salvage*, and of *demurrage*, the labour employed, and expence incurred

curred, with a view to the benefit of others, founds a claim to the losing party, although the ship should be wrecked at any future stage of the adventure, or the owners prevented in any other manner from reaping the advantage intended.

But there is one, and that the most important source of contribution, in which no indemnification takes place, unless a gain be actually reaped.—In cases of *jetson*, no contribution is due in order to make up the loss of him whose goods have been thrown overboard, unless the ship be actually saved *.

One reason of this seems to be, that the owner of goods made use of in a *jetson*, really abandons nothing, except what, independent of the jetson, he would have lost at any rate. If the ship be lost notwithstanding the jetson, the other parties not only reap no advantage, but *he incurs no loss by the jetson*. It is only where the ship is saved that he can be said to sustain a loss comparatively with the other proprietors of goods. But the *ransomer* risks a separate sum of money, totally distinct from his interest in the adventure; and if that sum be not refunded, he incurs a loss, whatever comes of the vessel.

There is another, however, and perhaps a more important reason of this difference; a reason which goes so far as to show that, in cases of jetson, it is the principle of *restitution* solely that operates, and not the principle of *recompence*; and consequently, that it is not only necessary there should

* See Voet *ad l. Rhod.* § 15. *Lex Mercat. Rediv.* 136. Foreign ord. *passim*.

should be a loss incurred on the one side, but an actual gain resulting from it on the other.

From the circumstances already stated with regard to these two principles of *restitution* and *recompence*, it is obvious that the latter of these, which is productive of obligation upon men, although they are not *actual gainers*, is much less extensive than the other. It proceeds upon the idea that one man acts *with the view to another's advantage;* from which circumstance he is entitled to trust for remuneration to the gratitude of him whose benefit was in view. In case of ransom and salvage, it was observed, the ransomer exposes to risk a separate subject, totally distinct from his share in the adventure. In cases of *jetson*, he merely abandons what he must have lost at any rate. But besides this, he seems, in the former case, to intend the advantage of others; in the latter, his own benefit merely. The ransomer, who exposes a sum of money to hazard, in order to recover the goods of others, might have avoided that risk, by ransoming merely his own property. And so far he exerts himself as a *factor* for others, and is entitled to trust to them for remuneration. But in a storm, no man can separate his own property from that of others, or avoid his single share of the common danger. He throws his goods overboard, therefore, with the effect perhaps, ultimately, of saving the whole ship, but with the immediate view of benefiting himself. He
has

has no title to be confidered as acting *factorio nomine*, from any confequential advantage that might have followed to others; and his only claim for indemnification arifes from the circumftance, that his lofs is productive of an *actual gain* to his co-adventurers.

The influence of thefe reafonings appears in fome queftions afterwards to be ftated upon the fubject of *jettifon*. The general point, that, in cafes of jetfon, no contribution is due unlefs it be the means of faving the fhip from the impending danger, is too trite to require illuftration*.

5. From the principles above ftated, it may be eafy to form a judgment of the manner in which a partial lofs muft be diftributed among the different parties concerned in a common adventure, according to the extent in which they have been enriched, or in which their benefit has been intended by it.

Contribution, or *average*, is accordingly of two kinds; *general* and *particular*.

General average is that contribution which takes place on occafion of damage incurred for the general intereft of the adventure at large; and it is borne by the proprietors of both fhip and cargo, according to the proportional value of each. *Particular average* is the contribution for loffes which have had a refpect to the advantage

---

* See *Dig. ad L. Rhod. For. Ordin. paffim.*

tage of the ship alone, or cargo alone; and it falls upon the one or other singly *.

Of *general average,* an example occurs, where a ship and cargo has been *ransomed* from an enemy. In the same manner, where a vessel has been taken and recovered, the *salvage* due to the recaptors being an expence incurred for the general benefit, must be refunded by a general contribution.

But the situation which affords the most illustrious examples of the operation of equitable principles, is where a *jetson* has taken place. In the exigency of a storm, pursuit by an enemy, and, in a variety of situations which may be figured, it must often become expedient that a part of the property should be thrown overboard, or otherwise exposed to additional danger, in order to save the rest. In these cases, if the vessel be saved, the proprietors of the whole

---

* There is another sort of claim which owners of ship have against the proprietors of cargo, that likewise goes by the name of *average,* though without much propriety: I mean a claim for pilotage and port charges, which is called *small* or *petty average.* This is not properly an equitable contribution in case of *loss* from the accidents of the voyage, but a matter of positive agreement between the owner and shipper, and entirely arbitrary. The shipper becomes liable for *primage and average accustomed;* it is an article of the bargain of affreightment. With this *petty average* the insurer has no concern.

In practice, one third of these expences of pilotage and port charges, falls on the ship, and two thirds on the cargo.

whole goods saved, and of the ship herself, ought to contribute to indemnify the sufferer, proportionally to the value of their respective properties; for in that proportion they derive a direct pecuniary benefit from the jettison *.

Lord KAMES, in his *Principles of Equity*, has adopted an idea that, in cases of *jetson*, goods ought to contribute, not according to their *value*, but their *weight*. He observes, that it is the heavy goods which occasion the danger; and if there were leisure for such a transaction, every owner of valuable goods would purchase an equal quantity of those that were heavy, and each would throw the same number of pounds weight overboard. Proceeding upon the same reasoning,
"the

* " Cum in eadem nave, varia mercium genera complures
" mercatores coëgissent, praetereaque multi vectores, servi,
" liberique, in ea navigarent, tempestate gravi orta, neces-
" sario jactura facta erat. Quaesita deinde sunt haec: An
" omnes jacturam praestare oporteat, et si qui tales merces
" imposuissent, quibus navis non oneraretur, velut gemmas,
" margaritas? et quae portio praestanda est? et an etiam pro
" liberis capitibus dari oporteat? Placuit, *omnes quorum in-*
" *terfuisset jacturam fieri, conferre oportere*, quia tributum ob-
" servatae res deberent: itaque *dominum etiam navis* pro
" portione obligatum esse. Jacturae summam pro *rerum*
" *pretio* distribui oportere; corporum liberorum aestimationem
" nullam fieri posse; itidem agitatum est, an etiam vestimen-
" torum cujusque, et annulorum, aestimationem fieri oporte-
" at? Et omnium visum est, nisi si quae consumendi causa im-
" posita forent: quo in numero essent cibaria, eo magis,
" quoad, si quando ea defecerint in navigatione, quod quis-
" que haberet in commune conferret." L. 2. § 2. D. *Ad leg. Rhod.*

" the Roman law," fays he, " appears uncouth
" in fome of its confequences; jewels, and I may
" add bank bills, are made to contribute to
" make up the lofs, although they contribute
" not in any degree to the diftrefs; nor is a
" fingle ounce thrown overboard upon their ac-
" count; nay, the fhip itfelf is made to contri-
" bute, though the jetfon is made neceffary, not
" by the weight of the fhip, but of the cargo."

The whole of this reafoning is founded on a fuppofition which has been already fhown to be erroneous; that in *jetfon*, as in other cafes of partial lofs, the obligation to contribute arifes from the principle, that benefit was intended, and that a *recompence* is due, whether any advantage *is actually reaped* or not. Upon this reafoning, it no doubt follows, that every commodity fhould contribute, not according to value, but weight; becaufe it is according to their weight, that they increafe the danger; and that the fhip, for the fame reafon, ought to be exempted.

But in cafes of jetfon, the contribution does not arife from any idea that the lofing party is entitled to a *recompence*, for having acted *factorio nomine*; but merely that he may claim *reftitution*, fo far as his lofs has been directly converted to another's gain. Upon Lord KAMES' fuppofition, many abfurdities would follow. Put the cafe, that a valuable jewel is thrown away in the hurry, and is to be contributed for by weight.

weight. The reſt of the cargo confiſts of a L. 1000 bill of exchange, having no ſenſible weight, and ſome *Cwts.* of coals, the whole of which, taken together, are not worth the loſs incurred. If goods are to contribute by weight, the bill of exchange will contribute nothing. The coals may be all given towards the loſs, without ſenſibly indemnifying the owner of the jewel. Here the holder of the bill will be the only gainer; the proprietor of the jewel will loſe a part; and the owners of the coals will loſe their all. Would this be an equitable diſtribution? Or can we preſume, that the owners of bulky commodities would ever conſent to any jetſon upon ſuch terms?

The modern nations of Europe, accordingly, have, in this reſpect, almoſt unanimouſly adhered to the principle of the civil law. The ſhip contributes as well as the goods; and both according to their value: and money and jewels are underſtood, with very few exceptions, to be liable, as well as the heavieſt and moſt bulky commodities.

In every caſe of *general* average, the owners of ſhip ought to contribute, not only for the hull of the veſſel, her tackle and appurtenances, but in reſpect of the *nett freight.* The *nett freight* will be a clear gain to them, if the ſhip accompliſhes her voyage. By the ordinance of *Hamburgh*, accordingly, it is declared, that "the "owners

"owners of ship shall contribute for the whole amount of both *ship and freight* *."

The following Scotch case, (stated by Lord Kames), does not coincide with these principles, as it seems to imply, that the ship-owner shall not contribute for *freight* at all.

LUTWITCH *contra* GRAY.

In a shipwreck, part of the cargo being fished out of the sea, and saved, was delivered to the owners for payment of the salvage. The proprietor of the ship claimed the freight of the goods saved *pro rata itineris*. The freighters admitted the claim, but insisted, that as the salvage was beneficial to him, on account of his freight, as well as to them on account of their goods, he ought to pay a proportion of the salvage. His answer was sustained to free him from any part, *viz.* that the expence was wholly laid out on recovering the freighters goods; and therefore that they ought to be liable. *Jan.* 18. 1755.

Upon this case, his Lordship observes, that it seems to have proceeded on the erroneous idea, that no contribution was due, unless the sufferer had acted *factorio nomine*. Whereas here a much more powerful principle operates, that the shipowners had reaped a pecuniary benefit at the expence

---

* Ord. of *Coningsb.* 885.—Of *Copenhagen*, No. 1284. —Of *Genoa*, 137.—Practice of *Britain*.—Ord. of *Hamb.* No. 981.

pence of others; and it was therefore immaterial, whether that benefit was intended or not.

There are some exceptions to this rule, that ship and freight ought to contribute to the full; but these are not numerous.

The *ordinance of France* (No. 579.) says, that both ship and freight are to contribute for one half. The *Antwerp* regulation provides, that the owners of the cargo shall have an option to make the ship contribute, either according to her real value, or her whole contracted freight. These regulations seem applicable to *gross freight*, which includes a consideration for the outfit; but they are, surely, in a considerable degree imperfect.

Not only ought the ship and cargo to contribute, but all who have an ascertainable interest in their preservation.

A lender on bottomry, it should seem, is in the precise situation of a ship-owner. The extent of his interest in the hull of the ship, diminishes so far that of the borrowers. He ought, therefore, like the other owners of ship, to contribute towards a ransom, jetson, or other common disaster. In Spain, accordingly, where the great expence of fitting out a ship to the Spanish colonies, renders bottomry a very frequent contract, and where, consequently, it is better understood than in most other countries, a bottomry-bond contains this condition, that the lender shall

shall run, in partnership with the owner, the risk on the hull, keel, and earnings of the ship.

The French ordinance says, that those who lend money on bottomry, shall bear their proportion of all gross or general averages, but not of simple or particular averages, without an express agreement to that effect. *Ord. Fr.* No. 660.

From Mr MAGEN's Essay, it appears, that the rule upon this point, in several other European states, is far from being laid down with precision; and it does not appear to be always consistent with principles. In England there are, it is believed, no fixed rules universally established, for settling partial losses on a bottomry-interest.

The owner himself of the goods thrown overboard, must contribute his own share, in proportion to the extent of his property on board: For as he is indemnified by the contributions of his fellow-adventurers, the jetson is beneficial to him, as well as to the rest.

In short, every person, for whose benefit expence or trouble has been usefully incurred, with a view to indemnification, is liable in a *recompence* for such expence and labour; and every person who has directly reaped an actual pecuniary advantage from another's loss, is liable in *restitution*, whether his advantage was intended or not.

There are a few exceptions, both by the civil law, and the practice of modern Europe. Sailors are excused in respect of their wages; partly from humanity, it being thought hard to deprive them of any part of their small earnings; and partly from utility, that they may be induced, with less reluctance, to consent to a *jetson*.

The Roman law excepted passengers, in respect of their lives saved by the jetson; because the life of a freed man does not admit of a pecuniary estimation. A similar rule is adopted in modern Europe. Passengers are, besides, free from contribution, for the usual articles of money, jewels, and necessaries, which may be considered as appendages to their person. MOLLOY says, that, "in general, money, and jewels, and even clothes, and all things in the ship, (except a man's apparel in use, or victuals put on board to be spent), are liable to average and contribution." It is believed, however, to be a general rule with regard to such subjects, that what pays no freight, pays no average.

In estimating the interest on board, in order to contribution, a question may arise, whether regard is due to the value of ship and goods at the *port of loading*, or that of *discharge*. The Roman law adopted a distinction somewhat metaphysical upon this subject. The goods lost were to be estimated at their original cost; those saved, were valued at the price which they might probably bring; because, in the former case, the

the prime coſt aſcertains the *actual loſs* of the goods thrown overboard; and attention to the market-rate, at the port of diſcharge, is neceſſary to determine the extent of *actual profit* that ſhall accrue from that loſs.

The point ſeems to be in ſome meaſure arbitrary. It appears more reaſonable, however, that the loſs and gain ſhould both be judged of by the ſame criterion; and none of the modern ſtates have therefore followed the rule of the civil law, although they differ very much from one another upon the point.

By ſome regulations, the whole goods are eſtimated at their prime coſt, or values in the port of diſcharge, according as the veſſel has, at the time of the loſs, executed half her voyage or not. This diſtinction prevails in the *Conſolato del mare*, and in ſeveral foreign ordinances; thoſe in particular of Genoa, of Rotterdam, of Stockholm, and of Copenhagen. It appears likewiſe, from *Gerard Malynes*, to have been the old rule in England.

The greateſt number of modern mercantile ſtates, however, have been of opinion, that the whole goods, loſt and ſaved, ought to be eſtimated according to their value in the port of diſcharge. This is the rule adopted by the Hamburgh ordinances; by thoſe of Coningſberg, Antwerp, and France; by the Spaniſh Weſt Indian laws, and by the general practice of Britain.

* * * * *

It

It remains to be confidered, how far, in what cafes, and in what proportions, the underwriter is liable for that lofs, which may fall upon the particular proprietor whom he has infured.

In total loffes, this queftion was very fimple. In a wager policy, where a total lofs is incurred, the underwriter is liable to the extent of the bett. In *open policies upon intereft*, the infurer is liable for his whole fubfcription, fo far as it can be fhown there was intereft on board. And in *valued policies*, he is liable for the prime coft, as afcertained by the valuation.

But in cafes of partial lofs, the point is attended with a good deal of intricacy.

1. In *wager policies*, in the *firft* place, there can be no partial lofs. For a partial lofs is too indefinite, and admits of too great variety in kind, and in degree, to be laid hold of as the condition of a wager. Still lefs can there be room for that particular fpecies of partial lofs which is repaired by contribution, and goes under the name of *average;* becaufe the affured, having no intereft, can fhew no real lofs. In thefe wager policies, therefore, the underwriter can, from the nature of the thing, have no connection with any damage that is not total.

2. In the fame fituation are many *policies upon intereft*, in which the affured exprefsly ftipulates to be *free of average* altogether, or below

low a certain extent. When a policy is executed, free of all average whatever, the infurer is liable for no damage, repairs, or charges, unlefs they are fo great, as to defeat the voyage, and to entitle the aflured to abandon.

A variety of claufes, ftipulating a partial freedom from average, have been adopted in different places, in order to avoid troublefome and intricate proofs, in relation to damages of fmall importance, upon commodities of a perifhable nature. Thefe muft be varying every day, according to the exigencies of trade. The ordinance of Middleburg frees the infurer from all average under *one per cent.*; that of Amfterdam, from all under *three per cent.*

At the foot of Englifh policies, there is commonly the following claufe, which has been of very long ftanding.

"*N. B.* Corn, fifh, falt, fruit, flour, and feed, are warranted free from average, unlefs general, or the fhip be ftranded.—Sugar, tobacco, hemp, flax, hides, and fkins, are warranted free from average under 5 *per cent.*; and all other goods, alfo the fhip and freight, are warranted free from average under 3 *per cent. unlefs general, or the fhip be ftranded.*"

Both of thefe exceptions from the claufe, "free of average," are founded in the reafon of the thing. *A general average* takes place, where a lofs has been incurred for the fake of the adventure at large. It is an expence laid out for the advantage of the whole concern, and confequently

quently of the underwriters themselves, and is in a very different situation from other partial losses, which are not the subject of contribution. It would be absurd, that the insurers should stipulate to be free from an expence incurred for their advantage; and it might be dangerous, by inducing the assured to avoid such expence, and allow the loss to become total. In the *Mediterranean*, accordingly, where general clauses, " free of average," are very common, without any exception, these clauses are *construed* not to extend to the case of *jetson* *.

It might be dangerous, if the assured himself were liable for partial loss in case of *stranding*; for the situation of the vessel would afford a sufficient pretext for *abandoning*; and the assured might be induced, instead of incurring expence at his own risk, in recovering the ship, fraudulently to allow the loss to become total, in order to recover the whole value from the insurers.—It is extremely difficult, however, to decide what shall constitute *stranding*. In one instance, *Cantillon v. L. Ass. Co.* it is said to have been found, that a ship was *stranded*, because, in falling down the Thames, she had *touched the bottom*. Since this determination, the insurance-companies in *London* have entirely laid aside the exception of the ship being stranded, and consent to subject themselves to partial loss, only where it is borne by a *general average*.

Some

* *Targa*, 230. *n.* 18.

Some difficulty has arisen with regard to the meaning of the word *unless;* whether, in the clause, " unless general, or the ship be stranded," it is to be taken as an exception, or as a condition. This point was fixed by the following decision.

WILSON *v.* SMITH.

Smith insured *Wilson* on the ship *Boscawen*, and her cargo of *wheat*, with the usual *N. B.* " Corn, " fish, fruit, &c. free of average, *unless* general, " or the ship be stranded." The vessel met with a storm, in which she was forced to cut away her cable and anchor, was otherwise damaged, and obliged to run to the first port, and refit. The insurers paid the expence of repairs as a general average. After being refitted, the ship continued her voyage; and when she arrived at her port of discharge, it was discovered, that the wheat had received damage by the saltwater.

The assured claimed a particular average for this loss, as well as the general average for repairs.

Lord MANSFIELD said, the word " *unless*" means the same as *except*, and never can be construed as a condition, in the sense put upon that word by the assured; namely, that he was to be free from partial loss, unless in two events, *viz.* a *general average*, and the *stranding* of the ship; but that, if either of these events happened, then he was to be liable to all other average.—The words.

words can never mean to leave the infurer fubject to any particular average.—Judgment was accordingly given for the defendant.—3. *Burr.* 1550.

According to this decifion, which is undoubtedly founded in the meaning of the exception, it ought to be expreffed,—" *except* general, and " *unlefs* the fhip be ftranded."

The memorandum ufed at the port of *Edinburgh* differs little from the *London* form. It runs thus: " Corn, feed, falt, fifh, fruit, flour, " and provifions of all kinds, that are in their na- " ture perifhable, are warranted free from all " average, unlefs general, or the fhip be ftrand- " ed; and all other goods, the fhip and freight " are warranted free from average *under five per* " *cent.* unlefs general, or the fhip be ftranded."

The *Glafgow* form varies a good deal. It contains, in the body of the inftrument, a freedom from *all average whatever, under five per cent.* And the *N. B.* is as follows:

" *N. B.* Infurers are not liable for any average- " lofs upon grain, fifh, fruit, wine, provifions, or " other goods, which, in their own nature, are " liable to perifh or decay, by continuing long " on board, or being faulty or decayed before " fhipping; but the owners of fuch goods fhall " recover, on a general average, when any " part of them are thrown overboard, for the " prefervation of the whole; and on a particular
" average,

"average, when the damage happens by *strand-*
"*ing* or *bulging.*"

We may observe, that the expression of this last passage, limits the particular average for which the insurer is liable, to that which is *occasioned* by stranding or bulging. The *London* policy seems to imply, that if the vessel be stranded, the insurer shall bear all partial loss, whether occasioned by that misfortune, or by the perishable nature of the goods.

It is worthy of notice, that, in consequence of this clause, "free of average," it is necessary to adopt a different view of what constitutes the distinction between a total and partial loss. It was formerly laid down, that a total loss is *whatever defeats the voyage*. This will not hold, however, where, in the case of perishable commodities, the underwriter has secured himself by the memorandum above stated. Here the subject must be actually gone. For what is the underwriter's view?—To defend himself against the *perishable nature* of particular commodities, which renders them peculiarly liable to certain accidents. He means to be secure from all damage arising in consequence of that peculiar nature, whether such damage be great or small; whether it *defeats the voyage*, or only diminishes the price of the goods. The effect of the memorandum, therefore, is to prevent a loss from being considered as *total*, so long as the subject is in existence; in order to abandonment, it must be burnt, sunk,

sunk, captured, or otherwise completely destroyed. This is established by the two following cases.

Mason v. Skurray.

Insurance was made by the defendant on a cargo of *pease* on board the *Happy Recovery*, from *London* to *St Augustine*, with the usual memorandum, "*Corn*, fish, &c. free of average, unless general, or the ship be stranded." The pease arrived at the place of destination, but so much damaged, that their produce was three-fourths below the freight, which, in consequence of the ship's arrival, became due.

The defendant, by four or five witnesses, conversant in the settlement of losses, proved, that, in the case of goods falling under the memorandum, it was the *usage* to consider the underwriter as discharged, if the commodities arrive at the market. Lord Mansfield said, that, since the introduction of the memorandum, every case must depend upon the construction of it. It is expressed in general terms; but must be explained from *usage*. The witnesses all swear to the *usage*, that if the specific thing comes to the market, the memorandum is understood to free the insurer from all demands for a partial loss. The case *Boyfield v. Brown*, was decided before the introduction of the memorandum.—The jury found for the defendant.—*Hil.* 1780. *At Guildhall.* See *Mr Park's System, p.* 13.

Cockayne

Cockayne v. Frazer.

Frazer insured *Cockayne*, to the amount of L. 100, on the ship " *Three Friends*, and on " goods, &c. at and from St John's in Newfound- " land, to her port of discharge in Portugal :" With the usual *N. B.* " Corn, fish, &c. warrant- " ed free of average, unless general, or the ship " be stranded."

On 2d December 1783, the ship sailed from Newfoundland, with a cargo of *fish*. On 11th December the crew hove overboard 40 quintals, for the general preservation of ship and cargo, and on the 20th, 26 quintals more. They had extremely bad weather, till their arrival at Lisbon, on the 10th January 1784, when a survey was made, by the Board of Health, at the request of the captain, who was likewise consignee of the fish. It appeared to them (and was so in fact) that the fish were rendered of no value by the sea-damage.—The ship did not proceed on her voyage.

In an action on the policy, the defendant pleaded the general issue, and paid into court the sum of L. 16 : 19 : 6 ;—L. 8, 15 s. as general average on the cargo ; and L. 8 : 4 : 6, as particular average on the ship. Verdict for the plaintiff, with L. 51, 15 s. damages, subject to the opinion of the court on a case containing the facts above stated.

Lord

Lord MANSFIELD.—This, like most litigations, arises from mistaking the question, and not properly defining terms. This is a very old clause in policies on perishable goods. Particular losses are excepted from the obligation of the insurer, unless the ship has been stranded. The insurer continues liable for a *total loss*; but a total loss here is the loss of the thing, not any damage, however great while it exists. It is not a diminution of value that is engaged against, but the loss of the thing itself.

In common cases, when the voyage is obstructed, and not worth pursuing, it is a total loss. But the memorandum goes on the idea that the insurer is not to be liable for any damage however great. If the thing exists, though worth nothing, it is sufficient to excuse the underwriter.

BULLER, J.—That the voyage here was defeated might be very material in cases not within the memorandum. In *Mason v. Skurray*, the court thought it a total loss, and on that it went to a new trial. But, upon the second trial, it appeared clear that there never had been an instance in which a total loss had been paid for, where the thing existed, though of no value. *Postea* to the defendant. *Easter* 25. Geo. III. *B. R. MS.*

3. In open policies upon interest, and where there is no such stipulation as that now stated, to be " free of average," three situations may occur.

First,

First, The sums underwritten may exactly correspond with, and be equal to the interest on board. In this case of an equal insurance, every underwriter must be liable for a partial loss incurred by his assured, *proportionably to his own subscription*.

Secondly, In an open policy on interest, there may be an *over-insurance*, or *double insurance*. The nature of these was formerly considered; and it was observed, that, in cases of total loss, there must be a proportional deduction from different subscriptions, until the sums remaining become commensurate to the real value of the interest. The same rule is applicable in partial, as in total losses.

Thirdly, Suppose, in an open policy on interest, the subject to be *under-insured*, the sums underwritten to be *lower* than the interest on board. In such a case, the owner himself bears the risk of that portion of value which is not insured; he comes in the place of an underwriter, to that extent. A partial loss, therefore, falls upon the insurers proportionally to their different subscriptions, *considering the owner of ship or cargo as himself an insurer of the values not otherwise covered*. If a total loss had happened, it is plain he would have lost to that amount; and he must suffer a partial damage in the same proportion.

On the other hand, where there has happened a shipwreck, and a salvage, the insured, if there be an *under-infurance*, is for the fame reafon entitled to his proportion of the property recovered. He is an infurer *pro tanto*, and muft have the benefits as well as the rifks of that fituation.

4. The effect of a *valued* policy is *to afcertain the amount of intereft,* for which the underwriter muft be liable in the event of damage incurred.

In cafes of *total lofs*, we have feen, the valuation fixes the obligation of the infurer. If the fubject has been *bona fide overvalued*, the infurer muft notwithftanding pay the whole fum in the policy, having received a *premium* correfponding to that amount. If it is *undervalued*, the owner has himfelf to blame, and muft-fit down contented with an incomplete indemnification.

In *partial loffes*, in the fame manner, the damage muft, in general, be eftimated not upon the real worth of the fubject infured, but upon the valuation in the policy. With this view, in order to find out what proportion the lofs incurred bears to the prime coft, as afcertained by the policy, a comparifon muft be made between the values of the goods when damaged or found at the port of difcharge; and the difference between the values of found and damaged will fhow the proportion which the lofs bears to the prime coft. Thus, if a cargo of fugar, at any particular port, when in a found ftate, would give L. 1000, but when damaged would give only L. 500; the difference is L. 500, which fhows that the lofs fuftained is one half, upon the intereft infured.

But

But although the amount of loss is ascertained in this manner by the values at the port of discharge, yet *the difference* between sound and damaged goods at the port of discharge, is not the *sum which the underwriter must actually pay;* for this would involve him in the contingency of the rise and fall of markets, which is no part of the adventure insured. The insurer undertakes all perils of the sea, the dangers of the voyage ; but he never proposes to be answerable for the prudence or success of the merchants speculations in trade.

In the case above stated, therefore, while *the difference* is found at the port of discharge between the value of the damaged goods, and the price they would have brought, if sound,—it must not be supposed, that the sum so found, is the *actual loss* which the underwriters are to pay. It merely shews *the proportion* which the loss incurred bears to the value of the whole subject ; and the insurers are only liable for the *same proportion of interest*, appearing by the valuation in the policy. If therefore there is a third, a fourth, a fifth, of difference between sound and damaged goods at the port of discharge, the insurer pays a third, a fourth, a fifth, of the valuation in the policy.

For example, a hogshead of sugar is insured, *valued* at L. 25. When it comes to the market, it is found to be damaged, and sells for L. 20. A *hhd.* of sound sugar, of the same quality, sells,

sells, at the same time and place, for L. 30. The difference therefore between sound and damaged is one third, or L. 10. The insurer does not pay L. 10; but he pays one third of the L. 25, the value in the policy, or L. 8 : 6 : 8.

"Suppose," says Mr MAGENS, "10 *hhds*. of
"tobacco are insured, valued in the lump at
"L. 100; one hogshead is lost; on the amount
"in quantity of one *hhd*, the loss will be 10 *per*
"*cent.* on the interest, whether the nett pro-
"ceeds of the tobacco gives loss or profit :—for
"though the merchants 9 hhds, which are not
"damaged, should produce nett L. 100, the
"insurer cannot object, you insured L. 100,
"your tobacco has yielded you nett L. 100,
"and therefore you have no demand; this
"would be availing himself of the merchant's
"profit, to pay the sea-loss.——

"Again, suppose on linens, the valuation or
"invoice covered, is L. 100.—

At a gaining market, they would produce nett,
 if sound, - - L. 120 0 0
But being damaged, produce nett   108 0 0

The loss on L. 120, is   -   12 0 0

If L. 120 lose L. 12,—L. 100 loses L. 10 0 0

At a lofing market, they would produce nett,
if found, - - L. 80 0 0
Being damaged, produce nett 72 0 0

The lofs on L. 80, is - L. 8 0 0

If L. 80 lofe L. 8,—L. 100 lofes L. 10 0 0

" In both inftances, the average or damage
" is one tenth part, or 10 *per cent*. On the
" other hand, if the infurer were to pay the
" difference between found and damaged, at the
" port of difcharge, he would in the one cafe be
" L. 2 a gainer, and in the other L. 2 a lofer,
" by the circumftances of the market."

In certain cafes of partial lofs, however, upon a valued policy, it has been faid, that *the valuation muft be opened up.*

In order to underftand this, it is neceffary to diftinguifh between two different modes of valuation. A cargo is fometimes valued by the weight, meafure, or package; as when a cargo of tobacco is valued at fo much a *hhd*. And this may be underftood to take place wherever the nature of the cargo, and the manner in which it admits of menfuration or valuation, is pointed out in the policy; as where infurance is made " on 10 bales of linen, *valued at L.* 100;" this is evidently the fame as if the policy had
faid,

said,—"on linens *valued* at L. 10 *per* bale." This mode of valuing by weight, measure, or package, has the same effect as if each specified package was taken apart, and made the subject of a separate valuation.

But a cargo is often *valued generally*, without specifying, either its nature, or the mode in which it can admit of mensuration or valuation; sometimes along with the ship; sometimes at the sums underwritten. "On ship *Sally*, and goods "*per* said *Sally*, valued at the sums underwrit- "ten."—"On whatsoever goods and merchan- "dises loaded, or to be loaded, on board the "said ship—valued at L. 1000."

In the former case, where each package is valued separately, a very obvious expedient occurs, in order to ascertain the partial loss which the underwriter must bear. It is only necessary to take the separate subject, whether bale, parcel, package, hogshead, or ton, (according as it is described in the policy), to find the proportion between its value when sound, and in its damaged state, at the port of delivery; and to calculate the same proportion upon the valuation in the policy. So that here the valuation is still held as a proof of the interest; and the observation, "that, in partial losses on a valued policy, "the valuation must be opened up," does not appear to be applicable.

But

Partial Loss. 367

But where a *general valuation* has taken place, the cafe is very different. For example, when fhip and cargo are valued jointly, or, what is more common, where a whole cargo, confifting of a variety of different articles, is valued in the lump: Here the affured does not appear entitled to demand the proportion of damage incurred by any individual package of goods; for example, by any individual cafk of liquor, or hhd. of tobacco. He is only entitled to the proportion which the damage incurred bears to the value of the whole intereft; and it becomes neceffary, therefore, to enquire into the comparative values of all the different articles of which the cargo confifts.

Suppofe a cargo, confifting of liquors, broad cloth, and coals, to be valued, in a general fum, at L. 500, without any fpecification as to the number of cafks, bales, or tons. And let the real value be L. 1000, fo that the cargo is undervalued one half. Suppofe one of the cafks of liquor to be ftaved. In order to afcertain the amount of the affured's claim, and to find what proportion of the L. 500, ftated in the valuation, is due, it is neceffary to enquire, not only what proportion of damage is done to the individual cafk, but what is the comparative value of that cafk, with the broad cloth and the coals, which form the remainder of the cargo; confequently it is neceffary *to prove the actual values* of the whole. The fame thing muft happen in an

over-

over-valuation, and in every case whatever; for without *opening up* the policy, and going into the real values, we can never judge whether the insurance be *equal to the interest* or not.

In every instance of *general valuation*, therefore, a partial loss renders the valuing clause of no use; for it becomes necessary to prove the *actual values*, as in an open policy. It has become customary in those cases, where the real values must thus, at any rate, be proved, to disregard entirely the valuation, and to proportion the partial loss upon the real interest.

This distinction between the effects of a separate and a general valuation, is illustrated by the two following remarkable decisions.

Lewis *v.* Rucker.

The defendant insured " goods aboard a ship " the *Vrow Martha*, at and from *St Thomas Island* " to *Hamburg*." The goods (which consisted of sugars, coffee, and indigo) were " valued at " *L.* 30 *per hogshead*, the clayed sugars, and *L.* 20 " *per hogshead*, the Muscovado; warranted free " from average under *five per cent.* unless general, or the ship be stranded." The coffee and indigo were likewise respectively valued.

In the course of the voyage, the sea-water got in; and when the ship arrived at Hamburg, it appeared, that every hogshead of the sugar was damaged; which made it necessary to sell them immediately. And the difference between the price which

Of Partial Loss.

which they brought by reafon of the damage, and what they might have been fold for at Hamburg, if found, was as L.20 : 0 : 8 *per* hogfhead, is to L. 23 : 7 : 8 *per* hogfhead, (that is, if found, they would have been worth L.23 : 7 : 8 *per* hogfhead; as damaged, they were only worth L. 20 : 0 : 8 *per* hogfhead.)

In an action upon the policy, the defendant paid money into Court, by the following rule of eftimating the damage; he paid the like proportion of the fum at which the fugars were *valued in the policy*, as the difference between found and damaged fugars bore to found fugars at Hamburg. The plaintiff objected to this meafure for eftimating the damage.

To diftinguifh this cafe, by particular circumftances, the plaintiff called evidence to prove, that if he had kept his fugars for fome time, as he had intended to do, they would have born a much higher price; and therefore the lofs which arofe from the neceffity of their being brought to an immediate fale, owing to the fea-damage, ought to be included.

A verdict having been found for the defendant by a fpecial jury; upon motion for a new trial, Lord Mansfield delivered the opinion of the Court.

His Lordfhip ftated the rule adopted by the defendant and jury.—The defendant takes the proportion of the difference between found and damaged at the port of delivery, and pays *that proportion* upon the value specified in the policy; and has no regard to the price in money, which either the sound or damaged goods bore in the port of delivery. He says, the proportion of the difference is equally the rule, whether the goods come to a rising or a falling market. For instance, suppose the value in the policy L. 30;— they are damaged, but sell for L. 40. If they had been sound, they would have sold for L. 50; the difference is a fifth: The insurer then must pay a *fifth of the prime cost or value in the policy*, (that is L. 6.) *E converso;*—if they come to a losing market, and sell for L. 10, being damaged, but would have sold for L. 20, if sound; the difference is one half. The insurer must pay half the prime cost or value in the policy, (that is L. 15.)

To this rule two objections had been made. 1*mo*, That this was going by a different measure in the cases of partial and total loss; for upon a total loss, the prime cost or value in the policy must be paid; the answer is, that where there is a total loss of ship and cargo, or where any separate part of the cargo is entirely lost, there the insurer is liable for the prime cost, without regard to any subsequent estimate. But where a partial damage is incurred by the cargo, it is impossible to fix from the prime cost what is the amount of that damage. The only way is by calculation at the port of delivery, to find the proportion in which the goods are spoiled; and as

Of Partial Loss. 371

as the infurer pays the whole prime coft, if the thing be wholly loft; fo if it be only a third, fourth, or fifth, worfe, he pays a third, fourth, or fifth, of the prime coft or valuation of the goods fo damaged.

2do, The cafe had been entangled with difficulties, founded upon this being a valued policy. The effect of a valuation is merely to *fix the prime coft*.—To argue, " that there can be no adjuft-" ment of an average lofs upon a valued policy," is contrary to the very terms of the policy itfelf, which is fubject to average, if the lofs upon fugars exceed *five per cent.* If there can be no average lofs in a valued policy, the affured here cannot recover at all; for this furely is not a total lofs.

In oppofition to the meafure the jury have gone by, the plaintiff contends, that he ought to be paid the whole value in the policy, upon one of two grounds:

1ft, Becaufe the general rule of eftimating fhould be the difference between the price the damaged goods fell for, and the prime coft, (or value in the policy.) Here the damaged fold at L. 20 : 0 : 8 *per* hogfhead, and the underwriter fhould make it up L. 30. *Anfw.* This would involve the underwriter in the rife or fall of the market. It would fubject him in fome cafes to pay vaftly more than the lofs; in others it would deprive the infured of any fatisfaction, though there was a lofs. For inftance, fuppofe the prime coft cost or value in the policy L. 30 *per* hogshead; the sugars are injured. At a losing market, the price of the best is L. 20 *per* hogshead; the price of the damaged is L. 19 : 10. The loss is about a fortieth, and the insured would be to pay above a third.—Suppose they come to a rising market, and the sound sugars sell for L. 40 *per* hogshead, and the damaged for L. 35, the loss is an eighth; yet the insurer would be to pay nothing.

2*d*, Because the sugars would have sold for a higher price, if the damage from the sea-water had not made an immediate sale necessary. And here likewise the verdict seemed to be right. The indemnity proposed by insurance is for damage from the sea, and not from disappointment in speculations and schemes of trade. The obligation of the underwriter is incurred upon the ship's arrival and landing her cargo; and the adjustment of a loss cannot depend upon any events of a posterior date.—The rule discharged. 2. *Burr.* 1167.

Le Cras *against* Hughes.

This was an insurance " on the ship *St Domingo*, prize to Captain *Luttrel*, and *on goods by said ship, valued at the sums underwritten.*" There was no value put on the whole, in the body of the policy, but particular sums added to the subscribers names on the back of it. The ship was lost, one tenth of the goods only saved. The

Of Partial Loss.

The deduction for the goods faved, was appointed to be fettled by a broker; but a doubt arofe as to the mode of computing it. Whether one tenth of the *fum infured*, or one tenth of the *real value* fhould be deducted; whether the affured were to recover nine tenths of the real value; in fhort, whether it was to be treated as an open or valued policy. *Bonham*, the broker, faid, the practice was to pay the whole fum infured, in cafe of a total lofs on fuch a policy; but in cafe of a partial lofs, it was confidered as an open policy, and a proportion paid of the real value infured. When this was firft mentioned, the Court thought it a valued policy; but they directed *Bonham* to make the calculation both ways.

Lord MANSFIELD.—I at firft thought this like *Lewis v. Rucker*, and that an aliquot part fhould be taken, without going into the values. But they are not fimilar. That cafe is right, and fhould govern wherever the goods are defcribed and valued by the cafk or package. But here the value is afcertained only by the fum infured. The only purpofe of a valuing claufe, to fave the trouble of proving the value, is not anfwered in an average lofs upon fuch a policy as this, where the actual values muft be proved, to afcertain the proportion of what is faved to what is loft. The real values muft therefore be gone into. The conftant ufage has been as ftated by the broker.

In *Erafmus v. Banks*, (*Mich.* 21. *Geo.* II.) LEE, C. J. permitted the affured to fhew his whole

whole lofs, which was more than the fum infured. *Smith v. Flexney* (at G. H. 1747) was cited in that cafe, in which the plaintiff not being able to prove any intereft, was nonfuited. The computation muft be on the real intereft on board. Judgment for the plaintiff.—*Eaſt.* 24. *Geo.* III.—*MS.*

From the diftinction that has been attempted between a general and a particular valuation, we may find a fatisfactory folution of a difficulty ftarted by Mr *Magens*, in relation to policies warranting againft average under a certain fum. A London policy frees the infurer from partial lofs under 3 *per cent*. Suppofe then, fays Mr *Magens*, a merchant has fhipped a quantity of goods, and, on arrival, a fmall part are fpoiled, fo as to be worth nothing; if the damage be calculated on the whole, it may not amount to 3 *per cent.*; but if on the particular fubject damaged, it may be a total lofs.

It fhould feem, that where a particular package is feparately valued, a lofs may be calculated on that individual package apart; as where fugar is valued at fo much a cafk, if one cafk is damaged, it muft be confidered whether the lofs amounts to 3 *per cent*. upon that individual cafk. But if a cargo is valued in the lump, the amount of lofs upon the whole head muft be taken into the computation.

E L E-

OF INSURANCE.

PART III.

Of those Circumstances peculiar to Insurance, which extinguish the Obligations of Parties, and vacate the Policy.

HAVING examined how the obligations of insurance may be created, and what are their nature and extent; it remains to consider by what circumstances they may be dissolved, and the effect of the policy destroyed, either in whole or in part.

And here it is not proposed to enter upon the general modes by which all agreements indifferently may be extinguished; but only those which are attended with some peculiarity in their application to the bargain of insurance. For this reason it is scarcely necessary to observe, that when, on the one hand, the subject of the insurance

surance incurs no loss; or when, on the other, any loss incurred is paid for by the insurer, the obligation of this last is extinguished by the performance of all that was undertaken.

The great circumstance which is productive of peculiarity in destroying the effect of an insurance policy, is *breach of contract* upon the part of the assured: A circumstance arising from the *conditional* nature of the bargain.

In this agreement, the underwriter, it was formerly observed, for a consideration received, promises to indemnify the assured from loss, upon the existence of some future event. The event to which this obligation has a reference, must be fully understood between the parties. And its existence is a condition without which the insurer does not consent to bind himself. In relation to a mercantile adventure, the circumstances of this event may be of a complicated nature, and all those circumstances ought to be fully settled before the bargain can be complete. A policy of insurance explains, therefore, the nature of the *perils* which are to be undertaken, and the nature of the *voyage* or adventure, in the course of which they are to be undertaken. It mentions the place from which it is proposed that the vessel shall set out, the line of her voyage, the port to which she shall direct her course, and where the insurance is supposed to terminate; it likewise frequently contains a number of particular provisions, tending to diminish the risk of the adventure,

adventure, in favour of the underwriter. All those specifications of the voyage are limitations of the hazard undertaken by the insurer; and conditions of the agreement by which he becomes bound. It is necessary, in order to preserve the assured's claim of indemnity, that these conditions should be fulfilled.

What degree of exactness and literal interpretation is necessary in this respect; what extent of construction is due to the terms of the policy; and consequently what is held to be a breach of contract, it now remains to enquire.

1. In every insurance, the underwriter is very much at the mercy of the assured, both with respect to information, and the performance of those stipulations and conditions which may be agreed upon, in his favour. It has been formerly shewn how much it is therefore held incumbent upon the assured, to make a full and complete communication of all he knows with regard to the risk; and that, without such communication, the policy is null *ab initio.*

The same consideration requires that the assured should be kept with a very strict hand to the performance of those articles, and the fulfilment of those conditions which the underwriter may stipulate. The assured must not depart from that line of voyage which is pointed out by the policy, otherwise the insurer shall be free.

If any variation from the agreement shall take place, and a damage shall be incurred, *in consequence of that variation*, it requires no illustration that for such damage the underwriter cannot be responsible. A contrary rule would be subjecting him to the consequences of a breach of contract upon the part of the assured.

As little does it require argument to show, that the assured cannot, by changing the circumstances of the adventure from those expressed or implied in the policy, *increase* the risk undertaken above the risk understood.

But supposing a variation to be made from the exact terms of the policy, and supposing the varied course to imply no *greater risk* than the one insured; or, supposing that no loss happens *in the course of the variation*, but at some other period of the adventure; although in these cases it does not appear that the underwriter is a *loser* by the variation, it is, nevertheless, an established point that he becomes free, and that the policy is vacated. The risk run must not only be *no greater* than that understood, but it must be the *same*.

There is, it may be observed, great difference between certain species of agreements in respect of the obligation which lies upon the debtor to fulfil the contract by *specific performance*. Where the prestation undertaken admits of a value different from the mere pecuniary advantage to be reaped from it; where it may be supposed

posed to possess an estimation in the mind of the creditor, independent of the money it is worth; in every such instance the debtor is bound to *specific performance*. But where the value is merely pecuniary; where one prestation is as good as another of the kind; in this case the debtor may be freed from specific performance, by paying the damage and interest.

It may at first sight appear, that insurance is one of those contracts in which there is no room for a particular choice or estimation, independent of the pecuniary value. The underwriter, when he insures, has no affection or preference for one adventure above another, except so far as it has a relation to the premium offered. It might seem, therefore, that, in the same manner as a person who had borrowed a guinea might pay in silver, instead of the identical gold. So an assured might vary from the voyage specified, always taking care that the underwriter was no *loser* by the change; that he was not exposed to a *greater*, though a *different* risk from that underwritten.

But in reality an insurance differs in this respect, from most other contracts. It is a bargain in relation to a future uncertain event, and therefore partakes of the nature of a wager. A wager, it may be observed, is a trial of skill as to a question of probability. Each party is induced to wager by the different weight which certain views and considerations have upon different

ent minds; and the wager derives its origin not from those general views of a probability, in which men are disposed to agree, but from those peculiar views and modes of thinking in which one man is apt to be a good deal different from others. In examining, therefore, what is the inductive cause of a wager, and what is the *value, to each party*, of his *bett*, we are to consider, not what the probability *is* in reality, but what each party may *think* of it.

Risks are not the objects of preference from attachment and feeling, like a spot of ground, a horse, a medal: But they are the objects of very different estimation to the judgment or fancy. People may form, upon solid views of reasoning, very different opinions of the amount of a probability. Still more are they apt to be swayed by the operation of fanciful circumstances upon the imagination. Much has been said of the eagerness people often entertain to procure a particular ticket in the lottery. Some fanciful combination, often exceedingly ridiculous, determines them to undertake a particular risk. The probability of two events may be really the same, and yet appear very different to the minds of different men. It would be unjust, therefore, to substitute one risk in place of another, although the former, in the common apprehension of mankind, should be no greater than the latter; for it was the *peculiar views* of parties that were the inducements to the

the wager; alter the precife circumftances of the cafe, and the inductive caufe of the wager, the dependence which each man has upon his own peculiar views, no longer fubfifts.

Nay, it may be obferved, that we are not entitled even to fubftitute, what, in the common opinion of mankind, might appear a *better* rifk in place of a *worfe*; for the more defperate any wager is, we have the ftronger evidence that the wagerer was led by a *peculiarity of opinion*, and that he was the more fixed upon that precife rifk, and no other.

Suppofe, therefore, a perfon betts upon a race-horfe, and, before the race begins, that horfe is drawn, and another put in his place; the wagerer will not be liable for the rifk upon the fecond horfe, although he fhould be as fwift as, or fwifter than the other. In the fame manner, if I infure a voyage to the Baltic, and the fhip alters her deftination and fails to the Mediterranean; 1 am not fubject to the rifk, although the two voyages fhould be perfectly adequate to each other. In thefe cafes the principle is clear. In others, where the effect of real or fanciful circumftances, in varying the fuppofed amount of the rifk, may not be fo ftriking, the fame reafoning muft ftill, in fome degree, be applicable.

It may farther be obferved, that the particular fituation of parties, in the contract of infurance, makes it expedient, to enforce this rule,

that

that a variation from the policy shall liberate the insurer, whether the risk be increased or diminished. For otherwise, the assured, from his superior knowledge of every particular relating to the adventure, might, under the pretence of *varying*, without *increasing* the risk, practise numberless frauds, which the insurer would very seldom have it in his power to detect. It is necessary, therefore, to affix a severe penalty to the smallest variation from the line of voyage undertaken; lest the assured, under the pretence of an *innocent variation* of the risk, might contrive to *increase* it to the prejudice of the other party.

2. Having said so much, in general, with regard to the adherence that is requisite upon the part of the assured, to the strict letter of an insurance-policy; it remains farther to illustrate the subject by a view of the different sort of variations that occur, and which have the effect to destroy the obligation of the insurer.

Variations from an insurance-contract may be of two kinds. The assured may, in the *first* place, *exceed* the powers with which he is entrusted. He may take steps which are not authorised by the agreement; for example, he may sail to ports and places, with regard to which the policy is silent. He may be guilty of what, in the expression of insurance-law, is called an *alteration of*, or a *deviation from*, the line of voyage undertaken by the insurer. Or, in the *second*

cond place, he may be guilty of a failure in performing some of those terms and conditions that are expressly stipulated; for example, he may neglect to fulfil a clause by which the ship is warranted *to sail with convoy*, or *to sail before a certain day*. He may do more, on the one hand, than he is warranted to attempt; or less, on the other, than he has undertaken.

These different species of failure, which we may distinguish by the names of *variation* from the policy, and *non-performance* of it, seem to deserve a separate consideration.

Lastly, We may examine what effect a failure, with regard to the conditions of the contract, ought to have on the *restoration of premium*.

SECT. I. *Effect of the Assured exceeding his Powers, or of* Variation *from the Policy.*

1. Variation from the terms of an insurance-contract includes two species, which require to be distinguished from each other, *viz. alteration* of the voyage, and *deviation* from it.

It was formerly mentioned, that, after a policy had been subscribed by the underwriter, it was still competent for the assured to retract, by breaking up the voyage, and altering the destination of his vessel; and that, in consequence of such a measure, the assured was liberated from the policy, and entitled to recover his premium,

mium, allowing to the underwriter a small deduction upon the sum insured.

The same change of measures, the same alteration of the plan of the adventure, which entitles the assured to recover his premium, must of course liberate the insurer from hazard. When the one contracting party becomes free, the other cannot continue subject to obligation. Nor is it necessary for this purpose, that the *alteration* should imply fault, in either of the contracting parties. The case becomes precisely the same, as if a person has betted upon a particular race-horse, and before the race that horse is drawn, or dies, and another is substituted in its place. The risk is no longer the same that was meant to be undertaken.

It is said accordingly, in the ordinance of Antwerp, that " when it can be proved against " any one, either by charter-party, bills of load- " ing, affreightment, or otherwise, or even by " lawful witnesses, that he has *altered the voyage* " insured upon, and which it was declared in " the insurance was intended, then he shall " have no power to demand any thing in re- " spect of such insurance, by reason of the said " alteration *."

Upon

---

* It may probably occur, that an *alteration* of the voyage is not properly a *breach* of the contract: When the policy is receded from, *before the commencement of risk*, it is not properly *broken*; for it never was complete. But this inaccuracy

Upon precisely the same principles the underwriter must be freed from his obligation, where the general design of the voyage is not altered, but where, in the course of the adventure originally proposed, and after the risk undertaken has actually commenced, a variation is adopted from the terms of the policy. This is called a *deviation*.

Every variation from the policy, adopted after the risk has commenced, must imply either fault and misconduct, or fraud and dishonest intention somewhere. And here lies the distinction between a *deviation* and an *act of baratry*. If there is a departure from the policy with a fraudulent intention, it is baratry; if from mere negligence or misconduct, it is a deviation. Naturally, it was observed, the insurer is not liable for any departure whatever from the terms of his agreement; in other words, he is not responsible for the assured's breach of contract. He undertakes, by an express clause, the *baratry*, or fraudulent misbehaviour, of master and crew; but he is, in this country, liberated from risk, by a deviation, which implies mere fault.

An alteration of the voyage taking place previous to the commencement of risk, supposes the accession of the assured themselves. A deviation does not necessarily imply any such knowledge or

inaccuracy of method has been overlooked, in order to contract the doctrine of *alteration* with that of *deviation*; this being by far the most important view of the subject.

or concurrence. It may be concerted by the affured, or it may be the private deed of the mafter and ship's company. Baratry, therefore, is more properly oppofed to a *deviation*, than to an *alteration;* for, as was formerly fhown, there can be *no baratry with the acceffion of the owners;* and therefore it fuppofes, in general, a variation fubfequent to the commencement of rifk.

Several circumftances feem jointly neceffary to imply baratry. There muft be a breach of orders, or of the mafter's duty to the owner; it muft be for the private intereft of the mafter or crew; and it muft be evidently calculated to injure fome party concerned. The abfence of any of thefe circumftances feems to deftroy the idea of fraudulent intention, and to reduce the breach of the policy to a deviation. Any departure from the voyage, faulty as well as fraudulent, may be attended with difobedience of inftructions, wherever it is the private deed of the mafter or crew. A mere deviation or alteration may be calculated for the intereft of the mafter and crew; and no baratry will be inferred, providing the breach of the policy has the concurrence of the fhip-owners, or does not appear capable of producing any detriment to the different parties concerned. And however obvioufly prejudicial a departure from the contract may be to the underwriters, the imputation of baratry will be removed by the inftructions of the

the ship-owner*. The common cases of deviation are either, where, after the commencement of risk, the assured themselves make some variation in the voyage, or else where the master departs from his instructions, from some foolish and imprudent scheme of advantage to his employers; or, at least, if it is for his own convenience, interest, or pleasure, where he does not suppose it will be attended with prejudice to those concerned.

2. From the general views formerly stated, it follows, that every policy ought to contain an explicit enumeration of the principal circumstances which constitute the risk of the adventure insured.

The assured, it is obvious, must necessarily be acquainted with the nature and plan of the adventure; he must know the ports from and to which the vessel is to steer, and at which she is to touch in the course of her voyage. Of these the insurer can know nothing, farther than what he learns from the policy, or from the insurance-broker. Even with regard to the strength, situation and outfit of the ship, and the condition of the cargo, his means of information are, comparatively, very imperfect. There is no reason to presume, therefore, that any circumstance relating to the *peculiar risks* of the adventure, was in the view of the insurer at subscribing the contract.

---

* See the cases *Valleio v. Wheeler*, and *Nutt against Bourdieu*, under *Baratry*.

tract. In point of expediency, likewise, it is obvious, that parties are, by no means, on an equal footing, and that the danger of fraud and imposition is almost entirely upon one side.

A full delineation of the voyage, seems, therefore, an essential circumstance in a maritime policy. And both equity and utility require, that the instrument should be strictly interpreted against the assured; that the underwriter should be liable to no risk, to which he does not *expressly* subject himself. No obligation is inferred by construction merely; the assured has no implied powers; he cannot go beyond the instrument.

Neither, in carrying this rule into practice, is any latitude whatever allowed to the assured. The circumstances of the adventure, as pointed out by the terms of the policy, must be adhered to in the strictest and most punctual manner. There is no difference, in point of effect, between a great and a small variation from the policy: Such a distinction could admit of no accurate rule. To vary, in the smallest particular, from the original plan of the voyage, constitutes an *alteration:* In following out this original plan, to depart, in the minutest circumstance, from the line chalked out by the policy, infers a *deviation.* In this respect, the effect of an alteration and a deviation is the same.

Nor is it of importance, whether the underwriter is a loser by the variation, or whether the risk

risk be thereby, in the general opinion, *increased* or *diminished*. It must be the *same* that was insured.

This general principle, that an insurance-contract demands a strict interpretation of the instrument in favour of the insurer, and against the assured ; that the latter cannot exceed the strict letter of the policy ; and that the former is laid under no *constructive* obligation,—appears conspicuous in a variety of situations that may occur in the course of a mercantile adventure.

The most obvious illustration suggests itself, where the ship has departed from the line of sailing marked out by the policy, and understood by the insurer. The ports of commencement and termination of risk are expressed in every policy. It is implied, that the assured shall use all possible diligence and dispatch, in proceeding from the one to the other. The vessel, therefore, must follow the *most direct* and easy route ; and if she turns to the right or left without a good reason ; if she calls or touches at any port which is not expressly specified, the insurer's obligation is at an end.

The effect is the same, whether the vessel shall touch or not, at any port that is not specified, if she follows a scheme of trade, an object of advantage, that is in any respect different from the original meaning and intention of parties in the contract.

But the principles which regulate the doctrine of deviation, are not confined to the single case, where

where the ship varies the course of her voyage. The risk of a maritime adventure depends on a variety of other circumstances than the line of sailing. For example, it may be affected by the particular strength and construction of the vessel, which is the subject of the insurance. The insurer undertakes the hazard of one particular ship, and no other; and therefore the assured cannot, at his own option, change the ship, so as to transfer the security. A voluntary *change of the ship*, without good cause, would produce a variation of the risk run, from that held out by the policy, and like a deviation from the direct course of the voyage, must annul the bargain.

In stating the different adjudged cases which illustrate these positions, we may take those first in order, the principle of which is most obvious; proceeding to others that may appear more disputable.

And here little doubt can be entertained, that the insurer must be liberated, where there is a *prolongation* or *increase* of the risk run above that held out by the policy. As in the following decision.

Chitty *v.* Selwyn.

If a ship be insured "at and from a place," while it lies at that place, preparing for the voyage insured, the underwriter is liable; but if the voyage be laid aside, and the ship lies bye with the owner's privity, for five, six, or seven years,

years, the infurer is not liable. 2. *Atkyns.* —*Trin.* 1742.

In the fame manner where the veffel adopts a new fcheme of trade, or of advantage of any fort, different from what was the original object of the adventure.

Cock v. Townson.

The fhip *George* was bound from *Corke* to *Jamaica*, without a convoy, in the laft war. The captain, in concert with two other veffels, took the advantage of the night, and, being fhips of force, *cruifed*, and thereby deviated out of the direct courfe of their voyage, in hopes of a prize. Lord Camden and the jury held, that, from the moment the *George* deferted or deviated from the *direct voyage* to *Jamaica*, the policy was difcharged. *In C. B.*

Or, where a veffel, inftead of being infured from one fpecified port to another, is infured *to a market*, fhe is bound to profecute this object of her deftination, *as directly as poffible.* She cannot enter upon any other purfuit, fo as to protract the adventure at the rifk of the infurers. Such proceeding is analogous to touching at a port not fpecified, and vacates the policy.

Marshall, Hamilton, *and* Co. *againft* Crawford, Barns, *and others.*

In April 1784, the purfuers, merchants in *Greenock*, fitted out the fhip *Ceres, Jamiefon* mafter,

master, upon a voyage to Newfoundland, and the West Indies. When she sailed from *Clyde*, she had on board 206 carts of coals, 20 barrels, and 40 firkins of beef, beside some dry goods, the property of the captain. Mr *Jamieson* was instructed to take on board, at Newfoundland, about 300 casks of *fish*, and with his whole cargo to proceed to the West Indies. In the instructions it was added, " our great object for the
" *Ceres*, is, that she arrive in the *West Indies*,
" so as to take in a cargo for *Britain*, &c.—If
" on your arrival at *Barbadoes*, Mr *Thompson*
" gives you assurance of a *freight* at any of the
" neighbouring islands, you will immediately
" proceed there, and engage one if possible, to
" any port in *St. George's Channel*, or even to
" *Bristol;* should you meet with no encouragement
" there, you will then proceed to *Morant bay, Ja-*
" *maica,* leave the ship immediately yourself, and
" wait upon *Messrs Maclean and Muir,* at *King-*
" *ston*, and *Messrs Francis King and Co.* Manchi-
" neal, and *endeavour to secure a freight* for the
" ship, on the best terms possible."

The owners having received advice of the safe arrival of their vessel at Newfoundland, on the 3d July 1784, opened a policy at *Greenock*
" *on ship and freight,* at and from *Newfoundland,*
" until she arrives *at her port or ports of discharge*
" *in the West Indies,* and is there 24 hours safely
" moored. And the risk on the freight to con-
" tinue until the cargo is there safely discharged:"
" After

" After the rate of one guinea and a half *per* L. 100
" Sterling, *and one guinea per* L. 100 *additional,*
" *if the ship shall proceed to Jamaica.*"

Afterwards, on the 22d of July, they opened
" another policy at *Glasgow,* " on the *ship Ceres,*
" alfo *on fish,* per faid *Ceres,* at and from New-
" foundland, until the veffel fhall arrive at a
" market in the *West Indies, with liberty to pro-*
" *ceed to Jamaica, and there be safely moored, and*
" *said fish landed,* at two guineas *per cent.*; with
" one *per cent.* additional, *if the vessel shall pro-*
" *ceed to Jamaica.*"

From the proteft and evidence of the captain, it appeared, that the veffel had arrived in fafety in the *West Indies,* and difpofed of all her *fish* at *Barbadoes, Dominique* and *Martinique.* That had the captain been to load at any of thefe Iflands, he could have fold his coals; but that he had been inftructed to carry his coals to the port of loading for the homeward voyage. That he had no ballaft, nor had he taken in any at Newfoundland. The coals and beef had both been configned to the mafter, for fale, by the Company's factor at Newfoundland:

That the captain fought for a freight at *Barbadoes and Dominique,* without fuccefs; touched at *St Kitts,* with the fame view, after he had difpofed of his fifh; and proceeded to *Morantbay, Jamaica,* where he arrived on the 23d of July, having ftill on board the coals, and about half of the beef. The veffel was moored with three anchors. The captain left her, and went to *Kingston*, to receive further orders with respect to his port of loading; and returned two days after, having been informed, that it would probably be *Manchineal*. The vessel continued moored at *Morant-bay*, for seven days, and on the 30th July was wrecked in a hurricane.

The insurers on *ship*, both at *Greenock* and *Glasgow*, refused to pay the loss, upon this ground, that the risk insured was at an end before the accident happened, the vessel having *landed her fish*, and having been more than 24 *hours safely moored at Jamaica*. But the Judge-admiral repelled the defence.

The question having come by suspension before the Court of Session, it was argued by the assured,—that an insurance to *ports of discharge*, or *to a market*, must extend until the vessel arrive at her *last market, or last port of discharge*. In this case, the vessel being insured until safely moored at *Jamaica*, must be understood, consistently with the general object of the adventure, to mean, *at a market in Jamaica*. That when the vessel was lost, she had her coals, and part of her beef, on board, which she was not to discharge at *Morant-bay*, but at the port of loading for the homeward voyage.

For the underwriters it was argued, 1*st*, That *Jamaica*, in the expression of these policies, particularly in the *Glasgow* one, is contrasted with *West*

West Indies; and confequently, although the veffel was infured to a market among the *fmaller Weft India iflands,* yet her liberty to *proceed to Jamaica,* implied nothing more than a common adventure between two fpecified ports.

And when a veffel is infured to any country, kingdom, or ifland, generally, the infurance is underftood to terminate at the *firft port* in that country, *&c.* which the fhip makes*.

2*dly,* That fhe had difpofed of her cargo before going to *Jamaica.* That the *fifh* was her only

---

* The following cafe was omitted under its proper head, —*Termination of Rifk.* It illuftrates the pofition laft ftated: CAMDEN *v.* COWLEY.—*Eaft.* 3. *Geo.* III. Action on a policy of infurance, *on a fhip,* at and from *Jamaica* to *London.* The fhip was alfo infured from *London* to *Jamaica* generally, and was loft in coafting the ifland, after fhe had touched for fome days at one port there, but before fhe had delivered all her outward bound cargo at the other ports of the ifland.

In order to fhew when the homeward bound rifk commenced, it was neceffary to fhow at what time the outward bound rifk determined; and to prove, whether, by the cuftom of merchants, the outward bound rifk determined, when the fhip arrived, and moored 24 hours *in any port* of the ifland, (as the plaintiff, in the prefent caufe, contended,) or when fhe had been fafe 24 hours in her *laft port* of delivery.

Lord MANSFIELD, Chief Juftice, ruled, that infurance-brokers and others might be examined, as to the general opinion and underftanding of the perfons concerned in the trade, though they knew no particular inftance in fact, upon which fuch opinion was founded. A fpecial jury found a verdict for the plaintiff; and the Court afterwards refufed a new trial. *Blackft. Rep.* 417.

only cargo; and the beef and coals were not to be confidered in that view; but as having been kept on board for ballaft, and fhip's provifions. The *fifh* was the only cargo mentioned in the policy, or infured; and no claim had been attempted for the *freight* of the beef and coals.

3*dly*, The veffel had deviated, by *protracting the rifk*. The veffel was infured to *a market*, and the captain, inftead of going directly to that market, had gone out of his way in fearch of a freight homeward. He had neglected to take advantage of a market which offered in the *Weft Indies*; in failing to *St Kitts*, and in the delay at *Morant bay*, he had made the fale of the cargo (which was the object of the voyage infured) fubfervient to a different fcheme, of procuring a homeward freight, with which the underwriters were nowife concerned. The fhip was infured *to a market*, and not till fhe could procure a freight.

The Court of Seffion almoft unanimoufly gave judgment for the infurers, although the judges did not feem to be fully agreed upon the grounds of the decifion. But, upon a reclaiming petition for the affured, and anfwers, they were unanimous upon the third point, that the affured had varied the rifk; and they *adhered*. Nov. 1786. —*Collected from the printed papers.*

Not only is the affured prohibited from *increafing* the rifk, but even from *altering* it in any particular. It is not neceffary for the underwriter

writer to show, that he is a loser by the deviation; the hazard not only must not be augmented, but it must be *the same* that was undertaken. The reasons of this were formerly pointed out; that an insurance is a species of wager, which does not admit of equivalents, but requires a specific performance; and that a contrary rule would open a door to fraudulent encroachments by the assured, upon the underwriter, which the latter could seldom have it in his power to detect.

Fox *v.* Black.

The plaintiff was a shipper of goods in a vessel bound from Dartmouth to Liverpool. The ship sailed from Dartmouth, and put into *Loo*, (a place she must of necessity pass,) in the course of her insured voyage. But as she had not liberty, by the policy, to go to Loo; and although she suffered no damage in going into, or coming out of *Loo*, (for she was lost after she got to sea again), yet this was held to be a deviation; and a verdict was found for the underwriter.—*At Exeter Ass.* 1767. Before Sir Jos. Yates *.

But the most remarkable adjudged case, upon the subject of deviation, and which is decisive of this, as well as a variety of other points, is that of *Wilson and Co. against Elliot.*

The

---

* This judgment was first produced and appealed to in *Stevens & Co. v. Douglas*, before the C. of Session.

The ship *Kingston* was insured " from Carron " to Hull, with liberty to call *at Leith*." She called at *Morison's Haven*, about six miles from Leith; afterwards returned in safety into the original track of the voyage, but was lost, a few days after, off the coast of Northumberland. The Court of Session found, that there was no deviation, for this, among other reasons, that it did not appear the underwriters had suffered a prejudice. But the House of Peers reversed that judgment *.

The following case was originally produced and appealed to in the question *Wilson against Elliot*, before the Court of Session. It is without a date; and there is some ground to suspect, incompletely stated. But, as it has been frequently quoted in the Scotch Courts, to support very different opinions from what we have ventured to maintain, it seems to have sufficient demerit to deserve insertion, in the same state in which we find it.

Hog *and* Kinloch *v.* Bogle *and* Scott.

A ship lying in the harbour of *Dundee*, was freighted to carry a cargo of lead from Leith to Campvere, and insured "*from the frith of Forth*" to that port. A freight in the mean time came in the way, from where she then lay (*Dundee*), to

* This case shall be fully stated on a future occasion. See below *ejus sect*.

to *Campvere*, which she agreed to take, and give up the other, *viz.* that from *Leith*; the policy was not altered, either from inattention, or that they considered it in no way material, whether the vessel sailed from the frith of Tay or Forth, as the port of destination (Campvere) was the same in both cases. The ship was lost in her way out, and the matter issued in a law-suit before the Court of King's Bench.—The underwriters argued, that they could not be made liable, as *the ship had not sailed from the frith of Forth*, as specified in the policy. Lord MANSFIELD desired to know what *course* the vessel steered from Dundee, and particularly, whether she had come safe into the course, which is in general taken from the frith of Forth. It was proved, by the oaths of five witnesses, that *the ship came even with the precinct of the frith of Forth*, being two miles off the isle of May, and so continued in the very same course as if she had come from Leith, or any other port within the frith of Forth, for Campvere.—Lord MANSFIELD said, that that made the matter very clear. Had the vessel been lost between the frith of Tay and the isle of May, the insurers could not be liable; but having come in safety into the *course* taken in general by ships going from the frith of Forth, the place from which the insurance commenced, no matter from whence she came prior to that, the underwriters were unquestionably

questionably liable ; and he doubted not, but the jury would find it so; which they accordingly did.

This judgment has in Scotland been founded on, in favour of a general, extensive interpretation of the policy; and in particular to show, that a deviation is not effectual to vacate the contract, unless a loss has happened *in consequence* of it. But this application of the decision is, with submission, erroneous. The question here appears to have been, whether parties in the insurance had any view to the *particular period of the voyage at which the insurance was to commence*; whether they meant, that the adventure was to commence like the insurance, " from the frith " of Forth." Lord MANSFIELD thought there was no evidence that such a restriction was meant; it does not appear from the words of the policy. It is to be wished, however, the case had been more fully reported, and upon better authority.

At the same time that it seems established in Britain, by repeated decisions, as well as founded on solid principles, that the insurer shall not be obliged to shew a prejudice arising from any breach of the policy, yet it must be acknowledged, that it will not be easy to reconcile this doctrine with many of the foreign mercantile regulations.

3. When

3. When it is said, that the vessel must follow the *direct line* of voyage, between the ports and places pointed out in the contract, and the *precise plan* of the adventure, this expression requires some explanation. The *direct line* of voyage must be followed only so far as circumstances will permit.

If the vessel should be driven out of her direct course by unavoidable accident; by winds and seas; or if the risk should be protracted by an embargo, this will not infer a deviation: The insurer takes upon himself all such accidents, and their consequences: The variation is a matter of necessity.

But it is not a physical necessity alone, that will justify a variation from the direct course of the voyage. If the master alters his proposed route, from a reasonable apprehension of enemies, or pirates; of a shipwreck, or an embargo; or of any other accident equally fatal to the adventure; the measure is in fact a matter of necessity, as much as if it had originated from the violence of winds or waves.

" If," says Roccus, " a ship alters its course, or
" deviates from the direct track of its voyage,
" the insurer is no longer bound, unless indeed
" the master alters his course, from motives of
" necessity, such as to refit his vessel, escape
" a storm, or to avoid an enemy; in which
" cases, notwithstanding the alteration of the
" ship's

" ship's course, the insurers remain fully
" bound *."

" Real and imminent danger of shipwreck,"
say all the Commentators and foreign ordinances, " or of stranding, or falling into the
" hands of enemies or pirates; contrary winds,
" storms, a necessity of obtaining a port to stop
" a leak or repair damages; these are just and
" reasonable causes of deviating from the direct
" course of the voyage †."

This apology, it must be observed, for a departure from the direct course of the voyage, is very extensive. It is extremely difficult, or rather impossible to distinguish accurately between what is absolutely necessary, and what is merely expedient. And there seems no reason, in this instance, for attempting to draw the line. The master is, no doubt, in general, bound to adhere to his instructions, and is faulty in departing from the voyage insured. But wherever he can show good reason for having believed that the variation would be of advantage to all concerned; wherever he *acts usefully* for the adventure at large; the underwriters, in such a case, could they have been applied to, would have expressly authorised the measure; and they cannot object to a conduct which the law considers as founded upon their *tacit consent*. It is sufficient to justify

---

* *Roccus, Not.* 52.

† See *Stracca, Kuricke, Casariges, Valines.* For. Ordin. *passim.*

fy a departure from the direct course of the voyage, not only that it be *necessary*, but that it be *useful* to all concerned.

Upon principles perfectly similar, no variation from the direct course can be considered as inferring a breach of the policy, providing the variation in question is agreeable to the received *usage* of merchants and seamen, in such circumstances.

For, in the *first* place, the maxim holds, That we ought to trust to every artist in his own profession. The presumption is, therefore, that the line of voyage which is *usual*, is also *most prudent* and most proper. The shipmaster, who should follow the received practice, would be defensible on the footing of having made a variation that was *useful*.

But, 2*dly*, the contracting parties must be supposed to know the practice, in the particular adventure which is the subject of their agreement, and to approve of it, for the reason above mentioned. Unless there be an express stipulation to the contrary, what can be proved to be *customary*, must be supposed to have their tacit consent.

The assured, therefore, may follow, not only the *direct*, *necessary*, or *useful* line of voyage, but likewise that which is *agreeable to common usage*.

The first of these points, that a departure from the policy is justified by necessity, is perhaps too clear to require illustration. In the case *Motteux*

teux v. L. Afs. Co. formerly quoted, the vessel was insured " at and from Fort St George to London." And it was found, that under the insurance *at* Fort St George, she was at liberty to go to Bengal, to make the necessary repairs for her homeward voyage.

In *Guibert v. Readshaw*, (reported by Mr Park,) the *Nancy* was insured *from Rochelle to Africa*. Three days after she sailed from *Rochelle*, she met with a gale which strained her seams, and split her mizzen-yard and riggings. The crew came in a body to the captain, desiring, for the preservation of their lives, that he would make to some port to repair. The vessel being a new one, and the captain finding she had too little ballast, complied, and put into Lisbon, the nearest port; from whence, after taking in ballast, he proceeded on the voyage. It was found that this was no deviation *.

The case of *Grahame and Coulter against Macnair*, an appeal from Scotland, in which a ship insured " from *Virginia* to *Barbadoes*," had been wrecked among the *Bermudas*, turned upon certain points of evidence, whether Bermudas was in the direct line of the voyage, or near it; and how far any departure from the direct course had been voluntary, or the effect of stormy weather. *Appealed Cases*, 29th March 1770.

It

---

* *Hil. Vac.* 1781. Park's System.

It has been found, however, that where a shipmaster is constrained by necessity to leave the direct course of the voyage, *he must* follow the voyage of necessity as directly as possible, and execute it in the shortest and most expeditious manner.

LAVABRE *against* WILSON, *and* LAVABRE *against* WALTER.

These cases were actions on the same policy of insurance, on the *Carnatic*, a *French* East Indiaman. The voyage was described in the following words, " at and from port *L'Orient* to *Pondi-* " *cherry*, *Madras* and *China*, and at and from " thence, back to the ship's port or ports of dis- " charge in *France*, withli berty to touch, in the " outward or homeward bound voyage, at the " isles of *France* and *Bourbon*, and at all or any " other place or places what or where soever." And there was this additional clause in a subsequent part of the policy, *viz.* " And it shall be " lawful for the said ship in this voyage, to pro- " ceed and sail to, and touch or stay at any ports " or places whatsoever, as well on this side, as on " the other side of the *Cape of Good Hope*, without " being deemed a deviation."

The ship reached *Pondicherry* on the 23d of July 1777. She continued there till the 23d of August following; when, instead of proceeding to *China*, she sailed for *Bengal*; where, having passed the winter, and undergone very considerable

able repairs, she sailed from thence early in the year 1778, returned to *Pondicherry*, and, after taking in a homeward bound cargo at that place, proceeded in her voyage back to *L'Orient*; but was taken in October that year by the *Mentor* privateer. The direct voyage between *Pondicherry* and *Bengal* is usually performed in six or seven days; but the *Carnatic* was about six weeks in going to *Bengal*, and two months on the way back from thence to *Pondicherry*. Both going and returning, she either touched at, or lay off, *Madras*, *Massulipatam*, *Visigapatam* and *Yanon*, and took in goods at all those places.

The defence set up was, that the voyage to *Bengal* was not a part of the original adventure intended; and this was endeavoured to be proved by certain private instructions that had been found aboard the ship, and which gave strong reason of suspicion: At least the voyage from *Pondicherry* to *Bengal*, instead of proceeding to *China*, appeared to be a *deviation*.

The plaintiffs maintained, that, under the general liberty given by the policy, of touching at all places whatsoever, the vessel might go to *Bengal*, as well as to *China**. Lord MANSFIELD, however, having intimated a clear opinion, that the general words were qualified and restrained by

---

* Upon this point, the plaintiffs had several opinions of *Dutch* and *French* lawyers in their favour. See a case in *Bynkershoek*.

by the expressions "*in the outward or homeward bound voyage,*" and "*in this voyage,*" so as to mean *all places whatsoever in the usual course of the voyage to and from the places mentioned in the policy,*—this ground was abandoned. The alleged deviation was defended upon the footing of necessity, evidence being produced to shew, that the vessel needed repairs, and that *Bengal,* in the circumstances of the case, was the only proper place for that purpose.

Lord MANSFIELD, upon one of these cases, stated a point of law against the plaintiff, *viz.* that if necessity were admitted to have been the sole motive for substituting the voyage to *Bengal,* in place of that to *China,* still it was incumbent on the assured to have pursued that voyage of necessity directly, in the shortest and most expeditious manner; and that the delay in going from *Pondicherry* to *Bengal,* and the repeated stops by touching at different places, and trading there, were deviations, and not within the protection, which the supposed necessity afforded to the indirect voyage.

The jury, in both cases, found a verdict for the plaintiff. But upon motion for a new trial, the Court being clear, that the question was ill decided, the plaintiff submitted. *Douglas's Reports,* 19*th* November 1779 *.

That

---

* There was another case, *Bize against Fletcher,* founded upon a different policy on the same ship. In this policy the latitude

That *expediency* is sufficient to excuse a departure from the direct course of the voyage, may likewise be illustrated by a variety of explicit decisions in the *British* courts*.

Delancey and another against Stoddart.

This was an action at the instance of a merchant in the *West Indies*, against his correspondent in *England*, for neglecting to obey his instructions with regard to insuring a vessel, " the " *Friendship*, in a voyage at and from *St Kitts* to " *London*, warranted with convoy."

The case turned, in a great measure, upon a question of fact, what were the plaintiff's instructions, and how far the defendant had undertaken to execute them. But a point of law occurred, whether the owner had not varied from the destined voyage?

The jury having found a verdict for the plaintiff, the facts relating to this point, as stated by Mr *Justice* Buller, upon motion for a new trial, were in substance as follows:

The ship had been lying at *St Kitts*, and, on or before the 3d July 1781, had left port to take in her cargo. She let go an anchor at *Sandy-point*;

latitude given of sailing to different ports, was not confined in its interpretation by any clauses similar to those laid hold of by Lord Mansfield in the case of *Lavabre v. Wilson*. And a verdict of the jury in favour of the plaintiffs was acquiesced in by the defendant. See *Douglas's Reports*.

* See a foreign case on the same subject. *Rocc. Resp.* 50.

point; but as the wind blew frefh, fhe drove out, and could not come in again. She was obliged to bear away for *St Euftatius*; and, after making feveral efforts to return to *St Kitts*, without effect, it was judged expedient, that fhe fhould finifh her loading at *St Euftatius*; and the plaintiff fold her to a Mr Rofs. She afterwards failed with the convoy on 1ft Auguft, and foundered at fea.

It appeared that *St Euftatius* is in the direct road to London from *St Kitts*; and the convoy always looked into that port to take up any fhips that might be there. That if the *Friendfhip* had failed to St Kitts, fhe muft have gone by *St Euftatius*, but would not have ftopped there.

Lord MANSFIELD.—If a ftorm drives a fhip out of her voyage, and fhe does the beft fhe can to get to her port of deftination, fhe is not obliged to return back to the point from which fhe was driven; but here, the witneffes fay, fhe tried to get back to St Kitts, but could not; and it is eafier to go directly from St Euftatius to London, than to go back to St Kitts firft. No time was loft by taking in the cargo at St Euftatius. Every thing here was the effect of the ftorm.

WILLES, J.—The cafe is difficult. The veffel, when driven to St Euftatius, inftead of going on directly to London, ftays fome time to take in a new cargo. The veffel is fold, and loaded with tobacco, inftead of fugar, which was to have been her original cargo. So that there is a new *owner*, a new *cargo*, and a new *voyage*. Doubtful whether the jury had sufficient evidence before them. The verdict ought to be reconsidered.

Ashurst, J.—This was all one voyage, being the effect of the storm. The vessel might have gone back to St Kitts to finish her loading; but it was better for all parties she should finish it at St Eustatia.

Buller, J.—It was diminishing the risk to finish the loading at St Eustatia. Besides, the evidence says, it is *usual*, where a captain has not got a full loading at St Kitts, to take in the rest at St Eustatia. If, therefore, the policy would have protected the ship, during a *voluntary* stay at St Eustatia, to finish the loading, *a fortiori* it will do so, when the ship was driven by stress of weather. Rule discharged.—*Termly Reports*. Mich. 1785.

Dunlop *against* Allan.

In the beginning of the year 1781, *Hugh Dunlop* shipped a quantity of goods on board the *Castlesemple*, belonging to *Alexander Houston and Company of Glasgow*, for St Kitts. The goods were insured by *Richard Allan*, " from the load-" ing thereof in Clyde, until they shall arrive " at St Kitts, and there be safely landed."

When the vessel arrived, on the 9th of March 1781, in the neighbourhood of St Christopher's, the

the captain received information, that the island was in the possession of the French. He understood, at the same time, that, by the terms of capitulation, goods destined for that island might still be landed there; but that the rest of the cargo (which was destined for Jamaica) and the ship herself, would be liable to seizure. He therefore landed Mr *Dunlop's* goods *at Antigua,* from which they might be transmitted to St Kitts; and he proceeded with the greatest part of the cargo to *Jamaica.* The goods landed at Antigua were soon after consumed by an accidental fire.

Mr *Dunlop,* the shipper, pursued Mr *Allan,* the insurer, for the loss, before the Court of Admiralty.—The insurer defended himself upon the plea of *deviation*; but the Judge-admiral repelled the defence.

The cause having been brought before the Court of Session, it was argued for the insurer, that this deviation from the insured voyage to St Kitts, by landing the goods at Antigua, was not *necessary* nor *useful* to that part of the adventure, with which the underwriter was concerned. As to him, therefore, that step of the master must be considered as a *voluntary deviation,* and must vacate the policy. At least the insurer if he be subjected, should, at the same time, be found entitled to recourse against *Alexander Houston and Co.* who had reaped an advantage, in the preservation of
their

their ship and cargo, by that very measure which had produced a consequential prejudice to the insurer.

The Court approved of the determination of the Judge-admiral, which was in these words; "Repels the defences, finds the defender liable "in the sums sued for; reserving to him his re- "course against the persons by whose conduct "he has been made liable." *Fac. Collect.* 24*th November* 1785.

A *change of ship* is precisely in the same situation with a departure from the *direct course* of the voyage; and it must be justified by the same reasons of necessity, utility, or custom, which excuse any other variation of the risk. In the following case, we have an example of necessity justifying the original departure from the policy, and expediency, those measures which were taken in consequence of that departure.

Plantamour *against* Staples.

The defendant insured the plaintiff, " on the "ship *Duras*, at and from Marseilles to Madeira, "the Cape, Isles of France, &c. and all ports, &c. "in the East Indies, Persia, and elsewhere be- "yond the Cape of Good Hope, from place to "place during her stay and trade there, and un- "til her safe arrival back at her last port of dis- "charge in France, upon any kind of goods, "and also on the body, &c. of said ship."

A verdict was found for the plaintiff, subject to the opinion of the Court on the following case.

That the plaintiffs were interested in bullion and goods, shipped on board the *Duras*, consigned to correspondents in Pondicherry, with instructions to barter the same, and to make returns in Indian produce. The plaintiffs were likewise interested in the ship, which was lost at the Isle of France. A great part of the bullion, and some of the goods, (but damaged), were saved from the wreck, and, without any authority from the underwriters, were sent forward in another ship to Pondicherry, where they were sold, and the returns in India manufacture shipped on board another vessel, the *Pere de Famille*, which sailed in August 1778 for France. The *Pere de Famille* was condemned at the Isle of France, as unfit for the voyage; and the plaintiffs goods put on board another ship, the *Louisa Elisabeth*, which was captured by an English privateer, and condemned as a prize.

On the 29th August 1778, several of the underwriters agreed to run the risk on the goods saved, in any other ship, till their safe arrival in France. The defendant, and others, refused this; but paid the average loss on the *Duras*. *Question*, Whether the defendant is obliged to pay the loss sustained by the capture and condemnation

demnation of the ship *Elisabeth,* and her cargo? if not, whether the plaintiffs are entitled to any, and what return of premium? Lord MANSFIELD. There is not a particle of doubt. The best that could be done, was done. The shipping at Pondicherry is admitted to have been necessary; the goods must come back in the best way;—this was the best.—The policy is properly worded, and the underwriters liable.

BULLER, J.—The case of *Mills v. Fletcher,* is very applicable, which determines generally, that the captain has a power to do every thing for the good of all concerned. And here the object was trade. The *postea* to be delivered to the plaintiff. *Mich.* 22. *Geo.* III. *MS.*

With regard to the effect of *Usage,* in explaining the meaning of parties in the policy, the adjudged cases of the English courts are voluminous.

SALISBURY *v.* TOWNSON.

A ship insured from Liverpool to Jamaica, put into Douglas Bay in the isle of Man. It appeared that there were some instances of the Liverpool ships putting in there, but it was not the *settled, established, common,* nor *direct* course of the voyage and trade; therefore it was held a deviation, and discharged the underwriters from any

any loss that happened subsequent to the deviation *.

Pelly v. Royal Exch. Ass. Co.

The plaintiff insured the ship *Onslow* from London to any ports and places beyond the Cape of Good Hope, and back to London, and until moored for twenty-four hours in the river Thames.

The ship sailed the 27th December 1753, upon a voyage to China, and arrived at Canton; where the captain took out the sails and tackle, in order to refit his ship, and laid them up in a *bank saul*, upon an island called *Bank-saul Island*, where they were soon after destroyed by an accidental fire. It appeared to be the universal custom for all ships in the China trade to do so; that the liberty of doing this was considered as a great advantage, from which the Dutch were the only nation excluded. These facts were found by the jury, subject to the opinion of the Court, whether the policy insured against this accident.

Lord Mansfield, after taking time to advise, delivered the opinion of the Court. By the express words of the policy, the defendants have insured the tackle, apparel, and other furniture of the ship *Onslow* from fire during the whole

---

* Appealed to in the case of *Stevens & Co. v. Douglas*, before the Court of Session, and recognised by English writers.

whole of her voyage, without any restriction. Her tackle was burnt in China, during the voyage. The event therefore is within the general words of the policy, and it is incumbent on the defendants to show, from the manner in which the misfortune happened, that it was not one of the perils undertaken.

A rational system of construction has been adopted of the ancient inaccurate form of words, in which this contract is expressed; this must be the same among all mercantile nations.

If the risk is varied through the fault of the assured, or master of the ship, the underwriter is freed. But the master is not in fault, if what he did, was done in the usual course, or necessarily *ex justa causa*.

The insurer, in estimating the price at which he is willing to indemnify the trader against all risks, must have under his consideration, the nature of the voyage to be performed, and the *usual course and manner* of doing it. Every thing done in the usual course must have been foreseen, and in contemplation, at the time he engaged. He took the risk upon a supposition, that what was usual or necessary would be done.

It is absurd to suppose, when the end is insured, that the usual means of attaining it, are meant to be excluded. Therefore, when the goods are insured " till landed," without express words, the insurance extends to the boat, the usual method

of

of landing goods upon shore. If it is usual to stay so long at a port, or to go out of the direct way, the insurer is considered as understanding that usage. *Bond v. Gonsales,* 2. *Salk.* 443, was so ruled by *Lord Chief Justice* HOLT. If goods are insured on board one ship to a port, and from thence on board another ship, the first that can be got; the insurance extends through all the intermediate steps of removing from one ship to the other, as usual. For the means must be taken to be insured, as well as the end.

All this was determined in the case *Tierney v. Etherington,* quoted by the plaintiff, (circumstances of that case stated.)—What is *usual* in any adventure, is understood to be referred to, as much as if expressed.

The only objection is, that they were burnt upon a *bank-saul,* and not in the ship; upon land, and not in the sea. But many accidents might happen at land, even to the ship. It might be burnt while repairing in a dry dock.

This had been improperly compared to a deviation. For the insurance being to *China,* the reparation at *Canton,* and the circumstances attending it, must have been foreseen by the parties.

Per cur. Judgment for the plaintiff, 1. *Burr.* 23d *May* 1757.

Tierney v. Etherington.

In delivering the opinion of the Court, in the case, *Pelly v. R. Exch. Ass. Co.* Lord MANSFIELD stated the case of *Tierney v. Etherington*, as follows:

That was an insurance on goods in a *Dutch* ship, from *Malaga* to *Gibraltar*, and at and from thence to *England* and *Holland*, both or either beginning the adventure from the loading, and to continue till the ship and goods be arrived in *England* or *Holland*, and the goods there safely landed.

The agreement was, "That, upon the ar-
"rival of the ship at *Gibraltar*, the goods might
"be unloaded, and reshipped in one or more
"*British* ship or ships, for *England* and *Holland*,
"and to return one *per cent*. if discharged in
"*England*."

It appeared on evidence, that when the ship came to *Gibraltar*, the goods were unloaded, and put into a store-ship, (which, it was proved, was always considered as a warehouse;) and that there was then no *British* ship there. Two days after the goods had been put into this store-ship, they were lost in a storm.

For the defendant it was argued, that the insurance was only upon the Dutch and British ships; and that it did not extend to the store-ship, which is considered as a warehouse at land, and so not a peril at sea.

For the plaintiff it was infifted, that this was a lofs in the voyage: The policy is, for all loffes at Gibraltar, as well as to and from. If there had been a Britifh fhip there, and the goods had been put into a lighter, in order to go to a Britifh fhip, and had been loft in the way, that would have been a lofs within the policy. We have liberty to unload and refhip; and therefore have a liberty to ufe all means in order to do that.

LEE, *C. J.* faid,—it is certain that, in the conftruction of policies, the *strictum jus* or *apex juris*, is not to be laid hold of: But they are to be conftrued largely, for the benefit of trade, and for the infured. Now it feems to be a ftrict conftruction, to confine this infurance only to the unloading and refhipping, and the accidents attending that act. The conftruction fhould be *according to the courfe of trade* in this place. And this appears to be the ufual method of unloading and refhipping in that place: *viz.* " That when there is no Britifh fhip there, " then the goods are kept in ftore-fhips."

He added, that where there is an infurance on goods on board fuch a fhip; that infurance extends to the carrying the goods to fhore in a boat. So if an infurance be of goods to fuch a city, and the goods are brought in fafety to fuch a port, though diftant from the city, that is a compliance with the policy, if that be the ufual place to which fhips come.

Therefore,

Therefore, as here is a liberty given of unloading and reshipping, it must be taken to be an insuring the goods under such methods as are proper for the unloading and reshipping. Here is no neglect on the part of the merchant (the insured;) for the goods were brought into port the 19th, and were lost the 22d November.

This manner of unloading and reshipping is to be considered as the necessary means of attaining that which was intended by the policy; and seems to be the same as if it had happened in the act of reshipping from one ship to the other. And as this is the known course of trade, it seems extraordinary if it was not intended.

This is not to be considered as a suspension of the policy, during the unloading and reshipping from one ship to another. For as the policy would extend to a loss happening in the unloading and reshipping from one ship to another; so any means to attain that end, come within the meaning of the policy.

And accordingly a verdict was given for the plaintiff.

In the Easter term following, a new trial was moved for: But it was refused by Lord *C. J.* LEE, Mr *Just.* CHAPPLE, and Mr *Just.* DENNISON; Mr *Just.* WRIGHT, indeed, being of a different opinion, namely, " that it was a removal at the peril of the insured." 1. *Burr.* See the preceding.

NOBLE

Noble *against* Kennoway.

Infurance was made upon the ships, "the *Hope* and the *Anne*, at and from Dartmouth to Waterford, and from thence to their port or ports of difcharge on the coaft of Labrador, with leave to touch at Newfoundland; and upon any kind of goods and merchandifes; and alfo on the fhips *till they fhall be arrived at their port of difcharge, and fhall have moored at anchor twenty-four hours; and on the goods and merchandifes until the fame fhall be there difcharged and fafely landed.*"

The *Anne* arrived fafe on the coaft of Labrador, on the 22d of June, and the *Hope* on the 14th of July 1778. From the time of their arrival, the crews were employed in fifhing, and had taken out none of their cargoes, except at leifure hours, (partly on Sundays) fuch things as were immediately wanted. On the 13th of Auguft, an American privateer entered the harbour, (Temple-bay) and took both the veffels, there being nobody at that time on board either of them. The action was brought to recover the value of the goods. The defence was, that there had been an unneceffary delay in unloading the cargoes, in confequence of which they had been expofed to capture; and that the underwriters ought not to be liable for what had happened from the negligence of the infured. The plaintiffs refted their caufe on the words of the policy, and on the ufage of the trade; with regard

regard to which, they produced evidence to fhew that this had been cuftomary during the fhort time that fettlements had been eftablifhed on the coaft of Labrador; and that in the Newfoundland trade, which was perfectly fimilar, it is cuftomary to keep their goods on board feveral months, and only to unload their cargo when they could not fifh.

A verdict having been found for the plaintiff, a rule to fhew caufe was obtained; when Lord MANSFIELD and the whole Court, were of opinion, that every underwriter is prefumed to be acquainted with the practice of the trade he infures; and confequently he had no reafon to complain of the delay of landing the goods which had taken place in the prefent cafe: And that the evidence with regard to the practice of the Newfoundland trade was properly admitted with regard to the nature of the trade recently eftablifhed on the coaft of Labrador.—The rule difcharged.—*Douglas Reports,* 22. *November* 1780.

The following cafe is nearly connected.

PLANCHE *and* JACQUERY *againſt* FLETCHER.

The plaintiffs *Planché and Jacquery,* merchants in London, infured goods " on board the " Swedifh fhip called the *Maria Magdalena,* at " and from London and Ramfgate to Nantz, " with liberty to call at Oftend, being a general " fhip in the port of London for Nantz." The defendant

defendant underwrote the policy for L. 300, at 3 guineas *per cent.* The ship's clearances from the custom-house in London, and her other papers, were all made out as for Ostend only; but the ship and goods were intended to go directly from London to Nantz, without going to Ostend. Bills of lading in the French language, dated 18th July 1778, were signed by the captain in London, but purporting to be made at Ostend, and that the goods were shipped there to be delivered at Nantz. The policy was subscribed by the defendant on the 7th July, and the lading was taken in between the 24th July and 17th August. The proclamation for making reprisals on French ships, bore date the 29th, and appeared in the Gazette the 31st July. Two underwriters had signed the policy after the proclamation, at the same premium of 3 guineas; one on the 31st of July, and the other on the 7th August. The ship sailed on the 24th August, and was taken by a King's cutter on her way to Nantz. After her departure from Gravesend, the captain threw overboard all the papers he had received from the custom-house at London; they had been obliterated by the custom-house officers at Gravesend, and were no longer of any use. The ship was released by the Admiralty; but the goods, in which alone the plaintiffs were concerned, were condemned.

A verdict having been found at Guildhall for the plaintiffs, application was made for a new trial,

trial, upon two grounds; one of which was, That there was a fraud in the underwriters, the ship having been cleared out for Ostend, and yet never having been designed for that place *.

Besides the facts above stated, the plaintiffs produced evidence to shew, that all ships going with goods of British manufacture to France, clear out for Ostend, without meaning to go thither; and that this is universally understood by the persons concerned in that branch of commerce. The view was to evade certain French duties.

Lord MANSFIELD said, That *the clearance for Ostend could be no fraud upon the underwriters, being according to the established course of the trade.* Perhaps it was no fraud upon any body; for it was probable, that these evasions of the *French* duties were connived at by the *Fermiers Generaux.* But, at any rate, the evasion of a foreign revenue-law was no fraud in this country; one nation does not take notice of the revenue-laws of another †.

The

---

* The other was, That as hostilities were declared after the policy was signed, and before the ship sailed, the defendant ought to have had notice, that he might have exercised his discretion, whether he would chuse for a peace premium to run the risk of capture.

† As to the other objection, his Lordship observed, that in the circumstances of the case, every man, at the time the policy was underwritten, might have foreseen the war; and as other persons

The rule discharged. *Douglas's Rep.* 15th November 1779.

But it is in the case of *East India* ships, that most frequent and striking examples have occurred, of the effect of *usage* in interpreting the meaning of parties.

SALVADOR *v.* HOPKINS, *and* HEATTON *v.* RUCKER.

By the charter-party made use of between the *East India* Company, and the owners of ships taken into their service, the Company are at liberty to detain all such ships for twelve months after the expiration of the original agreement.

The *Winchelsea* was insured " at and from " *Bengal* to any ports and places in the *East Indies,* " *China, Persia,* or elsewhere, beyond the *Cape of* " *Good Hope,* forwards and backwards, and du- " ring her stay at each place, until her arrival at " *London,"*—" at a premium of *four per cent."*

The vessel was detained in the *East Indies,* in consequence of a new agreement with the presidency of *Bengal,* from March 1762, till some time in March 1764, when she was lost. The underwriters insisted, that the policies were void, because, at the time of subscribing, they were not expressly told of the new agreement, by which the ship was to be detained in *India* for a year longer than the enlarged time provided for

persons had underwritten at the same premium after war was actually proclaimed, it appears probable, that the defendant himself had the war risk in view when he signed.

by the charter-party, this last having expired on the 11*th of February* 1764.

There were nine causes on the same ship, which were at first decided differently; but on motion for a new trial, were all ultimately determined in favour of the assured,—upon these grounds: That the underwriters are *bound and presumed* to know the course of the *East India* trade, the terms of the charter-party, and the destination of *India* ships, (which are under the direction of the Company, and not of their owners.)—That, besides the liberty given by the charter-party, to prolong the ship's stay for one year, it is *very common*, by a new agreement, to detain her *a year longer;* for no ship comes home in ballast; and the longer a ship is kept, the more beneficial to the owners.—That the words of the policy are adapted to this usage, being without limitation of time or place.

All these particulars, the insurers might easily have learned at the India-house, and ought to have known.—But they had insured without asking questions about her stay. And there was strong evidence, that the difference of her staying one year longer, would not have altered the premium: For after the new agreement was known, she was insured at the same premium,—and none of the underwriters insisted to be off.

In *Salvador v. Hopkins*, and these other cases, in which a verdict had been found for the plaintiffs, the rule was discharged.

But

But in *Heatton v. Rucker*, where it had been for the defendant, the rule was made abfolute. 3. Burr. 12th *June* 1765, B. R.

The fame point, that, *in confequence of the ufage of the trade*, an infurance on India fhips is underftood to comprehend the *country voyages*, was determined or admitted in a variety of cafes;—*Prefton v. Greenwood;—Gregory v. Chriftie;—Jackfon v. Macaulay;—Moffat againft Ward;—Farquarfon v. Raymond*, and *Farquarfon v. Hunter*, all in the courfe of the year 1785.

4. So far the circumftances, which are neceffary to conftitute an alteration or deviation, and the general effect of either to vacate the policy, or, at leaft, to liberate the underwriter from his obligation, admit of no difpute. But it may be a matter of more doubt what fhall be the confequence, when there has been an intention to vary from the voyage undertaken; but that intention, by the interpofition of accident, prevented from being carried into execution.

Suppofe, for example, that the affured owners have taken on board *a confignment* to a different port from that fpecified in the policy; but the veffel is loft in that part of her courfe in which both voyages coincide. Or fuppofe the mafter has refolved to touch at a port not exprefsly mentioned, but the fhip is captured before he has carried that fcheme into execution: Will thefe infer fuch a variation as fhall free the infurer?

And

And here there seems to be room for a well founded distinction between an *alteration* of the voyage and a mere *deviation* from it. An *alteration* was explained to be " a variation in the plan " of the adventure, *adopted previous to the com-* " *mencement of risk* ;" but a *deviation* takes place " in the execution of the original plan, *after* " *the risk has commenced.*" From this distinction, it seems to follow, that an intention to *alter* the voyage shall destroy the contract; but an intention to *deviate* merely, must, in order to that effect, be actually carried into execution.

It may here, in the *first* place, be observed, that an alteration, though merely intended, and not executed, *may* produce considerable difference in the risk run by the underwriter: For it is a variation *in the plan* of the adventure; and every variation in this respect must produce a greater or less variation in the assured's preparation and outfit, and in the whole measures calculated for the voyage. In this manner the risk run *may* be different from that undertaken, although the vessel should scarcely have weighed her anchor.

Suppose a ship to be insured from London to the South Sea. She requires a thorough repair, a good stock of all kinds of supplies, a strong complement of men, and perhaps an armed force, for such a service. The insurer knowing all these things to be necessary, contracts upon the prospect of that particular hazard. But the assured

sured *alters* his plan, and sends his vessel only to the *Madeiras*; which, we shall suppose, requires a smaller force, and an inferior degree of reparation. The vessel is lost, or taken, while in the direct road both to the South Sea and Madeiras; yet she was not in the course of the adventure originally insured; for the preparation and outfit were different from what was expected, and, for any thing that appears, might be the cause of the loss. Consequently the risk run was, from the very inception of the voyage, from the moment the vessel weighed anchor, different from that which the insurer meant to undertake.

An intended deviation, on the other hand, as it supposes the original plan still to continue in view, and the departure from the policy to be adopted subsequent to the commencement of risk, seems to exclude, in a great measure, the idea of any variation with respect to the preparation or outfit. The voyage, therefore, continues the same with what was undertaken; the intention to deviate produces no difference in the insurer's risk, until that intention be actually carried into execution.

But, in the *second* place, a view much more important occurs. *Intention to alter* must vacate the policy, independent of any consideration as to the amount of risk; for by intending to alter the voyage, the assured has *receded* from his agreement.

It

It was formerly observed, that while matters continue entire, and before the risk has commenced, the assured may recede from the contract, by breaking up the adventure underwritten. He actually does this, when he alters the vessel's destination, and the concerted plan of the voyage. In such a case, if the vessel had arrived in safety, the insurer would have had no action to recover the premium; for the assured would have shown, that the contract was void, by his breaking up the voyage *re integra*. And it is impossible that the obligation of the underwriter can subsist, while the reciprocal obligation of the owner is at an end.

The fact, however, that the assured means to *retract*, can be ascertained from a proof of intention only; because his option, in this respect, must be exercised *rebus integris*, and previous to the actual commencement of the voyage.—It is a matter which is constituted by *deliberate intention* singly. And as intention to *alter* the plan of the adventure, will vacate the obligation of the owner, the same naked intention must put an end to that of the insured.

But in a *deviation*, there is no room for a supposition, that the assured means to recede; because, after the risk is once fairly commenced, the situation of parties does not admit the exercise of such a power upon his part, but he is bound to perform the contract in all points. As therefore an *intention to deviate* will not free the

the assured, there is no reason why it should liberate the underwriter.

Hence, in the case of an alteration, as the policy is null, whenever the insured adopts the resolution of breaking up the voyage, the underwriter is bound to restore the premium; and all things are restored to their original state, as if there had been no contract. But where a variation has taken place, after the commencement of risk, the insurer keeps the premium, although his obligation is vacated from the moment of the deviation.

It would be a greater hardship, therefore, upon the assured, to infer *a deviation*, than *an alteration of the voyage*, from naked intention.

From what has now been stated, one reason suggests itself, for what was formerly laid down, and illustrated by the decisions, *Valleio v. Wheeler*, and *Nutt v. Bourdieu*;—That there can be no baratry with the accession of the ship-owners. In fact, every departure from the policy, with the accession of the ship-owners, implies, not merely a deviation, but an alteration of the voyage. There is *no contract;* for the voyage insured has never existed; and there was, from the beginning, no room either for baratry, or for any other of those perils to which the insurer is understood to subject himself.

It remains to shew by examples, what has been the practice upon this nice and intricate point.

In the *first* place, it seems to be agreed, that an intention merely to *deviate*, has no effect until carried into execution.

Kemp *and* Andrews.

If, after a policy of insurance, a damage happens, and, afterwards, in the same voyage, a *deviation;* yet the assured shall recover for what happened *before* the deviation. For the policy is discharged from the time of the deviation only. *Shower*, 129.—2. *Salkeld*, 444.

Upon the same principle, the ordinances of many countries agree in declaring, that if the voyage be only *shortened*, the risk ends, and the premium is gained. In fact, to shorten the voyage, is to *terminate it by a deviation.*

" Insurers shall be discharged from risks, and
" shall gain the premium, if the assured, with-
" out their consent, send the ship to a *greater*
" *distance* than that mentioned in the policy,
" though it be in the same course. But the in-
" surance shall fully hold good, if the voyage be
" only *shortened.*" *Guidon, c.* 9. *art.* 12.

In the decision, *Cock* v. *Townson*, formerly stated, " it was held by Lord Camden, and the
" jury, that from the moment the ship *George*
" deserted or deviated from the direct voyage,
" the policy was discharged *."

So

---

* The same thing is laid down in the opinions of four eminent *English* Counsel, upon the case of the *Jeanie*, Buchanan

So much for the effect of intention merely to *deviate*. But with regard to an intentional *alteration*, the practice is very far from being equally uniform.

The general line of foreign decisions, in the first place, seems to be directly opposite to the principles we have ventured to lay down; and to establish a conclusion, that even an intention to *alter*, and to change the plan of the adventure, must be *carried into execution*, before it shall vacate the policy. There are three cases collected by *Bynkershoek*, which directly support this opinion. At the same time, these decisions assume principles so widely different from what are received in *Britain* at this day, that, it is believed, the *English* reader will not be disposed to allow them much weight in the determination of the point.

Case.—A ship insured at *Amsterdam*, " from " *Marseilles*, so far as the *Elbe*, with *power to call* " *at all such places as the master shall think proper*, " no place excepted," was taken in the *Mediterranean* by the *Turks*, and burnt. The insured having claimed payment of the loss, the insurers defended themselves on this single ground, that the ship had *altered her voyage*, or had certainly *determined* to alter it; for that he
who

chanan *against* Hunter-Blair, from which it appears, that the rule as to an *intentional deviation* is perfectly understood and established in *England*. See these opinions in *Weskett's Digest*.

who alters his voyage, or *intends* to go into any other port than that expressed in the policy, has no action; and the insurers proved the design of altering the voyage by the consignment; that the master had, at *Marseilles*, agreed to freight his ship for *Dunkirk*; that he sailed from *Marseilles* to *Alicant*, and there also freighted his ship for *Havre de Grace*, and that these two places not being expressed in the policy, here were therefore two new voyages meditated or intended, though not perfected. The insured did not deny this, but said, that the ship was insured from *Marseilles* to the river *Elbe*, " with liberty to " go to all ports and places, none excepted." The meaning of which, in mercantile usage, was (upon the evidence of a crowd of merchants and seamen) maintained to be, that the ship could go to and touch at all ports intermediate, between the places to which and from which the insurance was made; and she must, between *Marseilles* and the *Elbe*, pass by *Alicant*, *Havre* and *Dunkirk*. The insured added, that the ship was taken by the *Turks*, and burnt in the *Mediteranean*, and that she must certainly have sailed through that sea towards the *Elbe*; for as to other cities, towns, or ports, and whether it was lawful for her to go to them, it would indeed be a proper subject of enquiry, if at or about these other cities, &c. the ship had suffered the loss in question.

The

The infurers, on the other hand, infifted, that the general liberty in the policy did not imply a power of touching at all places in the route, with a view of trade, but merely from views of neceffity, and produced the opinion of fome perfons much verfant in infurances, in fupport of this conftruction ;—that befides, the *alteration* of the voyage appeared from the determination of the mind alone ; nor was it material in what place the fhip fuffered the *lofs*, the fole *refolution* of altering the voyage, not the *event*, being what ought to be regarded. The Chamber of Infurances at *Amfterdam,* and afterwards the *Scabini,* decided in favour of the infurers ; but the *Curia* altered the judgment.

When the queftion came before the Senate, moft of the Senators were of opinion, that the claufe of liberty to " touch at all places," extended farther than to cafes of neceffity; for otherwife it was quite fuperfluous ;—but what principally moved them was, that the fhip was deftroyed and burnt, when fhe was failing in the proper courfe towards the *Elbe*, and that the rifk or peril which the infurers took upon themfelves, muft be eftimated from the place where the lofs happened ; for that the *naked determination or bare refolution to alter the voyage did not hurt the infurers ;* the *event* of an alteration might have hurt them, but it was in vain to complain or enquire about a matter which plainly

was

was not effected or carried into execution.—Judgment for the assured. *Feb.* 28. 1708. *Bynkersh. Quæst. Jur. Priv. lib.* 4. *c.* 3.

It deserves notice, that were it not for the account given by *Bynkershoek* of the *principle* on which this decision proceeded, the judgment itself is defensible upon the general liberty granted in the policy, of *going to all ports and places.*

Case.—A ship insured from Amsterdam to London, having been taken in her course by a French privateer, was ransomed for a certain sum; and having afterwards proceeded on her voyage to England, and arrived at the Nore, from thence, instead of going to London, altered her course, and sailed to Lynn Regis in Norfolk; *which from the bills of lading appeared to have been all along the port of her destination.* In an action brought by the insured against the insurers for the ransom money, the insurers refused to pay, because the ship never came to London, the place expressed in the policy; the insurers, in order to be discharged, urged principally that here there was not merely an intention of altering the voyage, but that in fact it was altered; for that the said ship did not sail to London as by agreement it ought to have done, but to Lynn Regis; a place which was not mentioned in the policy, and therefore the contract was void. In answer to this the assured maintained,

maintained, that it was not requisite to express the place or port of the ship's unloading or discharging, but the place or point at which the ship might arrive; it being sufficient if it appears *how far* or *to what point* the insurer undertook the risk; the whole voyage, and part of the voyage, might be agreed for, and so the ship consigned from the Mediterranean to Amsterdam, might be insured to Amsterdam or to Cadiz; and if to Cadiz, it must be at the risk of the insurer to the height of, or as far as Cadiz; nor could he demand that the ship should necessarily enter the very port of Cadiz, although she might if she would: If, therefore, the ship be lost before her arrival at Cadiz, the loss is at the risk of the insurer; and so in the case that has happened, the ship could not sail to Lynn Regis, without first sailing to the mouth of the Thames; wherefore, so far she sailed at the risk of the insurer, and before she arrived there was taken by enemies and ransomed:—The ship might have sailed to London, according to the policy of insurance; but he who undertook a risk to London, has certainly undertaken it as far as the mouth of the Thames: And though the ship did not sail from thence to London, it is obvious that the insured did not thereby run a greater, but a less risk; and therefore it is of no consequence to him that the ship did not sail to London. If the ship had been taken at the mouth of the Thames, sailing to Lynn Regis, no action would have

have lain against the insurer; but such farther destination to Lynn Regis does not increase his risk. Judgment was given for the assured. *June* 27. 1720. *ibid. lib.* 4. *c.* 5.

Case.—Insurance was made at Amsterdam upon a ship on a voyage " from Lisbon to Hamburgh;"—the ship was lost near the coast of England; and the insurers refused to pay the loss; because from the bills of lading, it appeared that she was *destined* not for Hamburgh, but for Toningen in Holstein: The insured answered, That though the bills of lading indeed bore to Toningen, yet this was merely to protect the vessel from French privateers, Toningen being a neutral port, and that in fact Hamburgh was the real port of the ship's destination; but farther, and independent of this, the insured denied, that the voyage was altered, since the ship was lost between those places that were expressed in the policy; to wit, between Lisbon and Hamburgh; and that an alteration of the voyage was to be understood in the case only of some *prejudice* accruing to the insurer; such as, that he run a *greater* risk than he undertook by the policy on the voyage insured; it was lawful to stipulate that not the whole voyage, but even some part of it should be within the policy or risk of the insurer; and it is therefore nothing to the purpose, that the ship was truly destined for Toningen, and the insured had desired it so to be, since

since the ship was not lost between Hamburgh and Toningen, but between Lisbon and Hamburgh.—Judgment was given for the insured. *April* 12. 1714.—*ibid. c.* 10.

The following British decision is a little obscure; and it does not clearly appear, whether the *species facti* regarded an intention to alter, or to deviate. As the former, however, seems most probable, it must be considered as supporting the same side of the question with the Dutch decisions now stated. The case quoted in it, *Carter v. R. Exch. Ass. Co.* is clearly a case of *alteration*, not *deviation*. Both cases are delivered to us without circumstances, and, therefore, of less authority.

Foster *v.* Wilmer.

The insurance was "*from Carolina to Lisbon, and at and from thence to Bristol.*" It appeared the captain had taken in salt, which he was to deliver at Falmouth before he went to Bristol; but the ship was taken in the direct road to both, and before she came to the point where she should turn off to Falmouth; and it was held the insurer was liable; for it is but an intention to deviate, and that was held insufficient to discharge the underwriter. In the case of *Carter v. R. Exch. Assurance Co.* where the insurance was from Honduras to London, and a *consignment* to Amsterdam, a loss happened before she came to the dividing point between these

these two voyages, which the insurers were held to pay for. *Strange* 1249. 19*th Geo.* II.

On the other hand, there are a variety of recent cases which have been uniformly decided in England and Scotland, upon the principle that an *intention* to *alter* is sufficient to void the policy. From these the point seems to be, in this country, perfectly settled. Two or three of the most remarkable may be quoted in this place; the rest may be reserved for the illustration of some other question.

Wooldridge *against* Boydell.

The ship *Molly* being insured " at and *from* " *Maryland to Cadiz*," was taken in Chesapeak-bay, in the way to Europe. The assured brought this action against the defendant, one of the underwriters on the policy. The trial came on at Guildhall before Lord Mansfield, when a verdict was found for the defendant, and a new trial being moved for, the material facts of the case appeared to be as follows:— The ship was cleared from Maryland to Falmouth, and a bond given that all the enumerated goods were to be landed in Britain, and all the other goods in the British dominions. An affidavit of the owner stated that the vessel was bound for Falmouth. The bills of lading were " *to Falmouth and a market*," and there was no evidence whatever, that she was destined for Cadiz.

Cadiz.—It was contended in favour of a new trial, that this was like the cases of an intention to *deviate*, where a capture had taken place before the deviation was carried into execution, which did not vacate the policy.—And besides, it was urged, that by the expression " *a market,*" in the bills of loading, was meant Cadiz; and that " *to Falmouth and a market*" might be considered as meaning to the market at Cadiz, first touching at Falmouth.—It had appeared, however, in evidence, at the trial, that the premium to insure a voyage from Maryland to Falmouth, and from thence to Cadiz, would have exceeded greatly what was paid in this case.

On the other hand, it was argued, that here there had been no inception of the voyage insured, and, therefore, the cases quoted, of an intention to deviate, did not apply.

The Court distinguished between an alteration, such as took place here, and a mere deviation, the design of which was taken up in the course of the voyage. And here there was sufficient evidence that the vessel was never intended for Cadiz, the port mentioned in the policy. —The rule discharged.—*Douglas' Reports.* 13*th November* 1778.

Bain *against* Kippen.

Kippen made insurance for *Bain*, upon a vessel " at and from Rothsay, in the Frith of Clyde, " to the Isle of Man, and from thence to the " Broomielaw

"Broomielaw of Glasgow." There afterwards appeared reason to believe, that her destination really was to fish off the Isle of Man; an adventure attended with more hazard, and entitling the insurer to a higher premium.

The ship proceeded from Rothsay, in the Island of Bute, on her voyage to the Isle of Man; but having been, by stress of weather, driven back to the former island, she was there stranded and wrecked.

Bain having sued *Kippen* for the insured values before the Admiral-court, the cause was thence, at the defender's instance, removed into the Court of Session.

It was pleaded for the underwriters, that the voyage for which the vessel was really destined, being different from that specified in the insurance, no action can lie on the policy; for parties were not agreed; the risk undertaken was different from that understood. That such concealment, besides, of the vessel's real destination, was a fraud upon the insurer.

It was answered by the assured, That the vessel was admitted to have been wrecked in a course the same with that of the voyage covered by the insurance. Whatever intention there may have been to vary the voyage, it had never been carried into execution.—The Lords assoilzied the underwriter.

In a reclaiming petition, the assured having offered to prove that the destined voyage was not for the purpose of fishing, but truly such as was described to the defender, the Court allowed the proof to be adduced. *Fac. Coll. 20th November* 1783.

Buchanans *against* Hunter-Blair.

John and *George Buchanans*, merchants in Glasgow, in consequence of some misapprehension between them and their agent at Honduras, got insurance done upon their vessel, the *Jeanie*, " from Honduras *to Bristol*," while the agent had cleared her out *for London*. The vessel being wrecked soon after her departure from Honduras, the underwriters refused to pay the loss, because the voyage had been *altered*, the Jeanie being consigned to London instead of Bristol.

In an action at the assured's instance against the underwriters, before the Admiral-court, for the insured values, the Judge-admiral pronounced a decree to the following effect:—" In re-
" spect the pursuers did not disclose their direc-
" tions to their correspondent, relative to the
" ship's destination for the port of London, and
" set forth to them the embarrassment which
" might arise from the contrary orders that had
" been given, whereby the defenders might have
" had sufficient lights to determine whether, in
" these circumstances, they would have insured:
" Therefore

"Therefore dismisses the claim of the assured," &c.

In a reduction of this judgment before the Court of Session, it was pleaded, That this was a mere innocent mistake, without fraud, for which it would be hard to vacate the policy; and that the present case corresponded exactly to that of an incomplete intention to deviate, the vessel having been lost in the direct course both to London and Bristol. See the case *Foster v. Wilmer.— Bynkersh. Q. Jur. Priv.*

It was answered for the insurers, That a misrepresentation by the assured, of a fact that is *material*, like the ship's destination, must vacate the policy, whether it has arisen from fraud or error. That here the voyage undertaken had never commenced; and as the insured, by breaking up the voyage, was free from the payment of premium, so must the underwriter from the risks of the adventure. That this put a material difference between an intended alteration and deviation. And if it were to be found, that an insurance to one place covered a voyage to another, because the courses were the same for a part of the way, it would involve the most dangerous and extensive consequences, and deprive the insurers of all certainty as to the extent of what they had undertaken. The Lord Ordinary, (AUCHINLECK) and afterwards the Court, " approved of the Judge-admiral's decree, and
" assoilzied

"assoilzied the defenders." *Fac. Coll. July* 15. 1779*.

Considering this distinction therefore, between an intended alteration and deviation, as perfectly established, it will lead to an explanation of a variety of apparent inconsistencies in the foreign ordinances. Thus, where it is said, " If a ship "shall voluntarily go by Cape Verde, without in- "serting and declaring it in the policies, it shall "be deemed a change of voyage; and if she "should be lost, the insurer shall have nothing "to pay, whether she be lost *before* or *after* ar- "riving at the Cape de Verde islands." *Ord. of Spain.*—This must obviously relate to the case of an intended *alteration*, where the determination as to the Cape Verde islands had been taken up *before* the commencement of risk, and consequently the insurance would be null from the beginning.

5. In cases of variation from the voyage insured, it is not a sufficient defence to the assured, that the departure from the policy was the act of master or crew alone, and that the assured themselves were not accessory to it. This situation, it may be observed, can only occur where the assured is a *shipper of goods*; because the owner of ship, having the regulation of the adventure, cannot be supposed ignorant of any alteration projected,

---

* The insured acquiesced in this judgment, upon the advice of four eminent English counsel, whose opinions have been published at length in Mr *Weskett's Digest of Insurance.*

projected, from the course of the voyage specified in the policy.

It was formerly attempted to be shown, that the underwriter could never be liable beyond the terms of his contract; that every departure therefore, from the voyage insured, being contrary to the agreement, must have the effect *naturally* to vacate the policy, whether that departure was the consequence of *fraud* or of *mere fault*. It was observed, however, that parties might, by special clauses, extend the obligations of the underwriter beyond their natural limits: He is not naturally liable for *fraud* or *fault* of the assured's servants; because fraud and fault suppose a breach of the implied terms of the contract; but he may, by an express stipulation, subject himself to either.

It was farther observed, that a great difference had taken place between Britain, and the greater number of mercantile nations, in this respect. In the foreign states, the insurer subjects himself, either in express terms, or by construction, to the consequences both of *fraud* and of *negligence*; in Britain he takes upon himself the peril of *baratry*, by which is meant *fraud only*.

From this difference, very curious and important consequences follow; and upon the point now under consideration, whether the accession of the assured is necessary, in order to give a deviation the effect of vacating an insurance-contract,

tract, a marked opposition takes place between the law of *Britain*, and of most other countries.

In foreign states, the insurer undertakes for the *master's fault ;* therefore he undertakes for a *deviation by the master's fault ;* that is, every departure from the policy, to which the assured is not accessory.

Thus, by the ordinances of *Middleburgh*, " the " *insured must not cause the master* he has freight-" ed to alter his voyage, or to enter or touch at " any other port than what is expressed in the " policy, otherwise the assurance shall be void. " But the master may touch at other harbours, " whenever necessity requires it ; and *when he* " *acts to the contrary, without orders from the* " *assured, the assurance shall nevertheless remain in* " *its full value, reserving to the assurer his redress* " *upon the master."* § 14.

By the ordinances of *France*, " Insurers shall " be answerable for all losses or damages, which " shall happen at sea, by tempest, shipwreck, " stranding, running foul of other ships, *changing* " *the course*, or the voyage of the ship, jettison, " fire, capture, plundering, detention of princes, " declaration of war, reprisals, and generally all " other accidents of the sea." § 26. (1681.)

" However, if the change of the course, the " voyage, or the ship, proceed *from an order of* " *the insured*, without the consent of the insurers, " they shall not be answerable for the risks." § 27.

By

By the *Prussian* maritime laws, or ordinances of *Koningsberg*:—" When an insured ship, or
" goods, *with the knowledge and consent of the par-*
" *ties insured*, go to other places and harbours
" than those specified in the policy, the insurance
" shall be void, and the premium agreed upon
" fall to the insurer. *But, in case the master, ei-*
" *ther at the instigation of another freighter, owner,*
" *or any other person, or of his own choice,* shall,
" without any necessity, sail to other places than
" that to which he was bound; or, in case of
" danger, shall neglect to endeavour, as far as is
" possible, to get into a place of security, the in-
" surance shall remain in full force; but the in-
" surer shall have his redress against the master
" and ship, for any damage or prejudice occa-
" sioned thereby." § 30.

By the ordinances of the city of *Hamburgh*;
" When a master of a ship shortens his voyage,
" the risk is at an end, and the premium gained;
" but if he prolongs the same, as, for example, if
" he goes to any other place than what he was
" bound to, *and the same is done with the know-*
" *ledge and consent of the assured*, then the assurer
" is nowise answerable for any misfortune that
" may happen to ship or goods, in such circui-
" tous course." § 5.

By the regulations of *Stockholm*, " If the ma-
" ster shall, without actual necessity, *and with-*
" *out the consent and knowledge of the insured,*
" go

" go to places and ports not specified in the po-
" licy, *the insurance is not invalidate thereby*, but
" the insurer may obtain redress against the ma-
" ster." § 11.

By the ordinances of Rotterdam, " the assu-
" red cannot give any orders to the captain for
" altering the voyage, or to go into any port,
" contrary to the tenor of the policy; and the
" assured, *if such alterations of the voyage are
" made by his order*, shall lose the right of his de-
" mand upon the insurer." § 51.

" When a captain, without necessity, *and
" without any orders from the assured*, hath alter-
" ed the voyage, or has run into, or touched at
" any other port or road, *the assurance is to re-
" main in its force*. However, the assured being
" satisfied by the assurers for the loss sustained
" by means thereof, shall be obliged, at the same
" time, to give up to the assurers all the claim
" he may have upon the captain on that score."
§ 52.

By the ordinances of *Amsterdam*, " the insu-
" red *on the cargo* may not cause the master,
" whom he has freighted, to enter, or to make
" any other port, nor to alter his voyage,
" but according to the policy, otherwise the in-
" surance shall be null, although it had been
" inserted in the policy, that he might touch at,
" and make all places any where; but the ma-
" ster may touch at other ports than those men-
" tioned in the policy, when necessity requires
" it.

" it. *And doing otherwise, if it be without order*
" *of the insured, the insurance shall nevertheless*
" *remain valid, saving to the underwriters the*
" *right of having recourse on the master; but if*
" *the insurance be made for the owners or pro-*
" *prietors of the ship, it shall, in such case, be*
" *null.*" § 6.

In conformity with these regulations, a variety of cases are to be found in the Commentators, and particularly in every page of *Bynkershoek;* of which the following is a sufficient example:

Case.—A merchant in Sweden got his vessel insured at Amsterdam, " from Elsineur to Am-
" sterdam." The ship *deviated* to the coast of Norway, for the sake of convoy, and was afterwards lost.

In an action upon the policy, the underwriter, among a variety of defences, pleaded the deviation. It was answered, that, by the *Ord. Amst.* the insurance subsisted, *if the master deviated, without orders from the assured*, which there was reason to suppose had been the case here. Several senators maintained, that the ordinance alluded to related to the case of *assured shippers* only, and not to *assured owners*, who appoint the master, and ought to be responsible for him. But the majority thought it applied to both. And although the owner was, by the Civil law, liable for the conduct of the master;
yet

yet it was allowed for the infurer to relieve him, in part, from that obligation, by undertaking for the mafter's *fault*, which he had done in this cafe, by the ufual claufe for that purpofe in the policy. The prefent deviation in this cafe cannot imply *fraud* * in the mafter, but *fault* only; and the infurer therefore was refponfible for it. The Senate of Holland gave judgment for the affured †. (1717.)

In Britain, the contrary opinion is univerfally underftood to be law; and it has been eftablifhed confiftently with principles, and with the fpirit of an Englifh policy: for in Britain, the infurer undertakes no breach of contract, except what arifes from *fraud*. He is not refponfible for the *faults* of mafter or crew, any more than he is for thofe of the affured themfelves. *Every* departure from the policy, (unlefs it amount to *baratry*), is equally beyond the terms of the bargain, whether it arifes from the mafter, or from his employers.

This conclufion may be gathered from a variety of adjudged cafes in the Englifh courts. But in the two following memorable inftances, the point was exprefsly decided. Thefe two cafes likewife afford illuftrious precedents upon the whole doctrine of alteration and deviation.

STEVEN

* In Holland, an affured *owner* cannot infure againft *baratry* of *mafter*, but *fault* only. See above.
† *Bynkerfh. l.* 4. *c.* 8. *Queft. Jur. Priv.*

Steven and Co. *against* Douglas.

John Douglas, merchant in Glasgow, insured *Steven and Co.* to the amount of L. 80 Sterling " on goods, by the *Belfast Trader*, at *and from* " *Belfast to Greenock or Port-Glasgow.*" On the 11th December 1770, the vessel had sailed from *Belfast Loch;* and on the 12th, the same day on which the policy was underwritten, she was totally wrecked on the coast of Scotland, near the village of *Girvan* in *Ayrshire*, and every person on board perished.

In an action on the policy, before the *Dean of Guild* of Glasgow, Mr *Douglas* pleaded deviation, or rather that the vessel had never sailed on the voyage insured. A proof was allowed; but the pursuer stopt it, by an *advocation* of the cause to the Court of Session.

It came before Lord Kennet, as Ordinary. The underwriter gave in a condescendence* of the facts he pleaded in defence; in which he set forth, that a wilful variation vacates a policy;—that the vessel, in this case, had not sailed on the voyage insured from *Belfast to Clyde*, but on a different voyage, from *Belfast to Lochryan and Clyde ;*—in the course of which, and during the deviation, she was lost; that this variation was not only known to the ship-owner, but public in Belfast eight or ten days before the insurance.

The

---
* A particular.

The assured, without admitting the facts alleged, denied that they were relevant*. He argued, that the underwriter had not specified enough to infer an *actual deviation*, but only an *intention to deviate*;—that, supposing it proved that the ship sailed for *Lochryan*, and that this was a deviation, yet that the assured having acted *optima fide*, and communicated all the intelligence they had, the policy must be valid; and if a deviation has taken place, *without the assured's accession*, it is the underwriter who must be liable in the first place, and may make good his recourse against the owner or shipmaster, as he best can ;—that if the shipmaster deviates, to the prejudice of the assured, it is a *deceit* or *imposition* on them, and therefore *baratry*. It is not less a *deceit* that the ship-owners are accessory.

Authorities founded on *Magens' Essay*, § 46.; *Ord. of Amst.* No. 517.; *of Middleb.* No. 177.; *of Rotterd.* No. 258.; *of Stockh.* No. 1042.; *Beawes' Lex Merc. Red.* Many of these make the distinction between an assured *owner of ship* and *shipper of goods*.

The *Lord Ordinary*, wishing to have the opinion of mercantile people, a case was made up, by parties, substantially agreeing with the defender's condescendence; and upon it, three merchants

---

* Inferred the conclusion of law founded upon them.

chants in Edinburgh, converfant in infurances, Mr *Alexander*, Mr *Houfton*, and Mr *Kinnear*, gave a report in favour of the affured.

The Lord Ordinary found, " that the defend-
" er has not condefcended on any thing fuffi-
" cient to free him from payment of the fum un-
" derwritten; therefore refufes a proof, and de-
" cerns againft him, &c."

In a reclaiming petition, Mr *Douglas* produced a variety of authorities to prove the effect of a variation. *Coke v. Townfon* ; *Salifbury v. Townfon*; *Fox v. Black*; *Burr. vol. 4. p.* 347.; *M'Nair v. Coulter*; *Roccus, p.* 165. and 207. with the opinions of fome perfons in England converfant in infurance-law.

At advifing this petition with anfwers, it feemed to be the opinion of feveral judges, that an *actual deviation* was neceffary to vacate the policy. And great doubt was expreffed of the poffibility of proving actual deviation, when nobody had been faved from the wreck ; and it behoved to be uncertain what was the effect of intention, and what of ftrefs of weather.

Several were inclined to adopt the opinion, that in order to vacate a policy, the affured muft be acceffory.—And the different fituation, in this refpect, of an affured owner of fhip, and fhipper of goods, was mentioned.

A judge, high in office, faid he was moved by the opinion of the London underwriters, and by the nature of the contract, to think otherwife.

The

The voyage insured is " from Belfast to *Clyde,*" not " *to Lochryan.*" The assured may recover against the shipmaster, not against the underwriter; *because there is no contract.*

This last opinion prevailed. And the Court first allowed Mr *Douglas* to produce a fuller *condescendence*, and upon advising it with answers, " allowed a proof;" recommending it to parties at the same time, to procure full information with regard to the London practice. The pursuer reclaimed;—but the Court adhered.

Upon proof, it was completely established, that although the vessel had been advertised for Greenock, and her clearances, as well as the bill of loading sent to *Steven and Co.* had been for that port only, the ship-owner, a Mr *Mitchell*, had taken in a *consignment of hides, and a terce of beef, for Stranraer, at the head of Lochryan;* that these had been loaded uppermost to be first discharged. A Dublin newspaper was produced, to prove that the wind was W. S. W. for a track of time, before and after the 12th December. And three shipmasters swore, that, *in such a wind,* the proper course to Clyde is away from the coast of *Ayrshire,* and to the east of the *Rock of Ailsa.* The defender produced satisfactory and undisputed evidence of the London practice in his favour.

Informations being ordered upon the proof, the pursuer stated, that there was no proof of either the assured, or his agent at Belfast, *knowing*

ing any thing of the intention to vary from the policy; and that the evidence of actual deviation was not conclusive.

The Court were almost unanimous, from the consideration, chiefly, of the *London* practice, that, in order to vacate a policy, it was not necessary the assured should be accessory. A great majority thought it sufficiently proved, from the whole circumstances, that the intention to vary had here actually been carried into execution. One judge observed, ' It is sufficient, to have the effect of a ' deviation, that the vessel was *destined for Stran-* ' *raer.* This is the circumstance founded on by ' the *London* insurers. " If *bound* for *Stranraer*," say they, " the policy is vacated."—No matter ' where she was lost.'—

The Court " found the deviation from the " voyage to Greenock proven; therefore sustain- " ed the defences," *&c. Dec.* 20. 1774.—The pursuer reclaimed upon this point, that there was no sufficient evidence of actual deviation. The Court, upon advising the petition, with answers, refused the desire of the petition, and adhered*.

WILSON *and Co. against* ELLIOT, *and others.*

Wilson and Co. merchants in *Glasgow*, having occasion to send some tobacco to *Hull*, applied to the Shipping Company at *Carron*, for freight. Having

* Collected from the printed papers, and notes of the counsel for *Steven and Co.*

Having forwarded their tobacco, they were advised by that Company, " that it was shipped " aboard the *Kingston*, which would sail next " day." At the same time, bills of loading were sent, but neither the letter covering these bills of loading, nor the bills themselves, nor any letters prior or subsequent, nor any advertisement, made mention of the vessel's being to touch at any port on her way to *Hull*. She sailed on the 4th February 1774.

On the 9th February, Mr *Wilson* applied to an insurance-office in Glasgow for a policy on this adventure; and having observed, that these coasting *Carron* vessels sometimes touched at different ports in their voyage, he conceived his order in the following words: " Please insure " for my account, *per* the *Kingston*, George Fin- " lay master, from *Carron* to *Hull, with liberty* " *to call as usual*, fourteen hogsheads tobacco, " at L. 38, 10 s. *per* hogshead, value in all " L. 539." He did not restrict the broker to any premium.

The broker shewed this order to *Coulter*, a judicious and experienced underwriter, who refused to sign it, with the general clause of *calling as usual*, and desired an explanation. The broker, to remove this objection, observed, that he supposed these vessels usually called *at Leith;* upon which Mr Coulter agreed to sign the policy, if filled up, " with liberty to call *at the* " *port of Leith*." The broker accordingly, without consulting the owner of the goods, filled up the policy, "*with liberty to call at the "port of Leith;"* upon which it was underwritten by Mr Coulter. It was afterwards subscribed by other underwriters, without knowing these circumstances. The merchant, however, got no account of this alteration of his order, till some days after the insurance was made, and a loss incurred. The ship sailed from *Carron*, did not call at Leith, but, by direction of the owners, went into *Morison's Haven*, a port about six miles beyond *Leith*, where she staid four days, and took in goods. She afterwards returned from *Morison's Haven* into the direct course of her voyage; and was on the 10th February totally lost off *Holy Island*.

The assured shipper of goods sued the underwriters, the owners of ship, and the insurance-brokers, before the Court of Admiralty in Scotland.

In the question between the assured and underwriters, the Judge-admiral " having con-
" sidered the whole circumstances of the case,
" and, in particular, that *it is not alleged* by the
" defenders, *that the pursuers were in the know-*
" *ledge of the ship being intended to put into Mo-*
" *rison's Haven*, repels the defences, &c." He afterwards allowed a proof, which, however, the underwriters declined to adduce; and he pronounced the following judgment: " Finds, that
" in

" in all cafes of infurance of goods on fhip-
" board, (belonging to others than the owners,
" and mafter of the fhip,) it is a general rule in
" law and practice, that the infurance fhall be
" effectual, although the lofs may have happen-
" ed in a deviation from the courfe of the voy-
" age, upon which infurance is made, *the in-
" fured not knowing of, nor confenting to fuch de-
" viation;* and finds, that at the making of in-
" furance upon fuch goods on fhipboard, it may
" be agreed between the parties, that, in the
" event of a deviation not allowed of in the po-
" licy, the infurance fhall then ceafe and ter-
" minate, and not be further effectual for the
" remaining part of the voyage; but finds, that,
" in the prefent cafe, there are not facts fuffici-
" ent to infer, that it was agreed the infurance
" was to terminate, and be no further effectual,
" in cafe of a deviation for the remaining part
" of the voyage; and further, having confidered
" that the fhip the *Kingfton*, after going into *Mo-
" rifon's Haven*, and failing from thence, did at-
" tain to, and was in the direct courfe of the
" voyage from *Carron Wharf* to *Hull*, where fhe
" was wrecked; finds, upon the whole, that the
" defenders are liable, &c."

The caufe was brought by fufpenfion before the Court of Seffion; and Lord ALVA reported it to the whole Lords, when one of the grounds of the Judge-admiral's decifion, *that the devia-*

tion had been without the knowledge of the assured, was entirely given up.

For the underwriters, it was argued, That this was an intentional deviation from the course of the voyage insured, which must vacate the policy; *Pelly v. R. Exch. Ass. Co.; Macnair against Grahame and Coulter; Coke contra Townson; Salisbury contra Townson.*—The risk has been increased; for Morison's Haven is a more dangerous port than Leith;—calling there implied a different cargo, and perhaps greater delay in loading. But it is immaterial what was the hazard of calling at Morison's Haven; it was not the precise adventure undertaken. If the ship had refrained from calling at Morison's Haven, it is a question whether she would have met with the storm. In this case, to touch at Morison's Haven, or any other port but Leith, was even particularly provided against; for *Coulter* refused to sign, with a general liberty of calling; and the insertion of *Leith*, in particular, implies an exclusion of every other port.

The assured argued, that a policy ought to meet with an equitable construction in their favour; and therefore a deviation ought not to vacate the policy, when it appeared to have been productive of no prejudice to the underwriter. In this case, the variation was rather nominal than real; Morison's Haven was so near, it could scarcely be said to be out of the course insured. And no advantage was taken of the underwriter;

underwriter; for the rifk was not increafed, the ufual premium of a voyage from Carron to Hull being the fame, whether they had liberty to touch at Morifon's Haven or not. And no lofs did in fact arife to the infurers from the fuppofed deviation, as the veffel had returned to, and was loft in the courfe of the voyage infured. When this is the cafe, it has been decided, that a deviation fhall not vacate the policy; *Kinloch and Hog v. Bogle and Scot.* Neither can the infurers found upon the argument, that the lofs may have happened in confequence of the delay at Morifon's Haven; for the veffel was allowed to call at *Leith*, without any limitation of time in ftaying there; the rifk of the voyage being prolonged, by calling at *a port* in the courfe of it, was clearly undertaken by the infurers; and it made no difference of hazard, whether that port was *Leith* or *Morifon's Haven.*

Befides, the underwriters were guilty of fault, and improper conduct, in perfuading the broker to vary from what they knew to be his inftructions; particularly after they knew that the fhip had failed, and her deftination confequently was irrevocable. An infurance-broker is the agent of the underwriter, and under his influence.

The opinions of a great number of merchants and infurers at London and Leith were offered in favour of the affured.

Obferved on the Bench.—" No prejudice in-
" curred by going into Morifon's Haven.—Dan-
" gerous

"gerous and inconvenient to merchandife, were
"an interpretation fo literal to be adopted.—
"The going into Morifon's Haven not fo im-
"portant as to conftitute a different voyage (as
"had been the cafe in *Steven againft Douglas*).—
"Improper behaviour of the infurers, particu-
"larly after they knew the veffel had failed.
"The Judge-admiral's decree, however, goes on
"a wrong ground."

The Court, by a great majority, "Having
"confidered the whole circumftances of the
"cafe, repelled the defences," &c. *

In a reclaiming petition, the underwriter ftrongly urged,—That although a policy ought to meet with a fair conftruction, according to the meaning of parties, yet the inftrument is the medium by which that intention muft be judged of. It is immaterial what is the real rifk attending the deviation; whether greater, equal to, or even lefs, than that of the voyage infured; it muft be *the fame* individual rifk; for otherwife it may be greater in the infurer's opinion. Befides, the fituation of parties calls for a ftrict adherence upon the part of the affured. There can be no difference between a great and a fmall deviation; this admits of no rule, and would involve infurance in total uncertainty. It is a miftake that a deviation cannot vacate the policy, unlefs the lofs happen in the courfe of it. The contrary has been found; *Fox v. Black.*

* Lords Hailes and Monboddo of a contrary opinion.— Lord Kames doubtful.

Black.—*Kinloch v. Bogle* is not applicable. The insurance is void from the moment of the deviation, and cannot revive without a new bargain.

Neither is there any room for blame upon the insurers, because they refused to sign the policy, as it was first drawn out, agreeably to the broker's instructions. The broker is not the agent of the underwriter, but of the assured, to whom he must be responsible, if he departs from his order; and he must judge for himself how far he can do this with propriety. There is no collusion alleged in the present case. It is unreasonable to find fault with any man for refusing to sign a contract, until the conditions of it are rendered agreeable to his own inclination.

Upon advising this petition, with answers, the Court, by a great majority, *adhered* *; March 7. 1776 †.

The underwriters appealed; and the House of Peers " ordered and adjudged, that the interlo-
" cutors complained of be *reversed;* and it is
" declared, that the respondents are entitled to
" a return of the premiums paid by them to the
" appellants." 25th *Nov.* 1776.

The assured's claim against the ship-owners and the insurance-broker, was submitted to arbitrators, who found the *broker* liable.

SECT.

---

* Lords KAMES, MONBODDO, HAILES, *alter.* Lord KENNET doubtful.

† From the materials of the late Mr Professor *Wallace*, collected in order to a report of the case.

Sect. 2. *Effect of the Assured falling short of the express Conditions of the Policy, or of* Non-performance.

1. The principles formerly mentioned, with regard to the effect of a *variation* from the terms of a policy, may be applied with still greater force, or rather, their application is more obvious, in cases of *non-performance;* the latter being a departure from an *express*, the former from an *implied* obligation only.

If the assured is not at liberty to *touch at any port* that is not precisely pointed out;—if he can execute no measure, with regard to which the policy is silent; much less can he be permitted to violate the *express provisions* of the agreement. That neither party shall assume a latitude of interpretation, is consistent with expediency in matters of insurance: That they shall adhere to the declared conditions of the policy, is agreeable to those rules which govern the explanation of ordinary contracts.

2. Since a strict adherence to the terms of an insurance-policy, is incumbent upon parties, it becomes of importance to fix, with precision, *what is* a part of the policy, and *what is not.*

In

In the communications that take place with regard to the subject of the bargain, to ascertain what expressions and clauses are to be considered as essential conditions of it, and call for an implicit observance.

There may be various communications between the assured and the underwriter, which are not to be considered in that light. It is proper, and perhaps requisite, that the assured should make a full discovery of his intelligence, with regard to the nature of the subject, and the extent of the risk. He may explain his intentions and views in the adventure; he may discover his belief and opinions, his wishes and expectations, his hopes and apprehensions with regard to it. By so doing, he may intend to give the insurer every opportunity of forming a fair and complete estimate of the peril he undertakes; but without proposing to preclude himself from such variations in his system of conduct, as circumstances may render necessary, or to produce a reliance upon the literal terms of the information he communicates. Such *representations of facts*, intended merely to communicate information concerning his views, are carefully to be distinguished from *warranties*, or essential conditions of the contract.

In treating, upon a former occasion, of the effects of fraud and error, an opportunity was taken to consider how far the assured is responsible for the truth and accuracy of those *repre-*

sentations of facts. He must not, it was observed, mislead the underwriter by intelligence that is *false*, or that is *materially erroneous*. What is held to be a *material* error in a *representation* of facts, was likewise illustrated by decisions in several different cases.

In distinguishing a *representation*, or what is intended merely as a piece of collateral intelligence, from a *warranty* which must be strictly adhered to, as a condition of the contract, the chief object must be to find a precise and accurate rule. The rule laid down by Lord MANSFIELD, and by the practice of England, is precise, accurate, and simple. "Whatever is written on the *same paper* with the policy, is a *warranty*." This holds even as to clauses upon the back or margin of the policy.

On the other hand, every *verbal communication*, and every clause engrossed *upon a separate paper*, is held to be a mere extraneous representation. A separate writing does not form a warranty, although it should have been shown to the underwriters at the time of signing; nay, even though it should have been *rolled up* in the policy, or *wafered* to it.

The decisions, to be quoted upon this head, will likewise serve to illustrate with what punctitious strictness an express warranty must be complied with.

PAWSON

Pawson v. Ewer.

Pawſon v. Ewer, Pawſon v. Snell, and Pawſon v. Watſon, which were all actions on the ſame policy, were argued on a motion for a new trial, in the Court of King's Bench. The caſe was this:

The broker who made the inſurance, ſhewed to ſome of the underwriters a paper *detached* from the policy, containing inſtructions relative to the force with which the ſhip was to ſail, *viz.* "12 *guns, and* 20 *men.*" There were no guns or men on board when the policy was ſubſcribed. Mr *Thornton*, the firſt underwriter on the policy, had ſeen the paper (and he had paid.) *Watſon* and *Snell* had not ſeen it; *Ewer*, who had ſubſcribed after them, had; but they all underwrote at the ſame premium, for ſuch a veſſel as that in queſtion, when ſailing without force.

The ſhip actually ſailed with only 10 guns, (four pounders,) and ſix ſwivels; and with only 16 men, and ſeven boys, beſides paſſengers. It was proved, that boys are entered on the ſhip's books, and conſidered on ſhipboard as men; and that 10 guns and 16 ſwivels are of greater force than 12 guns. That, upon the whole, the ſhip was of more force than ſhe would have been, if the written inſtructions had been ſpecially adhered to.

There were verdicts for the plaintiffs; but, on the motion for a new trial in one of the cauſes, which was to determine the reſt, it was contended, on the part of the defendant,—That the inſtructions

structions shewn to the first underwriter, (upon whom in general all the others rely,) being in writing, were to be considered as a *warranty*, which must be strictly complied with; and that it had not been complied with in this case. The counsel for the plaintiff, on the contrary, maintained, in the *first* place, that the written paper *being separate from the policy*, was only a *representation*, and that it was sufficient to comply with it in substance, or to do what was equally beneficial to the underwriters. But, in the *second* place, that the terms had been strictly complied with; for that swivels were a species of guns, and boys, in the maritime sense, were reckoned men, or seamen, as opposed to passengers.

Lord MANSFIELD said,—There is no distinction better known than that between a warranty or condition, which makes part of a written policy, and a representation of the case. Where it is a part of the written policy, it must be performed; as if there be a warranty of convoy, there must be a convoy; (nothing tantamount will do, or answer the purpose;) it must be strictly performed, as being part of the agreement; for there, it might be said, the party would not have insured without convoy. But, as by the law of merchants, all dealing must be fair and honest, fraud infects and vitiates every mercantile contract; therefore, if there is fraud in a representation, it will void the policy, as a fraud, but not as a part of the agreement. If, in a life policy,

policy, a man warrants another to be in good health, when he knows, at the fame time, he is ill of a fever, that will not void the policy; becaufe, by the warranty, he takes the rifk upon himfelf. But, if there is no warranty, and he fays " the man is in good health," when, in fact, he knows him to be ill, it is falfe. So it is, if he does not know whether he is well or ill; for it is equally falfe to undertake to fay that which he knows nothing at all of, as to fay a thing is true, which he knows is not true. But if he only fays, " he believes the man to be in " good health," knowing nothing about it, nor having any reafon to believe the contrary, there, though the perfon is not in good health, it will not void the policy; becaufe the underwriter then takes the rifk upon himfelf.

It is not the ufage to confider *inftructions* as a part of the policy; and it does not appear, that, in this cafe, the underwriters had confidered the circumftance of the veffel having *twelve guns and twenty men*, as a condition they wifhed ftrictly adhered to; otherwife, *why did they not take care to have that put into the body of the contract.* Befides, the different infurers, thofe who knew this circumftance, and thofe who did not, had all underwritten at the fame premium. It was clearly only a *reprefentation* of the fact, that the veffel *was a fhip of force;* and, fo far as feemed *material*, the information which it was intended to convey,

convey, appeared to have been well founded.—
The rule difcharged.

Afterwards, a Counfel having afked, at the requeft of the underwriters, whether it was the opinion of the Court, that, " to make written in-
" ftructions valid and binding as a warranty,
" they muft be inferted in the policy?" Lord
MANSFIELD anfwered, " That it undoubtedly
" was."—*Cowper's Reports,* May 16. 1778. B. R.

BEAN *againſt* STUPART.

The plaintiff infured a fhip, called *the Martha,* " at and from *London* to *New York,*" the voyage to commence from a day fpecified; and on the margin of the policy were written thefe words,—" *Eight nine-pounders, with cloſe quar-*
" *ters,* 6 *ſix-pounders on her upper decks,* 30 *ſea-*
" *men, beſides paſſengers.*"—The fhip was taken by an *American* privateer.

In an action upon the policy, the defence fet up was, that there were not 30 *ſeamen* on board the fhip; and, in fact, it appeared upon the evidence, that, to make up that number, the plaintiff reckoned the fteward, cook, furgeon, fome boys and apprentices, and fome perfons defcribed as men learning to be feamen; and that only 26 perfons had figned the fhip's articles. It alfo appeared, that there were feven or eight paffengers on board.

It fcarcely feemed to be difputed, that this claufe being written on the fame paper with the policy,

policy, was a *warranty*, and not a *reprefentation;* and therefore required to be ftrictly complied with; and Lord MANSFIELD delivered his opinion to that purpofe*.

A fpecial jury found a verdict for the plaintiff; and the defendant having obtained a rule to fhew caufe, why there fhould not be a new trial,—upon argument before Lord MANSFIELD, the rule was difcharged. *Douglas' Reports,* 13*th November* 1778.

In a note to the decifion *Bean againft Stupart,* in Douglas' Reports, the following cafes are ftated.

" At the fittings at Guildhall, after *M.* 19. *Geo.* III. in a caufe of KENYON and ASHTON *v.* BERTHON, the following words were written tranfverfely on the margin of the policy, " *In port* " 20th *of July* 1776." The fhip was proved to have failed the 18th of July; and Lord MANSFIELD held that this was clearly a warranty; and though the difference of two days might not make any material difference in the rifk, yet

as

---

* Witneffes were examined to explain what is generally underftood by the word *feamen;* and it was eftablifhed, that, at the Cuftomhoufe and *Greenwich* hofpital, boys are included in that word. Lord MANSFIELD obferved, that, in the prefent cafe, the term *feamen* feemed to be oppofed to *paffengers,* and not to boys and landmen; and, in that fenfe, the word feemed to include boys as well as men. There was another point, fufficiently clear, decided in this cafe,—That in the circumftances, the affured was entitled to abandon.

as the condition had not been complied with, the underwriter was not liable.

"But, 1*mo,* Though a written paper be *wrapt up in the policy,* when it is brought to the underwriters to subscribe, and shown to them at that time; or, 2*do,* Even though it be *wafered* to the policy, at the time of subscribing, still it is not in either case, a warranty, or to be considered as a part of the policy itself, but only as a representation."

"The first of these points occurred in a cause of PAUSON *v.* BARNEVELT, tried before Lord MANSFIELD at Guildhall, at the sittings in Trinity term 18. *Geo.* III. where the policy was the same as in the case *Pawson v. Ewer.* The counsel for the defendant offered to produce witnesses to prove that a written memorandum inclosed, was always considered as a part of the policy. But his Lordship said it was a mere question of law, and would not hear the evidence; but decided that a written paper did not become a strict warranty, by being folded up in the policy."

"The second occurred in BIZE *v.* FLETCHER, tried at Guildhall after *E.* 19. *Geo.* III. where it appeared that at the time when the insurers underwrote the policy, a slip of paper was wafered to it, describing the state of the ship as to repairs and strength, and also mentioning several particulars of her intended voyage; which particulars, in the event, had not been complied with

with. Lord MANSFIELD ruled that this was only a reprefentation; and if the jury fhould think there was no fraud intended; and that the variance between the intended voyage, as defcribed in the flip of paper, and the actual voyage, as performed, did not tend to increafe the rifk to the underwriters, he directed them to find for the plaintiff, who accordingly had a verdict."

3. Of the different conditions ftipulated by the underwriter, fome are intended to diminifh, or remove, the war rifk, or peril of capture. Such are the warranties that the fhip fhall have *convoy* ;—that fhe fhall *have convoy and arrive ;* that fhe fhall be a *neutral fhip ;*—or *a flag of truce.* Others are calculated to avoid the *fea rifk* in particular fituations ; fuch is the condition that the veffel fhall *fail before a day* certain.

Thefe warranties are expreffed in two different ways. Sometimes in the form of an abfolute condition, without which there fhall be no infurance. At other times, they are optional to the affured ; and are introduced not as a circumftance effential to the bargain, but which fhall have the effect to alter the terms of it, by producing a return of premium, if the condition be not fulfilled. Thefe two modes of introducing a condition have the fame effect with regard to the view now under confideration. It feems proper

proper, however, to explain separately the different warranties above mentioned, before examining those general points in which they all agree.

4. The most important warranties that occur, are those intended to secure underwriters, in time of war, against the extraordinary risk of capture by the enemy. In time of war, the peril of capture becomes infinitely greater to merchantmen than any other danger whatever; and the premium upon insurance rises accordingly. It obtains the name of the *long premium*, in opposition to the *short* or *peace premium*. Of these warranties the most common and the most important is a warranty of *convoy*.

By a *convoy* is understood a force consisting of one or more armed ships in hostility with the enemies of the vessel insured.

They must likewise be commissioned by the public to undertake her defence. It is not satisfying a clause of convoy, that a merchant-man accidentally sails in company with a man of war, and is protected by keeping her company. The armed ship must be instructed by Government to act for the special security of the vessel insured.

Thus, in the case *Hubbert v. Pigow*, (to be afterwards stated) the *Arundel*, the vessel insured, failed in company with the *Glorieux* man of war. It was found that the *Glorieux* was not one of the convoy appointed by Government, and therefore that the assured had not fulfilled

the

the condition. Afterwards, in a subsequent question upon the same case, *Hubbert v. Bainbridge,* upon new evidence being produced, it appeared that the *Glorieux* actually was a part of the convoy, and a verdict was found for the assured.

Hubbert *against* Newnham.

The *Withywood* was insured " at and from " Jamaica to London, *warranted to depart with " convoy for the voyage."* She sailed from Salt-river on the 27th July; and arrived at Bluefields on the 29th. Admiral *Graves,* with the convoy, had left Bluefields on the 26th, four days before the usual time: But the *Withywood* there fell in with the *Endymion,* a 44 gun-ship, which had been sent by Lord *Rodney* to assist Admiral *Graves,* but had never *joined* or *received orders* from the latter. The *Endymion* appeared to lie to for the *Withywood,* but they never spoke together. When the *Withywood* came up she failed; and was generally in sight till the 7th August, when the fleet was seen. And on the 9th the *Endymion,* having received orders, towed the *Withywood* into the fleet.

The *Withywood* having foundered in the great hurricane off Newfoundland, Lord Mansfield held that the *Endymion* was not convoy, and the underwriters not liable. Verdict for the defendant.—1783.——MS.

The object of stipulating for convoy, must, undoubtedly, be to obtain a security against the war-risk, during the whole voyage; and the presumption is, that when no particular part of the adventure is mentioned, the whole is intended. Were a *partial convoy* sufficient, the clause of convoy would become perfectly elusory: It would be impossible to fix a line, at which it could be said the condition had been fulfilled; and the assured might confine his performance to so small a part of the voyage as would totally destroy the security intended. To sail *with convoy*, therefore, and every other stipulation for convoy, means convoy *for the whole voyage*, unless the contrary be expressly provided.

" Warranted to depart with convoy," has been resolved to import, by the usage of merchants, a continuance with that convoy *as long as may be.* Lucas, 287.

Lilly *and others against* Ewer.

A policy was made on the *Parker galley*, " at " and from *Venice* to the *Currant Islands*, and at " and from thence to *London*," at a premium of five guineas *per cent.* " to return L. 2 *per cent.* if " the ship sailed with convoy from Gibraltar, and " arrived." The ship touched at *Gibraltar* on her way home, and sailed from thence under convoy of the *Zephyr* sloop of war, but the convoy was destined only to go to a certain latitude, about as far as *Cape Finisterre;* and accordingly the

the ſhip and convoy ſeparated, and the ſhip arrived ſafe at *London*. The only queſtion in the cauſe was, Whether, by the terms of the policy, the condition for the return of premium was, a departure from *Gibraltar, with ſuch convoy as could be met with*, for whatever part of the voyage that might happen to be, or, a departure *with convoy for the voyage*. In an action at the inſtance of the aſſured, againſt an underwriter, for return of premium, which came to be tried at *Guildhall*, before Lord MANSFIELD, and a common jury, a verdict having been found for the plaintiff, a rule was obtained to ſhew cauſe why there ſhould not be a new trial.

The evidence adduced in the cauſe, principally related to the uſage with regard to the interpretation put by merchants upon the expreſſion, *ſailing with convoy*. The plaintiff produced a reſpectable merchant, who underſtood, that *ſailing with convoy*, had a diſtinct technical meaning from *ſailing with convoy for the voyage*. The captain proved, that, at the time when he left *Gibraltar*, no other convoy was to be had. Contrary evidence was produced of the uſage, in favour of the defendant; and it was obſerved, that the natural import of the words ſupported his plea. Even if the words were doubtful, they ought to be conſtrued againſt the aſſured who made uſe of them. It was alſo ſaid, that when *partial convoy* was meant, it had of late been a frequent practice, eſpecially in voyages to the *Levant,*

vant, to specify how far the convoy was to come; as " *convoy to the Cape, convoy to Lisbon,*" &c.

Lord MANSFIELD, from the words, had been strongly of opinion, that the policy meant a departure with convoy for the voyage. The parties could not mean a departure with convoy, which might be designed to separate from the ship in a minute or two; though, when convoy for the whole of a voyage is clearly intended, an unforeseen separation is an accident to which the underwriter is liable. His opinion had been influenced by the proof of usage upon the part of the plaintiff; however, he had learnt that people in the city were dissatisfied with the verdict, and think the evidence of the plaintiff's witnesses was founded on a mistake. Critical niceties ought not to be encouraged in commercial concerns; and wherever additional words are rendered necessary, doubts and criticisms are multiplied.—The rule made absolute.—Verdict for the defendant. *Douglas's Reports, 6th February* 1779.

A variety of phrases have been made use of in the expression of this warranty; such as, " warranted *with convoy*;" " *to sail* with convoy;" " *to depart* with convoy;" " *to join convoy.*"

With regard to all these, the general observation seems applicable, that the intention of the clause is, to be protected during the whole voyage; and the underwriters are not to be cut out

of

of their complete security by the difference of a word. It seems to be settled, that *to sail with convoy*, *to depart* with convoy, and warranted *with convoy*, mean the same thing. In the case of insurance on the ship *Commerce (Dunmore against Allan,)* lately decided by the Court of Session, in which the vessel was insured, " war-" ranted with convoy," there was produced evidence, that this construction was agreeable to the usage of merchants in Scotland; and the Court of Session were unanimously of opinion, that it was necessary for the ship *Commerce*, not only to meet convoy, but to sail with convoy from the port of rendezvous.

In the case *Manning v. Gist*, at Guildhall, (to be afterwards stated), there were two policies on the same ship. In the one, she was *warranted with convoy for the voyage;* in the other, she was warranted *to depart with convoy*. The Court thought the warranties were substantially the same, and took the causes both together.

With regard to the expression of *joining* convoy, unless it is mentioned at what part of the voyage the junction is to happen, the same interpretation ought to be put upon it; and the underwriter ought not to be misled by the difference of a word. To join convoy, must be interpreted at the port of rendezvous.

Although, however, in general, by convoy, is to be understood *convoy for the voyage*, yet this rule admits of certain exceptions.

It

It was formerly observed, that both the assured and underwriters, must be supposed to know, and to approve of the usual and customary procedure in the course of any adventure insured. "Unicuique in arte sua credendum;" the usages of merchants, and seafaring people, therefore, in relation to a sea-voyage, must be for the advantage of all concerned, and must be considered as receiving the tacit consent of parties. Thus it was formerly mentioned, that a vessel might, without vacating her insurance, vary from the *direct* or *nearest* course, providing such variation was agreeable to *uniform practice*.

Upon similar principles, although, in general, a clause of convoy implies *convoy for the whole voyage*, from the port of loading, to that of discharge; yet, where a certain regular convoy is customary for the protection of that trade in which the ship insured is engaged, both parties must obviously have contracted with a view to that particular convey, and no other. If therefore it is the practice for such convoy to attend the merchant-man during a part of her voyage only, that partial attendance will be sufficient to implement the condition of the contract. Both parties are supposed to know the circumstances of the trade they insure; and neither can the assured be supposed to promise, nor the underwriter to expect, any other convoy than

than what general practice, in the course of that trade, has pointed out.

If therefore the customary convoy is not stationed at the port of loading, it will be necessary for the vessel insured to go in quest of her consort, at the place of rendezvous. Thus, in insurances from London, the convoy is often not to be obtained from the Thames, but at the Downs, or even at a more distant port along the coast. In insurance from Jamaica, the convoy is usually stationed at Bluefield's bay. In these cases, the warranty is fulfilled, if the merchantman joins convoy at the Downs, Bluefields, or any other port of rendezvous.

In the same manner, no doubt, when it is *customary* for the convoy to separate before arrival at the port of discharge, such separation, at the accustomed point, is not a failure of the warranty. Sometimes a provision for this purpose, is made by an express clause, that the vessel shall " join convoy *at the rendezvous*." But it seems to follow from the reason of the thing, without any stipulation whatever.

It is an obvious consequence from these reasonings, that a vessel, while she sails in quest of the convoy, to the port of rendezvous, is, in the mean time, under the security of the insurance. If the end is undertaken, the means must be undertaken by which that end is to be accomplished. And if she be taken or wrecked, before she arrive at the rendezvous, the underwriter must be be liable. In the same manner, she is covered by the insurance, after the convoy leaves her, from the *usual point of separation*, till she arrives at her port of discharge.

It likewise naturally follows, that although a vessel goes out of her *direct* or *nearest* course, in quest of the *usual convoy*, at the place of rendezvous, such procedure does not imply a deviation; because an agreement of convoy implies the assent of parties to every means that is *customary*, in order to carry that agreement into effect, and to obtain the convoy stipulated.

LETHULIER's *Case.*—The defendant, at London, insured a ship from thence to the East Indies, *warranted to depart with convoy*. In an action on the policy, the plaintiff shews, that the ship went from London to the Downs, and from thence with convoy, and was lost:—After a frivolous plea and demurrer, the case stood upon the declaration, to which it was objected, that there was a departure without convoy; *et per cur.* the clause, " warranted to depart with con- " voy," must be construed according to the *usage* among merchants; *i. e.* from such place where convoys are to be had, as the Downs, &c. HOLT, *C. J. contra*, we take notice of the laws of merchants that are general, not of those that are particular usages; it is no part of the law of merchants to take convoy in the Downs. 2. *Salkeld,* 443. *Mich.* 4. *W. and M. in B. R.*

BOND

Bond v. Gonzalez.

A policy was to insure the *William Galley* in a voyage from Bremen to London, warranted with convoy. She sailed under convoy of a Dutch man of war, to the Elbe, where they were joined by two other Dutch men of war, and several Dutch merchant ships; whence they sailed to the Texel, where they found a squadron of English men of war, and an Admiral. After a stay of nine weeks, they set out from the Texel, and the Galley was separated in a storm, and taken by a French privateer, retaken by a Dutch privateer, and paid L. 80 salvage. It was ruled by HOLT, C. J. that the voyage ought to be according to *usage;* and that their going to the Elbe, though in fact out of the way, was no deviation; for till the year 1703, there was no convoy for ships directly from Bremen to London ; and the plaintiff had a verdict. 2. *Salkeld* 445. *Feb.* 14. 1704.

Gordon v. Morley, *and* Campbell v. Bourdieu.

On an insurance from London to Gibraltar, *warranted to depart with convoy*, it appeared there was a convoy appointed for that trade to Spithead; and the ship *Ranger* having tried for convoy in the Downs, proceeded for Spithead, and was taken in her way thither. The insurers insisted, that this being in time of a French war, the ship should not have ventured through the Channel, but have waited in the Downs

Downs for an occasional convoy; and many merchants and office-keepers were examined to that purpose. But the Chief Justice held, that the ship was to be considered as under the defendants insurance to a place of *general rendezvous*, according to the interpretation of the words warranted to depart with convoy, *Salk.* 443, 445; and if the parties meant to vary the insurance from what is commonly understood, they should have particularised her departure with convoy from the Downs.—The juries were composed of merchants, and, in both cases, found for the plaintiffs, on the strength of this direction. *Strange,* 1265. 20. *Geo.* II.

For the same reasons, the particular *strength* of a convoy does not appear material. Parties must be supposed to have had in view the *usual* convoy, or that convoy which Government shall consider as expedient and proper for the service.

Manning v. Gist.

The *Elisabeth* was insured " from Tortola to " London; warranted to sail on or before the " 10th of August, *with convoy for the voyage.*" There was another case between the same parties, in which the ship was " warranted *to de-* " *part* with convoy." The court thought the warranty the same in substance, and took them both together.

It appeared that the *Cyclops* man of war was sent from St Kitts to take care of the vessels at Tortola,

Tortola, and carry them to latitude 19. to meet the Commodore, and the rest of the fleet. The *Cyclops* was to go no farther than latitude 19. There could be no other convoy from *Tortola*, as the whole fleet could not pass that way.

The *Elisabeth* lost her consort, after sailing from *Tortola*. It was proved that she neither could make *Tortola*, nor *Basse-terre*, the rendezvous.—Verdict for the assured plaintiff.—On motion for a new trial,—

Lord MANSFIELD said,—In a policy warranted with convoy, the force is never stipulated, but left to Government. The agreement must be construed by the voyage. *Basse-terre* is the general rendezvous; but, from Tortola, vessels cannot conveniently go to *Basse-terre*; and the convoy cannot, without great risk, go to Tortola. The *practice* therefore is, to send a ship to Tortola, to bring the vessels to a certain latitude; and this latitude must vary in different cases.—Rule discharged. *East.* 22. *Geo.* III. *MS.*

By a ship *having convoy*, must farther be meant, that she sails in such a situation as admits of her receiving that protection and assistance, which an armed force is capable of affording. To this effect, two circumstances seem necessary:

1st, That the armed ship, and the vessel insured, set sail together. What distance may be sufficient for the purposes of protection, is a point that must vary a good deal in different cases, and does

does not admit of an accurate rule. But one thing may be laid down as sufficiently established, that from whatever point the convoy is warranted,—whether from the port of loading,—from the general rendezvous,—or from any other point in the course of the voyage,—according to general usage, or special agreement;—from that point the vessel insured and convoy must sail, or attempt to sail, together. It is not enough that she overtake the convoy during the voyage, nor that she sail before it, and be overtaken. She must *join* at that point where the warranty is stipulated to commence; and she must make an *inception of the voyage* at the same time. A contrary rule would destroy entirely the utility of a clause of convoy; for, if the vessel insured may sail *any part* of the way without her convoy, where shall this power stop? If she may sail half a league, why may she not proceed a whole league, or two leagues? In short, the same holds in this, as in every other warranty; unless the condition be interpreted strictly, it can be of no use.

Taylor *v.* Woodness.

The defendant insured the plaintiff with a warranty of convoy. It appeared, that the Commodore had made signals the night before, for sailing from Spithead to St Helen's, and had made repeated signals next morning from 7 o'clock till 12; notwithstanding which, the ship

ship insured had neglected to sail with him, and did not sail till two hours after; she was taken by a privateer. In an action on the policy, the plaintiff was nonsuited. *Hil.* 4. *Geo.* III. *at Guildhall. Park's System,* 399.

Dunmore *against* Gildart.

Insurance was made " on the *freight* of the " *Anna*, from her loading ports in Jamaica, to " Clyde, *warranted to sail with convoy,* on or " before the first August." The facts appeared to be as follows.

The *Anna* took in her loading at *Savannah la Mar*, which is on the south side of Jamaica, only about three miles distant from *Bluefields*, and on the opposite side of a small cape. Most of the other merchantmen that were lying at Savannah, sailed upon the 23d or 24th July, to join the convoy at *Bluefields*. The *Anna* was not then ready; but on the 23d, the captain went over land to *Bluefields*, and got sailing orders from Captain *Moriarty* of the *Ramillies*, Admiral *Graves's* own ship.

The convoy sailed from *Bluefields* on the evening of the 25th, and steered westward past *Savannah*, continuing in sight of the harbour of *Savannah* from four to five o'clock of the afternoon of the 25th. At that time the *Anna* was completely ready to sail, and waited for a wind to carry her out, having her anchors up, and her pilot on board; but was becalmed. It deserves

serves notice, that the wind from the land usually failed in the day-time.

She continued unmoored, and, by two o'clock of the morning of the 26th, got clear off the reef of *Savannah la Mar*, and proceeded after the fleet with all possible dispatch. In the afternoon of the same day, a frigate from the north side hove in sight; and in the evening, the captain got sight of the fleet commanded by *Admiral Pigot*. He continued in sight of this fleet the 27th and 28th; lay to with them a part of the 28th; and, on the morning of the 29th, joined the fleet under the command of *Admiral Graves*, which was the regular convoy. The Anna was afterwards lost in the great hurricane off Newfoundland.

The case came on at Guildhall before *Mr Justice* BULLER, who would not suffer it to go to a jury; saying, the point was settled by recent decisions, and the plaintiff allowed himself to be non-suited. 1783. Never moved in since. *MS.*

2dly, The assured ship must not only have joined, but she must have got *sailing orders;* without which it is impossible she can understand signals, or act in concert with the convoy, so as to enjoy the protection intended.

" If any assurance," says the ordinance of Hamburgh, "be contained in the policy, that
" the ship is to depart with convoy, then, for
" fulfilling that condition, it is required,—that
" the convoy be actually at enmity with the ene-
" mies

"mies of the ship on which the insurance is made;—that the captain who is under protection, have received a *letter of instructions* from the commander of the convoy;—that he be ready to put to sea along with the convoy, as soon as he is informed, and knows that it will depart." A variety of English cases, which serve to illustrate this, among other points, shall be afterwards stated.

5. The species of warranty hitherto mentioned, that a vessel shall have the protection of *convoy*, affords by no means a complete security against the *war-risk;* but there is a condition sometimes stipulated, which entitles the owner of a ship to be insured upon the *short premium*, as it entirely removes from the underwriter the peril of capture. This is a condition, that the ship shall "*sail with convoy, and arrive.*"

It is generally executed as a stipulation for a return of premium, " if the ship fails with convoy, *and arrives.*"

The only point that seems to have admitted of doubt, with regard to this species of warranty, is, Whether the condition *of arrival* applies to the *ship only*, or to both ship and goods? The answer is, that the original intention of the warranty was to provide against the *war-risk*, and therefore it is enough if the *ship arrives;* and it is of no consequence, although the goods or the vessel have suffered *sea-damage*.

Simmond *against* Boydell.

A policy was underwritten in these words, "at and from the port or ports in Grenada to London, on any ship or ships that shall sail on or between the 1st of May, and the 1st of August 1778, at 18 guineas *per cent. to return L. 8 per cent. if she sails from any of the West India islands, with convoy for the voyage, and arrives.*" At the bottom there was a written declaration, "that the policy was on sugars, (the Muscovado valued at L. 20 *per* hhd.) for account of L. Q. being on the first sugars which shall be shipped for that account."

The ship *Hankey* sailed with convoy within the time limited, having on board 51 hogsheads of Muscovado sugar, belonging to L. Q. She arrived safe in the Downs, where the convoy left her; convoy never coming farther, and indeed seldom beyond Portsmouth. After she had parted with the convoy, she struck on a bank called the *Panfand* at Margate, and eleven of the 51 hhds. of sugar were washed overboard, and the rest damaged. The vessel was got off, and arrived at her port. The sugars saved were taken out at Margate, and, after undergoing a sort of cure, were carried to London in other vessels; and the forty hogsheads being sold, produced L. 340, instead of L. 800, which was their valuation in the policy.

The defendant, infurer, had paid into court the value of the fugars loft, and a return of L. 8 *per cent.* on L. 340. The plaintiffs, the ured, infifted, that they were entitled to a return of L. 8 *per cent.* not only on the fugars faved, but on the valued price of the 11 hogfheads of fugar which were loft, and on the difference between what the remainin 40 hogfheads produced, and their valued price. A verdict having been found at *Guildball* for the plaintiffs, rule was obtained to fhew caufe why there fhould not be a new trial.

For the plaintiffs, it was infifted, that the word *arrives*, applied only to the arrival of the fhip. That in policies of this fort, the intention is, that the underwriters fhall take the war-rifk upon themfelves; but that, if the veffel is protected by convoy from that rifk, and actually arrives, they fhall then return as much of the premium as was meant to cover the war-rifk. That it never could be meant by the word *arrives*, that all the goods fhould arrive in a found ftate, which, in fo long a voyage, was a thing impoffible. The very ufe of the word in the fingular number, fhewed the general underftanding that it was meant to apply to the fhip.

On the other fide, it was contended, that the words in the policy muft be applied to the fub-ject-matter of the infurance, which, in this cafe, was *on goods*, not on the fhip; and therefore the
condition

condition of arrival muſt be applied to them. But they had not all arrived at *London ;* nor any part of them, in the veſſel in which they ſailed from *Grenada ;* therefore the ſecond part of the condition was not at all performed ; or, at leaſt, only in part. Farther, if the underwriter were bound both to indemnify the aſſured for the loſs incurred by the diminution of his ſugars below the valued price, and likewiſe to make a return of premium on that diminution, the aſſured would be a gainer by the damage which his goods had ſuſtained. For, in the valuation of the cargo, the premium of inſurance was no doubt included.

The Court were unanimous, that the return of premium was due, if *the veſſel* eſcaped, independent of any claim of indemnity which the aſſured might have upon the underwriter for any damage ſuſtained by the goods.—The rule diſcharged. *Douglas's Reports,* 17*th November* 1779.

6. Another mode of relieving the underwriter from the war-riſk, is by introducing a condition, that the ſubject aſſured ſhall be *neutral* property. In order to implement this warranty, the ſhip or goods muſt be neutral in the conception of that nation from whom danger of ſeizure is apprehended ; and muſt be ſufficiently documented as ſuch.

The principal queſtion upon this ſubject relates to the evidence, which ſhall be ſufficient to ſhow, that the warranty has not been complied with,

with. If a veffel has been condemned in a foreign court, what weight is due to their fentence of condemnation, and whether may other evidence be adduced to refute or explain it.

It has been held, that a fentence of condemnation by a foreign court is conclufive, if fufficiently explicit. But if it be ambiguous, extraneous evidence may be admitted to explain the ground upon which it proceeded.

BERNARDI *againſt* MOTTEUX.

By an arret of the *French* Court, (26th July 1778,) "All veffels taken, of whatever nation, "whether neutral or allied, from which any pa- "pers have been thrown into the fea, fuppreffed, "or abftracted, fhall be declared good prize, to- "gether with their cargoes, upon the mere proof, "that fome papers have been thrown into the "fea, without any neceffity of examining what "thofe papers were, by whom thrown, and even "though a fufficient quantity fhould remain on "board, to juftify, that the fhip and its cargo be- "long to friends and allies."

The defendant infured the plaintiff on freight and cargo of the fhip *Joanna*, at and from *Venice* to *London*, "warranted neutral fhip and pro- "perty." It appeared, that a *French* frigate having ftopped her, while under *Venetian* colours, had ordered the captain to bring aboard his mufter-roll, paffport, and bills of loading, which
the

the captain had been unwilling to do; but having been obliged to comply, he had, in coming aboard the frigate, dropt into the sea the box containing his muster-roll, his patents, and passport, and only produced his bills of loading.

The sentence of the *French* Court mentions these circumstances, and states, as the ground of condemnation, " that the bills of loading con-
" tained goods for the account of sundry persons
" in *Venice*, consigned to sundry merchants in
" *London*, whither he was bound. That *these*
" *goods going into an enemy's country, and the loss*
" *of the papers which had fallen into the sea, had*
" *raised suspicions*."

In an action on the policy, it was stated for the opinion of the Court, whether this sentence was conclusive evidence against the plaintiff, that the vessel was not neutral. The defendant refused to allow the *arret* above mentioned, and the *proces verbal* on which the sentence was founded, to be made part of the proceedings. But the majority of the Court thought, that the sentence of condemnation was ambiguous, and therefore that evidence might be adduced to shew the real ground on which it proceeded. Judgment for the plaintiff. *Douglas's Reports*, 27th *January* 1781.

BARZILLAY *v.* LEWIS.

By certain *French* ordinances, it is enacted, that if more than one-third of a ship's crew are enemies

enemies to the King of *France*, the ship shall be confiscated; that the property of a ship shall not be held as transferred from an enemy to an ally, until she has been within a port of the latter; and by treaty, it is settled, that a passport shall be held to be fraudulent, unless the ship was in the port from which it has been procured.

A *French* ship, *L'aimable Agathie*, was taken by an *English* vessel, carried into *Liverpool*, and condemned as prize. She there got the name of the *Three Graces*. She was purchased by a *Dutch* Company, and sailed with a cargo for *Amsterdam*. The crew consisted of four *Danes*, one *Dutchman*, two *Swedes*, one *Portuguese*, one *Hamburger*, one *Norwegian*, one *Irishman*; the captain, a *Dane*.— She was insured by a *Dutch* name, " warranted " *Dutch*." In the course of her voyage, she was taken by a *French ship*, carried into *St Maloes*, and there released, as being *Dutch*; but this sentence was reversed on appeal, by the Parliament of *Paris*.

On motion by the plaintiff, to set aside a nonsuit, Lord MANSFIELD said,—The sentence of the *French* Admiralty, whatever it means, is decisive. It seems to be upon the ground, that the vessel is not *Dutch*. The warranty is, " that the " ship is *Dutch*," to the effect of being protected against the *French*. That she shall be neutral with respect to *France*.

It

It is of no consequence, whether she was condemned upon the principles of the law of nations, or upon the municipal regulations, which particular states may have introduced with regard to their marine. The *Dutch* owners were bound to know what entitled their ship to neutrality. She appears to the underwriters to be *Dutch*, and they insure her as such; but when sifted in the *French* courts, she is found not to have the requisites. She has no such pass as is required by Treaty. And what shows the grounds of the sentence, she is condemned by her *English* name. The sentence certainly proceeded on her not being *Dutch*; and this is conclusive.

WILLES, J.—The passport is collusive, and there is no ambiguity in the condemnation; therefore it ought not to be opened.

ASHURST, J.—If the condemnation were on a ground *collateral* to the policy, the plaintiff might go into evidence to set it aside. But clear here it was on her not being completely documented as a *Dutch* ship.

BULLER, J.—Under the warranty of a neutral ship, the party warranting must see, that she is completely documented, and comply in every respect with the marine regulations.—Rule discharged. *Trin.* 22. *Geo.* III.

In another case, *Mayne v. Walter*, (formerly stated,) the vessel, " warranted *Portuguese*," was condemned,

condemned, for having, contrary to a particular regulation of *France*, an *Engliſh* ſupercargo on board. As this was a ground of condemnation, unconnected with the warranty,—in an action on the policy, judgment was given for the aſſured plaintiff.

Several other caſes might be ſtated to the ſame purpoſe; but the doctrine appears too clear, to require farther illuſtration*.

7. There remains ſtill another warranty of conſiderable importance; where a veſſel is warrantted *to ſail on or before a particular day*. It takes place generally in thoſe adventures, the ſucceſs of which depends upon catching the opportunity of trade-winds, or avoiding the tempeſtuous weather incident to particular ſeaſons of the year, in the warm latitudes.

When a veſſel is " warranted to ſail before a " day,"—ſhe is underſtood to fulfil the warranty, if, before that day, ſhe has made a *bona fide inception of the voyage*.

Bond *v.* Nutt.

The ſhip *Capel*, in the Weſt-India trade, was inſured " at and from Jamaica to London; *war-* " *ranted to have ſailed on or before the 1ſt of Au-* " *guſt* 1776, at fifteen guineas *per cent.* to return " five *per cent.* if departs with convoy, and eight

" *per*

---

* There are two caſes, *Salucci v. Woodmaſs, Hil.* 24. Geo. III. and *Pallucci v. Woodmaſs, Hil.* 25. Geo. III. upon the ſame point.

"*per cent.* if with convoy for the voyage, and
" arrives."

The ship was completely laden, for her voyage to England, at *St Anne's* in Jamaica; and sailed from *St Anne's* bay on the 26th of July for *Bluefields*, in order to join the convoy there; *Bluefields*, the rendezvous of convoy, being out of the direct course to England. She arrived off *Bluefields* on the 28th or 29th of July, where she was immediately stopped by an embargo laid on all vessels being in any part of Jamaica, and was detained there till the 6th of August, when she sailed with the convoy for England, but was separated, and taken by an American privateer:—Upon these facts the jury found a verdict for the defendant.

Upon motion for a new trial, it was argued, in support of the verdict;—1*mo*, That the ship, although she departed from *St Anne's* before the 1st of August, did not depart *from Jamaica* in terms of the warranty; for *Bluefields* is in Jamaica as well as *St Anne's*: 2*do*, If the departure from *St Anne's* was a fulfilment of the warranty, then the going to *Bluefields* was a deviation.

It was argued, on the other hand, that the departure from the port of discharge, with every thing ready for the voyage, was a complete departure from Jamaica, and touching at *Bluefields* for the sake of convoy, was no deviation, being the most prudent course of sailing to England;
and,

and, therefore, being a variation from the direct courfe for a juftifiable caufe.

Lord MANSFIELD wifhed to hear the fecond ground more fully pleaded; after which, the court, confidering the great importance of the queftion, upon which no lefs than L. 100,000 depended, took farther time to advife. Afterwards his Lordfhip delivered the opinion of the Court;—We are all fatisfied the truth of the cafe is, that the voyage from Jamaica to England began from *St Anne's*. That when the fhip failed from *St Anne's*, fhe had no view or object whatfoever, but to make the beft of her way to England; and fhe touched at *Bluefields* only, as being the fafeft and beft courfe (under the then circumftances) of her navigation to England. The value of this queftion, admitted on both fides, fhews, that every other fhip, under the fame circumftances, looked upon the touching at Bluefields, where the convoy then lay ready, to be the fafeft courfe of navigation from Jamaica to England; and that it would have been unwife and imprudent for any fhip not to have touched there. The great diftinction is this: That fhe failed from *St Anne's* for England by the way of *Bluefields;* and that it was not a voyage from *St Anne's* to *Bluefields*, with any object or view diftinct from the voyage to England. If fhe had gone firft to *Bluefields*, for any purpofe independent of her voyage to England, to have taken in water, or letters, or to

have

have waited in hopes of convoy coming there, none being ready; that would have given it the condition of one voyage from *St Anne's* to *Bluefields*, and another from *Bluefields* to England. But here, under all the circumstances, we think she had no other object than to come to England directly by the safest course. Therefore the rule for a new trial must be made absolute. *Cowper's Reports*, 10th *May* 1777. B. R.

THELLUSON *against* FERGUSSON.

A French ship, *L'aimable Gertrude*, was insured " at and from Guadaloupe to Havre, *war-* " *ranted to sail on or before the* 31*st of December*." The ship took in her complete lading and provisions for France; and all her clearances and papers, at a port called *Point à Pitre* in Guadaloupe, and sailed on the 24th October for *Basse-terre*, where there is no port, but only an open road. The town of *Basse-terre* is the residence of the French Governor. The ship arrived there at night, when the captain went on shore, and next day waited on the Governor, who would not permit him to depart; and to prevent it, took his ship's papers from him. At this place he was detained till the 10th of January, when he set sail with a convoy; but was taken by an English vessel.

The captain swore, that notice had been given by the Governor, that a convoy was expected at *Basse-terre* on the 25th of October; that he
wrought

wrought night and day to get ready before that time ; and that when he failed on the 24th, he was ſtill in hopes of meeting with the convoy at *Baſſe-terre.*

The defendant produced a paper called *le role d'equipage*, which was one of the ſhip's clearances at *Point à Pitre*, and contained theſe words: " Permis au Sieur *Jean Jaques Lethuillier*, " commandant le navire *L'aimable Gertrude de* " *Havre, de s'en ſervir pour faire ſon retour au* " *dit lieu, paſſant à la Baſſe-terre pour y prendre* " *les ordres du Gouvernement*, en obſervant les " ordonnances et reglemens de la marine."

On another paper, called *le congé*, which was read on the part of the plaintiff, there was written at the bottom as follows: " *Vu de relache à* " *la Baſſe-terre, Guadaloupe, pour y attendre un* " *convoi pour France.*"

The captain ſwore, that he underſtood the only reaſons for the condition in the muſter-roll, that he ſhould go to Baſſe-terre, were, that the convoy was to be at that place, and that he might take ſuch diſpatches as were ready for Europe. He had not objected to it, becauſe, in the regular courſe of his voyage to France from *Point à Pitre*, he muſt have gone that way cloſe under the guns of *Baſſe-terre*, in order to avoid *Montſerrat*, there being no other road, except they were to keep quite to the leeward, which is not the cuſtom. If he had arrived there in the day-time, he would not have caſt anchor,

but

but would have sent his boat for the dispatches; but having arrived at night, his ship had been detained, contrary to his intention and expectation.

The defendant's counsel, to invalidate the captain's testimony, besides the *role d'equipage* or muster-roll, produced the captain's protest on his arrival at Dover, which contained these words: " Whereupon he (the captain) waited " on the proper officer at *Point à Pitre*, for his " muster-roll, and was answered it could not be " granted, *but on condition* that he should sail " first to Basse-terre, *and there wait the directions* " *of the Governor.*" It appeared likewise from the protest, that the captain had thought the insurance forfeited by his stay at Basse-terre.

A verdict having been found at Guildhall for the plaintiff, it was argued in favour of a new trial, principally on the following ground: That the departure from *Point à Pitre* was not to be considered as a *bona fide* and *complete* inception of the voyage for Europe: For that it was merely a *conditional* inception of the voyage, and appeared from the muster-roll and other evidence, to have depended upon the orders which the captain was to receive at *Basse-terre*. That it differed therefore materially from the case of *Bond v. Nutt*, in which the act of the captain in going to Bluefields was voluntary, and for the benefit of the concerned[*].

For

---

[*] There was another ground founded upon in this case, in consequence of the following clause of the captain's deposition.

For the plaintiff it was said, that this case was not so strong as *Bond v. Nutt*, because *Bluefields* was out of the straight course of the voyage in that case, whereas here *Basse-terre* was in the direct way to France; so that the captain must have gone by that place at all events, and although there had been no such words in the muster-roll, as those relied on by the defendant's counsel. The only purposes for which those words were inserted, were, that he might be sure of convoy, which was expected to be at *Basse-terre*, and to carry any government dispatches that

sition. " At the time the ship was first pursued and taken, " she was steering her course towards Brest. Her course was " not altered upon the appearance of the vessel by which " she was taken. Her course was at all times, when the " weather would permit, directed to Brest; for which port " he was instructed to sail, although the destination was for " Havre de Grace by the ship's papers. She was *not* before " nor at the time of the capture, sailing *beyond or wide of* " Havre de Grace."

From this it was maintained, that the vessel had never sailed on the voyage insured. But, on the other hand, as the captain had farther declared, " that he had sailed towards " Brest, as the safest way in time of war, of getting to " Havre, which still continued to be the place of the ship's " destination." And as, supposing that the voyage towards Brest would have been a *deviation*, it had been merely *intended* and *not executed*, the vessel having been taken before the dividing point.——From these considerations this defence seems to have met with little attention, and was dropped before the final conclusion of the proceedings, in the different cases depending on this policy.

that might be ready; the voyage to Europe was not less commenced on that account.

Lord MANSFIELD said, that the delay at *Basse-terre* was to be considered as an accident, which did not vary the *bona fide* commencement of the voyage. That in consequence of the expectation of convoy, he would have gone to *Basse-terre* at any rate, independent of the clause in the muster-roll. The rest of the Court were of the same opinion, that there was a *bona fide* inception of the voyage from *Point à Pitre.*—The rule discharged.—See *Douglas's Reports*, 21*st April* 1780, where it appears that a similar determination was given in actions against twenty other underwriters upon the same policy. *Thellufon v. Staples,* &c.

EARLE *against* HARRIS.

Action on a policy of insurance. A verdict having been found at Guildhall for the plaintiff, on motion for a new trial, Lord MANSFIELD reported the facts.—The policy was on the Leghorn galley, " at and from Leghorn to Jamaica, " with liberty to call at the Windward Islands, " and from thence to Liverpool; *warranted to* " *sail from Jamaica, on or before the first of Au-* " *gust next.*" The ship had taken in her whole lading and papers, and set sail from the port of *Savannah la Mar,* on the first of August, and went to *Bluefields,* which is at the distance of about five miles, and is the general place of rendezvous

dezvous for convoy. On the 25th of July, an embargo had been laid on all the ships in the island by the Governor, and inserted in the public newspapers of that date. On the first of August, as soon as the ship had crossed the bar, going out of the harbour of *Savannah la Mar*, the captain returned in a boat, and there made a protest against loss or damage to be sustained from the embargo; which protest he could not have made at *Bluefields*. At that place, the ship was detained till the 9th of August, when convoy arriving, the embargo was taken off, and she sailed for England with the convoy; but was afterwards separated from it, and taken by an American privateer.

The captain was examined at the trial, and admitted, that he had heard of the embargo; but said he thought it was only meant to prevent ships from departing without the protection of convoy; that he expected to meet with convoy at Bluefields on the first of August, and that the embargo would immediately cease, and leave him to pursue his voyage the same day without interruption.

The point upon which the case seemed to turn, was, whether this was to be considered as a *bona fide* inception of the voyage, so as to bring it under the case of *Bond v. Nutt*; or whether the sailing from *Savannah la Mar*, on the first of August, was merely colourable, and intended to answer the *letter* of the insurance.

Lord MANSFIELD, and a majority of the Court, thought that credit was due to the captain's declaration; and that there was no reason for setting aside the verdict, as contrary to evidence. The rule discharged.—*Douglas' Reports,* 21*st April* 1780.

8. It has been repeatedly observed, that a contract of insurance partakes of the nature of a wager. The underwriter becomes liable, in the event of a future contingency: He undertakes *a risk.* In judging of the value which each party sets upon his bargain, it is not enough to examine what is the amount of the risk in the general opinion of mankind, but what it is in the estimation of the individual wagerer. Insurance, therefore, does not admit of equivalents. The assured is not entitled to substitute one entire adventure, though as little or less hazardous, in the place of another; nor can he depart from any article, however trivial in the general opinion, which has been held up to the insurer; because he knows not what influence that circumstance may have had upon the insurer's conception of the complete risk. The same position was formerly shown to be strongly enforced by views of expediency.

The English lawyers distinguish between a *hypothetical* contract, and a *conditional* one. There is a condition understood in both; but in the former case; the condition is said to be *precedent,* in the other it is said to be *subsequent.* In what

what is called a hypothetical contract, the existence of the condition is understood to be absolutely necessary, in order to create an obligation upon the promiser. As, for example, when I promise to pay a sum of money, upon your performance of a certain deed. A conditional contract is where a promise is understood to be made by one party, upon condition that something shall either be actually performed by the other, or at least that he shall have done every thing in his power to make out the performance.

The obligation of the insurer is, according to this distinction, *hypothetical*, and the condition is *precedent*. This is justly inferred from the nature of the agreement, and situation of parties. From what has been said above, the assured must strictly execute what he has undertaken; and will not be permitted to discharge himself, by what may be considered as equipollent acts.

From this observation, it follows, that when a warranty has been undertaken by the assured, it is of no consequence, whether the failure shall arise from the fault of the assured, or from unforeseen and unavoidable accidents. The insurer meant to subject himself to a certain risk, from a view of the complex circumstances laid before him; and if any variation is made in those circumstances, the risk is not *the same*, and the event

event upon which he meant to bind himself, has not taken place.

This point, however, has been the subject of doubt, and formerly of some controversy; particularly in the case where a vessel has been insured, *warranted with convoy*. By a warranty of convoy, it seems to have been supposed, that the assured undertakes two things; that there shall be an armed force, ready, in proper time and place, to undertake the protection of the vessel insured; and that the vessel insured shall be ready, in every respect, to take advantage of that protection which her convoy may be capable of affording her. If there be a failure in either of those circumstances, the assured undoubtedly is guilty of a breach of contract, and there appears no hardship in considering the policy as void.

But if the condition has failed without any blame imputable to the assured: if, for example, he has been prevented by a storm or calm at sea, from actually joining, or, when joined, from receiving sailing orders;—does not the failure arise from those accidents, for all the consequences of which the insurer is liable? Does there not appear a hardship in annulling the assured's contract, and depriving him of his indemnity, in consequence of an event which it was not in his power to control? And shall not equity interpose, and relieve him, by a liberal interpretation of the condition?

The

The following decision seems to have proceeded upon such a view of the subject.

Victorin v. Cleeve.

The plaintiff insured on goods by the *John and Jean*, " from Gottenburgh to London, " *warranted to sail with convoy from Fleckery.*" In July 1774, the ship sailed from Gottenburgh to Fleckery, and there waited for convoy two months. On the 21st September, at nine in the morning, three men of war, who had an hundred merchant-ships in convoy, stood off Fleckery, and made a signal for the ships there to come out. There were fourteen ships, and the *John and Jean* got out by twelve o'clock, and one of the first, the convoy having sailed gently on, and being then two leagues a-head; and she came up with the fleet by six o'clock in the afternoon; but as it blew a hard gale, she could not get to either of the men of war for *sailing orders*. It was stormy all night, and at day-break the ship in question was in the midst of the fleet; but the weather was so bad, that no boat could be sent for sailing orders. A French privateer had sailed amongst them all night, and on the 22d, it being foggy, attacked the *John and Jean* about two, who kept a running fight till dark, which was renewed the next morning, when she was taken.

For the defendant it was insisted, that this ship was never under convoy; nor are vessels ever considered so, till they have received *sailing orders;*

ders ; and if the weather would not permit the captain to get them, he should have gone back. But the Chief Justice and jury were of opinion, that as the captain had done every thing in his power, it was a departing with convoy, and these agreements are never confined to precise words; as in the case of departing with convoy from London, when the place of *rendezvous* is Spithead, a loss in the going thither, is within the policy. So the plaintiff recovered. *Strange,* 1250, 19. *Geo.* II.

In this case, the vessel, it should seem, had formed a sufficient *junction,* according to the usage of the trade; but she had not got *sailing orders ;* this happened without the fault of the assured, and the warranty was found to be performed. Ought not the same rule to hold, if, by the storm, the vessel had been prevented from ever making a junction?

From a fuller and more just view, however, of the principles of insurance, the contrary doctrine is now completely established. It was formerly illustrated by adjudged cases in the instance of an *alteration* or *deviation* by the master or crew, or by the ship-owners, which vacates the policy, although without the fault, or even the knowledge, of the assured shipper of goods.

In several warranties, express or implied, the point cannot admit of doubt. Thus, there is an implied warranty in every insurance, that the ship
shall

shall be *sea-worthy*. Let us suppose, that every thing that could be expected is done by the assured to put her in that situation, but a latent defect has remained, which renders her, after all, insufficient for the voyage. Although there be no fault in the assured, yet as the warranty has not been complied with, the underwriter is free. *Mills v. Roebuck.*

A vessel is insured " from Jamaica to Lon-" don, *warranted to sail before a particular day.*" In the course of her outward-bound voyage she meets with storms and tempests, which occasion delay, and render it impossible to obtemper the condition. In such a case, the failure of the warranty has never been disputed.

In the case of a *warranty of convoy*, the point has likewise been expressly decided.

Hubbert *v.* Pigou.

Pigou insured *Hubbert* " on the ship *Arundel,* " at and from Jamaica to London, *warranted* " *to sail with convoy.*"

It appeared upon the trial, that Lord Rodney had, upon 12th July (1782), left orders for Admiral Graves to take ten ships of war under his command, and to convoy the West India fleet to England. Of these ten ships, the *Glorieux,* Capt. *Cadogan,* was to be one. Orders were accordingly given (July 22.) to Captain Cadogan, to put to sea immediately, as the fleet would be kept at *Bluefields,* (the general rendezvous), till his arrival with the *Glorieux.* Admiral Graves, however,

however, thought it advisable to sail from *Bluefields* on the 26th July, four days before the usual term for the departure of the fleet, with only five sail of the line, and fifty-one merchant-men, and (it appeared upon *this* trial) leaving no orders for the rest of the ships.

The *Arundel* sailed on 25th July, from *Morant Bay*, her port of loading, to *Kingston*, where she met with the *Glorieux*, and asked for *sailing orders*; but was told, that they were not necessary, as Admiral Graves would not be gone from *Bluefields*. She arrived at *Bluefields* on the 28th, in company with the *Glorieux*, and *Jason* man of war. Captain *Man* of the *Arundel* again applied for sailing orders; Captain *Cadogan* said he had none himself; but if they did not overtake the fleet, he would make out sailing orders. The *Glorieux* and *Arundel* sailed together in quest of the fleet, the former *acting as convoy*; and, on the 5th August, she brought the *Arundel* into the middle of the fleet, off *Cape Antonio* in *Cuba*, where she received sailing orders from Admiral Graves. She was afterwards separated, and taken.

The jury found a verdict for the defendant reluctantly. On motion for a new trial,—

Lord MANSFIELD.—Both parties are here free from blame. But there is a difference between a *hypothetical* and a *conditional* contract; the latter admits of equity, and where it cannot be performed literally, may be performed as nearly as possible,

possible. But in a hypothetical contract like this, if the event does not happen, there is no agreement.

The warranty of convoy does not begin except from the place of rendezvous; and the ship is protected by the policy, in sailing thither. The rendezvous may be fixed or changed by Government. Government likewise fixes the convoy; a man cannot chuse his own convoy.

Here, Lord Rodney appoints certain ships to put themselves under Admiral Graves' command, and become part of the convoy. In order to this they must have *sailing orders, which are material and essential*, as otherwise they cannot understand signals. On 26th July, Admiral Graves sails, without leaving orders for the ships that are left. He had not changed the rendezvous from *Bluefields* to *Cape Antonio*. The *Glorieux*, therefore, when she sailed from *Bluefields*, was not one of the convoy. The case is a hard one; but it does not admit of equity.

WILLES, J.—There is no fraud nor *laches* in this case; and therefore it is a hard one. No specific time for sailing is here mentioned, which should lead to suppose, that any particular convoy was in contemplation. On a liberal construction, it was sailing with convoy; for the *Glorieux* acted as convoy, and the warranty has been substantially complied with. The *Arundel* did all in her power to sail with convoy. Suppose, at *Bluefields*, the Admiral had been out of humour, and refused sailing orders, would that have voided the policy? There is only one case, (2. *Strange*, 1250,) which says, that *sailing orders* are necessary; and, in that case, it was found sufficient, that the party had done all in his power to procure them.—The verdict is wrong.

BULLER, J.—It is not necessary to say, whether sailing orders are necessary or not;—but it is better there should be sailing orders.

The condition of convoy must be literally complied with, otherwise there is no contract, though the assured has done his best. The *Glorieux* was no convoy; she did not sail under, and had no orders from Admiral Graves. It is immaterial what is the force of the convoy; but Government must appoint it. The Arundel did not *sail with convoy* appointed by Government.— Rule discharged, 19*th May* 1783 *.

9. From the foregoing doctrine, it must also be inferred, that it is of no consequence, whether the

---

* HUBBERT *v.* BAINBRIDGE.

A very great property depending on this insurance, the assured tried the question against another underwriter; and produced new evidence.

BULLER, J.—What passed on a former occasion is not to control the verdict of the jury. It now appears, that Admiral *Graves* had expressed his expectation, that the vessels left behind would join him off *Cape Antonio*. And there is reason to believe, that this was known to Captain *Cadogan* of the *Glorieux*. The *Glorieux*, therefore, was under orders, and one of the convoy.—Verdict for the plaintiff, in which the underwriters acquiesced, 1783. *MS.*

the failure of the assured to perform a warranty, has occasioned, in fact, any particular loss or inconvenience to the insurer. The question is not, whether the insurer has actually suffered any thing from the non-existence of any particular condition; but whether the circumstances of the bargain have taken place, in such a manner, as to render the hazard strictly the same, for which he meant to be responsible.

De Hahn *v*. Hartley.

The plaintiff, an underwriter, having paid a loss on the ship *Juno*, raised an action for repetition. The jury returned a special verdict, of which the material points were as follows:

On 14th June 1779, *De Hahn* insured *Hartley*, on the ship *Juno*, "at and from *Africa*, to her "port or ports of discharge in the *British West* "*Indies*." On the margin of the policy were written these words,—" Sailed from *Liverpool* "with 14 six-pounders, swivels, small arms, *and* "50 *hands, or upwards;* coppersheathed."

The *Juno* had sailed from *Liverpool* on the 13th October 1778; but, instead of 50, she had then only 46 hands on board; and she arrived at *Beaumaris* in the *Isle of Anglesea*, in six hours after leaving *Liverpool*. At *Beaumaris*, she took in six hands more, and continued to have 52 hands, during the rest of the voyage. During her passage from *Liverpool* to *Beaumaris*, it is specified in the verdict, that she was equally safe, as if she had had 50 hands on board.—She was taken by enemies, in the course of the insured voyage, on the 14th March 1779.

The counsel for the plaintiff was stopt by the Court.

For the defendant, it was argued, that the marginal note in this case was not to be considered as a *warranty*, like that in *Bean v. Stupart*, and other cases on the point. For in those, the note had always been a warranty of a fact with relation to the voyage insured. But in this, it has no relation to the voyage; it relates merely to the force of the ship at *Liverpool*, long before the risk commenced. The policy is " at and " from *Africa* to the *West Indies*;" but the marginal note, so far as it has not been adhered to, applies to the circumstances of the vessel, at a period antecedent, when she " sailed from *Li-* " *verpool.*"—So far as relates to the *coppersheathing*, which may apply to the adventure insured, the marginal note may be held to be a *warranty;* but as to the number of hands, when she sailed from *Liverpool*, it can be nothing more than a representation.—And has been substantially complied with.

The Court held, that this clause being a warranty, must be *literally* complied with. The distinction attempted between the different parts of the marginal note, is without foundation. Judgment for the plaintiff.—*Termly Reports, Trin.* 1786.

In the same manner, where a ship is insured under a warranty, which is calculated to secure her against the peril of capture; if the warranty is not performed, and a loss is incurred, the underwriter is not responsible, although the loss should have arisen from a cause totally unconnected with that hazard, against which it was the view of the warranty to provide.

WOOLMER v. MUILMAN.

This was an action for recovery of a total loss on a policy of insurance made " on goods and " merchandises on board the ship *Bona Fortuna*, " at and from *North Bergen*, until her arrival at " *London, warranted neutral ship and property.*" She was lost *in a storm.*

It was expressly stated, that the vessel, at and before the time she was lost, was not neutral property. Lord MANSFIELD said it was too plain to argue. Judgment for the defendant, 3. *Burr.* 17*th June* 1763.

A variety of cases, in relation to a condition of convoy, occur in illustration of the same principle. If a vessel is warranted with convoy, and does not actually join convoy, the contract is void, and the insurer is liable for no loss, from whatever cause it may be incurred. Neither is it of any moment, that she has overtaken the convoy before a loss has happened; for the agreement being rendered void, cannot revive by any subsequent change of circumstances.

DUNMORE

Dunmore and Co. against Allan, Campbell, and others.

There were two policies of infurance upon fugar, the property of *Robert Dunmore and Company*, on board the fhip *Commerce*, deftined for *Clyde* from *Jamaica*. In the one policy, which was fubfcribed by *Allan*, and others, at *Glafgow*, the rifk was defcribed thus:—" Beginning the ad-
" venture upon the faid produce, *at and from* the
" loading thereof, at the loading ports in *Ja-*
" *maica*, and to continue and endure until faid
" *Commerce*, with faid produce, fhall (*with li-*
" *berty to join convoy at the rendezvous*) arrive at
" *Greenock* or *Port-Glafgow*, or at their port of
" difcharge in *Great Britain*, and until faid pro-
" duce be there fafely landed." The claufe fpecifying the premium, with the condition of infurance, runs thus: " After the rate of 15
" guineas for each L. 100 Sterling, *warranted*
" *with convoy*, with L. 5 *per cent*. additional, if
" it does not fail on or before the 1ft Auguft
" current."

The other policy, fubfcribed at *Greenock*, by *Campbell*, and others, was in thefe words:—" Be-
" ginning the faid adventure upon the goods and
" merchandife, at and from the fhipping there-
" of on board faid *Commerce*, at her port or ports
" of loading in *Jamaica*, and continuing until
" faid *Commerce* fhall arrive at her port of dif-
" charge in *Clyde*, and until faid goods and mer-
" chandife are there fafely landed: The faid
" *Commerce*

" *Commerce to fail with convoy for Britain,* on or
" before the firft inftant; or, if after that date,
" to pay five guineas *per* L. 100 additional pre-
" mium; the faid *Commerce* having *liberty to
" join convoy at the rendezvous.*"

Admiral *Graves,* with the convoy appointed for the *Jamaica* trade, failed from *Bluefields,* upon the 25th of July 1782, being fix days fooner than the ufual departure of convoy.

On the 29th of July, the *Commerce failed* from *Montego Bay,* on the oppofite fide of the ifland; and having ground to believe, that the convoy were already failed, fhe proceeded after them, and joined them on the 20th of Auguft, when fhe received her *failing orders.*—After failing in company with them for fome time, fhe was feparated in a hurricane; again joined the fleet, was again feparated, and taken by the *Alliance,* an *American* frigate.

The caufe having come, (by fufpenfion,) before the Court of Seffion, the principal grounds maintained by the affured, feemed to be thefe:—That in practice it was *cuftomary* for veffels ftationed upon the north fide of *Jamaica,* inftead of going round to *Bluefields,* to wait for convoy at *Negril Point,* or fomewhere off the weft end of the ifland; therefore it was not neceffary to join at *Bluefields.* That, from feveral cafes, particularly *Victorin v. Cleeve,* Strange, 1250, it appeared fufficient, if a claufe of convoy was adhered to fubftantially.—And a diftinction was attempted

tempted between the expressions, warranted *with convoy*, and warranted to *depart* with convoy. The underwriters produced a certificate, that, by the *Glasgow* practice, these expressions are held to be synonymous. And they quoted a variety of recent cases, to show the literal adherence required by the *English* Courts, and by mercantile practice, to a clause of convoy.

Lord BRAXFIELD Ordinary, decided in favour of the underwriters, by " *suspending the letters* " *simpliciter.*"

Upon a reclaiming petition and answers, it was observed upon the Bench.—The vessel insured is protected by the policy, while sailing to the place of rendezvous. If she does not take advantage of this power, so as actually to *join convoy*, she has herself to blame. The condition of the contract is not implemented; the policy is void *ab initio*, and cannot revive in consequence of any subsequent junction. A vessel is no more at liberty to set sail after her convoy, than she is before it. Where would a latitude in this respect end?—The Court unanimously adhered. 1786.—*Fac. Coll.*

The same point was formerly illustrated by a variety of examples in cases of *deviation*.

10. It is not inconsistent with what has now been observed, that when the terms of a warranty have been strictly complied with by the assured, and the adventure has been commenced upon those terms, the insurer is not liberated from

from his obligation from any change of circumstances, occasioned by unavoidable accident, in the course of the voyage. Such changes constitute a part of that risk which the insurer has undertaken, and for which the premium is given.

Thus, where a vessel is warranted *neutral;* she is neutral when the risk commences, but she becomes otherwise in the course of the voyage; the warranty is held to be fulfilled; for this is an accident in the course of the adventure insured.

Eden *against* Parkinson.

The plaintiff insured the ship the *Yonge Herman Hiddinga* and her cargo, at and from L'Orient to Rotterdam, warranted a neutral ship and neutral property. The ship sailed from L'Orient on the voyage insured on the 11th December 1780, having the insured cargo on board; and both the ship and cargo were at that time neutral property, and continued so until the 20th of December 1780, when hostilities commenced between the English and Dutch. The vessel was taken on the 25th of December, and condemned as lawful prize.

These were the principal facts of a case submitted by a jury at Guildhall to the opinion of the Court. It was contended for the plaintiffs, that the warranty was complied with by the neutrality of the ship and cargo at the time when the voyage commenced. For the defendant,

ant, that this warranty was intended to be coextensive with the voyage; and that it was the same with an insurance against war-risk.

Lord MANSFIELD said, that the risk of future war is taken by the underwriter in every policy; like every other risk that arises in the course of the voyage. There is an implied warranty in every insurance, that the vessel is good and sufficient for the voyage; but this only relates to the time of her sailing. If she becomes insufficient during the voyage, it is at the risk of the underwriter. In the same manner, if a ship is warranted neutral, it means when the adventure commences; if she becomes liable to capture in the course of the voyage, it is one of those accidents for which the underwriter is answerable. The *postea* to be delivered to the plaintiff. Douglas's Reports, 26th June 1781.

In the same manner, in cases of *convoy*, it is enough if the condition be once fulfilled, by the vessel insured having made an actual junction, having got her sailing orders, and making an inception of the voyage with her convoy. Any separation that may afterwards happen is an accident in the course of the adventure insured. It is like a *deviation from necessity*, which does not vacate the agreement.

JEFFERY v. LEGANDRA.

A vessel was insured " from London to Cadiz, " warranted to depart with convoy." In an action

action on the policy, the jury found that the ship departed from the port of London, in company with the convoy; and that they failed together as far as the *Isle of Wight*, where they were separated by stress of weather. That the convoy put into *Torbay*, and the insured ship into *Fowey* in Cornwall. That three days afterwards, the wind setting right to bring the convoy down the Channel, the ship sailed out of *Fowey* to meet the convoy, but it did not come; and the insured ship was driven by another storm on the coast of France, and captured.

It was held by the whole Court, that the words " warranted to depart with convoy," mean only that the vessel insured shall depart with convoy from his first port, and shall not leave it through any fault of the master. And here the master had done all in his power to continue in company with the convoy.—Therefore judgment was given for the plaintiff.— 3. *Lev.* 320.—*Carthew*, 216.—2. *Salk.* 443.— 1. *Shower.* 320.—4. *Mod. Rep.* 58.

This principle is carried so far, that if the vessel insured has actually *joined* convoy, and is within the rendezvous at the time of sailing; if she has her *sailing orders*, is in every respect ready to depart with the armed force, and *makes an effort* for that purpose;—the attempt to sail along with the convoy is considered as a sufficient inception of the voyage; and, although,

from

from the accidents of wind and tide, it should prove ineffectual, is held a fulfilment of the warranty.

PHYNNE and another against WEBSTER.

Insurance was made " at and from London " to Quebec, *warranted to sail with convoy for the* " *voyage.*" The convoy lay at Portsmouth, and the ship at *Stokes' bay*, which is within the place of rendezvous; and she had got sailing orders from Captain ——— of the *Assistance*. On hearing the signal for sailing, she weighed; but the wind failing, and the tide being spent, she could not get away along with the convoy. She therefore followed next tide; but never came up with them, and was captured.

It was held that there was a sufficient performance of the warranty; as the ship had *joined* at the place of rendezvous, and her *not sailing* with the convoy arose from an event not within the power of man to control.—*At Guildhall, —after Hilary,—*1783.—*MS.*

CHAP. III.

Of the Premium, and of the Return of Premium, when the Policy is vacated.

SO much with regard to the obligation of the underwriter; the duration and nature of the risk for which he is liable; the extent to which he is subjected when a loss has been incurred,

curred, and the circumstances which vacate the policy, and destroy his responsibility: It remains to consider the effect of the same circumstances upon the corresponding obligation of the assured.

I. That, whenever the underwriter has run the complete hazard prescribed by the contract, he is entitled to the whole consideration stipulated, it is unnecessary to observe. When the insured voyage is completed, the underwriter has, indisputably, earned his whole premium.

On the other hand, where the intended agreement of insurance has not been carried into effect, and where consequently the insurer has run no risk at all, he can have no title to the premium for which he has given no equivalent.

But the insurer may, in certain cases, be entitled to the whole consideration, although he may not have run the whole, but only a part of the corresponding hazard; supposing that he has been prevented by the fault of the assured. If two persons enter into a bargain, and after it is completed by all the legal solemnities, one of them wishes to recede, the other is not, without his own consent, to be deprived of the advantage arising from the stipulation; and he who is ready to perform, may exact performance, although the other party should decline to receive the equivalent consideration in terms of the bargain. It is not precisely necessary that the insurer should run the whole risk, but only, after
the

the bargain is once complete, that the contrary was not his fault;—"*quod per eum non ſtetit.*"

From theſe principles, it follows, that wherever the contract of inſurance is null and void *ab initio*, the aſſured may demand a *return of premium*.

Among thoſe circumſtances which deſtroy the contract entirely, the intervention of fraud or of error, produces one very important claſs.

Where a perſon has been led to execute an inſurance by direct fraud; by a mutual error in the material qualities of the ſubject; or even in conſequence of any miſtake ariſing from the fault of the other party, which may effect his eſtimation of the riſk;—the bargain is void from the beginning; and as no hazard is run on the one ſide, no premium can be due on the other.

It has, however, been the ſubject of ſome doubt, how far, in caſes of very palpable and groſs impoſition, the aſſured ought to be allowed to recover the premium; and whether he ſhould not incur a forfeiture of it as a penalty. The regulations of Florence declare, in caſe of fraud with regard to the ſtowage of goods, that " the inſurers ſhall not " be under any obligation, and yet ſhall be entit-" led to the premium." There is a ſimilar regulation at Antwerp, with reſpect to over-inſurances. And from the votes of the Commons in 1747, it ſeems to have been intended in England, to impoſe the ſame penalty upon every ſpecies of fraud in inſurance.

It

It must be admitted, that the assured cannot be allowed to found upon his own fraud or omission, in order to annul the contract, when the event has turned out favourable to the insurer. If the vessel arrives in safety, the assured cannot maintain that circumstances had been concealed by him, that therefore the contract is null, and the premium to be returned. But, on the other hand, where the assured is *in petitorio*;—where the vessel is lost, and, against an action on the policy, the underwriter pleads the defence, that the conduct of the assured was fraudulent;—this defence tends to cut down the contract entirely; and for the insurer to retain the premium, would be inconsistent with his own argument, for the nullity of the agreement supposes that he neither can sustain loss, nor reap any benefit from that deed.

The point has been settled accordingly in England, by repeated decisions.

In *Whittingham v. Thornborough*, where the assured was fraudulent, by procuring the name of a leading underwriter as a *decoy*, " the policy " was decreed to be delivered up, and the pre- " mium to be repaid." In *D'Acosta v. Scanderet*, where very material advices had been concealed, " L. MACCLESFIELD decreed the policy to be " delivered up, with costs ; but the premium " to be paid back, and allowed out of the " costs."

WILSON

Wilson v. Ducket.

In action on a policy of infurance on a fhip, with a claim for money had and received to the plaintiff's ufe, it appeared that the firft underwriter was only a decoy to draw in others; it being agreed that he fhould not himfelf be bound by figning the policy. The jury found a verdict for the affured plaintiff for L. 10 premium, on the count for money had and received to his ufe, though they found againft the policy as fraudulent. The trial was had under a decree of the Court of Chancery, where the infurer, being there complainant, had offered to pay back the premium.

With the concurrence of the Court and the Counfel, it was agreed to bring this queftion before the Court, whether, upon a policy of infurance being found fraudulent, the premium fhould be retained by the infurer, or returned to the affured. Befide the cafes *Whittingham v. Thornborough*, and *D'Acofta v. Scanderet*, the plaintiff's counfel cited a cafe *Rucker v. Hollingbury*, in which the mafter of the rolls had been of an opinion oppofite to the two former decifions.

Lord MANSFIELD faid,—There muft be fome miftake as to this laft cafe; for the practice of Chancery was certainly agreeable to the two former. Thefe were all in Chancery; and it did not appear there was any common law decifion upon the point.—In this inftance, his Lordfhip looked

looked upon the offer made by the complainant's bill in equity to be the fame thing, as if he had brought the money into Court.—
3. *Burr.* 1361.

A deficiency with regard to the ſtatutory requiſites, forms another general claſs of circumſtances, which render an inſurance void from the beginning, and which, therefore, ought naturally to deſtroy the underwriter's right to the premium. When the policy has not been, in proper time, drawn out on ſtamped paper; when it relates to a wagering intereſt, or to an illicit trade;—the inſurer runs no hazard, and is not entitled to the conſideration.

By one of the acts, however, impoſing a ſtamp-duty on policies of inſurance, the premium is, in all caſes of contravention of the ſtatute, declared to belong to the inſurer. 5. *Geo.* III. *c.* 46.

In thoſe policies which are null, as contrary to ſtatute, it generally happens, that both parties are acceſſory to the evaſion of the law; for example, in a wagering policy, or an inſurance of illicit trade. In ſuch inſtances, a court of juſtice will reprobate any claim upon the contract; but if it is once carried into execution, the judge will refuſe to interpoſe, in order to reſtore parties againſt the conſequences of their own improper conduct.

Thus *Lowry* procured inſurance from *Bourdieu*, on a ſhip bound to the *Eaſt Indies*, with the view of securing himself in payment of a sum due by the captain; the assured had paid the premium. After the vessel had arrived, he raised an action to recover the premium, upon the ground that this had been a wager-insurance. The Court thought, that both parties were guilty of a breach of the law, and it was proper to assist neither. "*In pari delicto, melior est conditio* "*possidentis.*" Besides, if money has been given for an illegal purpose, it can only be recovered while the contract continues *executory*, but here it has been *executed*.

But the most important examples of a null insurance, are founded on the circumstance, that this contract is not complete, nor fully binding on the assured, until a performance has been made by the underwriter; that is, until the insured voyage has commenced, and the underwriter has begun to run the hazard. Until the adventure has commenced, the assured has a power to retract. He exercises this power whenever he alters the voyage, or departs in any article from the express or implied conditions of the agreement. For example, where, before the commencement of hazard, the plan of the voyage is changed, and it is resolved to touch at ports not specified, or to prosecute a destination different from what was understood. Where the vessel is warranted *neutral, with convoy,* or *to sail before a day,* and she fails in the performance of these declared conditions.

Where

Where the affured has thus receded from the bargain, by altering the plan of the voyage before the commencement of rifk, the contract is totally annulled; the underwriter is not liable in indemnity, and the affured recovers his premium.

On the other hand, wherever the bargain is completed;—where it relates to a legal intereft; where it is executed agreeably to ftatute; where it has not originated in mifreprefentation or concealment; and where there has been a beginning of performance:—In other words, where the infured hazard has commenced, the premium is gained by the underwriter. From the moment that the rifk commences, the affured has no longer a power to recede. If he perfifts in the adventure to a conclufion, the underwriter is liable for accident in the courfe of it, and earns his whole premium, by being expofed to the whole hazard. But if the affured, after the commencement of rifk, chufes to depart from the voyage undertaken, ftill the infurer is not, without his own confent, to be deprived of the benefit of his contract; and though, from the fault of the affured, he does not actually run the whole rifk, he is entitled to retain the confideration. In every cafe of *deviation*, therefore, or departure from the policy fubfequent to the commencement of rifk, although the infurer's obligation is at an end, yet the premium is gained.

The principle that a premium is due by the affured, in confideration of a correfponding rifk,

undertaken

undertaken by the infurer, has led to a queftion, whether, in certain cafes, the hazard of a voyage may not be confidered as divifible; fo that an apportionment of premium may be made according to the length that has actually been proceeded in the ftipulated adventure. In general, it fhould feem, that the adventure defcribed in any fingle policy, is to be confidered as one complex whole, which the infurer undertakes in confideration of the entire premium. It does not appear, that parties have formed any idea of a fubdivifion of the rifk, correfponding to a fubdivifion of the premium. Confequently, if the voyage be once commenced, there can be no room for an apportionment.

But there is one cafe, in which parties muft have formed a conception of the adventure as divifible; wherever one part of it depends on a condition, and another does not; for, when this occurs, the two parts of the infurance are in a very different fituation. The exiftence of that part which is conditional, is perfectly uncertain.

For example, infurance is made "from *London* "to *Jamaica*, and from *Jamaica* to *London*, war-"ranted with convoy in the homeward voyage." Parties muft be prefumed to have confidered thefe two infurances, out and home, as two feparate rifks; for the condition may fail, and confequently, the infurance home be null. And if they were to be viewed as one rifk, this abfurdity would

would follow, that the insurer could not be subjected for a total loss in the outward voyage, because it is impossible at that period to say, whether the condition of convoy homeward shall be fulfilled or not.

It is not enough, however, to afford room for a partial return of premium, that the adventure be partly conditional. Because it is not sufficient the voyage be divisible; it is farther requisite that there be some *data*, in what manner to make the division, and how to *apportion* the premium on the risk actually run. For this purpose, a proof must be adduced, that mercantile people, in the circumstances of each case, consider a certain proportion of the premium as adequate to the different branches of the adventure. Without these two circumstances, an adventure *partly conditional*, and a proof of mercantile *usage*, it seems to be established that no apportionment can take place.

STEVENSON *v.* SNOW.

This was a case referred at *nisi prius* before Lord MANSFIELD, for the opinion of the Court, upon an action brought by the plaintiff, the insured, against the defendant, the insurer, for a return of part of the premium.

It was an insurance " upon a ship at five gui-
" neas *per cent.* at and from London to Halifax
" in Nova Scotia, warranted to depart with con-
" voy

" voy from Portsmouth ; that is to say, the Ha-
" lifax or Louisburgh convoy."

Before the ship arrived at Portsmouth, the convoy was gone. Notice of this was immediately given by the insured to the underwriter ; and, at the same time, he was desired either to make the long insurance, or to return part of the premium.

The insured acquiesced in the payment of one and a half *per cent.* as the ascertained premium between London and Portsmouth ; and demanded a return of premium upon the other part of the adventure between Portsmouth and Halifax, as the condition had not been fulfilled, and therefore the policy so far was void.

The jury find, that the usual settled premium between London and Portsmouth, is one and one-half *per cent.* They also find, that, in circumstances like the present, it is customary for the underwriter to return part of the premium ; but the quantum uncertain.

For the plaintiff, it was argued, that as the underwriter had not run the whole risk, he ought not to retain the whole premium. It was answered for the defendant, that the contract was entire, and could not be divided into parts ; the premium was given in consideration of the whole voyage complexly ; it was impossible to apportion it, and to say with certainty what part of the premium the contracting parties might consider as corresponding to one part of the voyage,

and

and what to another. That whenever the rifk had once commenced, the whole premium was gained. If the veffel had been loft between London and Portfmouth, the underwriter would have been liable for the whole lofs; the voyage therefore was commenced, and the whole premium due.

It was replied, the voyage here is not one entire rifk, but divifible. There is one voyage from London to Portfmouth, and another from Portfmouth to Halifax. If the fhip had been loft between London and Portfmouth, the infurer would have been liable; but he would have been entitled only to a proportion of the premium correfponding to the rifk run. See Ord. *Coningfb.* and *Stockb. Magens, vol.* 2. *p.* 190. 266.

Lord MANSFIELD was clear that the rifks were divifible. The other Juftices, DENNISON, FOSTER, and WILMOT, were of the fame opinion. The one voyage was pure, the other conditional; and the condition had not exifted.—*Per Cur.*—Judgment for the plaintiff. 3. *Burr.* 17*th Nov.* 1761.

TYRIE *v.* FLETCHER.

Fletcher infured *Tyrie* upon "the fhip *Ifabella*,
" at and from London, to any port or place
" where or whatfoever, for twelve months, from
" the 19th of Auguft 1776 to the 19th of Au-
" guft 1777, both days inclufive, at L. 9 *per*
" *cent.* warranted free from captures and feizures
" by

"by the Americans, and the confequences
"thereof." In all other refpects, it was, in the
common form, againft all perils of the fea, *&c.*
The fhip failed from the port of London, and
was taken by an American privateer about two
months afterwards.

The plaintiff having brought an action for a
return of part of the premium, by confent a
verdict was found for the plaintiff, fubject to the
opinion of the court.

For the plaintiff it was argued, that as only a
part of the rifk had been run, only a part of the
premium was due. *Stevenfon v. Snow.* That
was a policy upon a voyage; but it was eafier
to apportion the rifk in a policy upon time like
the prefent, than in a policy upon diftance. In
the cafe of *Bond v. Nutt,* the underwriters paid
into court a part of the premium, in proportion
to that part of the voyage from which they held
themfelves difcharged. The conftruction of the
policy under thefe circumftances ought to be,
that it was an infurance for twelve months, at the
rate of fo much *per* month; as the rifk was only
run for two months, the premium advanced upon the other ten ought to be returned.

It was argued for the defendant, that the policy was one entire rifk; and that, as foon as
the fhip failed from the port of London, that
rifk commenced, and the entire premium was
due. In the cafes *Stevenfon v. Snow,* and *Bond
v. Nutt,* there were two diftinct voyages. If a
policy

policy upon time may be divided into months, why not into weeks or days. The present case is not distinguishable from an insurance upon a life for a year, with an exception of suicide, where the party destroys himself within a month. No one ever thought of requiring a return of premium in that case, because the risk is entire; so it is in the present case.

Lord MANSFIELD said, there were two general rules established, applicable to the question. 1*st*, That where the risk has not been run, whether its not having been run was owing to the fault, pleasure, or will of the insured, or to any other cause, the premium shall be returned. 2*dly*, That if the risk has once commenced, there shall be no apportionment or return of premium.

In the case of *Stevenson v. Snow*, there were two separate voyages or risks insured. The example of a life-policy, quoted by the defendant, is precisely in point.

In the present case, parties, instead of insuring from two months to two months, or for any other proportions of time, had made no division of time at all. It is one entire contract from August 1776 to August 1777, and supposes the insured to have meant to give one entire sum.

ASTON, J.—This is one entire contract. In the case of *Bond v. Nutt*, the voyage was divisible, *viz. at* a port in Jamaica, and *from* that port, conditionally, if she sailed before a certain day.

Willes and Ashurst, J. of the same opinion. Judgment for the defendant. *Couper's Reports,* 18*th Nov.* 1777.

Loraine *against* Thomlinson.

The plaintiff had underwritten L. 200 on a policy effected at Newcastle, whereby the ship the *Chollerford* was insured against capture by the enemy *for twelve months*, in the coasting trade between Leith and the Isle of Wight, beginning the 13th of March 1779, and ending the 13th of the same month 1780, at the rate of 15 *per cent. per* month.

The ship was lost in a storm, within the first two of the twelve months for which the insurance was made. And the plaintiff brought an action for the premium, which, according to the usage of Newcastle, had not been paid *per* advance. The defendant tendered L. 3 as the premium for two months, upon this ground; that as the insurance was at so much for each separate month, the premium was only due for that number of months for which the risk had continued. A jury, at the assizes for Northumberland, returned a verdict subject to the opinion of the Court upon this point.

It was argued for the defendant, that this was not one entire contract for a year, but an insurance from month to month, for twelve months. If the policy had been for a year or twelve months, and the premium a gross sum, the Court could

could not have apportioned it, becaufe the rifk in one month might be greater than in another; but here the parties have apportioned the premium. The only purpofe that they could have for mentioning the monthly proportion, muft have been to afcertain the fum to be returned, in cafe of capture within the year. If it had been meant to be an entire contract, the premium would have been fixed at L. 18 *per annum,* without any mention of months.

Lord MANSFIELD and the Court were very clear. His Lordfhip faid, that it was an infurance for twelve months, for one grofs fum of L. 18. They have calculated this fum to be at the rate of 15 s. *per* month. But what was to be paid down? Not 15 s. for the firft month, and fo for month to month, but L. 18 at once.

The *poftea* to be delivered to the plaintiff. Douglas' *Reports,* 1*ft February* 1781.

BERMON *againft* WOODBRIDGE.

In a policy of infurance on the French fhip *Le Pactole* and her cargo, the voyage was defcribed in the following words: " At and from Hon- " fleur to the coaft of Angola, during her ftay " and trade there; at and from thence to her " port or ports of difcharge in St Domingo; and " at and from St Domingo back to Honfleur." The claufe refpecting the premium was as follows.—" Slaves valued at 800 livres *per* head ; " the fhip at L. 1450 Sterling ; other goods, *&c.*
" as

"as interest may appear, at a premium of L. 11 *per cent.*"

The ship sailed to Angola, and from thence to the West Indies. On her way from Angola she put in at Cayenne on the coast of America, and from Cayenne went to Martinico, confessedly out of the course to St Domingo. The captain attempted to justify this deviation upon the footing of necessity; but the jury were clear it was not necessary. Upon their declaring that opinion, it was contended for the plaintiff, that the voyage insured ought to be considered as composed of three distinct parts, viz. *1st*, from Honfleur to Angola; *2d*, from Angola to St Domingo; *3d*, from St Domingo to Honfleur; and that as the last of these had never commenced, there ought to be a return of premium upon it. The jury having likewise found upon this point for the defendant, a new trial was moved for.

Lord MANSFIELD, in delivering the opinion of the Court, said,—The question depends on this, whether the policy contains one entire risk on one voyage, or whether it is to be split into six different risks; for by splitting the words, and taking *at* and *from* separately, it will make six instead of three risks, viz. 1. *at* Honfleur; 2. *from* Honfleur to Angola; 3. *at* Angola, &c. Here the insured and insurers consider the premium as an entire sum for the whole, without division; it is estimated on the whole at 11 *per cent.* And,

And, which is extremely material, there is *no contingency*, at any period out or home, mentioned in the policy, which, happening or not happening, is to put an end to the insurance. The two cases of *Stevenson v. Snow*, and *Bond v. Nutt*, which had been founded upon, were quite different from this. In these cases, the two parts of the voyage were separated from each other, by a condition being annexed to one of them, which made it a contingency, whether that part of the insurance should take effect or not. The two cases of *Tyrie v. Fletcher*, and *Loraine v. Thomlinson*, were very strong on the other side; for if you could apportion the premium in any case, it would be in insurances on time. Therefore we think this an entire risk, one voyage, and that there can be no return of premium. The rule discharged. *Douglas' Reports*, 2d *July* 1781.

MEYER *v.* GREGSON.

The defendant insured the plaintiff "*at* and "*from* Jamaica to Liverpool, warranted *to* "*sail on or before the first of August*, at 20 gui- " neas *per cent.* to return 8, if she sails with con- " voy." The ship did not sail till September, and was lost.

In an action at the assured's instance for return of premium, the underwriter paid 8 guineas into Court, by way of making a return for convoy. The jury found a verdict for 8 guineas more,

more, which was allowing the underwriter to retain 4 guineas for the risk *at* Jamaica. Motion to set aside the verdict, and enter a nonsuit.

Lord MANSFIELD.—It appears from the evidence, that the risk *at* Jamaica is different on different sides of the island; and it would be endless to apportion it. Besides, parties have expressly divided the risk with respect to convoy; they stipulate a premium of twenty guineas to return 8, if she sail with convoy. But there is no such division with respect to the time of sailing, so that it seems to have been intended as an absolute warranty. In *Stevenson and Snow,* the Court went on its being expressed so as to constitute two voyages; the usage being to have convoy from Portsmouth only, and the risk from London to Portsmouth being exactly known.

WILLES, J. thought the premium should be apportioned.

ASHURST, J. agreed with Lord MANSFIELD.

BULLER, J.—The parties do not appear to have considered it as two risks, so the Court cannot do it for them. All insurances from Jamaica are *at* and *from*; and although in many instances the voyage has not begun, yet it never has been supposed that a return of premium should take place. The jury had found no usage. The rule for setting aside the verdict made absolute. *East.* 24. *Geo.* III. *MS.*

LONG

Long v. Allen.

The defendant infured the plaintiff, on a fhip the *Jamaica, at* and *from* Jamaica to London, "warranted to depart with convoy for the voyage, and to fail on or before the firft of Auguft,—at a premium of 12 guineas *per cent.*" The fhip failed on the 31ft July 1782, but without convoy for the voyage. In an action for return of premium, (amounting to L. 50, 8s.) the jury found the facts above ftated; and farther, "that in infurances *at* and *from* Jamaica, with a warranty as in this policy, when the fhip does not fail before the day fixed, or does not fail with convoy, it is the ufage to return the premium, deducting one-half *per cent.*" Queftion, for the opinion of the Court, Whether the plaintiff is entitled to recover?

Lord MANSFIELD.—The law is clear, that if the rifk be once commenced, there can be no return. Hence, in a queftion where diftinct rifks are infured by the fame inftrument, my opinion has been to divide the rifks. I am aware there are great difficulties in apportioning, and therefore the Court have generally leaned againft it. But when there is *ufage*, the difficulty is removed.

WILLES and ASHURST, J. concurred.

BULLER, J.—Since Lord HOLT's time, a greater latitude has been adopted in admitting parole evidence, and with regard to the effect of *ufage* in the conftruction of a policy. Ufage will make

make places within the policy which are not within the words. It will explain and even control a policy. The ufage here found is univerfal; and though the fum of one-half *per cent.* may in fome cafes be a fmall allowance for the rifk *at* Jamaica, yet the underwriter is aware of that. In *Meyer v. Gregfon*, there was no ufage proved. The *poftea* to the plaintiff, *Eaft.* 25. *Geo.* III. *MS.*

When the policy is null from the beginning, fo that the underwriter runs no rifk, and the affured recovers the premium, the former is allowed to retain one-half *per cent.* upon the fum infured, as a confideration for keeping an account of the tranfaction.

II. Although the premium is expreffed in the policy to be paid by advance, yet it is not fo in fact; but is ufually retained in the hands of the affured, or of the infurance-broker, until the iffue of the adventure, when a final adjuftment can take place between the parties.

Infurance is, in general, executed by the intervention of a *broker*. The broker is, in the firft inftance, the agent of the affured, from whom he receives an order of infurance, which he fhows to different underwriters; and if they agree to undertake the rifk, he draws up a formal policy in terms of the order, for their fubfcription.

If the broker neglects to take proper meafures for getting the order executed, after having undertaken

dertaken it; or if he varies from the terms of it, he muſt be reſponſible to the merchant, his employer. See *Delancey againſt Stoddart*, in *Termly Reports, Mich.* 1785. *Wilſon againſt Elliot.* In this reſpect, he ſeems bound to uſe the ſame degree of diligence with any other factor.

Where a policy is effected by means of a broker, the underwriter muſt be ſuppoſed to look to the broker for payment of the premiums, from the date on which they are underſtood to be due. This is believed to be agreeable to the general practice of Britain, as well as founded in the reaſon of the thing; though I know no caſe, either Engliſh or Scotch, in which the point has been expreſsly decided. In the following, (collected by *Mr Park*,) it became indirectly the ſubject of enquiry.

Milton, a broker at Newcaſtle, had procured inſurance for *Bland*. *Milton*, becoming bankrupt, his aſſignees ſued *Bland* for premiums advanced by *Milton* for his behoof. One queſtion that aroſe was, Whether credit was given to the aſſured, or to the broker, when the premium was not paid down at the time the inſurance was made? *Milton* ſwore, that, in May 1764, he had been told by the underwriters, that they would have nothing to do with the aſſured, which was conſidered at Newcaſtle as the London practice·

tice: That, from that time, he had always acted on this plan, and had paid, since that time, L. 1000 to underwriters, which he had never received. London brokers were then called, who said they understood the underwriters look to them only; and that the underwriters did not once in ten times know who the assured were; and that, in cases of failure, the underwriter came upon the effects of the broker; the broker upon those of the insured.

In most parts of the kingdom, however, this responsibility of the broker does not commence immediately on the execution of the policy. The delay of payment of the premium, whether it is to be considered as an indulgence to the assured, or a matter of right, supposes that the broker should be allowed a reasonable time to exact payment. The period allowed for this purpose varies so much in different parts of the island, is so fluctuating, and depends so little on principles, that nothing need here be said with regard to it.

Although the whole expence of insurance must ultimately be borne by the assured, yet, in the office now mentioned of collecting the premiums, (which necessarily falls upon the broker, from the responsibility connected with his employment,) he appears to act immediately as agent for the underwriter. For the trouble and risk

risk attending the business, he is therefore indemnified by a commission of so much *per cent.* upon the premiums. The amount of this commission varies exceedingly in different situations.

In this manner, the broker is factor or agent for both parties, the assured and the underwriter; for the assured, by procuring insurance upon his order; and, for the underwriter, by collecting the premiums.

Every factor or agent has a *lien* for a balance due to him, upon the goods of his principal. This was found by Sir JOHN STRANGE, Master of the Rolls, in the case of *Kruzer et al. v. Wilcox et al.*; where his Lordship decreed, " That a " factor has a *lien* on goods consigned to him, " not only for incident charges, but as an item " of mutual account for the general balance due " to him, so long as he retains the possession. " But if he parts with the possession of the goods, " he parts with his *lien;* because it cannot then " be retained as an item for the general account." There was another case, *Gardiner v. Coleman*, decided in the same manner.

An insurance-broker, therefore, as a factor for the assured, seems to have a *lien* upon the policy, while it remains in his custody, for a balance due by his employer.

Thus, Mr *Amyand* had got insurance in his own name upon goods the property of Mr *Meybohm.*

Lord

Lord MANSFIELD said—"Suppofing Mr *Amyand* to have made his infurance, not upon his own account, but as agent for *Meybohm*, ftill, as *Amyand* has poffeffion of the policy, and appears to have been a creditor of *Meybohm*, upon the balance of accounts between them, at the time when he made the infurance, he is entitled to retain the policy." *Godin v. Lond. Aff. Company.* 1. *Burr.* 489.

In the following cafe, it may, perhaps, be doubted, whether the Court of Seffion have not gone a greater length in fuftaining the broker's claim of retention.

LESLIE and THOMSON *againft* DAVID LINN.

Leflie and Thomfon, infurance-brokers in Edinburgh, were employed by *Maclean*, a merchant in Leith, to get infurance on a fhip done for him at Glafgow. The brokers, in effecting this infurance, had the policy taken out in their own names. Accordingly, a lofs having happened, one of the underwriters granted his bill for his fhare, in favour of *Leflie and Thomfon*. This bill, however, was by him tranfmitted to *Maclean*, who had previoufly got the policy into his cuftody, upon which *Maclean* indorfed and delivered it to *Linn*.

Leflie and Thomfon infifted for delivery of the bill to them, on this ground: That *Maclean* having

ving been previously endebted to them, they, with a view to avail themselves of the possession of the policy, for operating their payment, in the event of a loss, had accepted the commission from *Maclean*, and, for their farther security, had the policy made out in the above manner. In a competition with regard to this bill, appearance having been made for *Linn*, they, in support of this claim,

Pleaded: The bill in question being payable to them, and not to *Maclean*, the indorsation in favour of *Linn*, by the latter, cannot confer the special privileges competent to indorsees of bills of exchange. *Linn*, therefore, in this competition, stands on the same footing as *Maclean* himself would have done; and the question is, which of the parties has right to the contents of the bill, as a part of the insured values payable by the underwriters?

An insurance-broker is to be considered as a factor acting on commission; and as it is established, that a factor is entitled to retention of the subject of his factory, for satisfaction of debts due to himself by his constituent; so it is lawful for an insurance-broker to retain possession of the policy, for security or payment of debt owing to him, by the party on whose commission he acts. This rule is founded on the practice of merchants; and in *England* has been exemplified by a judgment of the Court of King's Bench, *Godin v. Lond. Affur. Co.* In this particular case, the policy was made out in the names of *Leslie and Thomson*, and therefore, though *Maclean* actually got it into his custody, the effect respecting the latter is the same as if it had still remained in the possession of the former.

Answered: The power of retention competent to a factor, is not disputed. But an insurance-broker acting in his proper sphere is not a factor. If indeed the insured, besides commissioning him to make the insurance, which is his peculiar office, were farther specially to authorise him to retain the policy, and, in the event of a loss, to recover the sums underwritten, then he might so far assume the character of factor, and plead the privileges of such. But whilst his employment is not thus extended beyond its proper limits, his commission is strictly confined to the effecting of the insurance, by making the bargain with the underwriters; upon his doing which, it is his duty instantly to deliver up the policy to his employer, who may have immediate occasion for it, as in the event of his transferring the cargo so insured to a purchaser. As for the policy in this case, being framed in the name of the insurance-brokers, that circumstance must pass for nothing, as being unauthorised by *Maclean*.

The *Lord Ordinary* " preferred *David Linn* to " the principal sum and interest contained in " and due by the accepted bill produced."

The

The Court, however, *altered* that interlocutor, and preferred *Leslie and Thomson*. *Fac. Coll. July* 4. 1783.

In the fame manner, the broker has a fimilar right of retention, for money due by the underwriter, upon the premiums in his hands.

INDEX.

APPENDIX X.

No. I. *Form of a London* POLICY *on Shipping and Merchandise.*

IN the name of God, Amen. *Messrs A. B. and Co.* as well in their own names, as for and in the name and names of all and every other person or persons, to whom the same doth or shall appertain, in part, or in all, doth make assurance, and cause *themselves, and them, and every of them,* to be insured, lost or not lost, *at and from Hull to Hamburgh, upon any kind of goods, and merchandise; and also upon the body, tackle, apparel, ordnance, munition, artillery, boat, and other furniture of and in the good ship, or vessel, called the Prince Gallitzin, a Russian ship,* whereof is master under God, for this present voyage, *Jacob Tretiacoff,* or whosoever else shall go for master in the said ship, or by whatsoever other name or names, the same ship, or the master thereof, is, or shall be called, or named. Beginning the adventure upon the said goods and merchandises, *from the loading thereof aboard the said ship at Hull, or elsewhere,* upon the said ship, &c. and so shall continue and endure during her abode there, upon the said ship, &c.; and further, until the said ship, with all her ordnance, tackle, apparel, &c. and goods and merchandises whatsoever, shall be arrived *at Hamburgh,* upon the said ship, &c. until she hath moored at anchor twenty-four hours in good safety; and upon the goods and merchandises, until the same be there discharged and safely landed. And it shall be lawful for the said ship, &c. in the voyage, to proceed and sail to, touch and stay at, any ports or places whatsoever, without prejudice to this insurance. The said ship, &c. goods and merchandises, &c. for so much as concerns the assureds and assurers in this policy, are, and shall be valued at——. Touching the adventures and perils, which we the assurers are contented to bear, and do take upon us in this voyage; they are of the seas, men of war, fire, enemies, pirates, rovers, thieves, jettisons, letters of mart, and counter-mart, surprisals, takings at sea, arrests, restraints, and detainments of all kings, princes and people, of what nation, condition, or quality whatsoever; baratry of the master and mariners, and all other perils, losses, or misfortunes, that have, or shall come to the hurt, detriment, or damage of the said goods and merchandises and ship, &c. or any part thereof. And in case of any loss or misfortune, it shall be lawful to the assureds, their factors, servants, and assigns, to sue, labour, and travel for, in and about the defence, safeguard, and recovery of the said goods and merchandises, and ship, &c. or any part thereof, without prejudice to this insurance; to the charges whereof, we the assurers will contribute, each one according to the rate and quantity of his sum therein assured. And it is agreed by us the insurers, that this writing, or policy of assurance, shall be of as much force and effect, as the surest writing or policy of assurance heretofore made in Lombardstreet, or in the Royal Exchange, or elsewhere, in London; and so we the assurers are contented, and do hereby promise and bind ourselves, each one for his own part, our heirs, executors, and goods, to the assureds, their executors, administrators, and assigns, for the true performance of the premises, confessing ourselves paid the consideration due unto us for this assurance, by the assured, at and after the rate of five guineas *per cent*. In witness whereof, we the assurers have subscribed our names and sums assured, in London.

> *N. B.* Corn, fish, salt, fruit, flour, and seed, are warranted free from average, unless general, or the ship be stranded; sugar, tobacco, hemp, flax, hides, and skins, are warranted free from average, under five pounds *per cent*. and all other goods; also the ship and freight are warranted free of average, under three pounds *per cent*. unless general, or the ship be stranded.

No. II. *A* POLICY *from Fire, used in Scotland.*

WHEREAS *A. B. merchant in* ———— has paid the sum of *twelve shillings and eight pence* to the Society of the ———— Assurance Company, against losses by fire, and has agreed to pay, or cause to be paid to them, at their office in ———— *the sum of twelve shillings,* at the term of *Martinmas* 1787, and the like sum of *twelve shillings,* at the said term of *Martinmas,* yearly, during the continuance of this policy, for insurance from loss or damage by fire, for *goods not hazardous in his shop, stone, slated, or tiled, called* ———— *situated in the Middle Street of Newcastle, only not exceeding six hundred pounds.*

Now know ye, That, from the date of these presents, and so long as the said *A. B.* shall duly pay, or cause to be paid, the said sum of *twelve shillings,* at the term and place aforesaid, and the Directors of said Society for the time, shall agree to accept the same, the stock and fund of the said Society shall be subject and liable to pay to the said *A. B.* his heirs, executors, or assignees, all such his damage and loss, which he the said *A. B.* shall suffer by fire, *not exceeding the sum of six hundred pounds,* according to the tenor of the printed proposals, issued by said Society, bearing date the 20th May 1783. In witness whereof, we (———— ———— Directors of the said Society for the time being) have subscribed these presents at ———— the 23d day of October, in the year of our Lord, one thousand seven hundred and eighty-six years.

No. III. *A Scotch* POLICY *on Lives.*

IN the name of God, Amen. Know all men, by these presents, that we, the subscribers, merchants in ———— have assured, likeas each of us, for ourselves, do, by these presents, assure, to and in favour of Mr *A. B.* merchant, as agent for *C. D.* Esq; of —— the several sums of money annexed to our respective subscriptions underwritten, upon the life of *E. F.* valued at —— pounds Sterling; which said *E. F.* is at present residing in ———— and is understood to reside in Great Britain

Britain or Ireland, during the continuance of this assurance; and the condition of this assurance is such, that if the said *E. F.* shall die, or depart this life, by any ways or means whatsoever, (suicide and the hands of justice excepted,) at any time on or between the 1st day of May 1784, and the 1st day of May 1785, both days inclusive: That we the subscribers, for ourselves, severally, and our several heirs, executors, administrators, or assigns, and not the one for the other or others of us, engage and promise, that we, respectively for ourselves, our respective heirs, administrators, or assigns, shall pay, or cause to be paid into the said *A. B.* for behoof of the said *C. D.* or his heirs, administrators, or assigns, the full sum or sums of money, which we have hereunto subscribed; hereby confessing ourselves paid the consideration due unto us by the assured, after the rate of ―― pounds Sterling, for each hundred pounds Sterling subscribed by us. And it is agreed, that this writing of assurance shall be of as much force and effect as the surest policy, or writing of assurance, made in London; and also, that in case of any dispute or difference arising relative to this policy, it shall be referred to two indifferent persons, one to be chosen by the assured, and the other by the assurers, who shall have full power to adjust the same, with power to them to chuse a third person to be oversman and umpire between them; and their award shall be obligatory upon both parties. At ―――― 1st day of April 1784, in presence of these witnesses, *G. H.* merchant in ―――― and *J. K.* his clerk, by whom these presents are written.

INDEX

INDEX OF THE CASES.

A.

	PAGE.
Arnold *v.* Godin,	103
Affievedo *v.* Cambridge,	318

B.

Betts againſt Carman, (note),	38
Barbour againſt Fletcher,	86
Bates againſt Graham,	91
Boyfield *v.* Brown,	285
Barclay and Collier,	311
Bize againſt Fletcher,	411—474
Bynkerſhoek, (three caſes from him on the ſubject of intended alteration of the voyage),	437, &c.
Bean *v.* Stupart,	474
Bain againſt Kippen,	445
Buchanans *v.* Hunter-Blair,	447
Bond *v.* Gonzalez,	487
Bernardi againſt Motteux,	497
Barzillay *v.* Lewis,	498
Bond *v.* Nutt,	501
Bermon againſt Woodbridge,	543

C.

Carter *v.* Boehm,	77—52
Court *v.* Martineau,	82
Cazalet and others *v.* St Barbe,	302
Cockayne *v.* Frazer,	359
Chitty *v.* Selwyn,	394
Cock *v.* Townſon,	395—436
Camden *v.* Cowley, (note),	399

D'Acoſta

INDEX.

PAGE.

D.

D'Acosta v. Scanderet,	56—531
D'Acosta v. Firth,	299—263
Davis v. Gildart,	273
Dean v. Dicker,	314
De Paiba v. Ludlow,	315
Daubony v. Read,	316
Delancy against Stoddart,	412
Dunlop against Allan,	414
Dunmore against Allan,	483
Dunmore against Gildart,	491
De Hahn v. Hartley,	519
Dunmore and Co. against Allan, Campbell, and others,	522

E.

Elton v. Brogden,	162
Edmonston v. Jackson,	297
Earle against Harris,	508
Eden against Parkinson,	525

F.

Fitsherbert v. Mather,	68
Fitzgerald v. Pole,	325
Fox v. Black,	401
Foster v. Wilmer,	443

G.

Grieve against Young,	65
Gregson v. Gilbert,	186
Grant v. Parkinson,	261—228
Glover v. Black,	235
Gregory v. Christie,	ib.
Godin v. the London Assurance Company,	274
Goss v. Withers,	289
Gavin Kempt and Co. v. Glen,	305

Guibert

		PAGE.
Guibert v. Reidſhaw,	- - -	408
Grahame and Coulter againſt Macnair,	-	ib.
Gordon v. Morley, and Campbell v. Bourdieu,		487

H.

Herdman, M'Iver and M'Allum,	-	51
Hodgſon v. Richardſon,	- -	58
Henkle v. R. Exch. Aſſ. Co. (note),	- -	97
Hamilton v. Mendes,	- -	292
Hanbury and King,	-	310
Hog and Kinloch v. Bogle and Scot,	-	402
Hubbert againſt Newenham,	- -	479
Hubbert v. Pigou,	- - -	515
Hubbert v. Bainbridge, (note)	- -	518

J.

Johnſton againſt Sutton,	- -	19
Jones againſt Schmoll,	- -	189
Jenkins v. Mackenzie,	- - -	321
Jalabert and Nevill v. Collier,	- -	323
Jeffery v. Legandra,	- - -	526

K.

Kay againſt Young,	- - -	62
Knight v. Cambridge,	- -	156
Kent v. Bird,	- - -	236
Kulen Kemp and others v. Vigne,	-	238
Kemp and Andrews,	- - -	436
Kenyon v. Berthon,	- - -	475

L.

Lampro (Samuel),	- -	51
Lewen v. Swaſſo,	- -	178
Lockyer v. Offley,	- - -	200
Lynch v. Dalzell,	- -	221
Le Cras v. Hughes,	- -	226—372

Lawry

	PAGE.
Lawry and another *v.* Bourdieu,	236
Le Pypre *v.* Farr,	253
Lane and Caswell *v.* Collier,	286
Lutwitch *v.* Gray,	347
Lewis *v.* Rucker,	368
Lavabre against Wilson, and ditto against Walter,	409
Lilly *v.* Ewer,	480
Lethulier's case,	486
Loraine against Thomlinson,	542
Long *v.* Allen,	547
Leslie and Thomson against David Linn,	552

M.

Mayne *v.* Walter,	81
M'Dowal *v.* Fraser,	85
Motteux *v.* London Assurance Company,	95—408
Mills *v.* Roebuck,	99
March (Earl) *v.* Pigot,	107
M'Nair *v.* Coulter and others,	255
Milles *v.* Fletcher,	295
Manning *v.* Newnham,	303
Mason *v.* Skurray,	358
Marshall, Hamilton and Co. *v.* Crawford, Barns and others,	395—121
Mollison *v.* Staples,	221
Manning *v.* Gist,	483
Ditto *v.* ditto,	488
Meyer *v* Gregson,	545
Milton (assignees of) *v.* Bland,	550

N.

Nutt and others, assignees, &c. of Hague, a bankrupt *v.* Bourdieu,	171
Newby *v.* Reid,	272
Noble against Kennoway,	128—425

Pray

P.

	Page
Pray and others v. Edie,	245
Perseverance (case of),	126
Pringle v. Hartley,	306
Pond v. King,	320
Planché and Jacquery against Fletcher,	23—426
Plantamour against Staples,	416
Pelly v. Royal Exch. Ass. Co.	419
Pawson v. Ewer,	471
Pawson v. Barnevelt,	474
Phynne and others against Wetster,	528

R.

Rook v. Thurmond,	57
Robertson v. Ewer,	192
Richardson and Co. v. Stodart, &c.	197
Roche v. Thomson,	205
Roebuck v. Hammerton,	220

S.

Stewart against Morison,	59
Shirley against Wilkinson,	64
Stewart against Dunlop, (note),	71
Seaman v. Fonnereau,	73
Stackpole v. Simon,	87
Sparrow v. Carruthers,	124
Stamma v. Brown,	160
Saddler's Company v. Badcock,	223
Storey v. Brown,	288
Spencer v. Franco,	312
Salisbury v. Townson,	418
Salvador v. Hopkins,	429
Steven and Co. against Douglas,	456
Simmond against Boydell,	494
Stevenson v. Snow,	537

INDEX.

PAGE.

T.

Thomas (le) case of,	90
Tongue v. Watts,	118
Thellusson v. Fletcher,	217
Tierney v. Etherington,	422
Taylor v. Woodnets,	490
Thellusson against Fergusson,	504
Tyrie v. Fletcher,	539

V.

Valleio and Echalai v. Wheeler,	169
Vincentio de Medicis (case of),	252
Victorin v. Cleeve,	513

W.

Whittingham against Thornborough,	48
Watt against Ritchie,	92
Waples v. Eames,	120
Wilson v. Wordie,	258
Whitehead and Bance,	315
Wilson v. Smith,	355
Wilson and Co. v. Elliot,	403—460
Wooldridge against Boydell,	444
Woolmer v. Muilman,	521
Wilson v. Ducket,	532

ERRATA.

Page vii. Preface, between *Sir William* and *Burrow*, insert *Blackstone, Sir James*.
—— 6. at the bottom, for *11th* read *12th* century.
—— 129. Notes, for *extent* read *event*.——for *will* read *shall*.
—— 159. line 2. for *agreeable* read *agreeably*.
—— 181. ——1. for *whole general* read *whole of the general*.
—— 337. for *hards* read *yards*.
—— 406. Note, for *Cafariges*, read *Cafaregis*.
—— 409. line 3. the words *he must* should not be put in Italics.
—— 434. —— 8. from the bottom, for *injured* read *injurer*.
—— 459. for *East of the rock of Ailsa*, read *West*.

www.ingramcontent.com/pod-product-compliance
Lightning Source LLC
Chambersburg PA
CBHW031937290426
44108CB00011B/585